THE PRACTICAL
ASTRONOMER

COLIN A. RONAN

BONANZA BOOKS
NEW YORK

Published 1984 by Bonanza Books
distributed by Crown Publishers, Inc.

Library of Congress Cataloging in Publication Data
Ronan, Colin A.
  The practical astronomer.
  Reprint. Originally published: New York:
Macmillan, 1981.
  Includes index.
  1. Astronomy – Popular works. I. Title.
QB44.2.R67   1984   520   84–24248
ISBN 0–517–467593

h g f e d c b a
Printed and bound in Spain.

THE PRACTICAL ASTRONOMER

CONTENTS

CONTENTS

ACKNOWLEDGEMENTS

I would like to thank the following people for special pictures and assistance; however, any errors in the book are my responsibility.
Colin A. Ronan

Mr. Ron Arbour, Mr. Richard Baum, Mr. Paul Doherty, Mr. Tony Feldman, Mr. Peter Gill, Mr. Ron Ham, Mrs. Enid Lake, Mr. Patrick Moore, Mr. Harold Ridley, and Mr. Reg Spry.

The author and publishers would also like to thank the following people for illustrations reproduced.

For special help with photographs and artwork:
Mr. G. Amery, Mr. H. J. Arnold, Mr. L. F. Ball, Professor R. D. Davies, Mr. Storm Dunlop, Mr. Harry Ford, Mr. B. W. Hadley, Professor R. Hanbury Brown, Commander H. Hatfield, Mr. Michael Holford, Mr. J. McConnell, Mrs. Ann Ronan.

Photographs
Aerofilms Ltd. *46.*
J. Allan Cash Ltd. *17, 23, 46, 47, 181.*
Ann Ronan Picture Library *14, 32 left, 36, 48 above, 86 left & above right, 108, 110, 120 left, 130, 136, 137, 138, 139, 142 below, 143 top, 145 above & below right, 154 above, 156 left, 163 above & right, 170 above, 172 below, 173 centre & bottom, 174, 176 right, 186 top & centre, 187 above, 195 below.*
Mr. Ron Arbour *8, 162 left, 200 left.*
Association of Universities for Research & Astronomy, Inc., The Kitt Peak National Observatory *76 right, 140, 146 right, 166 below right.*
Australian High Commission *12.*
Bell Laboratories *197 above.*
Bibliothèque Nationale *66.*
Big Bear Solar Observatory *156.*
British Museum, Courtesy of the Trustees *22 left, 27 above, 44 centre & right, 45 above.*
Camera Press Ltd. *13, 33 above, 39, 40 above right, 41 above left, 72 below right, 98 below right, 179 below.*
Canterbury Cathedral, Courtesy Dean & Chapter *24 below left.*
Central Office of Information *185.*
CERN *183 below.*
Chatterton Astronomy Dept., University of Sydney *76 left.*
Mr. Dennis di Cicco/Sky & Telescope Magazine *94 above.*
Mr. Storm Dunlop *162 top.* Photo by late W. E. Pennell & supplied by his son R. Pennell.

Mr. Harry Ford *148 centre below.*
Mr. Peter Gill *74, 148 left.*
Hale Observatories *32 centre, 48. below, 73 above, 83 below, 87 centre & left, 89 below right, 100, 143 centre, 162 below right, 163 below left, 165 above, 166 below right, 169 above, 186 bottom centre & right, 187 below, 189 above & below right, 190 right, 192, 193, 194 above left, 195 above.*
Mr. Ron Ham *200 below centre & right.*
Commander H. R. Hatfield *28 above, 29 above, 33 below centre.*
Mr. Alan Heath *104.*
Michael Holford Library *22 right, 42 above, 43 below, 44 left & 171 right* (all Science Museum Photos) *43 above* (British Museum Photo) & *145 below left.*
Institute of Geological Sciences, London *148 above & below right, 149.*
Institute of Opthalmology *42 below.*
Mr. Gustav Lamprecht *159 below right.*
Lick Observatory *88 below, 91, 94 & 95 below, 96 left, 98 left, 99, 100 & 101 above, 130, 164 above, 186 bottom left, 189 below left, 191, 192 right, 194 above right.*
Norman Lockyer Observatory, Sidmouth *138, 146.*
Lowell Observatory *129 above.*
Lunar & Planetary Laboratory, University of Arizona *101, 130.*
Lund Observatory *168.*
Mansell Collection *27 below, 98 above.*
Mr. Ben Mayer *87 right.*
Meteorological Office Library *155 above* (photographer & copyright R. N. Hughes), *155 below* (photographer & copyright Dr. J. A. Lang).
Mr. Alan McClure *140.*
Mr. John McConnell *29 left & 102.*
Mr. Dennis Milon *146 right, 147 left & right, 158 left, 161 below left.*
Mr. Patrick Moore *200 above right.*
Mount Wilson Observatory *100 below left, 169 above, 190 left.*
Mullard Radio Astronomy Observatory Cambridge *89 below left.*
NASA *20, 90, 92 above right, above left & below, 93 above left & above right, 97 below right, 98, 100 below right, 119 right, 121, 124 centre & below, 125 centre & below, 126 centre left, 130, 132, 133, 134, 170 below, 171 left, 176 centre, 184 above.*
National Gallery, Courtesy of the Trustees *25.*
National Maritime Museum, London *65, 68 below, 80 left, 129 below, 134, 137.*
National Radio Astronomy Observatory, Parkes, NSW *194 below.*
New Mexico State University

Observatory *127 bottom.*
Novosti Press Agency *127 top.*
Nuffield Radio Astronomy Laboratory, Jodrell Bank *161 right.*
Oakridge National Laboratory, USA *184 below.*
Oxford Scientific Films Ltd. *16 & 26.*
Professor J. M. Pasachoff *28 below, 29 right, 33 below right.*
Queens' College Cambridge, Courtesy President & Fellows, photographer Mr. J. Gibbons *24 left above.*
Mr. Harold Ridley *146 left.*
Royal Geographical Society *21.*
Royal Greenwich Observatory, Hailsham *138.*
Royal Observatory Edinburgh *40 below right, 73 below left & right, 75 above, 164, 165 below, 166 above, 167 left & right.*
The Royal Society, Courtesy of *173*
Sacramento Peak Observatory, Association of Universities for Research in Astronomy, Inc. *33 below left.*
Mr. William Sager *154.*
The Science Museum, London *11, 14, 15, 19 above & below, 24 right, 34, 70.*
Science Research Council *72 above right.*
Space Frontiers Ltd. *116–117 centre, 118 left & right, 119 left, 122 left, 123 above, 125 above, 127 centre right.*
Mr. R. Spry *72 left.*
Union Observatory, Johannesburg *145 top left.*
United Kingdom Atomic Energy Authority *183 above.*
US Naval Observatory, Flagstaff, Arizona *140, 142 centre, 169 below.*
Vision International *45 below.*
Dr. R. L. Waterfield *138, 140.*
Yerkes Observatory *80 right, 83 above right, 138.*

Artwork
Harry Clow, Ted Hammond, Aziz Khan, Edwina Keene, Jeff Ridge, Roger Taylor, John Thompson, John Woodcock, Martin Woodford.
Mr. Richard Baum, Mr. Paul Doherty, Mr. W. E. Fox, Mr. J. Hedley Robinson.

81 fig. 5 The Eclipsing binary Algol – from a light curve by Joel Stebbings *182* fig. 3 Light curve of Cephei – after a diagram prepared by the British Astronomical Association *134* Drawing of the Earth's atmosphere – Times Atlas p. xxxiii. *153* Layers of Earth's atmosphere after a drawing in *Exploring the Atmosphere* by G. M. B. Dobson (O.U.P. 1968).

INTRODUCTION

THE CELESTIAL SPHERE AND CHARTING STARS

Astronomy, the study of the heavens, has a long history. The stars have always held a fascination for man and through them he has attempted to understand the mysteries of the universe. This scrutiny has revealed unimaginable distances in space and time, and the relative insignificance of the Earth in the context of our galaxy and beyond.

Whether you are scientifically minded or not astronomy is an exciting subject. It is not always necessary to have access to sophisticated equipment to be an active astronomer, and in fact some major discoveries have been made by amateurs.

Our scheme in this book will be to explore the universe, following in the steps of the astronomers of the past as well as making use of the latest results of space research. To begin with we shall use only our eyes, as the early astronomers did. Later we shall make use of binoculars, telescopes and other equipment to build up a picture of the universe.

As a start, just look up at the night sky and you will see a black backdrop sparkling with stars. The sky is black because obviously the Sun is not shining to give us the blue sky of daylight. And the stars are visible because they are not blotted out by the bright light of day. But what is the true shape of the sky? This was one of the basic questions early astronomers asked and their first conclusion was that it was shaped like a giant dome, stretching high above their heads. This may seem a very simple explanation – too simple even. However, we are judging the early astronomers' beliefs with the benefit of hindsight. Today spacecraft have gone to the Moon, Mars, Jupiter and other planets and we know that the stars are at different distances from the Earth. But this is all modern knowledge.

Faced with just the visual evidence when you look at the night sky, how can you *know* what the sky is like? The answer, of course, is that you cannot. You can only describe what you see and work from there.

Suppose, to begin with, we accept the idea that the heavens are a dome. Look at the sky on and off during the night, and what do you see? To do this pick out a few stars which look as though they are arranged in some kind of pattern. You do not have to know any patterns or constellations to do this; just choose a group which you find easy to recognize. Each time you go out you will see that the group you have chosen has moved across the sky. So either the dome of the heavens is rotating, or the Earth on which you are standing is slowly rotating. Early astronomers believed the heavens rotated and the Earth stood still. To them the Earth seemed just too fixed and solid to be a moving body. They argued it must be stationary for, after all, if it moved what would happen to the air? Should we not find it rushing past us, so that we were constantly experiencing a gale? We shall see later (page 14) how an experiment can be done to see what really is happening, but at the moment let us consider the sky seeming to turn.

What is the point in the sky around which the dome of the heavens appears to rotate? If you live in a northern hemisphere country, the point is not difficult to find. There is a bright star very near to the north pole, called the Pole Star or Polaris. You will find it by looking northwards, and you will notice how the entire body of the heavens seems to go round it as if it were a pivot. In the southern hemisphere there is no star equivalent to Polaris in brightness near the pivot-point, but there is a dim star close to it. This can be located by looking southwards, and the sky seems to move around this dim star called Sigma σ Octans.

Having found the pivot-points of the heavens we can discover something else. If you observe your pivot-point you will find it always stays at the same height above your horizon, night after night. But if you travel due north or south it will change. In the northern hemisphere as you go north, so the Pole Star will seem higher in the sky, and if you go south it will appear lower and nearer the horizon. The opposite happens in the southern hemisphere; the pivot-point moves higher as you go further south. Of course it is necessary to travel a good 1,000 to 1,500 km north or south before the change becomes really obvious. Such a variation in the pivot-point or 'celestial pole', as it is usually called, is important because

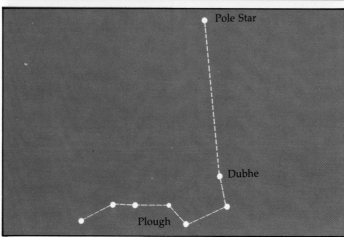

above
Amateur astronomer's photograph of the Plough or Big Dipper, which is almost always visible in the northern hemisphere.

below
It is easy to find the Pole Star by following a line up from the bright star Dubhe at the end of the Plough.

opposite
The position of the Pole Star depends on the whereabouts of the observer. Within the Arctic Circle the Pole Star appears very high in the sky because the angle at which we see the Pole Star is at its greatest. The further south the observer the lower the Pole Star, until at the equator it is on the horizon and the Plough is less often visible.

Pole Star

Dubhe

Plough

To Pole Star

80°

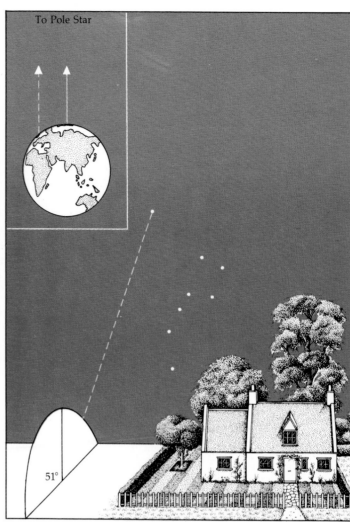

To Pole Star

51°

To Pole Star

30°

To Pole Star

9

The diagram shows how latitude and longitude are used to find the precise location of London and New York. The principle of mapping places on the Earth's surface is also applied to charting the position of stars in the sky.

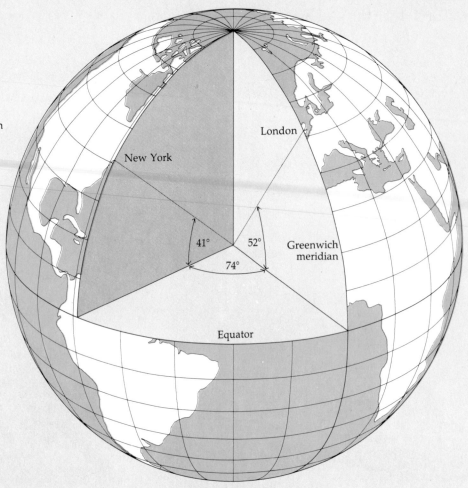

New York

London

41°   52°

74°

Greenwich meridian

Equator

The celestial sphere
If we imagine the Earth at the centre of the celestial sphere, then the celestial equator is on the same plane as the Earth's equator. The north and south celestial poles are on the continuation of the line joining the Earth's poles, and the ecliptic is inclined by 23½° to the celestial equator. By using the astronomical co-ordinate system we can fix the position of star X at a right ascension of 6 hours and a declination of +45°.

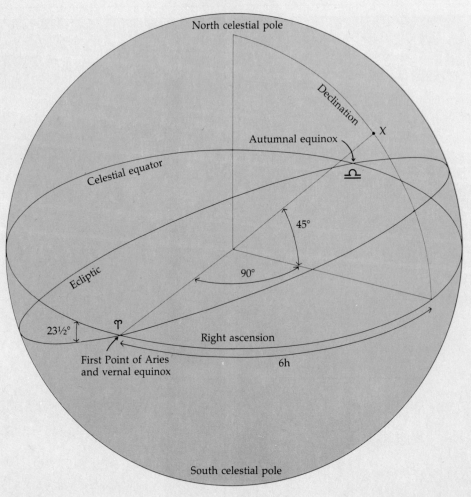

North celestial pole

Declination

X

Autumnal equinox

♎

Celestial equator

45°

90°

Ecliptic

23½°

♈

Right ascension

First Point of Aries and vernal equinox

6h

South celestial pole

Astronomers at work in the original observatory at Greenwich. The observatory was founded in 1675 by Charles II, who appointed John Flamsteed as the first Astronomer Royal. Flamsteed was given the job of producing a reliable star catalogue which could be used by British sailors for navigation.

it proves that the heavens are not dome-shaped. If they were, then you could move so far south or north that the pole would lie close to the horizon and the bottom edge of the dome would be visible. But no bottom edge is ever seen. If you go to the equator where the celestial poles lie on the horizon you will still see an entire starry sky at night.

Having now discovered that the first astronomers were wrong, can we decide what shape the heavens are? The one shape that would fit what we have so far discovered is a sphere. A sphere of stars surrounding the Earth would have the two celestial poles – one at the north and one at the south – about which it would appear to rotate. What about the Earth itself, lying at the centre of this sphere? Is it spherical too, as the Greek philosopher and mathematician Pythagoras suggested in the sixth century BC? There are all kinds of evidence to support this theory, as we shall come to later (pages 102 and 134). But what about the heavens?

Astronomers now know that the heavens are not really like a sphere. The stars appear to be fixed on the inside of a giant globe, but this is nothing more than an optical illusion. The stars are, in fact, all at different distances from us, stretching out into space a vast way – a fact realised by Chinese astronomers at least 1,800 years ago, because they thought of all celestial bodies floating in empty space. But for some astronomical purposes, for instance when we want to measure the star positions, it is still convenient to imagine that the

stars themselves are all fixed on the inside of a sphere. We picture the Earth positioned inside this giant or 'celestial sphere'.

Charting stars on the celestial sphere is carried out in a similar way as mapping places on the Earth's surface. On the Earth, we fit a 'grid' of lines from which we measure places. We draw in the Earth's north and south poles and the equator, the line cutting the Earth in half between the poles and separating the northern and southern hemispheres. Then we draw a line from the north pole to the south pole through Greenwich, just south of London. This is the 'Greenwich meridian', and where it crosses the equator is the starting point of our measurements. To find the position of any place, say New York, we draw a meridian through the place (see the drawing) and then measure the angle westwards along the equator between the Greenwich meridian and the meridian through New York. It is 74°. This gives the longitude. We still have to find the distance of the place north or south of the equator. New York is north of the equator, and the angle along its meridian, measured upwards from equator to pole, gives us the latitude. New York's latitude is almost 41° north. So we can give the position of New York by quoting two co-ordinates – Latitude 41° north, Longitude 74° west. That gives us New York's position without any possibility of confusion.

To chart the positions of stars a similar system is used. On the celestial sphere we draw the north and south celestial poles, and the

celestial equator, half way between them. But what do we use instead of the meridian of Greenwich as our fixed point on the celestial equator? The most convenient thing to do is to use the Sun's apparent path as our guide. During a year the Sun appears to move across the background of stars; its path is known as the 'ecliptic' (because it is connected with determining eclipses – see pages 28–29). In the northern hemisphere spring, this path cuts the celestial equator as the Sun moves north of it. During the northern summer the Sun stays north of the equator (which is why it is summer), then it dips in the autumn crossing through the celestial equator again. When the Sun is on the celestial equator, night and day are equal in length, and each crossing point is often referred to as an 'equinox'.

The crossing point of ecliptic and celestial equator which the Sun reaches in the northern spring is the 'vernal equinox' – (also known as 'The First Point of Aries') and denoted by the symbol ♈. Using this as our 'Greenwich' equivalent we can measure the position of any star. Astronomers use the term 'right ascension' (abbreviated 'RA') for the celestial equivalent of longitude and express their measurements, which are made only in an eastwards direction, in hours, minutes and seconds of time instead of degrees. This is because the celestial sphere appears to rotate with time (we imagine the Earth as stationary). The whole way round the celestial equator (360°) is taken as 24 hours, so the star at X will have a right ascension of 06 hours 00 minutes 00 seconds. The astronomical equivalent of terrestrial latitude is called 'declination', and this is measured in degrees and fractions of a degree. Thus the declination of star X is $+45°$ 00' 00'' (where 00' means zero minutes of arc and 00'' zero seconds of arc, one minute of arc being 1/60th of a degree, and one second of arc 1/60th of a minute of arc). A minus sign before the declination would mean the star lies south of the celestial equator. So the position of X in the sky can be precisely specified, just as easily as a place on the Earth.

There is one difficulty that astronomers have which geographers do not. Unlike Greenwich, the vernal equinox does not stand still. The ecliptic and equator move so that the crossing point goes backwards or precesses. This precession is small – only 50'' (or 0.014°) per year – and need not trouble us in this book.

CHAPTER 1
THE SUN:
ASTRONOMY IN
DAYLIGHT

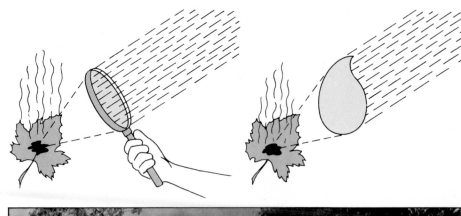

Our lives on Earth depend on the heat and light provided by the Sun. Without this, the terrestrial scene would be desolate and cold. The Sun is also our nearest star and as such is of great interest to astronomers; by studying it they can learn facts about stars in general.

Solar study is convenient because you can do some astronomy in daylight, but as the Sun is so bright and hot, special precautions must be taken when observing it.

The first rule about observing the Sun is **never** to look straight at it. Only on rare occasions when there is fog or mist, can you look at the *setting* Sun, but these are exceptions. The general rule is **never to observe direct**. The reason is obvious: the Sun is very bright and its glare alone can damage your eyes. It is also hot and the heat rays it emits can blind you. So take care never to observe the Sun direct through a telescope or a pair of binoculars. There are safe ways to observe the Sun and these are described on pages 34 and 35.

What is the Sun? First of all, we know it is a round object up in the sky which gives out heat and light. So much the earliest astronomers knew, but their opinions began to differ when it came to size and distance. We can, of course, measure the apparent size of the Sun, as they did, and we shall find it is about half a degree in diameter. But is it a globe of coal in the sky a few thousand metres above the ground, or hundreds, thousands, or even millions of kilometres away? To settle the question the ancient Greek astronomers Aristarchos (about 280 BC) and Hipparchos (about 130 BC) tried to measure the distance. Aristarchos' method was simple and you can try it, although you will have to use trigonometry and must not expect to get an accurate result.

Aristarchos realized that while the Sun gave out its own light, the Moon only shone because it reflected

The heat of the Sun's rays concentrated through a magnifying glass can set fire to a dry leaf. It is thought that forest fires can begin in the same way as a result of the Sun's rays being concentrated by raindrops.

Measuring the distance of the Sun by Aristarchos' method will show you that the Sun is much farther away than the Moon.

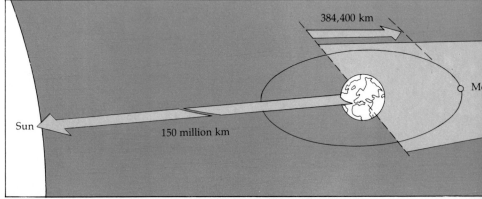

The Moon at first quarter.

the light of the Sun. So he waited until the Moon was at first quarter, that is until half its disc appeared lit up; he then measured the angle between the Moon and the Sun (see diagram). Put two pegs or pins in a board to get the Sun's direction, and then two pegs or pins in line with the Moon. You can then measure the angle MES with a protractor. Using trigonometry (which is very convenient, but was not invented in Aristarchos' time) the distance ES (Earth to Sun) is found from the formula ES = ME ÷ cosine MES. ME is the distance of the Moon, which Aristarchos knew and you can also find it (pages 90–91), or you can take it as 384,400 km. It is not possible to obtain an accurate result, partly because it is extremely difficult to determine when the Moon's disc is exactly half illuminated, and partly because your means of measuring the angle between the Sun and Moon is very crude. Even Aristarchos got it wrong: the Sun is nearly 400 times further off than he thought. But what Aristarchos' measurement showed him, and yours should show you, is that the Sun is certainly much further off than the Moon.

The problem of measuring the Sun's distance has challenged astronomers ever since Aristarchos' time, and all kinds of methods have been used. The latest measurements, using radar techniques, show that its average distance is almost 150,000 million km. This is a very important distance in astronomy, for once it has been established it can act as a yardstick for almost every other astronomical distance. It is known as the Astronomical Unit (usually abbreviated A.U.).

Knowing the distance of the Sun, and observing that it covers about ½° in the sky, it is possible to calculate its diameter. This works out to 1.39 million km, or 109 times the diameter of the Earth. This giant body is a huge ball of hot gas, kept together by the force of gravity acting on the 2×10^{27} (2,000 million million million) tonnes of its material. Because it shines by its own light, the Sun is a star and it is by far the nearest star to us. The next nearest star is 272,000 times further away. The amount of energy poured out by the Sun is equivalent to 1×10^{20} (100 million million million) single-bar electric heaters, yet it is not a specially large or powerful star. But the small fraction of this energy captured by the Earth (2.0×10^{-9} or 2 thousand-millionths) is still enough to support life all over the planet.

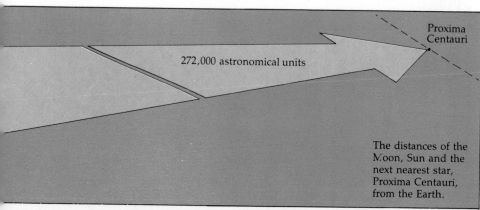

Proxima Centauri

272,000 astronomical units

The distances of the Moon, Sun and the next nearest star, Proxima Centauri, from the Earth.

NIGHT AND DAY

In earliest times when it was thought that the Earth was flat, people believed the Sun passed underneath the Earth at night. Another theory was that the rotation of the celestial sphere caused the Sun to rise and set.

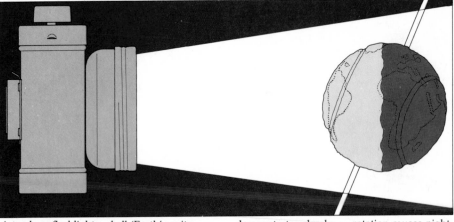

A torch or flashlight shining on a tennis-ball 'Earth' on its knitting-needle axis demonstrates clearly how the Earth's rotation causes night and day.

We now know that it is the Earth, not the celestial sphere, which rotates once every 24 hours, and which gives us the experience we call night and day. It is easy to make a model to show this. Take a ball – an old tennis-ball is ideal – to represent the Earth. With a felt-tip pen draw on it the main land masses – North and South America, Europe, Asia, Africa and Australia. Next insert a long knitting-needle through the north and south poles; the knitting-needle represents the Earth's polar axis and as you turn it, so the model Earth will rotate. You now need a source of light to represent the Sun and the most suitable is an electric torch which gives a focused beam. Now switch off all the lights in the room (and if you are doing the 'experiment' in daytime, pull the curtains too!) and shine the torch at the model Earth. Half the globe will be illuminated. On this half it is daytime. On the dark side it is night and, as you rotate the globe, you will see how different continents pass from daylight into night, and from night into daylight. To simulate the Earth's rotation properly, you should rotate the globe in an anti-clockwise direction, so that to an observer on your 'Earth', the Sun (the torch) appears to rise in the east and set in the west.

Night and day can be simulated in another way, using the same model. Fix the globe in position and do not rotate it. Now take your torch or whatever light source is being used, and move it round the fixed Earth in a clockwise direction. The effect will be just the same as rotating the Earth in an anti-clockwise direction. An observer on your model Earth could not tell which was really happening; whether the Earth was rotating or the Sun moving round it. The sequence of night and day will follow without change whichever happens. Of course, if it is the Sun which is going round the Earth it would have to be

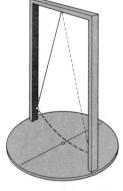

A demonstration of the Earth's rotation using Foucault's pendulum in the Panthéon, Paris 1851.

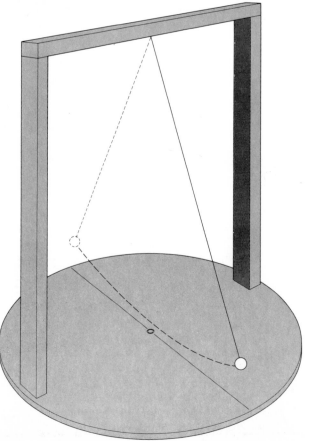

A model pendulum shows that when the frame is rotated, the pendulum's swing changes relative to the frame.

opposite
You can repeat Foucault's experiment yourself. Place a piece of paper, as shown above, underneath the pendulum. Set the pendulum swinging along the centre line and after quarter of an hour you will see that the direction of swing has changed.

The Foucault pendulum is released along the zero line at the Science Museum, London; a flame is used to burn through the retaining thread in order that the pendulum starts to swing smoothly. The pendulum is 24.98 m long and the bob weighs 13.62 kg. The plane of swing turns by about 11¾° each hour.

moving at a great speed. Even taking Aristarchos' incorrect and far too small value for the Sun's distance, the Sun would have to race through space at 4×10^7 km per hour (24 million miles per hour) to orbit the Earth every 24 hours, and this seems unlikely, to put it mildly. Yet how can we be sure that the Earth moves?

There is experimental evidence that the Earth is rotating, as was first demonstrated by the French physicist Léon Foucault. In 1851 Foucault hung a pendulum, consisting of a 5 kilogram bob suspended from a steel wire, from a cellar roof in his Paris house. He then set the pendulum swinging. Once set going the pendulum would continue to swing in the same direction irrespective of whether the Earth is moving or not. But, of course, if the Earth *was* rotating, then Foucault's house and cellar would move round, but would not drag the pendulum with them. The result was that the direction in which the pendulum was swinging changed with respect to the room. The direction of swing appeared to move round to an observer.

You can see what happened by making a model. Out of wood or any convenient material (Meccano, for instance) make up a small frame and fix it on a flat base. Have the crossbar high enough (15cm or more) to allow you to hang a thread from the middle. Make the thread into a pendulum by tying a metal nut or some other object to the end. Set the pendulum swinging and then, slowly and carefully, rotate the base, making sure you do not shake the pendulum. You will find it continues to swing in the same direction relative to the room but not relative to the frame.

To test this on the Earth itself you need a long pendulum, as long as you can conveniently make it. A string with a heavy weight on the end will do as your pendulum. Suspend this from the ceiling or from as near to the ceiling as you can, with the weight close to the floor. On the floor place a large sheet of paper with a straight line drawn along the middle, and some lines drawn close to it but crossing at angles of 2°. A couple of lines will do. Make sure windows and doors are closed and set the pendulum swinging along the centre line. After 10 minutes and then a quarter of an hour, look to see the direction of the swing. You will see it has changed.

A larger better pendulum to demonstrate this is often to be found in a local science museum.

OBSERVING THE RISING AND SETTING SUN

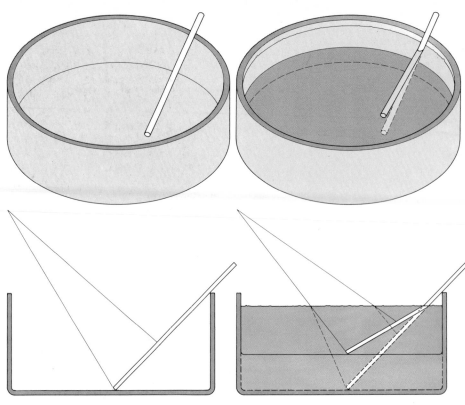

The Sun appears at its most dramatic when it is rising or setting. At these times its disc seems to us to be distorted. To explain this visual effect it is necessary to understand the principle of the refraction of light.

In ancient Greece scientists believed that we were able to see, because the eye emitted rays of light. According to their theory, when these rays hit an object, they transmitted an effect back to the eye. This is wrong. We now know that other early Greek philosophers were correct when they thought of light as something emitted from a source of light to the eye. However, both schools of thought discovered the phenomenon of 'refraction', whereby rays of light are bent when they pass from one substance to another substance not equally dense. The great Greek astronomer Ptolemy, who worked at Alexandria about AD 130, demonstrated this with what he called a 'baptistir' or deep bowl. It is worth repeating Ptolemy's demonstration if we want to understand the distortion we see when the Sun rises and sets.

Now let us examine what happens when the Sun is rising or setting. At these times it appears close to the horizon where the density of the air differs greatly. The air near the ground is denser than the layer of air just above it, and the layer of air above that is less dense still, and so on upwards until the Earth's atmosphere peters out at some 400 km. So the Sun's light passes through many layers of differing density. Now consider what happens when the Sun is setting. When the Sun is at A, light from the top of the disc is going through the air at a different angle than that from the lower part. So the rays are bent by different amounts before they reach the observer's eye. The result is that the bottom part of the Sun's disc appears to be lifted up. In consequence the Sun's disc appears slightly compressed.

As the Sun sinks lower towards the horizon, so the distance the light

above
To repeat Ptolemy's demonstration, place a drinking straw in a

glass. When the glass is filled with water the straw appears to bend; this effect is caused by

refraction of light because water is denser than air.

below
A sunset showing the compression of the Sun's disc.

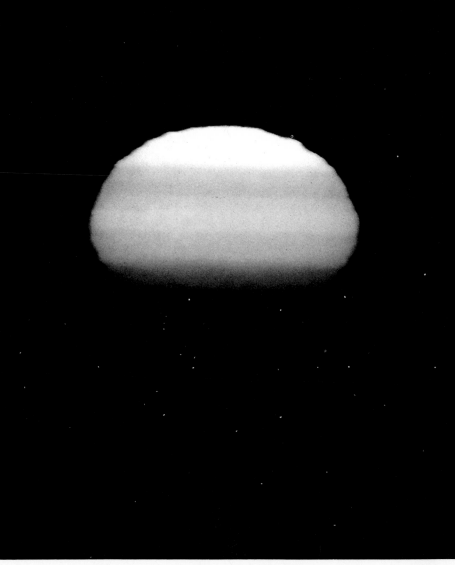

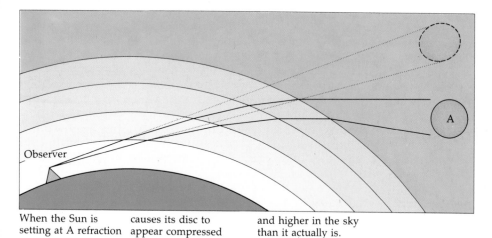

When the Sun is setting at A refraction causes its disc to appear compressed and higher in the sky than it actually is.

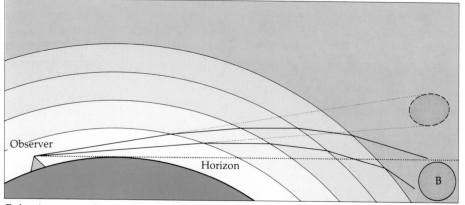

Observer

Horizon

Refraction causes the Sun to be still visible to the observer a few minutes after it has actually sunk below the horizon at B.

below
The Midnight Sun in the Lofoten Islands, Norway.

travels through the layers of air becomes greater and the distortion of the disc more pronounced. This is something well worth watching out for, but do take care that you try to observe it only through fog or haze: do not look directly at the setting Sun on a bright day or in a clear sky.

You may wonder why we see the Sun, and the Moon for that matter, as a disc when it is high up in the sky. After all the light from the upper part of the disc is coming through a higher and so a thinner layer of air than light from the bottom of the disc. So why does the Sun not look squashed? The reason is that the 'differential refraction' between the layers is very much less than close to the horizon because the light has less air through which to travel and so the effects are not so marked. We see what seems to be a perfectly round disc. The refraction of the air does, however, lift Sun, Moon and stars so that they appear a little higher in the sky than they really are.

For those who live in countries not too far from the north pole – such as the north of Norway, Sweden and Greenland or the northernmost parts of Canada – or those travelling south to the edge of the Antarctic continent, there is the wonderful phenomenon of the 'Midnight Sun'. This only happens at summertime, when the Sun is close to the most northerly or southerly parts of its path among the stars (pages 10–11). Then it reaches a high enough declination to be seen from within the Arctic Circle or Antarctic Circle. For a short time the Sun can be seen for 24 hours.

You can use your model of the Earth on its axis to demonstrate this. Use your source of 'sunlight' as before and tilt the Earth's polar axis over until the sunlight lights up the area around the north or the south pole. Now rotate the Earth. You will find that the polar regions always remain illuminated throughout the entire rotation. If you imagine yourself on the Earth within this polar region, you will see that the Sun will appear at its highest at midday (i.e. when you are on the side facing the Sun). When you have been carried to the far side by the Earth's rotation and it is midnight, you are still lit by sunlight, but the Sun appears low down nearer the horizon. You will also notice that at the opposite pole, the Sun never rises at all during the 24 hours. It is winter in that hemisphere and at the polar regions perpetual night.

SOLAR AND SIDEREAL DAYS

The regular motion of celestial objects has provided man with methods of measuring time. The movement of the Sun gives us solar time, but the Earth's rotation can also be measured with reference to the stars.

The Sun, like all celestial bodies, rises in the east and sets in the west. What does it do in between? The short answer is 'go and look'. If you live in the northern hemisphere the Sun will seem to travel upwards in the sky moving from the east towards the south. When it appears due south, it has completed half its journey, and it is at its midday position. Then it moves towards the west, sinking lower and lower in the sky until, in due course, it sets. In the southern hemisphere, the Sun will move from the east northwards, not southwards; at midday it will have reached its highest apparent position northwards. Thereafter it will move north-westwards, sinking in the sky until it sets in the west. Anyone who wants to build a house with the living-room facing the Sun must ensure that this room faces south in the northern hemisphere, and north in the southern hemisphere. House builders and architects have been known to make mistakes over this!

What you see if you observe the rising and setting Sun is the solar day. And if you count the number of solar days in a year, you will find that there are 365 whole days. (There are, in fact, 365¼ solar days in a year but we are concerned only with 365 – the number of whole days – at the moment.) The Earth rotates so that it can fit in 365 complete revolutions about its polar axis every time it completes one circuit or orbit of the Sun. Take your model of the Earth (the tennis-ball with the knitting-needle through it) and fix your light representing the Sun in the middle of the room. Now if you walk once round the 'Sun' in a circle, imagine that you rotate the 'Earth' 365 times.

Next consider the starry sky, the celestial sphere, represented in your room by the walls, floor and ceiling. When you orbit your Sun (lamp) once, how many times has the Earth rotated on its axis? It has rotated 365 times with respect to the Sun, but how many with reference to the stars? To solve this problem, mark a dot in red or some other easily visible colour on your 'Earth'. Now have the dot facing one wall, and begin to move in orbit. As you orbit, make sure the red dot on the Earth keeps facing the same wall of the room (i.e. the same group of stars in the sky).

Ophiucus

The Earth's orbital movement accounts for the difference in time between the solar and sidereal day. As the Earth moves in orbit different constellations are visible in the night sky during the year (*above and below*).

Orion

A sidereal day is 4 minutes shorter than a solar day: an observer will see a particular star at the same position 4 minutes earlier on successive nights.

You will see that as you move, so the Sun begins to creep up over the horizon. When you are half-way round, although the red dot on the Earth is still facing the same wall (part of the sky), the Sun is now in the way – indeed it is at its midday position. Continue and the Sun will sink to the other horizon. Complete the orbit and the stars will once more be in the red dot's sky with the Sun behind. What has happened? Although the Earth has not rotated on its axis, the very act of orbiting once round the Sun has caused the Sun to appear to rise, reach noonday position, and set. In other words with respect to the stars, a collection of which we have taken as our reference point (a particular wall in

the room), we obtain one extra day every year due to the Earth's revolution round the Sun. In fact there are 365¼ solar days in the year and 366¼ star days or 'sidereal days' in the year.

This all means that the sidereal day is shorter than the solar day. The difference is just about 4 minutes. You can check this for yourself by going outside and timing when a particular star appears due south. (You can mark the south point with a stick stuck in the ground.) Then go out on the next night, but some 5 minutes earlier and note precisely the moment the same star is due south. You should find that it 'souths' 3 minutes 56½ seconds earlier (56.556 seconds to be precise).

Astronomers use sidereal time for observing purposes. If you have a telescope mounted so that you can set it at a certain declination and right ascension then you can point it to any star you want (pages 70–71). However, as we saw (page 11) right ascension is measured from the vernal equinox, and it is necessary to use sidereal time to tell us where the vernal equinox is. The reason for using sidereal time is not only that we are observing stars and will find it more convenient to use star time, but also because, technically, the sidereal day begins when the vernal equinox is due south. So if you know the sidereal time, you can estimate where the vernal equinox is; even if you cannot see its position in the sky, you know the angle at which it lies. Hence you can work out where in the sky a star of particular right ascension will be, so that you can observe it with your telescope.

If you want to be very precise, as professional astronomers have to be, there are special corrections which have to be made because the vernal equinox is moving, due to precession (page 11). This motion must be taken into account, as well as another movement of the equinox due to a slight nodding movement or 'nutation' of the Earth's polar axis, if sidereal time is to be determined accurately. We do not need these corrections here but they are found in astronomical tables (page 198).

A nineteenth-century astronomical clock showing both solar and sidereal time.

Astronomers find it convenient to use sidereal time because they are more concerned with the time it takes the Earth to rotate once with respect to the background of distant stars than with respect to the Sun.

left
An atomic clock. The most accurate time-keeping today is done by atomic clocks, not by observing the stars, because the Earth's motion is not perfectly regular. An atomic clock uses vibrating atoms in place of a pendulum, balance spring or a piece of quartz.

Orbit the model Earth around the 'Sun' without rotating it. Point X always faces wall A and you will find that the orbital movement causes X to experience a complete day.

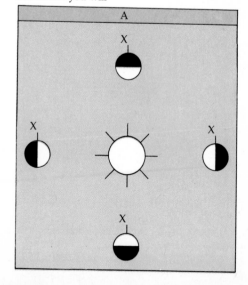

THE SEASONS

Everywhere on Earth the pattern of life is governed by recurring seasonal changes. These changes are determined by the tilt of the Earth's axis.

A gnomon, the simplest of all astronomical instruments, in use on the Moon during the Apollo 17 mission. The gnomon was used to establish the local vertical Sun angle and as a scale. The colour bands enabled the colours on the Moon to be correctly determined.

The seasons vary throughout the world. In the more temperate areas in both northern and southern hemispheres four seasons are recognized – spring, summer, autumn (or fall) and winter. At the north and south poles there are only two seasons – winter and summer – while in equatorial and tropical countries the seasons are usually divided into those periods which are dry or rainy.

The seasons can be observed by the simplest of all astronomical instruments, the gnomon, which in its earliest form is nothing more than a stick stuck vertically into the ground. Simple though it is, it can provide quite a lot of information. So set up a gnomon in the garden, or mount a stick vertically on a board and take it to the window. You must be sure that the window, or the patch of garden, lies in the right direction so that the Sun's midday beams can strike the gnomon to cast a shadow.

Watch the shadow of the gnomon as the morning progresses. You will see that besides changing direction, the shadow changes length. As the morning wears on, so the shadow gets shorter and shorter. When the Sun is due south, the shadow will be at its shortest. Of course you can use your gnomon to tell you where south is. When the shadow is at its shortest, then the Sun lies in the direction of due south, so if you draw a line from the tip of the shadow through the gnomon and extend the line out on the other side, the extended line will point due south.

Mark the tip of the noonday shadow, either by sticking a used matchstick in the ground or making a mark on your board. Watch the noonday shadow off and on over the next eight weeks or so. You will notice that it is growing either shorter or longer. Continue observing, and after some weeks (how long will depend on the date on which you started) – you will notice a change. Suppose the shadow reaches its shortest length, it will then begin to lengthen each day. Six months later, it will reach its longest midday length, and once more it will shorten.

What does this lengthening and shortening mean? The length of a shadow depends on the height of the object which is casting it and on the height of the light source. The gnomon is a fixed height, so the length of the shadow it casts can depend only on the height of the light source which is the Sun. When the noonday shadow is, say, getting shorter each day, this indicates that each day the noonday Sun is higher in the sky. Conversely, if the noonday shadow gets longer day by day, then the noonday Sun is sinking lower in the sky.

Experience will show you that the shadow is shortest in mid-summer and longest in mid-winter, and this is true in whichever hemisphere you live. Why? You can find the answer by looking again at the drawing of the celestial sphere (page 10). Note the ecliptic, the Sun's apparent path in the sky. In the northern hemisphere spring it is at ♈, the vernal equinox. Then it moves upwards above the celestial equator until it comes to its highest point, its highest declination. After this it begins to lose declination. In the interval between its highest declination and moving downwards, the Sun is virtually at a standstill. This is called a solstice (in the northern hemisphere, the 'summer' solstice).

In the southern hemisphere spring begins when the Sun crosses the 'autumnal' equinox ♎, as the northern hemisphere people have named it. It gets higher in the southern hemisphere skies due to its greater southern declination. At this time, it is of course getting lower in northern hemisphere skies.

When the Sun is high in the sky there are longer hours of sunlight than when it is lower, because with a high path, the distance which it travels is longer. The part of the Earth's surface where it is summer also receives more of the Sun's radiation than does the part which is experiencing winter. This will become clear if you use your model Earth again. Set up a light source for the Sun and then hold the Earth so that the northern part of its polar axis is tilted away from the Sun. The total solar radiation is not equally distributed. The southern hemisphere gets more than the northern and for longer each day; the air and surface are heated and it is summer. It is winter in the northern hemisphere: the north polar regions receive no light, and the Sun rises later and sets earlier than in the summertime. Now tilt the Earth's axis the other way, so that the northern part of the polar axis is tilted towards the Sun. Conditions are reversed. The northern hemisphere lands have the lion's share of the Sun's radiation and it is summer while the southern hemisphere experiences its winter.

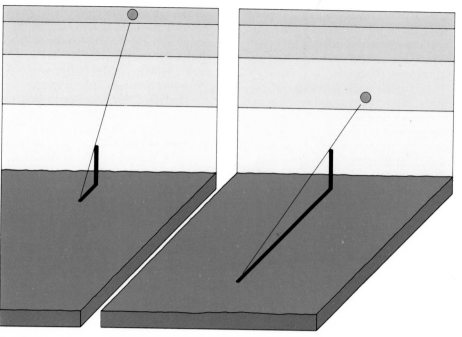

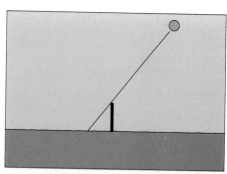

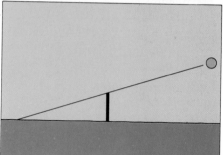

The shadow cast by the gnomon grows shorter as the Sun climbs higher in the sky. At noon when the Sun is due south, the shadow will be at its shortest.

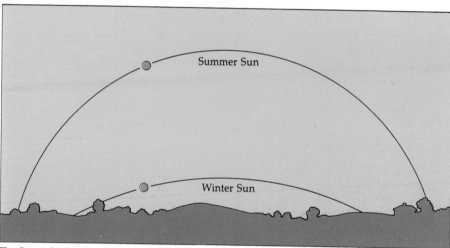

Summer Sun

Winter Sun

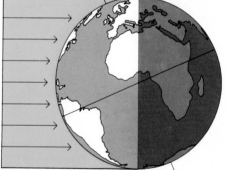

The Sun is higher in the sky in summer than in winter. There are more hours of sunlight in summer because, being higher, the Sun travels a greater distance across the sky.

Borneo tribesmen use a gnomon to measure the length of the noonday shadow to determine the season.

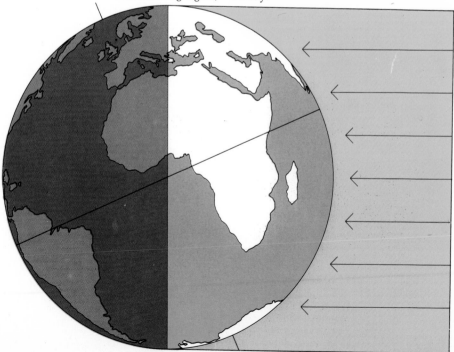

The seasons occur because the Earth's axis is tilted by 23½° with respect to the plane of its orbit. The northern hemisphere experiences its summer when it is tilted towards the Sun (*right*). When the northern hemisphere is tilting away from the Sun, it is winter (*left*).

MAKING SUNDIALS AND USING THEM

People have always needed to tell the time and sundials are the oldest form of timekeeper. They are sunclocks and rely on the position of the Sun in the sky to record the passing hours.

Sundials can be either portable or fixed, and they appear in a wide variety of shapes and sizes. Many are quite easy to construct. The earliest of all sundials is one based on the gnomon. It is easy to turn your simple gnomon (page 20) into a primitive sundial. You will already have marked the noonday shadow lengths and these lie due north (in the northern hemisphere) and due south (in the southern hemisphere). This point will be twelve o'clock noon on your dial. What about the other hours? You can mark them in using a clock to find where the Sun's shadow falls each hour.

The earliest astronomers had no clocks they could use, so how did they mark up a sundial? Take the earliest known sundial, the Egyptian one made in the reign of Pharoah Thutmose III in the 15th century BC. This is quite easy to make out of three pieces of wood, but how can one mark in the hours without a clock? Midday is straightforward enough, but what about the others? To do so we have to make some decision about the hours themselves. In the twentieth century, we have equal hours; every hour of the day and night throughout the year is equal. Such a scheme of reckoning hours arrived in the western world soon after the first mechanical clock appeared in the early fourteenth century, since equal hours were ideal for a mechanical clock to keep. Previously every civilisation had used unequal hours, which were quite unsuitable for any mechanical timekeeper.

The reason for using unequal hours was the changing length of the day throughout the year. Most civilizations decided that there would be a certain number of hours in the

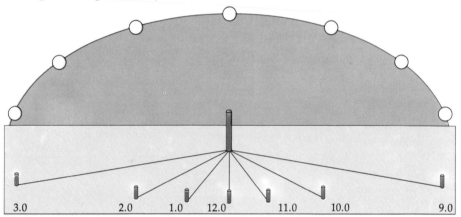

A primitive sundial can be made by using a gnomon and marking the shadow every hour.

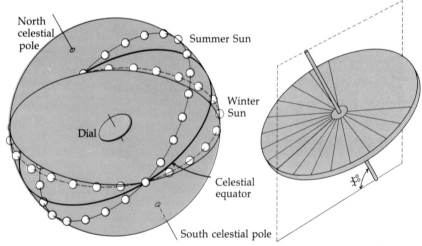

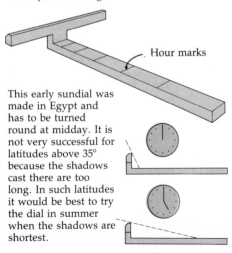

A Roman hemicyle dial invented by Berossus about 290 BC. The style is missing.

Hour marks

This early sundial was made in Egypt and has to be turned round at midday. It is not very successful for latitudes above 35° because the shadows cast there are too long. In such latitudes it would be best to try the dial in summer when the shadows are shortest.

The equatorial dial is the simplest of all dials and can be used to mark out the hour lines in most other types of dial. The dial plate of the equatorial dial is parallel to the celestial equator and the style is aligned with the celestial poles. Both faces of the plate are used according to the height of the Sun in the sky.
The hour lines are marked out at 15° intervals and $x°$ corresponds to your latitude. Sundials can be made from Plastikard, which is available from most model shops. Divisions should be marked with a water-resistant paint.

right
An eighteenth-century equatorial compass sundial with windvane and universal altitude adjustment.

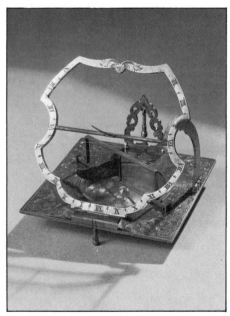

day (often twelve), and the same number during the night. But since the days are shorter in winter than in summer, the daylight hours would each be shorter in winter. They would, in fact, vary from day to day, gradually lengthening as summer approached, and then shortening again as winter came. To mark out a dial with these hours, it might be best to do so on the longest day of the year, marking the position of the shadow cast by the sundial's gnomon by light from the rising Sun, and later that cast by the setting Sun.

Then, with a mark for the noonday Sun, one can mark out twelve equal hour lines. The time the Sun's shadow takes to move from one hour mark to the next varies with the season. So in summertime the interval between two marks would be equal to 1¼ hours of the average or 'mean' time we use today, and in winter equal to only three-quarters of an hour. For this reason these hours were often known as 'temporary'.

There is, of course, no reason why the sundial (sometimes just called a 'dial' for short) should have a flat base on which the shadows fall. It could have a curved surface, as in the famous type of ancient dial known as the 'hemisphere of Berossus', after its designer, the astronomer-priest Berossus (sometimes spelled Berosus or Berossos) who lived about 290 BC. But whatever dial one does construct, the temporary hours can be marked as just described. On the other hand, it is possible to mark up a sundial with our present-day equal hours by calculation. It is not very difficult, although for some types of dial one must use a little trigonometry.

Today we have 24 hours in every day and night period. During this period the Sun appears to move right round the entire sky although, of course, from any particular place on the Earth's surface, it can only be seen for part of this time. This means that the Sun moves through 360° in 24 hours, or 15° in every hour. With this in mind we can do as dial-makers have done since equal hours were adopted, and mark the hours out by calculation. The easiest type of dial on which to do this is the **equatorial dial**.

The equatorial sundial is so called because its dial plate is parallel to the celestial equator. The 'style' or gnomon which casts the shadow is

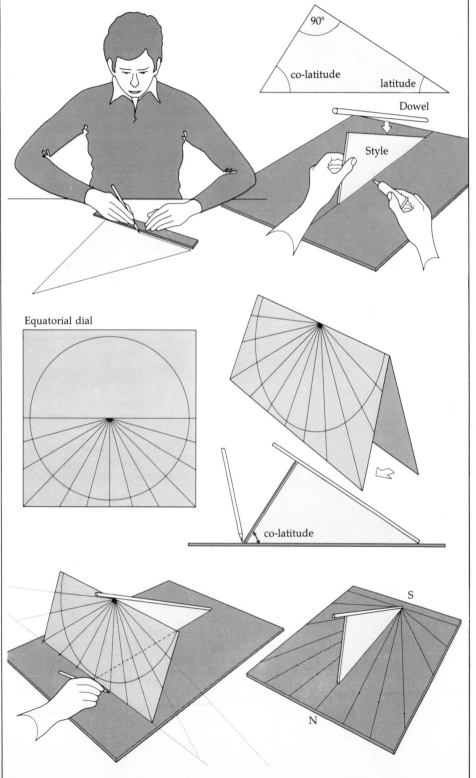

Equatorial dial

left
A horizontal dial can be marked up using an equatorial dial. The angle between the equatorial dial and the horizontal dial is the co-latitude (90°-latitude). Use a dowel for the top of the style which should make an angle with the dial plate equal to your latitude.

above
The horizontal sundial, Kew Gardens, London.

23

perpendicular to the dial plate. To mark out equal hours is simple. One first draws a line on the dial plate to represent the direction of the Sun at midday, and then marks off hour lines at 15° intervals. To set up such a sundial you must tilt the dial over so that it makes an angle of x degrees with the ground (i.e. with a horizontal plane). The number of degrees of x corresponds to your latitude. If in London, x will be 51°30′, in New York $x = 40°55′$ and in Sydney, Australia, $x = 33°55′$ (south). The equatorial sundial has a strange limitation which is that it does not work when the Sun is on the celestial equator, i.e. when it is at one of the equinoxes. At this moment the Sun's light is edge on to the dial plate.

More convenient to use is the **horizontal sundial**. Here there is no need to have two faces; the same one will do all the year round. Its hours are not at all at 15° to each other because the horizontal plate is inclined to the equatorial plane, and they are slightly altered in position. You can work out the positions mathematically. The formula is tangent A = sine latitude × tangent hour angle of the Sun. (A is the angle between the north-south line and the hour line you are drawing, and the hour angle of the Sun is 15° per hour, (30° for two hours, etc). But there is a simple way of marking out using the dial plate of an equatorial sundial. The drawing shows this. The one thing to be careful about is that the angle between the equatorial dial and your horizontal dial is correct. This should not be the latitude of the place where you are setting up the dial, but the co-latitude (90° – the latitude), i.e. 38°30′ for London, 49°05′ for New York and 56°05′ for Sydney.

Another useful type of sundial is the **vertical dial.** If you make one of these you can carry it outside in sunny weather and hang it on a wall which faces the midday sun. Once again, as in the horizontal dial, you can mark out the hour lines on the dial either mathematically or by using an equatorial dial as a marker. For the mathematically-minded the formula for hour lines is tan A = cos latitude × tan Sun's hour angle. (A has the same meaning as for the horizontal dial.) The diagram shows how to mark out the vertical dial plate. A square equatorial dial plate is more convenient than a round one.

Portable dials which will indicate solar time can take all kinds of forms. Probably one of the simplest to make

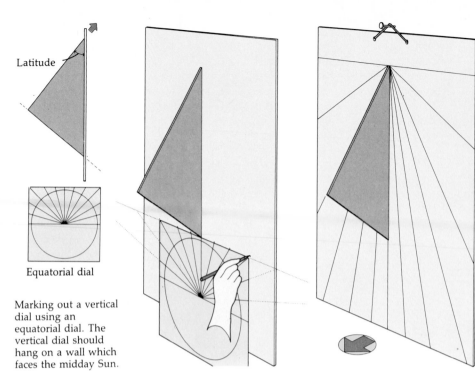

Latitude

Equatorial dial

Marking out a vertical dial using an equatorial dial. The vertical dial should hang on a wall which faces the midday Sun.

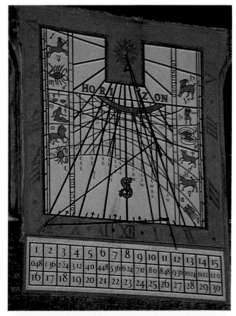

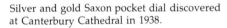

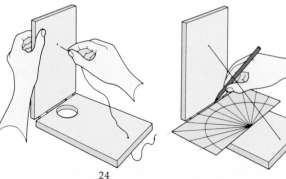

Silver and gold Saxon pocket dial discovered at Canterbury Cathedral in 1938.

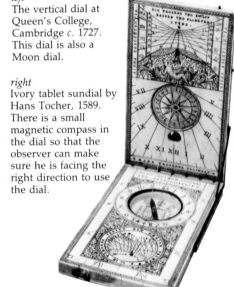

left
The vertical dial at Queen's College, Cambridge *c.* 1727. This dial is also a Moon dial.

right
Ivory tablet sundial by Hans Tocher, 1589. There is a small magnetic compass in the dial so that the observer can make sure he is facing the right direction to use the dial.

Co-latitude

Latitude

A portable dial can be made from two pieces of hinged wood. The lines are marked with an equatorial dial and the thread joining the two pieces acts as a style.

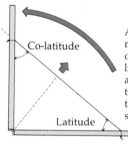

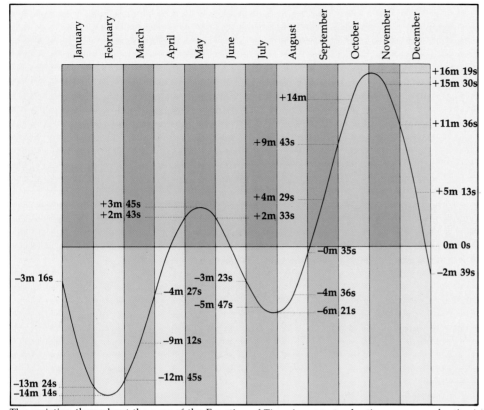

The variation throughout the year of the Equation of Time (apparent solar time – mean solar time) which can be as much as a quarter of an hour.

The chart shows months January through December along the top, with equation of time values:

+16m 19s
+15m 30s
+14m
+11m 36s
+9m 43s
+5m 13s
+4m 29s
+3m 45s
+2m 43s
+2m 33s
0m 0s
−0m 35s
−2m 39s
−3m 16s
−3m 23s
−4m 27s
−4m 36s
−5m 47s
−6m 21s
−9m 12s
−12m 45s
−13m 24s
−14m 14s

The Ambassadors 1533 by Hans Holbein the Younger. The objects shown in the painting reflect the interests of the two men in the arts and science: a pillar sundial and a polyhedral reclining sundial are included.

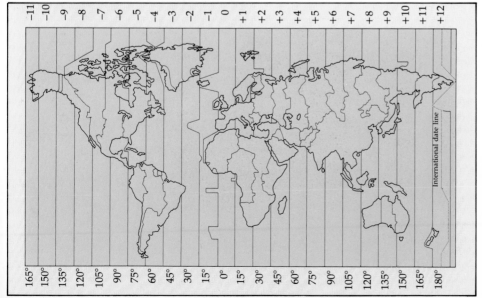

The Earth is divided into 24 time zones which each correspond to 15° of longitude. At the international date line, not only the hour but also the date changes.

is the folding horizontal dial. This is a horizontal dial with a lid which, when opened, stretches a thread from lid to dial plate. To give accurate time the dial must be set up facing the correct direction and it is best to have a small magnetic compass fitted into the dial plate. Or you could make a true pocket dial like one the Saxons used. Here you have a flat plate with a moveable peg as the style or gnomon. This will give you a rough indication of time – say 9 am, noon and 3 pm. You can mark it out using a clock as a guide or, alternatively, like a vertical dial, but putting the hours before one another. You will need three vertical rows of hours to cover the different lengths of shadow which will be cast at different seasons of the year. To use the dial, select the correct hole, insert the style, and turn the dial to face the Sun.

However accurately you make a sundial it will seldom give you the correct clock time because our hours are not based on the apparent motion of the real Sun but on the movement of what astronomers call a 'mean fictitious Sun'. This is because the true Sun does not move across the sky at a steady rate through the year. This erratic progress is due to two factors. First, because the Earth orbits the Sun in an ellipse instead of a true circle (page 134), it varies its orbital speed, with the result that the Sun appears to go fastest in the sky in December and slowest in June. Secondly, the Sun appears to move along the ecliptic, but our hours are worked out for the mean fictitious Sun which moves at a regular speed along the celestial equator. Because the ecliptic is inclined to the celestial equator, the rate of motion will differ depending on how far the eliptic lies north or south of the celestial equator. Combining both factors we get what is known as the equation of time, which is the difference between apparent Sun time and mean time. [The equation of time = (apparent solar time) – (mean time).] The equation of time may reach as much as 16 minutes 18 seconds, but it becomes zero four times a year.

The mean time used today depends on the 'time zone' in which we live. Greenwich mean time is the standard in Britain, in New York noon occurs 5 hours later and in Sydney 10 hours earlier. So if you live east or west of Greenwich your mean time will be different due to your geographical position. It is 1 hour for every 15° of longitude, or 4 minutes for every degree.

DETERMINING THE DATE OF EASTER

Calendars are based on the movements of the Sun and Moon. A basic problem in constructing a calendar is that the year does not consist of a whole number of lunar months; nor does it contain a whole number of days. Many ancient calendars were very inaccurate, sometimes with the seasons occurring in the wrong months.

There are two methods of making a calendar; one is to use the Moon and the other the Sun. The Sun gives us the year – the seasonal calendar – but the earliest calendars were based on the movements of the Moon. Periods defined by the Moon do not fit exactly into those determined by the Sun, and this gives problems in establishing the date of Easter (which is a lunar calendar festival) in terms of our solar calendar.

The Moon orbits the Earth once every month. The word 'month' is a corruption of 'mooneth' or monthly period. Ancient man used the Moon as his calendar guide because it was an easy timekeeper for him to reckon by. It showed phases every month (pages 94–95), apparently going through a cycle of changes of shape in a period of time which was not too long to remember. The cycle takes place every 29½ days (29.53059 days, or 29 days 12 hours 44 minutes 03 seconds, to be precise). Or we can record the time it takes for the Moon to complete an orbit round the Earth, and measure the sidereal month – the period in which the Moon moves from some fixed star back to the same star again. This is 27.32158 days (27 days 7 hours 43 minutes 4.5 seconds). In neither case can the period be divided exactly into the tropical or seasonal year of 365 days – or more precisely 365¼ days. Try dividing 365 and 365.25 by 29.5 and 27.3, and you will end up with odd fractions, which make it difficult for calculation and really mean that a lunar calendar and a solar calendar are incompatible from any practical point of view.

Easter is a festival based on a lunar calendar, since the Hebrews, like all early nomadic peoples, used a calendar of this kind. It is defined (in the Western churches) as the first Sunday after the Full Moon on or after the vernal equinox. (The Eastern churches of Greece and Russia use a slightly different lunar dating.) So to determine the date of Easter it is necessary to find the date of the vernal equinox, the dates on the solar calendar of the phases of the Moon (and these vary from one year to the next), and the dates on which the days of the week fall.

The vernal equinox occurs on March 21, so we must find on which day of the week the Full Moon occurs after this date. The sixteenth-century astronomer Christopher Clavius and his colleagues who drew up the Gregorian calendar we now use, worked out a set of rules for determining Easter. These make use of the Dominical Letter and the Epact assigned to each year – numbers which are sometimes given in diaries.

above
The Full Moon rising over Monument Valley, Arizona. The monthly phases of the Moon were used by ancient man as a calendar guide.

below
Easter is a festival based on a lunar calendar. Easter Day falls on the **first** Sunday after the Full Moon on or after the vernal equinox.

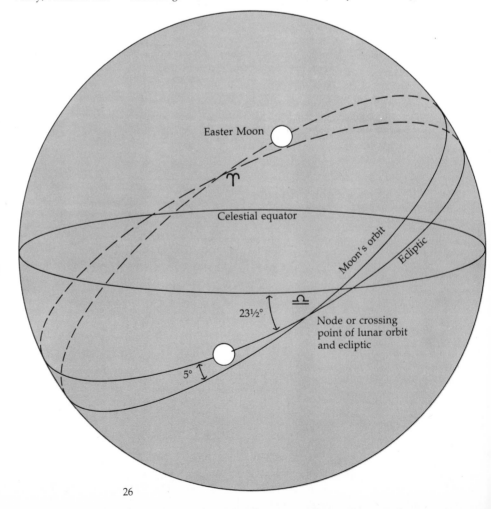

The Dominical Letters give clues to the days of the week and the dates on which Sundays fall. There are therefore seven Dominical Letters: A, B, C, D . . . . G. A is assigned to January 1, B to January 2, and so on with January 7 having G. The series then repeats; January 8 is A, January 9 is B, etc. Suppose the first Sunday in the year falls on January 4 (as it does in 1981), then as its Dominical Letter is D, D is the Dominical Letter for that year. No Dominical Letter is given to the extra day (February 29) of a leap year, so a leap year has two Dominical Letters, one for Sundays before the extra day and another for the Sundays after it. Thus the leap year 1980 has two Dominical Letters, F and E. Because there are 52 whole weeks and 1 day in an ordinary year, the sequence of Dominical Letters for succeeding years runs backwards.

The Epact is a number calculated from the fact that every nineteen years the phases of the Moon appear on the same dates. This was discovered by Meton of Athens about 430 BC. However, the Metonic cycle is not exact, and some corrections must be made when using it with the Gregorian calendar which is good (although not perfect) in long-term accuracy. Since 12 lunations (New Moon to New Moon) total 354 days (i.e. $12 \times 29\frac{1}{2}$) and these fall short of a tropical year (i.e. solar year) by 11 whole days (or 12 whole days for a leap year), the Epact has to take account of this 11- or 12-day difference. Indeed, the word Epact is derived from the Greek *epaktos* meaning brought in, as we are bringing in 11 or 12 days each year. Knowing the date of New Moon for any one year, the Epact can be worked out using lunations of 29 and 30 days alternately.

Computing the date of Easter in 1981 will show how the Epacts and Dominical Letters are used. For 1981 we have the Dominical Letter D and Epact 24. Consider the Epact first. The number 24 means that the first Full Moon in 1981 appears 6 + 15 days after the year begins. The Epact tells us that the Moon is 24 days old at the beginning of the year, so there are (30–24) or 6 days of that lunation left to run, while 15 more days take us to Full Moon in the following lunation. Thus the first Full Moon in 1981 is on January 21. Two further lunations, one of 29 days and one of 30 days, take us on another 59 days, so that there is a Full Moon on March 21. The next Full Moon will be 29 days later, i.e. on April 19.

What day of the week will April 19 be? The Dominical Letter D tells us that the first Sunday is on the fourth day, i.e. January 4. Therefore subsequent Sundays will be on January 11, 18, 25; February 1, 8, 15, 22; March 1, 8, 15, 22, 29; and on April 5, 12, 19, . . . So Easter Day is on April 19.

A Mesopotamian astronomical tablet containing observations and calculations of the New Moon for three consecutive years from March 23, 103 BC to April 18, 100 BC.

right
The illustration for the March calendar from the fifteenth-century Book of Hours, *Les Très Riches Heures du Duc de Berry*. The March signs of the Zodiac and the phases of the Moon are shown at the top of the picture.

Dominical Letters and Epact Numbers 1980–1990		
Year	Dominical Letter	Epact Number
1980	FE	13
1981	D	24
1982	C	5
1983	B	16
1984	AG	27
1985	F	8
1986	E	19
1987	D	0
1988	CB	11
1989	A	22
1990	B	3

ECLIPSES OF THE SUN

Although the Sun's diameter is almost exactly 400 times the diameter of the Moon, it is also about 400 times farther away, and so their apparent size is the same. If the Sun and Moon are in line, the Moon can therefore block out the Sun to cause an eclipse.

A most astonishing phenomen is the total eclipse, when the whole disc of the Sun disappears. This can be a terrifying sight. Day suddenly turns into night, the stars become visible, birds go to roost and animals settle down to sleep; the temperature drops and the whole world takes on a strange, eerie appearance, and buildings look as if they are made of cardboard. No wonder that in the past there were some countries where it was believed that the Sun had been swallowed by a monster. The people banged drums and gongs to frighten it away, or performed sacrifices to placate it, so that the Sun could be restored to its customary splendour. That the Sun did return must have made them feel that their efforts were worthwhile although, of course, we now know that a total solar eclipse can never last for very long. The maximum is 7 minutes 40 seconds but most are much shorter than this. All the same, even just a few minutes will seem long if you think that the Sun has gone for ever!

The nature of solar eclipses puzzled astronomers all over the world, because all one sees is that part or all of the Sun's disc disappears. Early Chinese astronomers suggested that the Sun underwent changes of power or brightness, and the early Greek philosopher Anaximander (6th century BC) also thought eclipses were due to the Sun and the Moon temporarily ceasing to shine. However, the true nature of solar eclipses eventually became known by the Chinese, Greeks and other civilizations and was found to be due to the motion of the Moon. Ancient astronomers realized that the Moon orbited the Earth, although not in precisely the same apparent path as the Sun. The Moon's orbit, they discovered, is tilted over 5° compared with the apparent orbit of the Sun – the ecliptic. This means that solar

eclipses will not occur every month, and you can readily make a model to see why this is so.

Once again use your model (page 14) of the Earth, with a knitting-needle for the rotation axis. You now need a long arm to represent the radius of the Moon's orbit (i.e. the Moon's distance). The long arm can be made of light wood or aluminium. If you want to make a scale model using a bead (about 1.8

cm in diameter) for the Moon and a tennis-ball for the Earth, then the arm should be 2 m long, but this would be rather unwieldy. Since we are only concerned with showing the principle of eclipses it will be quite satisfactory if the arm is only about 60 or 70 cm long. It should have a hole close to one end, large enough for the knitting-needle to pass through comfortably but not loosely. At the other end fix a long toothpick

left
A partial eclipse is visible to observers just outside the band of totality of a total eclipse, or when the Earth, Moon and Sun are not precisely aligned.

below
A total solar eclipse. Total eclipses are very important for the astronomer because parts of the Sun's atmosphere which are not normally visible, can be seen.

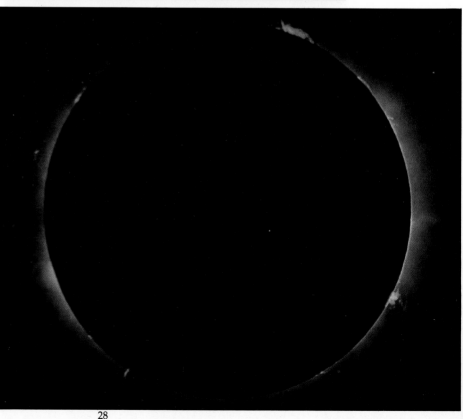

28

right

The diamond ring effect can occur at the beginning or end of a total eclipse. The effect is produced by a patch of sunlight shining through an irregularity at the edge of the Moon.

below left

Annular eclipse, Greece April 1976. When the Sun is nearest to the Earth and the Moon at its most distant, the Moon will obscure only the central part of the Sun's disc leaving a ring of light or 'annulus' round the edge.

below right

The total eclipse of 1973, showing the corona which is the outermost layer of the solar atmosphere. The corona extends tens of millions of kilometres into space.

and on the top of this fix your bead.

Now that you have a model of the Earth-Moon system, even though not to scale, it is possible to see how eclipses of the Sun occur. First switch on a table-lamp to represent the Sun, and turn off any other lights. Now align your Moon and Earth so that they are in line with the Sun. The Moon should now cast a shadow on the Earth. This is the condition for a solar eclipse. You will notice that the Moon's disc is dark as seen from the Earth: this is the condition of New Moon (pages 94–95).

We must now investigate what happens a few months later at New Moon. To do this keep your Earth-Moon system pointing in the same direction (i.e. to the same wall of the room) and walk a quarter of the way round the Sun. In other words you have moved 90° round the Sun. Remember to keep the Earth's polar axis in the same direction as it was before. Now rotate the Moon-arm until the Sun, Moon and Earth are lined up again. This time, though, tilt the Moon-arm down just a little to represent the changed inclination of the Moon's orbit with respect to the Earth. Now the Moon will not be casting its shadow on the Earth but just below it. A similar thing happens when the Moon-arm is tilted upwards a little; the Moon's shadow lies above the Earth. Thus the model demonstrates how the tilt of the Moon's orbit prevents there being a solar eclipse every month, even though the Sun, Moon and Earth are in line every month.

The Greek astronomers became well aware of this inclination of the Moon's orbit. What is more, by the time of the great Greek astronomer Ptolemy (2nd century AD), it was clear that the Moon's orbit was very complicated. We now know that all kinds of forces affect the orbit – the pull of the Earth, of the Sun and of the other planets, for example. But the main facts to appreciate when considering eclipses are, first, that the orbit is tilted and, secondly, that the orbit itself rotates. If we look at the problem from the point of view of an observer on Earth, we can see that eclipses of the Sun will only occur when the Moon is close to a point on its orbit where that orbit crosses the ecliptic. At any other point on its orbit the Moon will be too far to the 'side' for its small disc to blot out the Sun.

The orbits of the Moon round the Earth and of the Earth round the Sun are not circles but ellipses. In consequence, the Earth is further

from the Sun at one time of the year than at another, and the distance between the Moon and the Earth varies too. Viewed from the Earth this means that the apparent size of the Sun differs a little throughout the year, as does the apparent size of the Moon. As a result, even when the Moon is in a position to give a total eclipse this may not occur. If the Sun is at its nearest to us and the Moon at its most distant, then the Moon's disc will appear too small to cover the whole of the Sun's disc. The Moon will pass in front of the Sun but it will only obscure the central part of its disc, leaving a ring of light or 'annulus' round the edge. This is an 'annular' eclipse (a name that is sometimes mistaken to mean annual!). On the other hand, if the Sun is at its furthest, so its disc is at its smallest, and the Moon at its

nearest and thus displays its largest disc, there is a total eclipse. You can see, then, that whether an eclipse is annular or total depends on the relative distances of the Sun and Moon from the Earth, as does the duration if it is total.

An eclipse of the Sun occurs when the Moon casts its shadow on the Earth, but from how much of the Earth is such an eclipse visible? Another model will answer the question, so set up your tennis-ball Earth on its axis at as great a distance as possible from the table-lamp or, better still, a focusing torch. Next put your bead representing the Moon a distance of 2 m from the Earth and line it up so that it does cast a shadow on the Earth. You will see that the shadow is rather small, with a larger but less dense shadow around it. This shows that only a few

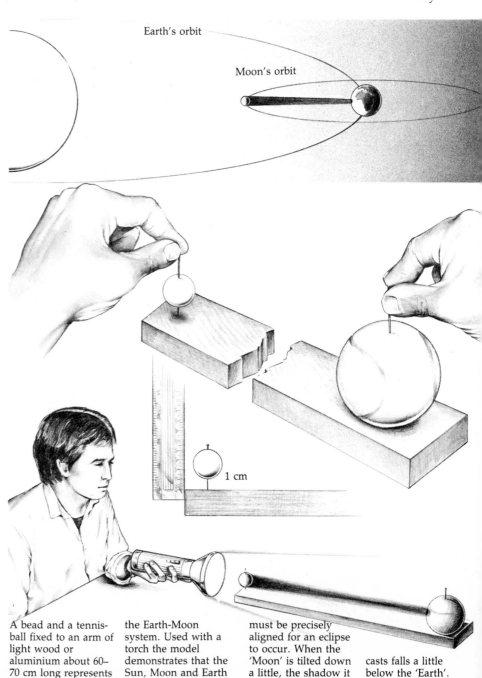

Earth's orbit

Moon's orbit

1 cm

A bead and a tennis-ball fixed to an arm of light wood or aluminium about 60–70 cm long represents the Earth-Moon system. Used with a torch the model demonstrates that the Sun, Moon and Earth must be precisely aligned for an eclipse to occur. When the 'Moon' is tilted down a little, the shadow it casts falls a little below the 'Earth'.

TABLE OF SOLAR ECLIPSES

Date	Type	Place	Maximum duration of totality
1980 Aug 10	Annular	S. Pacific & central S. America	—
1981 Feb 4	Annular	Pacific Ocean & Australia	—
July 31	TOTAL	U.S.S.R	2m 03s
1983 June 11	TOTAL	Indian Ocean, Indonesia, New Guinea	5m 11s
Dec 4	Annular	Atlantic Ocean & central Africa	—
1984 May 30	Annular	Mexico, S.E. U.S.A. & N. Africa	—
Nov 22	TOTAL	New Guinea & S. Pacific Ocean	1m 59s
1985 Nov 12	TOTAL	S. Pacific Ocean	1m 59s
1986 Oct 3	Central	N. Atlantic Ocean	—
1987 Mar 29	Central	Atlantic Ocean & Africa	—
Sept 23	Annular	China & S. Pacific Ocean	—
1988 Mar 18	TOTAL	Indonesia & Philippines	3m 46s
1990 July 22	TOTAL	Finland, U.S.S.R. & Alaska, U.S.A.	2m 33s

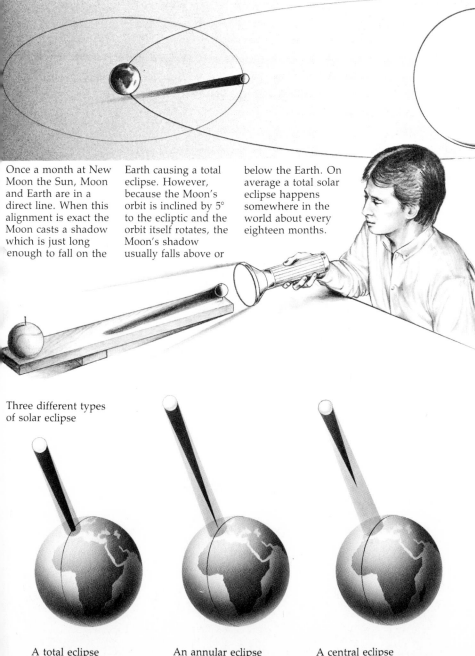

Once a month at New Moon the Sun, Moon and Earth are in a direct line. When this alignment is exact the Moon casts a shadow which is just long enough to fall on the Earth causing a total eclipse. However, because the Moon's orbit is inclined by 5° to the ecliptic and the orbit itself rotates, the Moon's shadow usually falls above or below the Earth. On average a total solar eclipse happens somewhere in the world about every eighteen months.

Three different types of solar eclipse

A total eclipse   An annular eclipse   A central eclipse

people over a small area of the Earth can ever see a total solar eclipse. Next, if you move your Moon bead slightly, you will see that the shadow quickly moves across the tennis-ball, and this is indeed what happens; the shadow giving totality moves rapidly across the Earth. (The effect is even more marked when you remember that the Earth is moving round the Sun as well.) If you are close to the area where totality is visible – in the area of the larger and less dense shadow – you will see a *partial* solar eclipse. Only part of the Sun's disc will be obscured; it will look as if a bite has been taken out of the Sun, and none of the dramatic awe-inspiring effects of a total eclipse will be seen.

Because of the movements of the ecliptic, of the Moon's orbit, of the Earth's polar axis and the rotation of the Earth, total solar eclipses never occur in the same place consecutively. Indeed they very seldom happen again in the same place. For instance, there was a total solar eclipse visible in a line running from North Wales across to County Durham in England in 1927, but the next one to be seen from the United Kingdom will not occur until 1999 and will then only be visible in Cornwall. The track of totality is never wide and usually no more than about 50 km. A list of important eclipses is given and if there is one not far away from you, you really must try to see it as it is indeed an amazing experience. In fact when you remember that something like 71% of the Earth's surface is ocean, to be able to see one conveniently on land will be very rare and such an opportunity is not to be missed.

As total eclipses last for so short a time some astronomers have recently taken to chartering a high-flying aircraft from which to make observations, flying well above any clouds along the path of the moving shadow of totality. Certainly this has prevented them from suffering the kind of disappointment experienced by colleagues who have frequently travelled abroad to observe an eclipse and then found it so cloudy that they saw nothing!

Drawings of three different types of solar eclipse are given. They show the shadows cast by the Moon to give a total eclipse, an annular eclipse, and a 'central' eclipse, where an observer on Earth notices an annular eclipse unless he is at the closest point on the Earth's surface to the Moon, when he sees a total eclipse of very short duration.

THE SOLAR SURFACE

Early astronomers observed dark patches on the Sun. One theory was that these spots were planets, but this was dismissed by Galileo, who noted that the spots moved across the Sun in the same direction and at the same rate. From these and other observations he concluded that the Sun rotated.

If you look at the Sun through haze or mist you will sometimes see one or two dark spots on its surface. Studying these provides information about the solar surface.

Such spots were observed by the astronomers of ancient China two thousand years ago, but they were not recorded in the West until the early seventeenth century; then Christoph Scheiner, a German astronomer, saw them but thought they were small planets orbiting the Sun. The West lagged behind China in making such observations because Europeans thought that the Sun was

a perfect body and could not have spots or blemishes on it. Galileo, who claimed that he had observed sunspots eighteen months before Scheiner, was certain that the spots were on the Sun's surface – he did not believe that the Sun was a perfect body – and he proved his point by careful observations. Both Scheiner and Galileo used telescopes for their researches and you can see what they did, if you use a telescope as described on page 34. (Do *not* use it to look at the Sun directly.)

Working with your telescope, you can prove just as Galileo did, that the sunspots do appear on the solar surface. If you watch the Sun's disc each day and find one or more sunspots, you will notice that as time passes they move across the Sun. The reason for this is that the Sun rotates, spinning on its axis once every 25 days. Galileo saw that as a

spot was carried round to the edge or limb of the Sun it began to lose its shape when seen near the centre of the disc and appeared squashed sideways. This is just what one would expect if the spot is on the Sun's surface, because the compression is an optical effect due to perspective as the spot moves to the limit of our vision before rotation causes it to disappear to the rear of the Sun. You can see a similar effect if you rotate your model of the Earth so that for instance, the continent of Africa, moves from the middle of the sphere to the edge.

If you make observations of the Sun's disc when there are a number of spots at different 'latitudes' on the solar surface, you will notice that those close to the solar equator move faster than those at higher latitudes. For example, while a spot near the equator takes 25 days to complete a

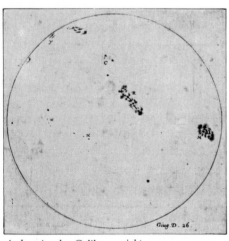

A drawing by Galileo of sunspots. In the early seventeenth century it was believed that the Sun was a perfect body and could have no blemishes on it. But Galileo was certain that sunspots were on the Sun's surface.

right
The 'butterfly diagram' which shows that at the beginning of a solar cycle sunspots appear at high solar latitudes; as the cycle progresses they appear at lower latitudes. The diagram also shows that as an old cycle ends a new one begins.

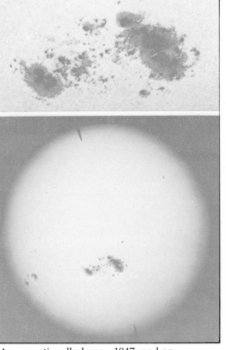

An exceptionally large sunspot group on the Sun's disc April 7 1947, and an enlargement of the group.

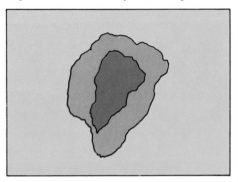

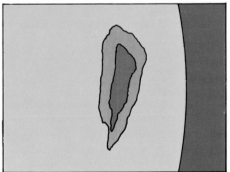

As the Sun rotates, sunspots appear to move across its surface. As a sunspot nears the Sun's limb the effect of perspective makes the spot seem compressed.

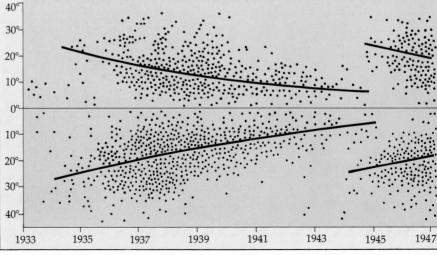

rotation, spots at latitude 30° take some 25.8 days and at 40° latitude 27.8 days. Spots are not usually found at latitudes lower than 5° or greater than 45°.

The number of spots on the Sun varies. A maximum number occurs every eleven years or thereabouts, this period never being much less than 10 years or more than 12. Spots frequently appear in groups of two or sometimes more, and at the beginning of a solar cycle (following on a minimum number of spots), the first ones appear at high solar latitudes. As the cycle progresses, the spots appear at lower and lower latitudes. You can observe all this by watching the Sun whenever you can, noting down numbers of sunspots and their latitudes (page 35) but, of course, to cover a complete solar cycle will take you eleven years!

Sunspots look black, having a dark central point or 'umbra' and a lighter surrounding area, the 'penumbra'. But sunspots are not dark: they do emit light and only appear dark by contrast with the bright disc or 'photosphere' of the Sun. The difference between the two occurs because a spot has a temperature of about 5,000°C and so is cooler than the photosphere at 6,000°C. Since cooler gas gives off less energy than hotter gas sunspots appear relatively dark.

Above the photosphere lie thinner parts of the Sun's atmosphere. You cannot see this in daylight unless you use special equipment on a mountain-top observatory, but it is visible during a total solar eclipse. Then it appears like a pearly-coloured crown around the eclipsed Sun and is known as the *corona* (Latin: crown). The corona extends some tens of kilometres beyond the photosphere, but its shape alters slightly with the progress of the sunspot cycle.

During a total solar eclipse you may also see one or more flame-shaped objects around the edge of the Sun. These are prominences – huge glowing clouds of hydrogen gas. They can be photographed at any time through a telescope but to do so you need either a very elaborate optical instrument, the spectrohelioscope or a special filter which is rather expensive.

Sometimes, on a very clear day when the air is steady your projected image will show that the Sun's photosphere looks mottled, like a rice-pudding. Heat pouring out from the Sun causes little lumps of bright, very hot gas to rise to the surface, cool, and when cooler and darker, subside again; this continual vertical circulation gives the rice-pudding appearance. 'Granulation' is best observed from telescopes sent up in high-flying balloons. Another noticeable feature on the Sun's disc are bright patches of hot gas called *faculae* (Latin: torches). These are associated with sunspots and can sometimes be seen when the spots are close to the edge of the Sun's disc. They undergo rapid changes in themselves but, like the sunspots, seem to follow the eleven-year cycle.

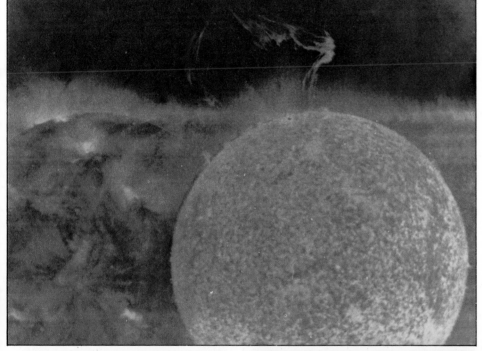

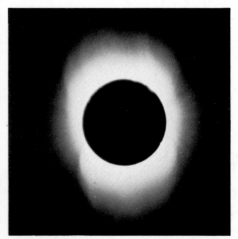

A huge solar eruption photographed from the orbiting space-station Skylab. Intensely hot rarefied gases are being sent over 300,000 km into the corona.

A photographic negative showing the spots as white, of a complex sunspot group and surrounding granulation of the photosphere. Such groups may be over 100,000 km long, but a granule only about 1,000 km across.

A prominence of hot hydrogen gas rising from the Sun to some 70,000 km above its surface. The photograph was taken by an amateur astronomer, Henry Hatfield.

The shape of the inner corona can be seen to change constantly with the progress of the sunspot cycle. At the eclipse of 1977 (*above*) it was near the solar maximum.

OBSERVING THE SUN

It is always dangerous to look at the Sun direct. However, there are safe ways of observing the Sun, based on the simple camera obscura.

The best way of looking at the Sun is to project its image onto a piece of white paper. You can easily demonstrate this by making a camera obscura. The name comes from the Latin *camera* meaning a 'chamber' or 'room', and *obscura* meaning 'dark'; in other words a 'dark room'. A darkened room in which you could stand and view scenes from outside was familiar to the Arabs and Chinese a thousand years ago, and it is not difficult to make a model of one to illustrate the principle.

Take a cardboard box and lid, put a piece of white paper on the inside of one end, and pierce a pinhole in the opposite end (Fig. 2). Light coming through the pinhole will project an image of an object outside the box onto the white paper. The image will be reversed and upside down. In a darkened room a mirror can be used to give you an upright image. If a larger hole is made in the box and a small magnifying lens inserted, the image will be brighter and can be made very sharp (Fig. 2). This latter is the principle behind the simple box camera, but there is a problem; in lifting the lid of the box light will be let in, making the image difficult to see.

However, a camera obscura is an excellent way of observing the Sun because the Sun gives an extremely bright image.

For a telescope you need a 'projection box'. This is a variation on the camera obscura with one side cut away and preferably slightly tapered in shape (Fig. 3). It should be light in weight otherwise it will pull the telescope downwards, and the opening in the side should be large

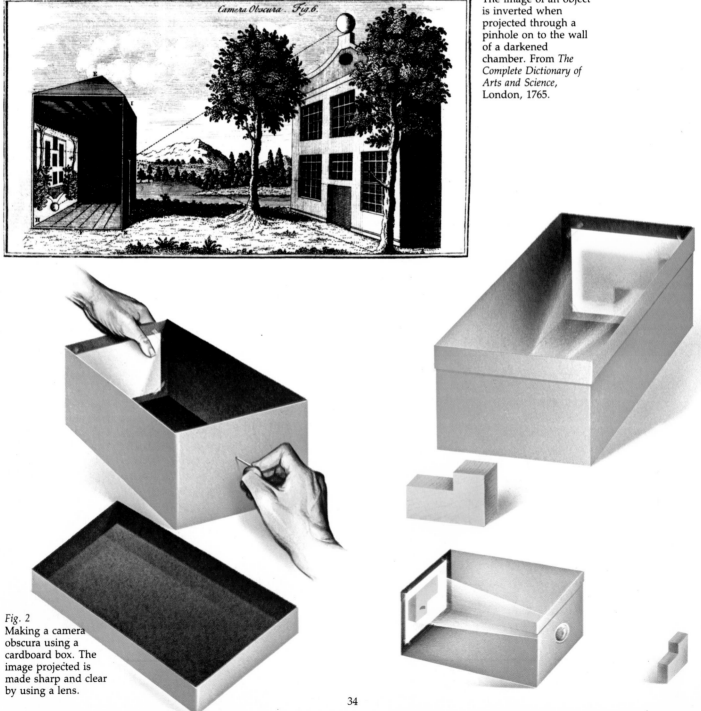

Fig. 1
The image of an object is inverted when projected through a pinhole on to the wall of a darkened chamber. From *The Complete Dictionary of Arts and Science*, London, 1765.

Fig. 2
Making a camera obscura using a cardboard box. The image projected is made sharp and clear by using a lens.

enough for your hand so that you can, for instance, plot the positions of sunspots.

It has been mentioned (page 32) that it is useful to plot the latitudes of sunspots, and the projection box is ideal for this. First mark down, on the piece of paper at the end of your projection box, the positions of any spots you can see. Then you can set about finding their latitude. To do this you need to know the east-west declination line on your drawing of the Sun. This line is easily determined: choose a small spot on the Sun's disc and adjust your telescope so that it lies at one edge of your field of view and mark this point on your drawing. Now keep the telescope still, and you will find

that the rotation of the Earth moves you and your telescope so that the image of this spot drifts across your field of view. When the spot has reached the other edge of your field of view, mark that point as well. You now have the east-west declination line. If you draw a line perpendicular to it, passing through the centre of the Sun, you will have a line to help in determining the heliographic longitude of sunspots.

The east-west declination line may or may not coincide with the Sun's equator. Whether it does or not depends on how the Sun's axis is tilted with respect to the Earth, and this varies throughout the year. However you can get an idea of the latitude of any spot if you know the

amount of this tilt. To measure the solar or 'heliographic' latitude accurately you will have to make use of some current tables of the Sun's position, axial inclination and so on, as well as using some trigonometry. (Such information and instructions are published for instance by the British Astronomical Association, page 200). You can also find the heliographic longitude of spots accurately in this way, too, but for a rough estimate, time the transit of spots across the centre line you have drawn. Then, because the Sun takes some 25 days to rotate once, i.e. to go through 360°, each hour between transits means a heliographic longitude between spots of 0.6° or 36 arc minutes.

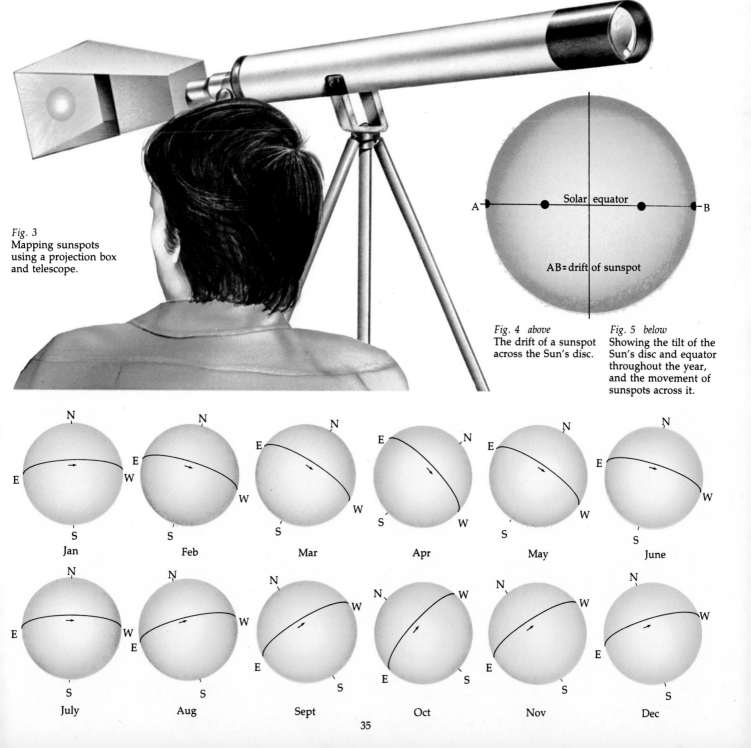

Fig. 3
Mapping sunspots using a projection box and telescope.

A⊢————— Solar equator —————⊢B

AB = drift of sunspot

Fig. 4 above
The drift of a sunspot across the Sun's disc.

Fig. 5 below
Showing the tilt of the Sun's disc and equator throughout the year, and the movement of sunspots across it.

Jan   Feb   Mar   Apr   May   June

July   Aug   Sept   Oct   Nov   Dec

HOW TO ANALYSE SUNLIGHT

Light can be broken down into the colours of the spectrum, and the first person to do this was Isaac Newton in the seventeenth century. These colours correspond to the various wavelengths which together make up white light.

Isaac Newton began to experiment during 1665 and 1666 to try to establish the nature of light. He was interested in knowing why light became coloured when passed through a prism. You too can repeat Newton's experiment quite easily but it is necessary to have two prisms. It is best to do as Newton did and use ones made of glass. But glass prisms are not easy to buy and if you cannot find any, it is possible to make them, although you will have to be content with plastic prisms filled with water. These do not disperse sunlight into its separate colours as effectively as glass prisms, but they will serve us well enough.

To make your own prisms you will need a sheet of transparent

plastic or Perspex. Transparent plastic can be obtained from a shop stocking model aircraft or model railways: it is called 'Plastiglaze' and you should buy the thickest sheet available. Whether Perspex or Plastiglaze is used, you should cut out pieces for each prism as shown in the drawing. These pieces must now be stuck together. For Plastiglaze use a polystyrene cement (liquid or in a tube), and for Perspex a special Perspex cement is the best adhesive. Stick the three sides and one end together, leaving one end open. Stand the half-completed prism on one end with the opening at the top, and fill it with water. Fill it as

full as possible but do not let the water overflow, and ensure that you can fit the triangular-shaped endpiece on without it getting wet. Once the prism is filled, apply adhesive to the edges of the endpiece and stick this to the open end. Do not move the prism until it is thoroughly dry. (It is wise to stand the unfinished prism in a bowl before you fill it with water so that if your sealing is not perfect you do not have water spilling everywhere when you move it!) You may find that you have trapped a small air bubble, but provided it is small, it does not matter.

Once you have made two prisms you are ready to repeat Newton's

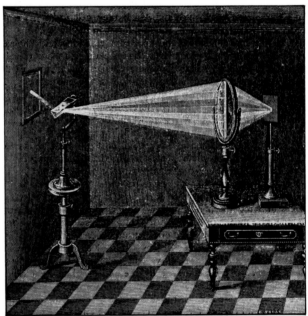

When light enters a prism, it is split into the colours of a spectrum. This spectrum combines to make white light again by passing through a lens, and then shines onto a small screen. The diagram (*below*) shows the same experiment using two prisms. Newton used this method to explore the spectrum.

Making a prism: instructions are in the text. All the pieces of plastic should be cut out separately and glued together; do not try to fold them over.

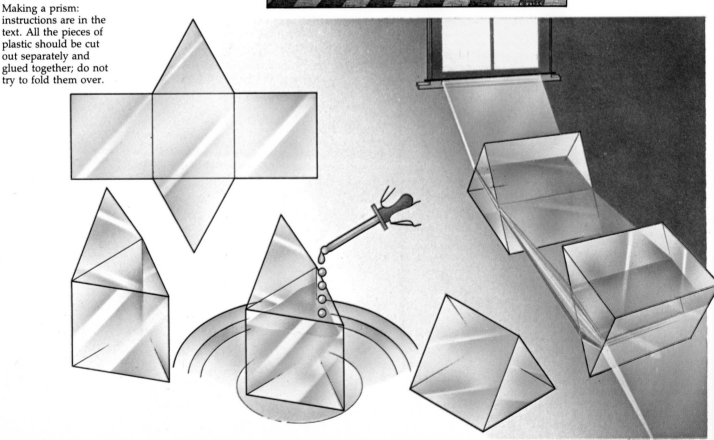

36

experiment. Choose a sunny day, close the curtains or blinds, but arrange them so that just a small strip of sunlight comes through. Allow this beam of sunlight to shine through one prism. The prism will split up the sunlight, dispersing it into its separate colours, from red at one end of the spectrum to blue and violet at the other. So far so good: this is a common enough effect which you have probably seen when the bevelled edge of a mirror reflects sunlight, the bevelled edge acting like a prism. Now take the second prism and turn it the opposite way to the first prism. Then place it close to the first one so that the coloured

beam reaches it. You will see that the colours are combined again to give 'white' light.

This experiment was important. It led Newton to understand that 'white' sunlight was composed of various colours. In 1802 an English scientist, William Wollaston made a 'spectroscope' with which he hoped to separate each of the colours of the spectrum. To achieve this he passed the sunlight first through a narrow slit, then used a lens to change the light from this slit to a parallel beam. The beam passed through a prism and was then examined with a small telescope. You can make such an instrument using one of your prisms,

a magnifying glass and either a small telescope, one side of a pair of binoculars or, failing these, a second magnifying glass. You also require a very narrow slit. Care must be taken in building this instrument if it is to work, but the result will be worthwhile; the drawing shows what has to be done.

There is another way of making a spectroscope which uses a 'grating' instead of a prism. The grating is a sheet of transparent material ruled with thousands of very fine lines. The lines are so close together that the gaps between them are comparable with the lengths of light waves (for light comes to us in the form of waves). You can see a 'reflection grating' in operation if you look at a reflected light beam from a long-playing record: the beam is split into its separate colours. The drawing shows how you can use a reflection grating to make a spectroscope, but it is necessary to buy the grating – an old record is not suitable. Such gratings are not cheap, but a supplier is given in the list of useful addresses on page 200.

Set up your spectroscope on a table and then feed sunlight to the slit. The easiest way to do this is by using a mirror. On looking through the telescope, or binocular or magnifying glass, you should see the coloured spectrum crossed by a great number of dark lines. These lines are a clue to gases present in the Sun.

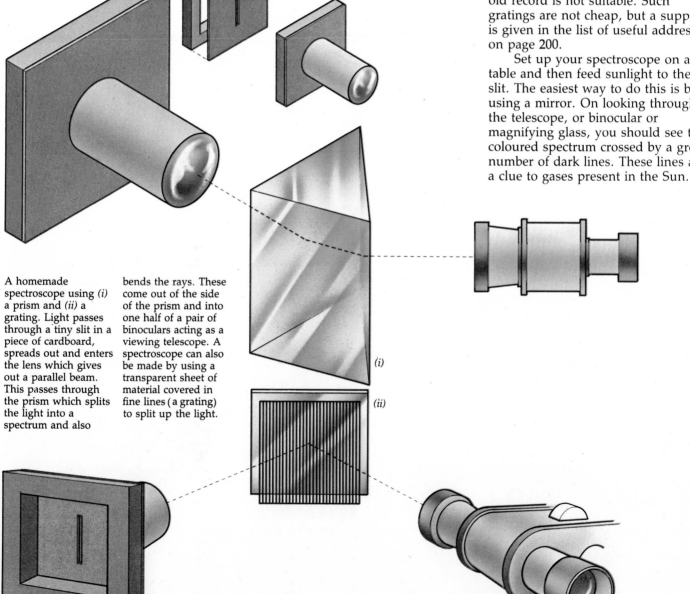

A homemade spectroscope using (i) a prism and (ii) a grating. Light passes through a tiny slit in a piece of cardboard, spreads out and enters the lens which gives out a parallel beam. This passes through the prism which splits the light into a spectrum and also bends the rays. These come out of the side of the prism and into one half of a pair of binoculars acting as a viewing telescope. A spectroscope can also be made by using a transparent sheet of material covered in fine lines (a grating) to split up the light.

(i)

(ii)

FRAUNHOFER LINES AND THEIR MEANING

The dark lines in the solar spectrum were first observed in the early nineteenth century. But at the time scientists did not realize that they provide important information about the composition of the Sun.

Wollaston noticed some of the dark lines in the spectrum. He believed that they might represent the boundaries between different colours of sunlight and did not study them further. However, the lines are of much greater significance than Wollaston guessed. In Germany the instrument-maker and physicist Joseph Fraunhofer built a beautiful precision spectroscope and studied the lines in detail, plotting the positions of 574 of them. But he, too, did not know what they were.

Eventually Fraunhofer and some other scientists, who had been interested in using the spectroscope for looking at sources of light other than the Sun, found a clue. If you have made a spectroscope, you too can find this clue. It is necessary to

observe a flame coloured by sodium, and to do this a gas flame is required. The flame of a gas cooker will do, but in a laboratory a scientist uses the flame of a bunsen-burner. This is a special burner which burns a mixture of gas and air and can be placed in a convenient position on a laboratory bench. In a laboratory an iron stand is used with the bunsen-burner and a sheet of metal gauze is placed on the stand. If you use a gas cooker you can stand the gauze (which you can buy from some large ironmongers or hardware stores) on one gas ring.

Once you have set up your

gauze, adjust the flame of the bunsen-burner or the gas cooker so that it does not come through the gauze, but is high enough to heat the gauze until it glows red hot. Next you want a lump of sodium, and this is easily obtained in the form of cooking salt. (Salt is sodium chloride). The aim is to burn the sodium (or salt) and to look at its flame with your spectroscope, so you should line up your spectroscope so that the light from the burning sodium will pass through the slit.

Now place your lump of salt on the gauze, and once it is glowing and burning look at it through the

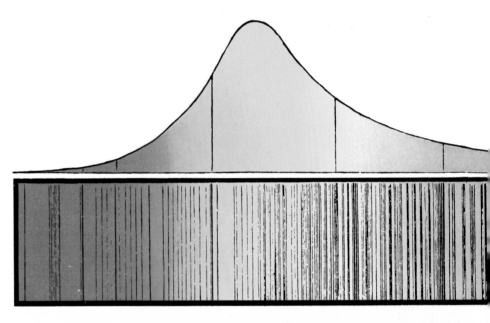

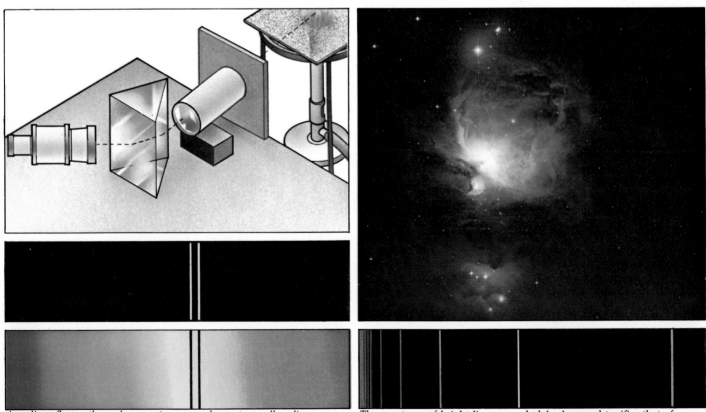

A sodium flame, through a spectroscope, shows two yellow lines. However, sunlight shining through the flame shows two black lines.

The spectrum of bright lines on a dark background typifies that of a nebula, in this case the Orion nebula, shown above.

spectroscope. What do you see? Not a bright coloured band of light but a yellow line where the yellow part of the coloured spectrum would be. You may, in fact, see two yellow sodium lines close together, but they need a spectroscope with a high quality glass prism to separate them clearly.

If you are unable to obtain the metal gauze required you will have to line up your spectroscope on the gas flame and ask someone to drop some grains of salt into the flame. These will burn with a yellow flame for a short time, and for that brief moment you will, if you are looking through your spectroscope, see the yellow line(s). Or, perhaps easiest of all, you can use your spectroscope to examine the light from a yellow sodium street lamp.

Look again at the spectrum of the Sun and you will notice lines; if you look at the yellow part you will see one (or a pair) of strong dark lines just where your yellow sodium lines were. Why?

The answer took some years for physicists, astronomers and chemists to discover during the last century, but in 1860 two German scientists, Gustav Kirchhoff and Robert Bunsen (the inventor of the bunsen-burner) solved the problem in their laboratory. They found that the continuous coloured spectrum was just the coloured radiation which is emitted by a dense body of gas or a dense solid like a lump of iron when it is heated so strongly that it glows with a bright, almost white, light. If you point your spectroscope at an electric light bulb you will get a continuous spectrum because the tungsten wire or filament inside the bulb is heated until it is incandescent.

Kirchhoff and Bunsen found that every chemical element had its own 'bright line' spectrum, just as sodium had. The lines which a glowing gas emits are characteristic of that gas – they are its 'fingerprint'. So the presence of certain lines on a spectrum will indicate that certain chemicals are present.

They also found that if you have a hot glowing source, like the Sun, giving a continuous spectrum, and the sunlight passes through some cooler gas – cool sodium vapour, for example, there are *dark* lines just in the same position as the bright lines occur if the gas were glowing on its own. Thus the dark lines in the solar spectrum are caused by gases round the Sun, which absorb some of the continuous spectrum. By examining those lines we can tell what chemical substances are present in the Sun. Stars display such lines in their spectra, too, so the same methods can be applied to them.

A solar spectrum with a curve above it to show where the main amount of the Sun's energy lies; this is in the orange and yellow of the spectrum. The spectrum is crossed by hundreds of lines named after Fraunhofer who discovered them. When he drew the spectrum, he started with red on the left, but it is now the accepted convention to draw the spectrum ending with red on the right.

The tungsten filament of an electric light bulb gives a continuous spectrum.

The continuous spectrum of the Sun.

OTHER SOLAR RADIATION

The Sun emits light which we can study by breaking it up into its separate colours. But the Sun also sends out heat to warm us. Does it therefore emit other rays, and if so what are they and how can we study them?

The first step in investigating other solar radiation was made in the latter years of the eighteenth century by the great observational astronomer William Herschel (1738–1822) who was born in Germany, but spent most of his life in England. Herschel's experiment was simple and effective and you can easily repeat it, using a prism and a thermometer. Choose a sunny window and place a cardboard screen with a hole in it against the glass. The screen will allow a small patch of sunlight to enter the room. (It may be necessary to close the curtains of any other windows.) Let the beam of sunlight fall on a prism and arrange a sheet of white paper so that the coloured spectrum produced by the prism falls on the paper.

Next take a thermometer (not a medical thermometer but an ordinary household one) and place its bulb in the path of the blue-green rays of the spectrum. The thermometer will register no change in temperature. Now move the bulb of the thermometer slowly towards the red end of the spectrum. When you reach the end of the spectrum continue a little further, and leave the thermometer there. You will see that it soon begins to indicate a higher temperature. Then try the thermometer at a couple of other positions further below the red and observe the temperature. You will find that after a certain point the temperature does not rise any more.

The experiment proves that the Sun is emitting not only visible rays but also invisible rays, rays to which your eyes are not sensitive. These rays lie below the red end of the spectrum and are called 'infrared' rays, because they are 'infra' or below the red. This radiation is also sometimes referred to as 'radiant heat'. The thermometer is sensitive to the infrared rays and that is why you can detect them.

Do these infrared rays behave like light rays? Can they be reflected? Can they be refracted or bent by a lens? If you put a mirror or sheet of tin-plate in the position where the thermometer registered the infrared rays, then you can use it as a surface to reflect the rays to the thermometer. William Herschel used a magnifying lens in front of a coal fire

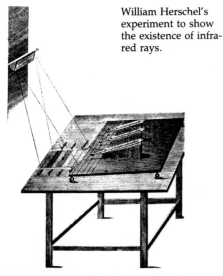

William Herschel's experiment to show the existence of infrared rays.

X-ray photographs of the Sun: the X-rays are being emitted by the Sun, we are not seeing through it.
left
Part of the Sun's disc with a flame-like cloud of hot hydrogen gas, which is giving out X-rays. The colours are not real but show different intensities of the X-rays translated onto special film.
right
The entire solar disc showing bright patches where the X-rays are being emitted.

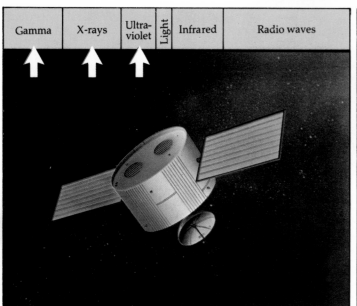

Gamma	X-rays	Ultra-violet	Light	Infrared	Radio waves

Space probes go outside the Earth's atmosphere and observe the universe using very short wavelengths: gamma, X- and ultraviolet rays.

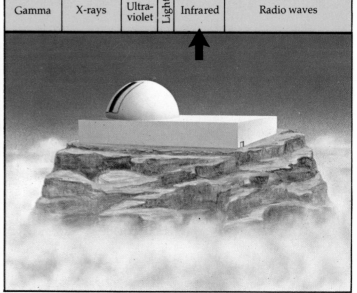

Gamma	X-rays	Ultra-violet	Light	Infrared	Radio waves

Infrared telescopes are placed on a mountain peak as the lower atmosphere absorbs most infrared rays entering it.

to concentrate this radiant heat on to a thermometer and proved that the rays are refracted by a lens just like ordinary light waves. You can repeat this experiment, using an electric gas, or coal fire, or even a candle.

Do any rays lie below the infrared? Herschel could not detect any nor were you able to do so with your thermometer. Yet there are rays, or waves, of invisible light there, but you need a special, very sensitive, very short-wave, radio receiver with which to detect them. This is because below the infrared there lie radio waves, and it is these which radio astronomers capture with their radio telescopes. The Sun and other stars all emit radio waves, although they are usually very faint because most stars are so far away. Radio waves from the Sun are, however, regularly studied.

What about the other end of the spectrum, beyond the blue and violet end? Are there rays there? Once

again you can test this, but a thermometer is no good. A very simple way is to use a white handkerchief which has been washed at a laundry or washed in one of those 'whiter-than-white' washing powders. Make sure the window behind your cardboard screen is open, and put a piece of the handkerchief at the blue end of the spectrum: it will look blue. Move it into the violet and it will look violet. Now move it where there is no light, just beyond the violet, and you will find that the handkerchief will glow gently with a bluish-white colour. This is because invisible rays from the Sun are striking it and making a dye in the washing powder glow (in fact it is this dye which makes white clothes washed in the powder look so white). The invisible rays lie beyond the violet and are called 'ultraviolet' rays or 'ultraviolet light'.

Ultraviolet light is absorbed by glass and little passes through it,

which is why the window behind your cardboard screen must be open. Photographic films are sensitive to ultraviolet light and if you mark the paper beyond the violet with an 'X' and photograph it, you will find that enough ultraviolet gets through your camera lens to give you a picture. The skin is sensitive to ultraviolet light and the body manufactures a dye to prevent these rays from penetrating too far – the dye is a substance called melanin and is what creates a suntan.

The Sun emits a great deal of ultraviolet, but only a portion of it permeates the Earth's atmosphere. Ultraviolet rays have a shorter wavelength than violet light and very short wavelength ultraviolet is absorbed by the atmosphere. X-rays, which the Sun also emits, are of even shorter wavelength than ultraviolet. None of these ever penetrate the atmosphere and can only be observed from up in space.

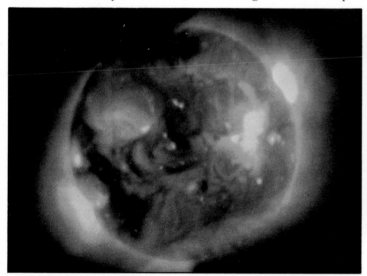

An astronomer works at the control console of the 3·8 m U.K. infra red telescope at Mauma Kea, Hawaii.

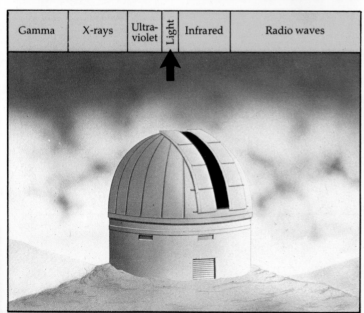

Gamma	X-rays	Ultra-violet	Light	Infrared	Radio waves

Large optical telescopes are placed on high ground to be above the denser, more polluted parts of the Earth's atmosphere.

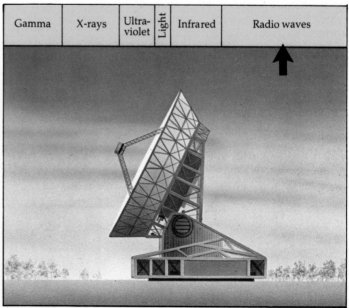

Gamma	X-rays	Ultra-violet	Light	Infrared	Radio waves

Radio telescopes can be built on the ground as radio waves penetrate the atmosphere quite satisfactorily.

CHAPTER 2
THE STARS

The people of ancient civilizations identified patterns among the stars. The modern astronomer can see these same patterns which appear to move across the sky every night.

From earliest times man has looked up at the night sky. Long before there was any street lighting, the stars could not be overlooked, as they are today by most people who live anywhere near a town, city or motorway.

When you go outside to observe the stars, allow your eyes to become accustomed to the darkness. After a few minutes you will find you can see more stars than just after coming outside. This is because your eyes have become 'dark adapted'. In daylight or under bright artificial lighting, the pupil of the eye contracts so that it does not allow too much light to reach the light-sensitive part of the eye, known as the 'retina'. But when you have been in the dark for a while, the pupils expand enabling you to detect dimmer light than at first.

When you go inside again the pupils will contract and it is best not to go straight into a bright light – shield your eyes with your hand for a moment to allow the pupils time to adjust. Dark adaption is important, and amateur astronomers usually use a red filter over a torch if they want to look at a star chart or make notes while at the telescope. The red light does not impair their dark adaption because the dark adapted eye is more sensitive to the green and blue-green part of the spectrum.

If you watch the stars you will see that the whole dome of the sky seems to turn. The stars move as a whole, always keeping their same relative positions in the sky.

As soon as he looked at the stars, man began to make up stellar patterns – he could recognize a shape that seemed to him like a plough, or a lion, or a hunter with a belt and a sword. And so the star patterns or 'constellations' were born. The kind of patterns men saw depended on what myths and legends were part of their folklore, and what animals they knew. The

A sixteenth-century celestial globe of papier mâché and vellum, showing Ptolemaic constellations. Attributed to Peter Apian 1495–1552.

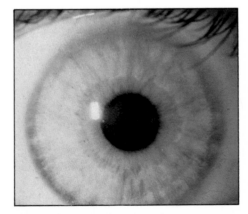
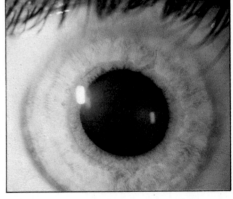

In light the pupil of the eye contracts; in the dark it expands to let in as much light as possible.

42

An eighteenth-century Arabic celestial sphere of brass, with silver studs representing stars.

A chart showing the constellations Corona Borealis, Hercules and Boötes. Copperplate by John Bevis for *Uranographia Britannica*, London 1750.

Egyptians favoured vast constellations and it is difficult now for us to know precisely which stars were grouped into which constellation, although we know that one of them represented a hippopotamus. The Chinese had their own constellations devoted to seasons of the year, mostly named after palaces and other objects connected with the imperial court.

Our constellations were invented in the Mediterranean area where the nights are usually clear. There is a lion, a fish, hunting dogs and a hare, but no tiger and no elephant. There are also heroes and heroines of local legends, Hercules, Andromeda and a Centaur, for instance. The origins of these constellations go back more than 2,500 years, yet the same stars are in the same groups today. In the light of this simple fact it is not hard to understand why people believed that the stars were eternal, fixed for ever in the same positions. Because we are now able to make precise measurements with ten thousand and more times the accuracy that ancient astronomers could achieve, we know that the stars are not fixed. They do move, but so very slowly that it takes a long time – some thousands of years – before any change can be detected in the night sky without a telescope.

However, ancient astronomers did notice that there were some celestial bodies which moved. The most obvious was the Moon, which, when it is full, shines with a very bright light. During a month it moved slowly eastwards among the constellations. The other moving bodies, which looked like bright stars although they never twinkled, but shone with a steady light, were called the 'wanderers' or, in Greek *planetes*, hence the word planets. The reason why they moved and sometimes wove an intricate path of loops among the stars was the main puzzle ancient astronomers had to solve (pages 108–111).

How many stars can you see in the night sky? On a dark clear night they seem to be countless in number. But in fact at any one time there are only about 1,500 stars visible without a telescope. With binoculars many stars too dim to be detected by the eye alone can be observed, and the total number visible rises to many thousands; with a small 7.5 cm aperture telescope the total reaches almost half a million and with a large professional telescope astronomers can photograph millions upon millions of stars.

THE CONSTELLATION FIGURES OF THE ZODIAC

The Zodiac is the name given to the band of constellations circling the celestial sphere through which the Sun, Moon and planets appear to move. We are familiar with the names of these constellations today because some people still mistakenly believe that they influence our lives.

In the earliest times there was a belief that the celestial bodies influenced certainly kings and emperors, and probably their subjects too. The ancient Egyptians thought of the sky and the Earth beneath it as gods. They had many other gods, of the elements or household for instance, and people believed they were continually at the mercy of the gods' pleasure or displeasure. The Mesopotamians, Greeks and Romans also credited their gods with great power. With the belief that the Earth and mankind were the centre of the universe, it seemed natural to suppose that the celestial bodies and their gods had a bearing on man's future. We now know that the Sun,

for example, does indeed affect us; it supports life on Earth and both the Sun and Moon are powerful tide-raising forces. But to the people of the ancient world the celestial bodies governed their destiny.

The effect which the celestial bodies were believed to have depended on the characters attributed to them, and the constellations through which they appeared to move. Thus the red-coloured Mars sometimes augured ill – it was a portent of pestilence or war – although in Babylonia it was

Venus which announced coming destruction. The influence of a constellation depended on its appearance: the constellations of Leo (the Lion) and Sagittarius (the Archer) had a male influence, Virgo (the Virgin), a female influence, and so on. Today we know the true nature of the planets (pages 116–129), and that the Earth is not the centre of the universe. We will also see that the constellations are not really the groupings they appear to be, as the stars composing them are at different distances from us and from each

above
The Sun God, Ra, flanked by baboons from the *Theban Book of the Dead, c* 1300 BC.

below
The constellations of the Zodiac. An observer on Earth will

see the Sun in the area of Aries and Pisces during March. These constellations are only visible in daylight at this time, while the main Zodiacal constellations in the night sky are Virgo and Libra.

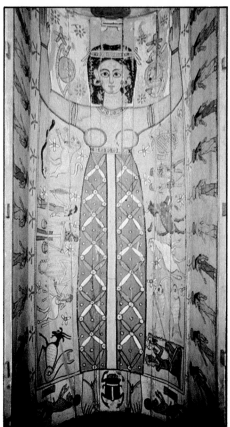

above
Egyptian wooden coffin, 2nd century AD. The painted

interior shows the sky goddess surrounded by the twelve signs of the Zodiac.

Armillary sphere with the signs of the Zodiac. Made by Hieronymous

Vulpariae, Florence, 1554.

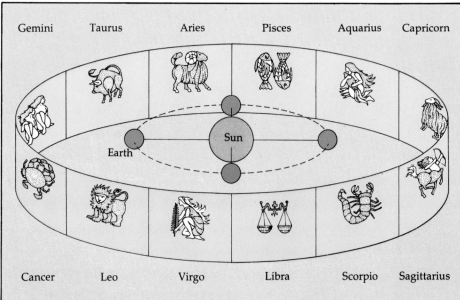

Gemini Taurus Aries Pisces Aquarius Capricorn

Earth Sun

Cancer Leo Virgo Libra Scorpio Sagittarius

other (pages 48–51). So it becomes clear that the stars are not fastened to a sphere as ancient peoples believed.

The constellations of the Zodiac do fulfil a useful function all the same, for they are the ones at which the observer must look to see the planets Mars, Jupiter, Saturn, Uranus and Neptune – and Pluto, although a telescope with an aperture greater than 25 cm is needed to see it.

There are twelve constellations of the Zodiac, and moving eastwards across the sky from the First Point of Aries, they are Aries, the Ram;

Taurus, the Bull; Gemini, the Twins; Cancer, the Crab; Leo, the Lion; Virgo, the Virgin; Libra, the Scales; Scorpio, the Scorpion; Sagittarius, the Archer; Capricorn, the Goat; Aquarius, the Water-carrier; and Pisces, the Fishes. There is a rhyme which expresses all this:

The Ram, the Bull, the Heavenly Twins,
And, next the Crab, the Lion stands,
The Virgin and the Scales,
The Scorpion, the Archer, the Sea-goat,
The Man who pours the water out,
The Fish with glittering tails.

The names of the constellations make it clear that the whole series is composed either of animals (the Ram, Bull, Crab, Lion, Scorpion, Goat and Fish) or people (the Twins, Virgin, Archer and Water-carrier). Only the scales do not fit into this category, called the 'zoo-circle' from the Greek *zoo-os* meaning living; a circle of living constellations, in fact.

The diagram shows the layout of the Zodiacal constellations on the celestial sphere, The constellations are connected with the seasons and the months of the year. In ancient times the Sun was in Aries in March but this is now no longer true. This is because of the precession of the equinoxes (page 11). The First Point of Aries has moved so that it is no longer in the constellation Aries, but in the constellation of Pisces: it has precessed or gone back by one entire constellation, or by one 'sign' as the astrologers would put it. There are many beautiful old books from medieval times which show the old system of zodiacal constellations, and the table below gives these as well as the present arrangement, which takes in the effects of precession.

The table shows the time when the Sun is in each constellation. To know which of the zodiacal signs will be in the night sky we need to look at a right ascension 12 hours different as this brings us to the other side of the celestial sphere. Thus in March/April the main zodiacal constellation is Virgo, and in November/December we get Taurus.

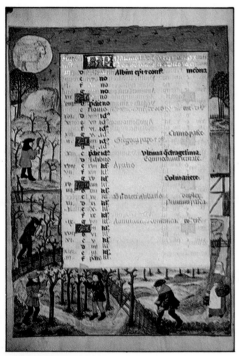

The March and April pages from the fifteenth-century *Bedford Missal.*

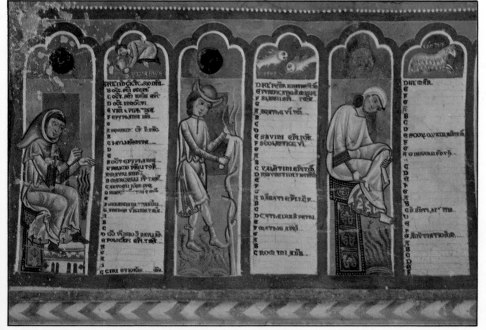

Detail of thirteenth-century fresco at Bominaco, Italy, of the months of the year. Aquarius, Pisces and Aries are shown.

Constellation	Medieval months
Aries	March/April
Taurus	April/May
Gemini	May/June
Cancer	June/July
Leo	July/August
Virgo	August/September
Libra	September/October
Scorpio	October/November
Sagittarius	November/December
Capricorn	December/January
Aquarius	January/February
Pisces	February/March
Constellation	Modern months
Aries	April/May
Taurus	May/June
Gemini	June/July
Cancer	July/August
Leo	August/September
Virgo	September/October
Libra	October/November
Scorpio	November/December
Sagittarius	December/January
Capricorn	January/February
Aquarius	February/March
Pisces	March/April

THE SEASONAL MOVEMENTS OF THE SUN AND STARS

The Sun apparently moves round the sky once every year, and passes through all the zodiacal constellations as it does so. Its apparent motion guides us so that we can make a seasonal calendar. But since the stars are not visible in the sky once the Sun has risen, how can we determine its whereabouts?

There are two main methods of doing this and which one we use will depend to some extent, on where we live. The most simple is to use the technique of heliacal risings and settings. This method (the name is derived from the Greek word *helios* meaning Sun) was used all over the Mediterranean area, and is of great antiquity. It can be used also in countries in higher latitudes, like northern Europe and North America. In essence it is simple enough. To determine the heliacal rising look eastwards just before dawn and notice which are the last stars to be visible before the Sun rises. A note must be made of these. For heliacal settings just the opposite is done. One looks westwards at sunset, and notes the first stars to appear in the

west just after sunset. Record these also. The night sky itself, just after the Sun has set, will also provide other evidence for you can find which zodiacal constellation follows westwards, just after sunset. Conversely, the sky just before dawn allows you to see which zodiacal constellation has risen just before sunrise. It is, of course, a basic requirement that you can recognise the constellations, or at least all the zodiacal ones, to use this method.

In the Mediterranean area heliacal risings and settings are a very convenient way of determining the Sun's position. In ancient Egypt they also made use of the heliacal rising of the bright star Sirius, which they called Sothis; its rising just

before the Sun heralded the beginning of the annual floods in the Nile delta and, indeed, the Egyptians believed it was the rising of Sirius that caused the floods. Because of the latitudes of the countries in the Mediterranean area, which lie approximately between 30° and 40°, the celestial pole is lower and closer to the horizon than it is in the countries of northern Europe and Canada. This means that the Sun and stars rise and set at a steeper angle than they do in higher latitudes, with the result that twilight is shorter and dawn comes faster than in more northern countries. This makes heliacal risings and settings ideal for determining the Sun's seasonal position. Places in Australia and New

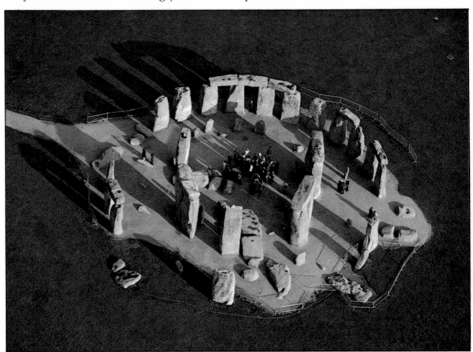

Stonehenge

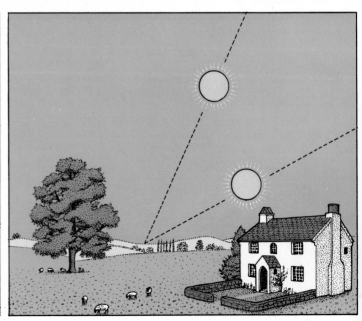

The rising and setting of the Sun at different latitudes. Near the equator the Sun rises high and sets steeply; in more distant latitudes the Sun does not rise so high and sets at an oblique angle.

46

Zealand have similar latitudes (south) to those of the Mediterranean countries.

In more northerly latitudes rising and setting occurs at a much more oblique angle; twilight is longer and the air is frequently less clear, consequently it is impossible to get results as precise as those obtained with the steeper Mediterranean path. For precision observing some other method is needed, and about 1500 BC, the people living in Brittany, England and the west coast of Scotland, took advantage of the sloping path and made different kinds of calendar observations. These entailed the use of large stones as guides or markers, which were laid out in the form of circles or ovals on the ground to make up an observatory.

These observatories of megalithic man were designed to allow him to watch for the extreme seasonal positions of the Sun and Moon. When the Sun is at its highest position in the sky at noon at midsummer (page 20), it rises at the furthest position in the north-east that it will ever reach and sets at the most north-westerly point it will ever come to. Similarly at mid-winter, when it is at its lowest in the sky at noon, it will rise at the most south-easterly point it ever reaches and set at its most south-westerly point. If, therefore, we lay out a ring of stones and use some distant stone or hill as a reference mark, we can note when it is midsummer and mid-winter by watching sunrise and sunset.

As far as the Moon is concerned, its path is more complicated than that of the Sun. Every month it crosses the ecliptic twice, and it is at these crossing points that eclipses can occur. The Moon makes the same pattern of movements as the Sun, because its apparent orbit is tilted with respect to the celestial equator just as the Sun's is, although by a different amount. However, the Moon goes through its cycle of changes almost 13 times faster than the Sun, because there are almost 13 lunar months in a year. In addition, the Moon's orbit rotates once every 18.6 years so there is also a cycle of changes of rising and setting positions to be taken into account. The megalithic astronomers knew all these changes because they observed carefully over very long periods, setting out their stone blocks – or sometimes wooden blocks – so they could see the changes.

It also seems likely that, knowing the changing seasonal positions of the Sun and of the Moon, they were able to tell when eclipses would occur. The giant stone-circle at Stonehenge was probably an 'eclipse computer' as well as an observatory for determining the seasons and a religious centre. The midsummer Sun still rises over the 'heel-stone' there.

Stone circles take up a large space and you also need a clear and wide horizon to show the rising and setting positions of the Sun. But if you do have space you can stick posts or stones in the ground to see the principle on which they worked.

The huge stone observatory at Carnac in Brittany comprises 2,730 standing stones over a distance of 4 km. They were erected so that the main stones could be aligned accurately to show the movements of the Sun and Moon.

Stone circles are used for determining when the Sun or Moon has reached the extreme points in its orbit. One standing stone uses a dip in the horizon as a reference point, but if there is no convenient mark on the horizon a distant stone is used instead.

DISTANCES OF THE STARS

The stars are a vast distance from the Earth. They are all bodies shining by their own light, and many of them are larger than the Sun, but they seem to us no more than tiny points of light. Even in the largest telescope they still appear as tiny dots because they are too far away to display a disc.

The first successful measurement of the distance of a star was not made until 1838, when the German astronomer, Friedrich Bessel, using a special telescope, managed to measure how far away the star 61 Cygni was. But 61 Cygni is comparatively near, and more distant stars had to wait until after the end of the nineteenth century before their distances were measured satisfactorily. It would be difficult, although not impossible, for a very experienced amateur astronomer today to measure the distance of even 61 Cygni, and so stellar distances are really something best left to the professional. Nevertheless, you can make a model and do a few simple observations which will show you the principle on which the professional astronomer works.

The professional measures star distances by a method which land surveyors, call 'triangulation'. It is a method they use when obtaining the distance of something out of reach and, of course, this is so in the case of a star.

Triangulation as it is now used was invented in 1533 by Gemma Frisius, and its principle is shown in the drawing taken from a book by Sebastian Munster, published in 1551. (It is easiest if you look at this and then at the modern diagram at the side.) The example Gemma Frisius gave was measuring the width of a river. As you see, he suggested beginning by choosing an object such as a tree (D in the modern diagram) close to the bank on the observer's side of the river, and a second object – another tree, say C – on the opposite bank. Measurements can be made by standing at position A on the nearside bank of the river and measuring the angle between the tree D and the one on the opposite bank C. This measures the angle DAC. In the diagram by Gemma Frisius, you will see the angles are measured with a kind of cross-shaped instrument. This was the 'cross-staff', an

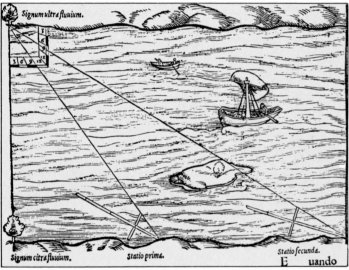

Fig. 1
This shows how to measure the position of a distant object by triangulation. The principle is explained in the text using the modern version of the diagram, *Fig. 2*.

Fig. 3
The Dumb-Bell nebula is a cloud of bright gas and stars, showing objects at different distances in space.

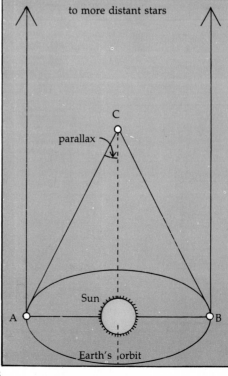

Fig. 4 left
Measuring the distance of a star by triangulation. AB is the diameter of the Earth's orbit. Using it as a base line, the parallax of a star at C can be obtained.

Fig. 5 right
Measuring stellar distances using the trigonometrical parallax method. For this you need an angle-observing instrument made from a cardboard disc, marked in degrees at the edge and glued to a wood block. A sighting bar with a pointer made from plastic is fixed to the wood block on a pivot so that it can swivel round.

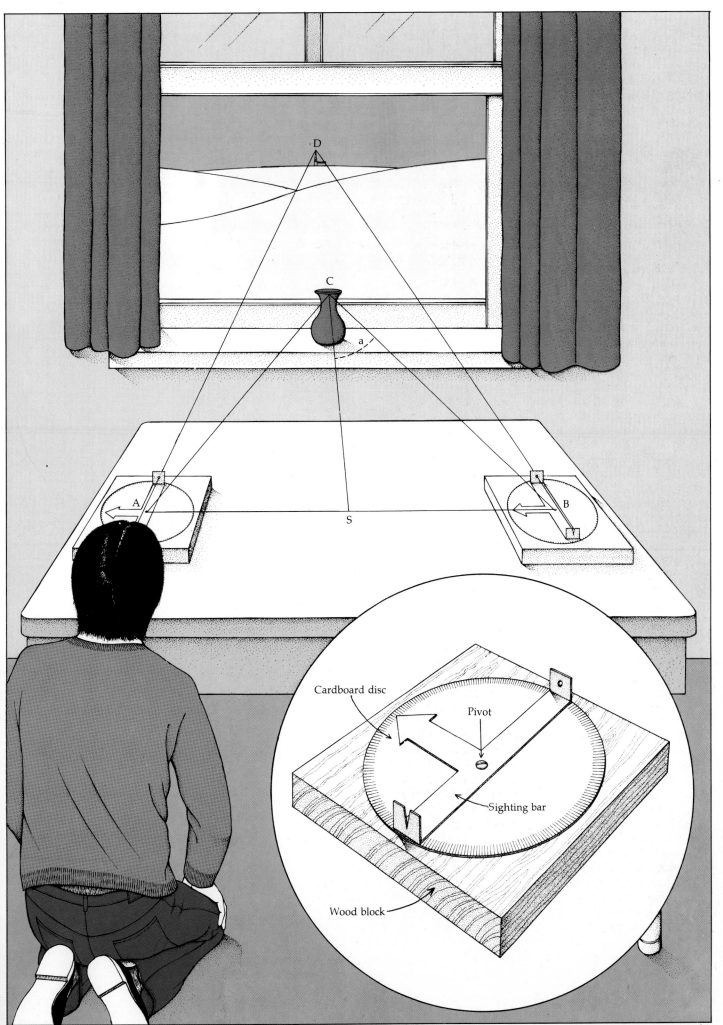

Cardboard disc

Pivot

Sighting bar

Wood block

instrument much used in his day, but when we come to try out the principle of triangulation we shall use a much simpler instrument.

Next, the observer moved further along the river bank to a new position B, making sure that he was in line with the tree D and the first position A. He then measured the angle between the tree D and the distant tree C once more. Thus he obtained the angle DBC. Lastly he very carefully measured the 'baseline', the distance between the two observing positions A and B.

The result of all this was that the surveyor knew the length of the side AB of the triangle ABC, and he knew angle DBC (because he had measured it) and the angle BAC (because BAC = 180° – angle DAC, which he had also measured). He could therefore find the width of the river (CD in the modern diagram) by trigonometry.

The distance of a star is measured in a similar kind of way, although in place of an object like D between us and the star the astronomer uses the background of very distant stars. Two separate sets of observations are made, the second set being made six months after the first set. This six-month interval means that the Earth has moved half-way round its orbit, so that the distance in space between the two sets of observations is the diameter of the Earth's orbit round the Sun. In other words the baseline AB is the huge distance 300 million km. As you can see from Fig. 4, the longer a baseline is, the greater the difference between the angles measured at the two different positions.

Because even the nearest stars are so far away, the astronomer needs the longest possible baseline, as otherwise it will be difficult to detect the angle between the two observing positions. In fact this is what happened when Copernicus put forward his theory that the Sun, not the Earth, was the centre of the universe. In 1543 there were no telescopes with which to make such measurements, and even when they were invented, it took almost 300 years before they were precise enough to detect the tiny angles involved. For instance, Bessel's measurement of 61 Cygni gave an angle of only 0.35 arc seconds or 0.0000972 degrees. Such a tiny angle is equivalent to the thickness of a single human hair seen at a distance of 30 metres, and that is for a comparatively nearby star.

You will notice in Fig. 4 that the drawing shows that the 'more distant

stars' have two lines pointing to them, one from A and one from B, yet both lines are parallel. This is because the more distant stars are so far away that they will appear in the same direction whether the observer is at A or at B. You can see something of this for yourself by going outside and standing about 7 metres away from a tree or a street lamp. Shut one eye and look at the pillar of the street lamp or the trunk of the tree and notice which object in the distance it seems to be in line with. Now close that eye and open the other one. You will still see the street lamp or tree, but now it will appear to have shifted with reference to the distant object. The street lamp seems to move because it is nearer,

but the more distant object appears stationary, whichever eye you use for looking at it.

The apparent shift of the nearby tree or street lamp is known as 'parallax', and when one measures distances in this way by using angles, the measures are called measures of parallax. So when an astronomer measures stellar distances as shown in Fig. 4, half the angle ACB is known as the parallax of a star. The angles are small, but if a star were near enough to give a parallax of 1 arc second (i.e. 1/3600 part of a degree) then the distance SC is known as a 'parsec' [i.e. a *par* (allax of one) *sec*(ond)]. Using the Earth's orbit as the baseline, a parsec turns out to be a distance of 30.857 ×

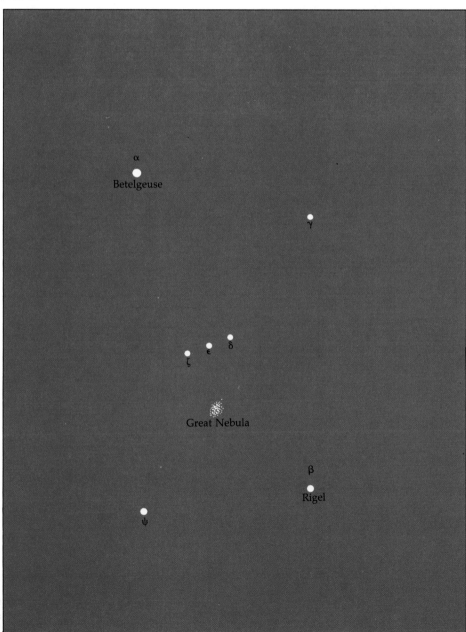

Fig. 6 above
In the constellation of Orion the pattern of stars is seen as a hunter, but the stars are in no way connected and only

form this image because of our view-point from Earth.

Fig. 7 opposite
Orion seen from above shows that the stars are at very different distances from us. The distance from Earth to the

nearest star in Orion is less than the distance between this star and the star furthest away in the constellation.

10^{12} km (or 30,857,000,000,000 km). This is an enormous distance by earthly standards, but it is still not far enough to reach the nearest star, whose parallax is only 0.763 arc seconds. (This is the star Proxima Centauri, visible only in the southern hemisphere and then needing a telescope to show it.) To express such great distances, astronomers use the 'light-year', which is the distance light travels in one year. A light-year (which is *not*, as some people wrongly suppose, a measure of time) is almost 10^{13} km, or 9.4607×10^{12} km (9,406,000,000,000 km) to be more precise. On this scale 1 parsec = 3.26 light-years.

You can get an idea of the scale of a light-year by glancing at the following distances. Once round the Earth = 40,000 km or 0.13 light-seconds; distance Earth-to-Moon = 384, 400 km or 1.3 light-seconds; distance Earth-to-Sun = 149,597,870 km or 8.3 light-minutes; distance Earth to Proxima Centauri = 4.27 light-years. These figures also mean that you never see the Moon as it is now but as it was 1.3 seconds ago, because light has taken 1.3 seconds to travel the 384,400 km from it to us; again we only ever see the Sun as it was 8.3 minutes ago, and Proxima Centauri as it was over 4 years ago. And the further we gaze into space, the further back in time we are looking. One could say that a telescope is a kind of time machine.

This method of measuring stellar distances by using observations made at the ends of the Earth's orbit, known technically as 'trigonometrical parallax', will only work with precision for stars closer than about 30 parsecs or 98 light-years, although it is possible to get results out to 98 light-years; after this the angles are too small to detect. Other methods, based on the true brightness of the different types of stars (pages 74–79) or on the way certain stars vary their light (pages 82–85), have to be used for distance measurement.

Although you cannot measure stellar distances yourself, you might like to check up the trigonometrical parallax method, using simple trigonometry and a simple angle-observing instrument. The drawing in Fig. 5 shows you how to make such an instrument, and with it you can measure some nearby object, using very distant objects for your background. First measure the angles DAC and DBC. Also measure the angles DAB and DBA. It then follows that CAB = DAB − DAC, and CBA = DBA − DBC. With this information you can find ACB (180° − CAB − CBA), and half of this angle = a = parallax. We shall write this angle as $\hat{a}$. You may wonder why we do not measure the angle $\hat{a}$ directly. The answer is we cannot – it is not practical to do so. And in astronomy D is so very far away that we have the situation illustrated in Fig. 4 where the angles DBA and DAB are both right angles and so make it unnecessary for you to measure them as you have to do in your experiment. When you have found angle $\hat{a}$, you must also measure the distance AB between your two observing positions. Halve this and you will get some distance we shall call x. You can now work out the distance SC by using the formula tan $\hat{a} = x \div$ SC, or writing it so that we can more readily find SC, SC = $x \div$ tan $\hat{a}$ You can find tan $\hat{a}$ (i.e. the tangent of the angle $\hat{a}$) either from tables used in trigonometry or direct from some pocket electronic calculators. You can then check your answer and observations by actually measuring the distance SC.

By measuring the distances of the stars astronomers can prove not only that the stars are not fixed on the inside of a sphere, as the ancients believed, but also that the constellations are not really groups of connected stars. In other words the stars in any particular constellation only look as if they are grouped together because we look at them from a certain position.

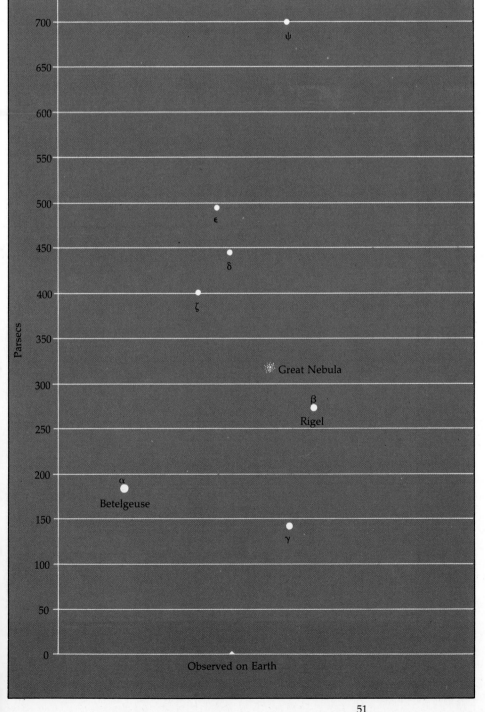

THE CONSTELLATIONS VISIBLE AT DIFFERENT TIMES OF THE YEAR

The following charts show which stars are to be seen at different times of the year.

The constellations visible in the night sky will vary from one season to the next, as we have just seen (pages 44–45). When you look into the sky you will see only some of the stars shown on the charts according to which direction you are facing. The maps will work as a general guide for observers in various latitudes although the central overhead points will vary somewhat. They are drawn for observers in latitudes around 52° north and between 46° to 24° south. No planets are shown because their positions vary depending on their orbits (pages 114–115). The star charts also indicate the different brightnesses or 'magnitudes' of the stars (pages 74–75).

To cover observations made from a wide range of latitudes the charts of the southern skies are drawn on a slightly different projection from those of the northern hemisphere.

Chart visibility times: For northern observers the times given are Greenwich Mean Time (GMT). For southern observers these same times refer to the local time in Sydney, New South Wales, Australia.

NORTHERN SKIES
The most striking constellation is Orion (the Hunter) with the three stars forming his belt. The bright red star, Betelgeuse, is his left shoulder and the bright blue-white Rigel is his right foot. Towards the east of Orion's other foot (κ Orionis) is Sirius, the brightest star in the sky. Gemini (the Twins) is another notable constellation, with the bright stars Castor and Pollux. Taurus (the Bull) is also clearly visible with its magnificent giant red star, Aldebaran, and the Pleiades star cluster, a scintillating sight through a pair of binoculars or a small telescope. Notice too the Milky Way, stretching across the sky from the north-western horizon overhead to the south-eastern horizon and also, nearly overhead, the beautiful 'W' of five stars which make up Cassiopeia.

Chart 1

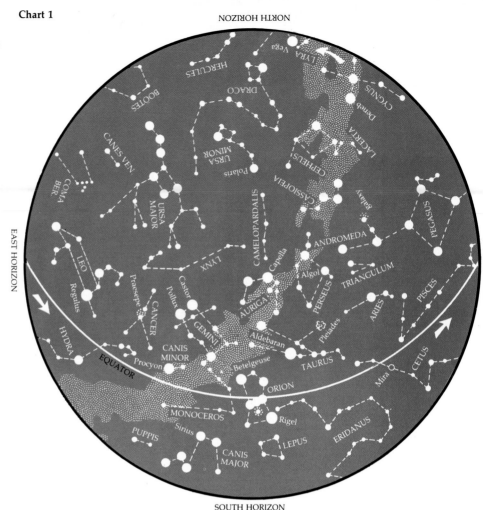

Chart 2

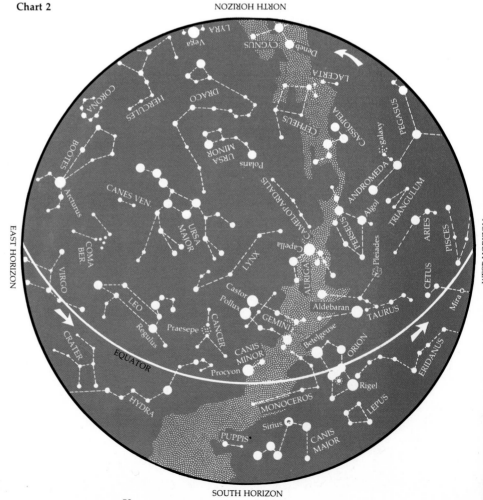

Chart 1

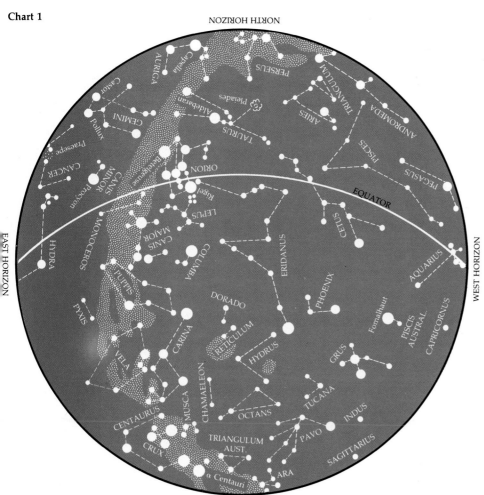

NORTH HORIZON

EAST HORIZON

AURIGA Capella PERSEUS TRIANGULUM ANDROMEDA
Castor GEMINI Aldebaran Pleiades ARIES
Pollux TAURUS PISCES
Praesepe CANCER Betelgeuse ORION PEGASUS
CANIS MINOR Procyon Rigel EQUATOR
HYDRA MONOCEROS CANIS MAJOR LEPUS CETUS
COLUMBA ERIDANUS AQUARIUS
PYXIS PUPPIS DORADO PHOENIX CAPRICORNUS
VELA CARINA RETICULUM HYDRUS Fomalhaut PISCIS AUSTRAL.
CHAMAELEON GRUS
CENTAURUS MUSCA OCTANS TUCANA INDUS
CRUX TRIANGULUM AUST. PAVO
α Centauri ARA SAGITTARIUS

WEST HORIZON

SOUTH HORIZON

SOUTHERN SKIES

There is much to see here. Orion (the Hunter) is visible, but standing on his head compared with the way he looks to northern observers, and Sirius is very high in the sky. So also are Carina (the Keel) and Vela (the Sail), forming two parts of the one-time constellation Argo (the Ship). Crux (the Southern Cross) is in the south-east and Tucana (the Toucan) in the south-west, with the really fine globular cluster 47 Toucanae (pages 164–165). The two extended, wandering constellations, the river Eridanus and Hydra (the Water Monster), are visible. Eridanus, stretching from Orion to between Hydrus (the Sea Serpent) and Phoenix, is almost overhead at Christmas and Hydra is low in the east in early January but higher later in the month, The Milky Way is very high late in January. The Large Magellanic Cloud is very high; the Small Magellanic Cloud is well above the south-western horizon.

Chart 2

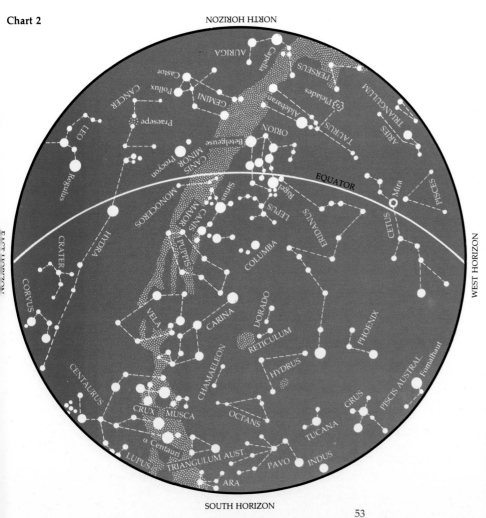

NORTH HORIZON

EAST HORIZON

AURIGA Capella PERSEUS
Castor Pollux GEMINI Aldebaran Pleiades TRIANGULUM
CANCER Praesepe TAURUS ARIES
LEO Regulus CANIS MINOR Procyon ORION Betelgeuse
Sirius Rigel EQUATOR PISCES
CANIS MAJOR LEPUS Mira
CRATER HYDRA MONOCEROS PUPPIS ERIDANUS CETUS
CORVUS COLUMBA
VELA CARINA DORADO PHOENIX
RETICULUM
CHAMAELEON HYDRUS PISCIS AUSTRAL. Fomalhaut
CENTAURUS MUSCA OCTANS GRUS
CRUX TUCANA
α Centauri TRIANGULUM AUST. PAVO INDUS
LUPUS ARA

WEST HORIZON

SOUTH HORIZON

53

Chart 1:
Times of visibility
December 21 at 22 hrs;
January 5 at 21 hrs;
January 20 at 20 hrs;
February 4 at 19 hrs;
February 19 at 18 hrs.

Chart 2:
Times of visibility
January 20 at 22 hrs;
February 4 at 21 hrs;
February 19 at 20 hrs;
March 5 at 19 hrs;
March 20 at 18 hrs.

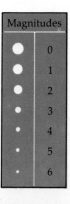

Magnitudes	
	0
	1
	2
	3
	4
	5
	6

NORTHERN SKIES

Many of the constellations remain the same as in January and February. The circumpolar stars are there, of course, and note Coma Berenices (Berenice's Hair), a lovely little constellation, down from the handle of the Plough (Big Dipper). By April, the constellation Boötes (the Herdsman) is fairly high with its bright yellowish star Arcturus.

You can use a sighting-tube – a long tube without lenses, easily obtained by using a cardboard tube made for sending charts and plans through the post – fix it on a stand and watch how the Pole Star moves round the north celestial pole. You can also see how the stars slowly move from east to west as the Earth rotates. If there are nearby street lights, a sighting-tube will also help you, after a time, to pick out some of the dimmer stars because it cuts out unwanted light and enables one eye to become dark-adapted.

Chart 3

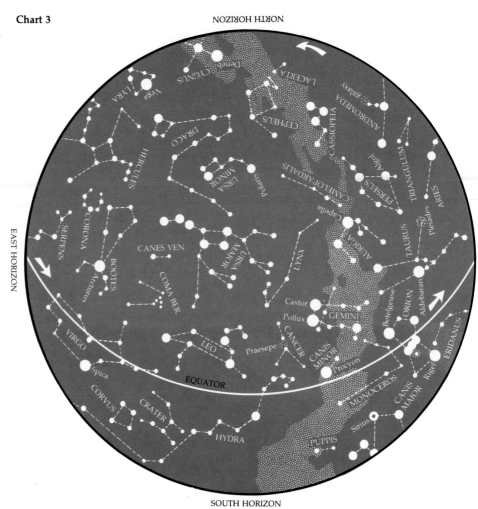

Chart 4

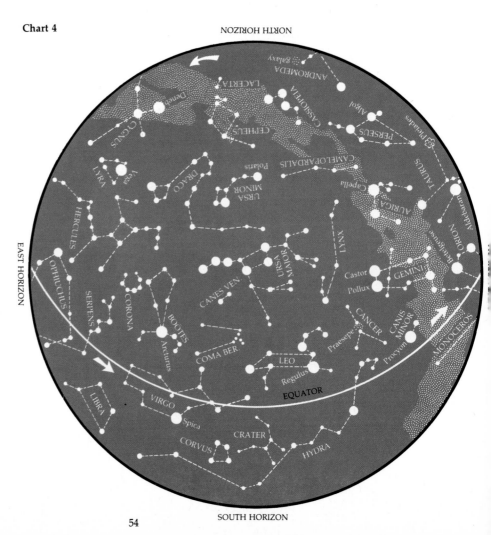

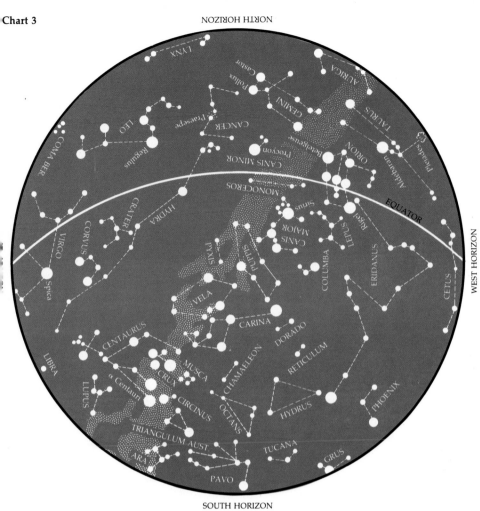

Chart 3

SOUTHERN SKIES

The constellations and objects mentioned in charts 1 and 2 are still visible, with Hydra high in the sky but Eridanus down nearer the western horizon by April. Corvus (the Crow) and Crater (the Cup), both small constellations, can be seen in the east a little closer to the horizon than Hydra. The Milky Way and Magellanic Clouds are fine and high and the constellation Centaurus (the Centaur, a legendary creature half-man, half-horse) can also be seen clearly eastwards of Crux. The brightest star, α Centauri, is multiple and, after the Sun, is the star nearest to us at 4.3 light-years.

Chart 4

Chart 3:
Times of visibility
February 20 at 22 hrs;
March 6 at 21 hrs;
March 21 at 20 hrs;
April 5 at 19 hrs;
April 20 at 18 hrs.

Chart 4:
Times of visibility
March 21 at 22 hrs;
April 5 at 21 hrs;
April 20 at 20 hrs;
May 5 at 19 hrs;
May 21 at 18 hrs.

Magnitudes	
	0
	1
	2
	3
	4
	5
	6

NORTHERN SKIES

Boötes (the Herdsman) is well up in the sky and so too is the constellation Virgo (the Virgin), with its beautiful blue-white star Spica. Northeastwards from Boötes is Hercules and, lower down and nearer the horizon, is the twisting constellation of Serpens (the Serpent). In June, north-east from Hercules, it is easy to see Lyra (the Lyre – the only musical instrument among the constellation names), containing the bright white star Vega. Also visible in June, although still not very high in the sky, is Cygnus (the Swan) which, with its spread wings, is a very easily recognizable constellation.

Chart 5

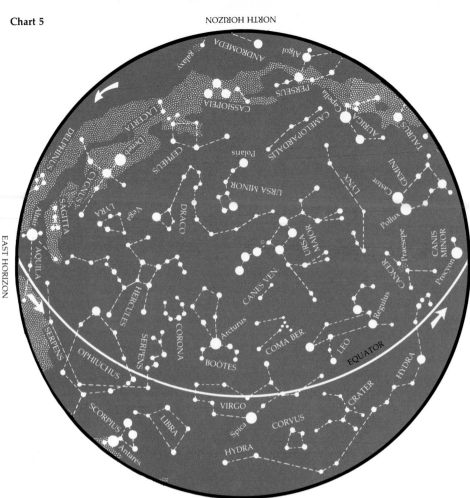

Chart 6

Chart 5

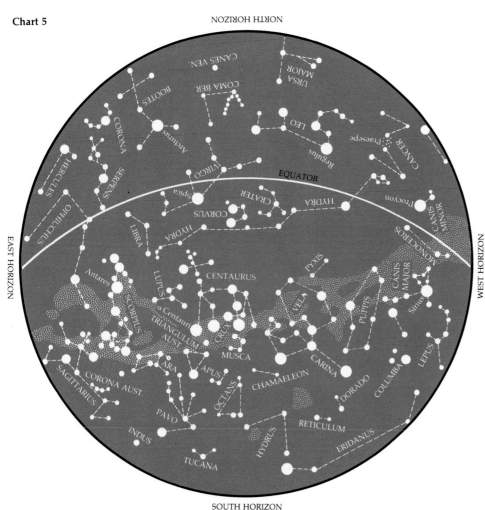

SOUTHERN SKIES

Crux and Centaurus are high in the sky, near the zenith – how near will depend on the latitude at which you are observing. The constellation Scorpius (the Scorpion) is also well above the horizon and lower down in the sky is Sagittarius (the Archer). In this region of the sky, you are looking towards the centre of our star-island or galaxy (pages 168–169). The Milky Way itself will be seen in an east-west line. Close to it are the constellations Ara (the Altar) and Triangulum Australe (the Southern Triangle), while south of Triangulum lies Pavo (the Peacock). In the west, fairly low down, are Canis Major (the Great Dog) with Sirius and Canis Minor (the Small Dog). Higher in the sky is Puppis (the Poop or Stern) and Carina (the Keel) of the one-time constellation Argo (the Ship). Carina is particularly interesting; its brightest star is Canopus or α Carinae, 500,000 times brighter than our Sun and second only to Sirius in brightness; and near the star θ Carinae is a vast nebula centred on the star η Carinae which exploded in 1843. It is well worth looking at with a telescope or binoculars.

Chart 6

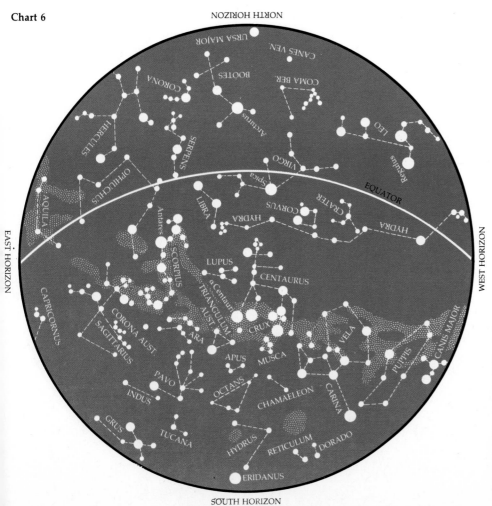

Chart 5:
Times of visibility
April 20 at 22 hrs;
May 5 at 21 hrs;
May 21 at 20 hrs;
June 5 at 19 hrs;
June 21 at 18 hrs.

Chart 6:
Times of visibility
May 21 at 22 hrs;
June 5 at 21 hrs;
June 21 at 20 hrs;
July 7 at 19 hrs;
July 22 at 18 hrs.

Magnitudes	
●	0
●	1
●	2
●	3
•	4
·	5
·	6

NORTHERN SKIES

Nearly overhead is Draco (the Dragon), another serpentine constellation, weaving its way between Polaris (the Pole Star) and Ursa Major (the Great Bear). Also near the zenith is Lyra with Vega shining brilliantly. Cygnus flies at a high altitude too and the white star Deneb (α Cygni) is very clear. Near Cygnus, but to the south of it, is Aquila (the Eagle), another constellation with outspread wings, looking a little like a cross. Hercules and Boötes are also high in the sky. In the east, you can readily see Pegasus (the Flying Horse) and Andromeda, with α Andromedae and α, β and γ Pegasi forming the justly famous 'Square of Pegasus' – a square of stars which is very easy to pick out. Higher in the sky than β Andromedae is a hazy patch of light. This is the Andromeda galaxy (pages 186–189), at over 2 million light-years the most distant object you can see with the unaided eye.

Chart 7

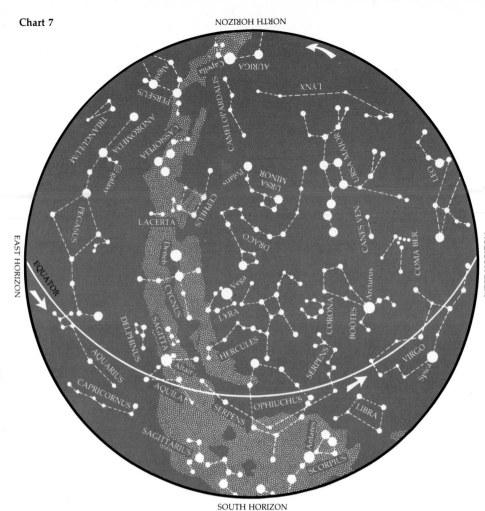

Chart 8

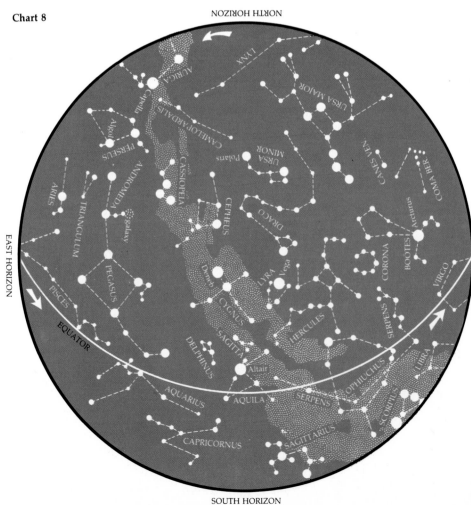

Chart 7

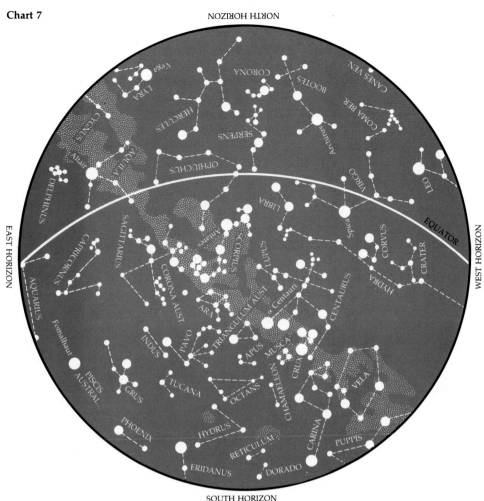

SOUTHERN SKIES
Scorpius is nearly overhead and Sagittarius and Centaurus are also high in the sky. So too is Grus (the Crane), whose three bright stars, α, β and δ form a triangle; but have a look at ε Grucis through binoculars – it is a beautiful double star – while δ Grucis is a double you can see with the unaided eye. Low in the west is Libra (the Scales), well known to northern observers, and in the east, but rather higher up, is Aquarius (the Water Carrier). Bright in the west is Fomalhaut (α Piscis Australis – the Southern Fish).

Chart 8

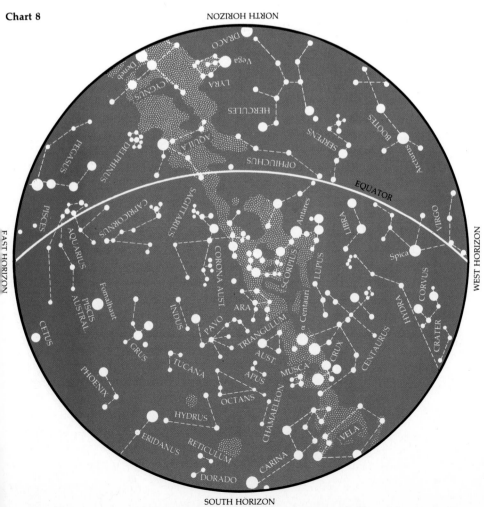

Chart 7:
Times of visibility
June 21 at 22 hrs;
July 7 at 21 hrs;
July 22 at 20 hrs;
August 7 at 19 hrs;
August 23 at 18 hrs.

Chart 8:
Times of visibility
July 22 at 22 hrs;
August 7 at 21 hrs;
August 23 at 20 hrs;
September 8 at 19 hrs;
September 23 at 18 hrs.

Magnitudes	
	0
	1
	2
	3
	4
	5
	6

NORTHERN SKIES

Things to look for during these times are variable stars. A notable one is the red star Mira (o Ceti). Situated in Cetus (the Whale), which is low down in the east, late at night in late September and earlier in October evenings, it needs a telescope of at least 5 cm aperture to detect it. With a variation period of brightness of about 332 days, it may still be too dim to detect, but you may be lucky. Another famous variable is Algol (the Demon) in Perseus (β Persei), which is also in the east but higher in the sky. A bluish-white star, it varies in brightness less than Mira and is always visible to the unaided eye. Its variation period is 2.86 days. Capricornus (the Goat) is visible in the south and during October Taurus (the Bull) becomes visible again.

Chart 9

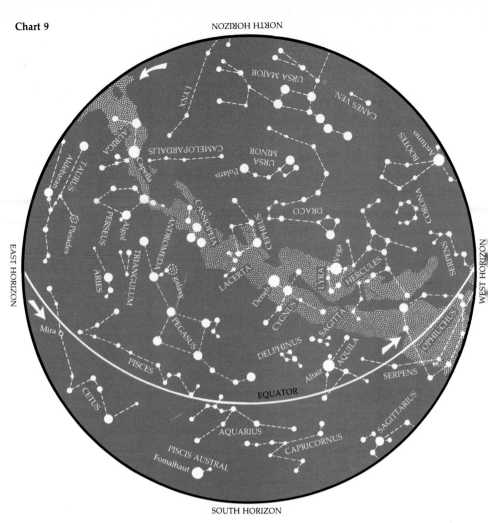

Chart 10

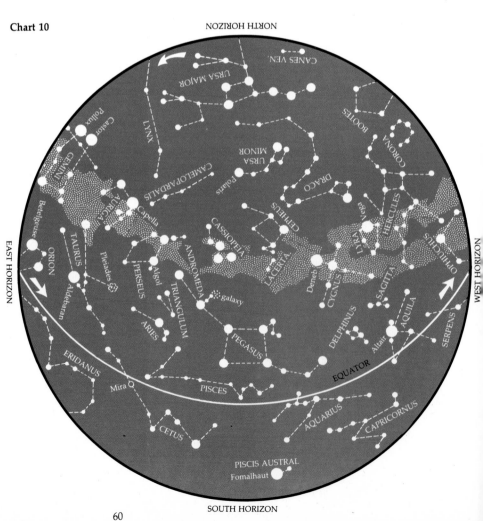

Chart 9

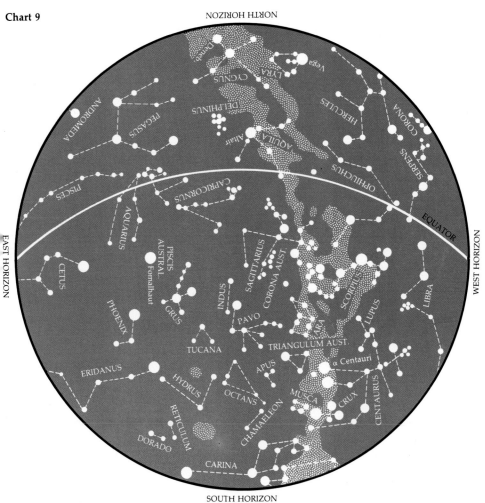

EAST HORIZON

WEST HORIZON

SOUTH HORIZON

SOUTHERN SKIES

Grus (the Crane) is very close to the zenith, while Sagittarius (the Archer), Pavo (the Peacock) and Hydrus (the Sea Serpent) are high in the sky. In the south are the tiny constellations of Tucana (the Toucan), Apus (the Bird of Paradise), Chamaeleon and Indus (the Indian). Octans (the Octant, an observing instrument) lies south too. The Magellanic Clouds are in the south too and both are worth looking at in some detail for they are the nearest galaxies to us. The Large Magellanic Cloud has some spiral arms in its outer regions; see if you can detect them, you will have to use a telescope.

Chart 10

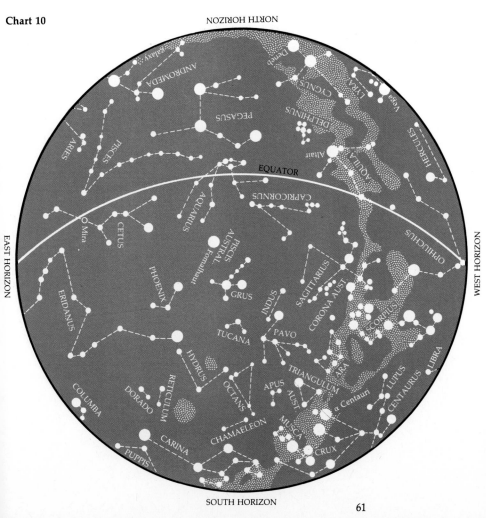

NORTH HORIZON

EAST HORIZON

WEST HORIZON

SOUTH HORIZON

Chart 9:
Times of visibility
August 23 at 22 hrs;
September 8 at 21 hrs;
September 23 at 20 hrs;
October 8 at 19 hrs;
October 23 at 18 hrs.

Chart 10:
Times of visibility
September 23 at 22 hrs;
October 8 at 21 hrs;
October 23 at 20 hrs;
November 7 at 19 hrs;
November 22 at 18 hrs.

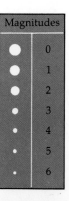

Magnitudes	
⬤	0
⬤	1
⬤	2
●	3
•	4
·	5
·	6

NORTHERN SKIES

The Milky Way, stretching from east to west, is a wonderful sight on a clear moonless night. The winter constellations, Orion (the Hunter), Taurus (the Bull), Andromeda, Pegasus (the Winged Horse), Gemini (the Twins), Auriga (the Charioteer) and Aries (the Ram), are now visible. Andromeda is high in the sky, but Orion is rather low to begin with. Cetus (the Whale) is reasonably high in the southern part of the sky, so look out again for Mira. Note also the state of Algol, for Perseus is high in the sky. Look too at the Plough (Big Dipper) and the multiple star Mizar in the centre of the handle. People with sharp eyes can detect its companion Alcor without any aids to vision. Seeing these stars was said to be an eyesight test for warriors in some North American Indian tribes.

Chart 11

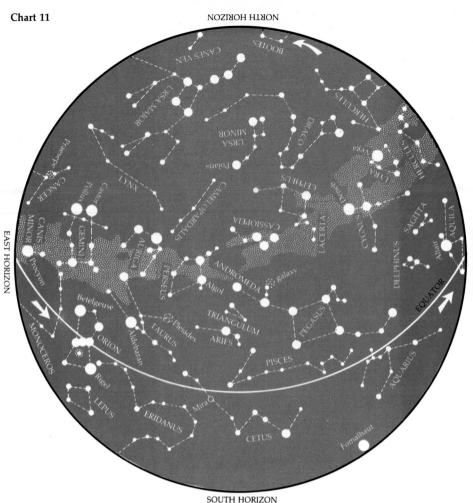

Chart 12

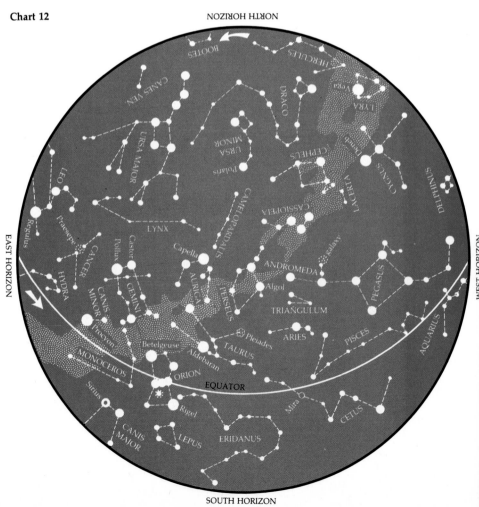

Chart 11

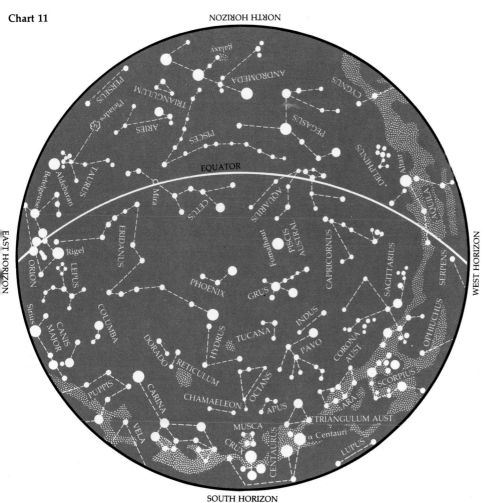

SOUTHERN SKIES

The Milky Way is very low down on the horizon, although the Magellanic Clouds can be seen well in the south. In the east are Puppis (the Poop) and Carina (the Keel). Orion (the Hunter) is just to the north-east but rather low down. Eridanus wends its way from the east up almost to the zenith, close to which is Phoenix. Grus (the Crane) is high up in the west and so is Piscis Australis (the Southern Fish), with its beautiful star, Fomalhaut, while Capricornus (the Goat) and Aquarius (the Water Carrier) are still visible in the west.

Chart 12

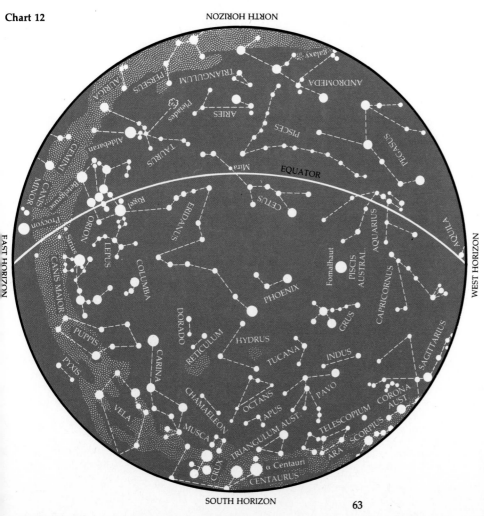

Chart 11:
Times of visibility
October 23 at 22 hrs;
November 7 at 21 hrs;
November 22 at 20 hrs;
December 7 at 19 hrs;
December 21 at 18 hrs.

Chart 12:
Times of visibility
November 22 at 22 hrs;
December 7 at 21 hrs;
December 21 at 20 hrs;
January 5 at 19 hrs;
January 20 at 18 hrs.

Magnitudes	
●	0
●	1
●	2
●	3
•	4
•	5
·	6

THE CIRCUMPOLAR STARS

The circumpolar stars are always above the horizon, although they can only be seen at night. As they appear to wheel slowly round the sky, an observer on Earth can easily use them to tell the time at night.

The number of circumpolar stars which are visible will depend on your latitude; for example, if you were at the north pole, all the constellations north of the celestial equator would be circumpolar. The charts show the circumpolar constellations visible between latitudes of 50° and the equator.

The night sky in the northern hemisphere can be seen as a huge clock face with the Pole Star, marking the celestial north pole, as its central fixed point and the Plough or Big Dipper as its hand. (In fact, the Plough takes approximately twenty-four hours to circle round the Pole Star.) To tell the time using these stars, you need a 'nocturnal' or star clock. This consists of a disc, marked off in months and hours, and an arm, which is like the hour hand of a clock. This arm is set parallel to the Pointers which you have to spot in the sky. They are the two bright stars (α and β Ursae Majoris) at the far end of the Plough's blade (or bowl of the Big Dipper) which point northwards directly to the Pole Star. The dial beneath the arm will indicate the time. Since the aspect of the circumpolar stars varies with the seasons, this hour dial must be set correctly for the time of year, by placing midnight against the date on which you are using the nocturnal.

Finding the south celestial pole – if you live in the southern hemisphere – is more difficult. The most obvious pointers are the two stars which form the body of the Southern Cross, Crux – that is α Crucis (Acrux) and γ Crucis. These do not point exactly to the south celestial pole, but about 8° to the side of it, towards the larger Magellanic Cloud. There is no bright star very near the south pole; the closest is σ Octans, of 5.5 magnitude.

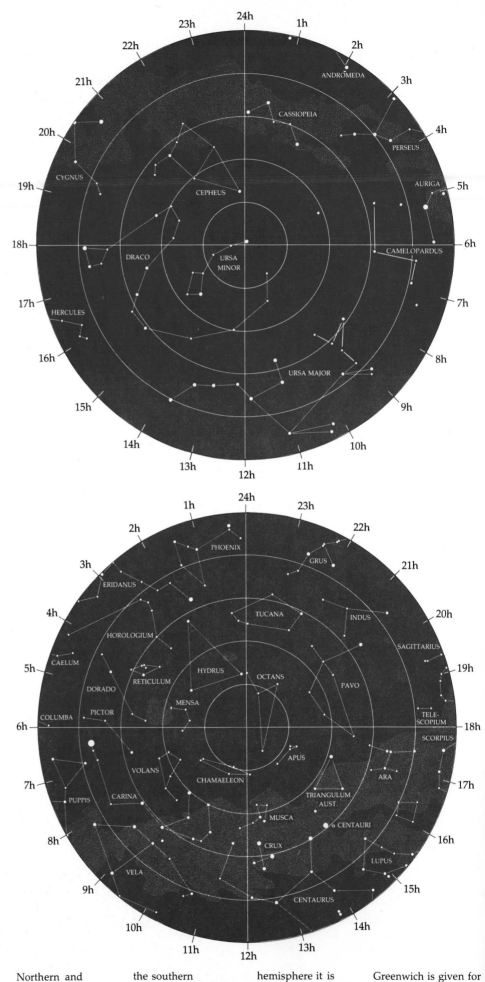

Northern and southern circumpolar star charts. When using a nocturnal in the southern hemisphere, align the arm with α and γ Crucis. For the southern hemisphere it is necessary to check your time zone. The time zone of Greenwich is given for the northern hemisphere.

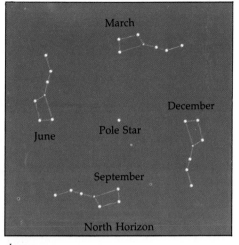

March

December

June

Pole Star

September

North Horizon

above

This diagram shows the position of the Plough (the Big Dipper) in March, June, September and December. The Pointers align with the Pole Star in the centre.

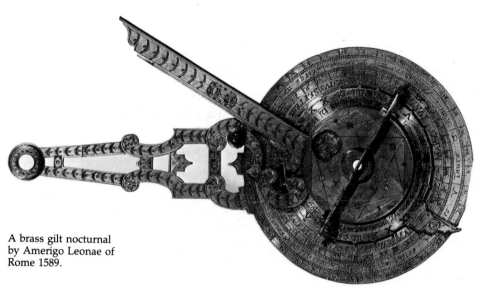

A brass gilt nocturnal by Amerigo Leonae of Rome 1589.

These are the various parts of a nocturnal with a side view below, showing how the nut and bolt fix the pieces together.

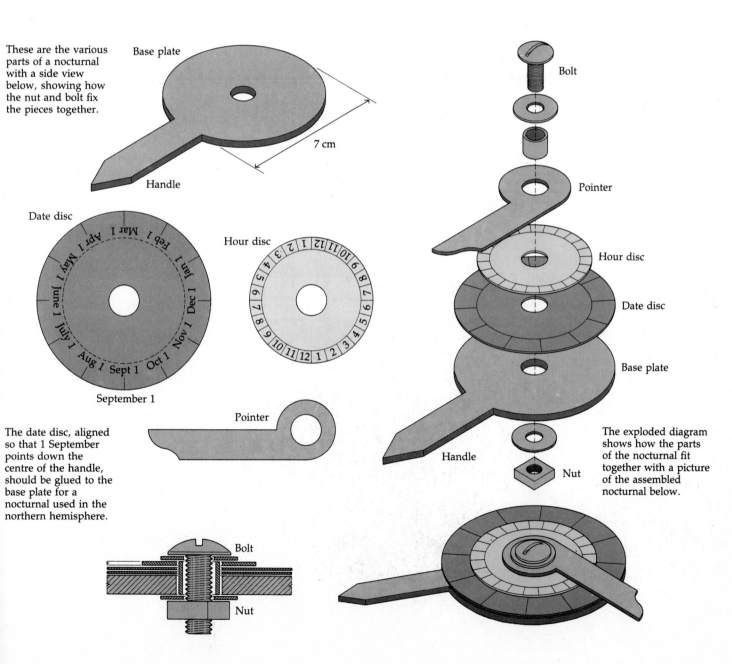

Base plate

Handle

7 cm

Bolt

Pointer

Hour disc

Date disc

Base plate

Handle

Nut

Date disc

Mar 1 Apr 1 May 1 Feb 1 Jan 1 June 1 July 1 Dec 1 Nov 1 Aug 1 Sept 1 Oct 1

September 1

Hour disc

Pointer

The date disc, aligned so that 1 September points down the centre of the handle, should be glued to the base plate for a nocturnal used in the northern hemisphere.

The exploded diagram shows how the parts of the nocturnal fit together with a picture of the assembled nocturnal below.

Bolt

Nut

INSTRUMENTS FOR MEASURING STAR POSITIONS

A planisphere is the sphere of stars transposed onto a plane or flat surface. An astrolabe shows the times of sunrise and sunset and the rising and setting times of certain stars.

The principle of the planisphere is as follows: imagine yourself observing the celestial sphere from below the south celestial pole, with a sheet of paper cutting through the celestial sphere at the celestial equator (Fig. 1). The sheet of paper gives a chart or 'projection' of the celestial sphere, and there are three important facts about it. First, the celestial equator appears as a circle on the paper, and therefore so do all circles on the sphere connecting stars of the same declination. Fig. 2 shows how the tropics of Cancer and Capricorn appear when projected onto a flat sheet of paper. Secondly, stars which are a certain number of degrees apart on the celestial sphere will be the same number of degrees apart on the planisphere chart. Thus stars A and B (Fig. 1) which are 90° apart remain 90° apart when plotted on the chart. Thirdly, you can chart not only all the northern hemisphere stars but also some southern hemisphere ones, for instance star C. If you viewed the celestial sphere from the north celestial pole, then you could make a planisphere chart of the southern hemisphere stars and a few northern hemisphere stars as well.

To make use of this chart (or 'stereographic projection' as it is technically called), we need to know what stars are visible at any one time. This means drawing in our horizon, and blocking out that part of the sky that would not be visible to us. At any latitude the celestial pole is exactly that number of degrees (referring to the latitude) above the horizon, looking north in the northern hemisphere and south in

In making a star chart, projections are used. These are a method of transferring points on a sphere onto a flat sheet of paper. The drawings below show how it can be done, the letters A, B, C, etc referring to points on the celestial sphere and A¹, B¹, C¹, etc to the projections of those points onto the paper.

The kind of projection used depends on its purpose and your viewpoint. These projections for a planisphere and astrolabe are made by looking from one pole of the celestial sphere and projecting onto a plane (sheet of paper) at the equator.

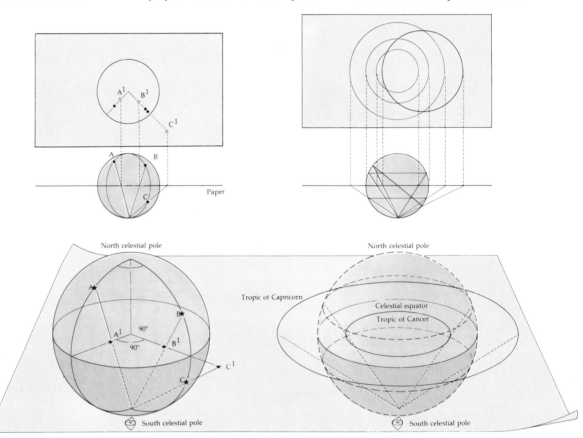

Fig 1
Projection of the celestial sphere.

Fig 2
Projection of the tropics, and equator.

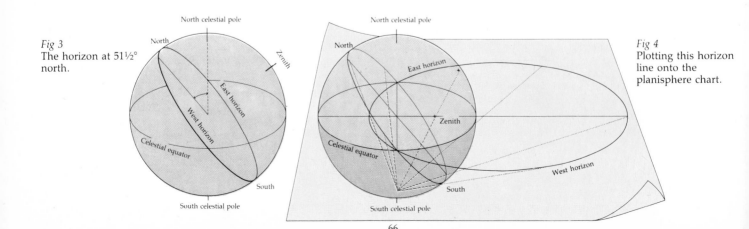

Fig 3
The horizon at 51½° north.

Fig 4
Plotting this horizon line onto the planisphere chart.

the southern hemisphere. Fig. 3 shows the horizon line in the northern hemisphere at a latitude of 51½° north (which is the latitude of London). Fig. 4 shows how this is plotted onto the planisphere chart. The result is an elliptical shape for the horizon because a circle is being projected *at an angle* (the latitude) onto a flat surface. Fig. 5 shows the horizon on the planisphere chart for a latitude of 51½° north. The elliptical nature of the horizon is clear, with the rings of equal altitude closer together north of the north celestial pole than they are south of it. Around the horizon, azimuths or compass directions are marked. These start at 0° (due north) and move round in clockwise direction.

To construct a simple planisphere you need a chart of the heavens (Fig. 6 gives you a simplified sketch). Plot in the brighter stars of first and second magnitudes and then some others to make up the constellation shapes. The table on page 202 gives you the coordinates (right ascension and declination) of these, but remember not to plot stars south of the tropic of Capricorn if you live in the northern hemisphere at a latitude more than about 50°.

Now make a mask in which the cut-away piece will show what area of sky can be seen from the latitude at which you live. For this, draw out your horizon as shown in Figs. 4 and 5 on a thick paper disc and cut out the sky area within the horizon.

Round the edge of the disc mark off the twenty-four hours of the day (Fig. 7). When you put the chart and mask together you can tell what stars are visible at any date or at any time, by matching the date on the chart with the time of day on the mask. However, if you live in a low latitude – 30° or less – then your star disc will need to be larger to cover those constellations visible close to your horizon. You may then find it more convenient to use the star charts on pages 52 – 63. Before you start drawing the star disc you should mark it out as shown in Fig. 6. Planispheres can be bought ready-made in some bookshops (page 198).

An astrolabe can be made in a similar way to a planisphere. It

Fig 5
Planisphere showing the horizon for 51½° north.

Fig 7
Mask showing cut-out for horizon and marked round the edge with the hours of the day.

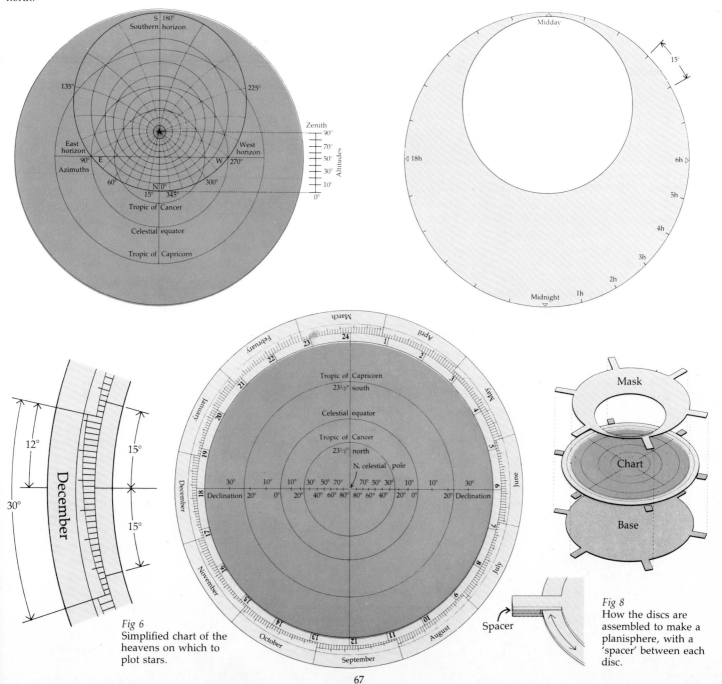

Fig 6
Simplified chart of the heavens on which to plot stars.

Fig 8
How the discs are assembled to make a planisphere, with a 'spacer' between each disc.

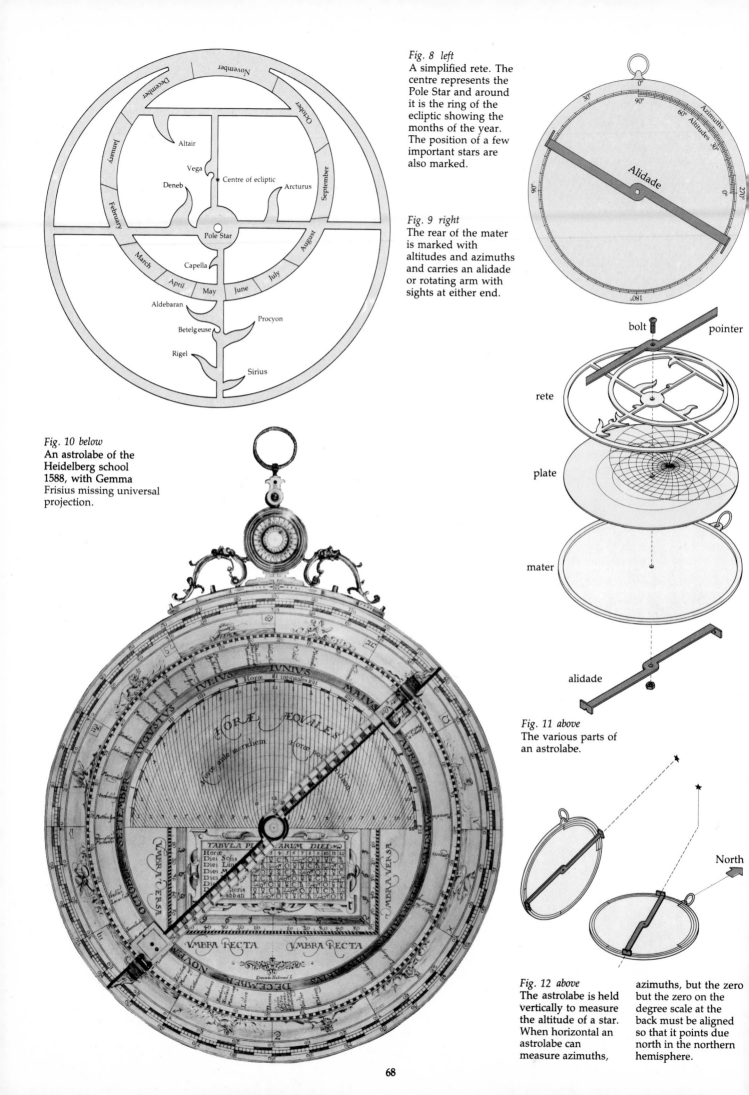

Fig. 8 left
A simplified rete. The centre represents the Pole Star and around it is the ring of the ecliptic showing the months of the year. The position of a few important stars are also marked.

Labels in Fig. 8: November, December, October, January, September, February, August, March, April, May, June, July, Altair, Vega, Deneb, Centre of ecliptic, Arcturus, Pole Star, Capella, Aldebaran, Procyon, Betelgeuse, Rigel, Sirius

Fig. 9 right
The rear of the mater is marked with altitudes and azimuths and carries an alidade or rotating arm with sights at either end.

Labels in Fig. 9: Alidade, Azimuths, Altitudes, 0°, 30°, 90°, 60°, 30°, 270°, 0°, 90°, 180°

Fig. 10 below
An astrolabe of the Heidelberg school 1588, with Gemma Frisius missing universal projection.

Fig. 11 above
The various parts of an astrolabe.

Labels in Fig. 11: bolt, pointer, rete, plate, mater, alidade

Fig. 12 above
The astrolabe is held vertically to measure the altitude of a star. When horizontal an astrolabe can measure azimuths, but the zero azimuths, but the zero on the degree scale at the back must be aligned so that it points due north in the northern hemisphere.

Label in Fig. 12: North

consists of a main part – the 'mater' which carries 'plates' – and a fretwork disc called a 'rete', pronounced 'reetee', (Fig. 8). The mater can be made from a disc and rings of card. Each plate is like the planisphere chart (Fig. 5) which has the celestial sphere and horizon on it but carries no stars, as these are on the rete. There is a separate plate for each latitude where observations are to be made. The rete is really a star map with the Sun's path or ecliptic marked on it. It is made like a piece of fretwork because in the days when the astrolabe was first made by Muslim astronomers (about AD 400), no suitable glass panels were available on which the stars could be drawn so the plate could still be seen below. Fig. 8 shows a rete for the northern hemisphere.

The back of the mater is used for calculations and for observing the altitudes of celestial bodies. Ours is marked with azimuths and altitudes (Fig. 9). Observations are made through a sighting arm or 'alidade'. (There is also an arm or 'rule' on the front of the astrolabe.) The mater has a protruding section at the top through which a ring is passed. By holding the astrolabe up by this ring and sighting through the alidade it is easy to measure an altitude (Fig. 12).

There are many things an astrolabe can calculate, but a complete set of instructions on how to make and use the instrument cannot be given in detail here. However, with a plate for your latitude, a rete as in Fig. 8 and a mater, you can make a simplified astrolabe. With this you can find times of the rising and setting of the Sun and of those stars on the rete.

To find the time of sunrise on a

certain date, for example, begin by setting the rete so that the date on the ecliptic touches the eastern horizon on the plate. Now set the rule to lie exactly at the place where the ecliptic and the horizon coincide and it will point to the time on the rim of the mater. To find the rising time of a star on a certain date, first rotate the rete until the star pointer lies on the eastern horizon. Next line up the rule so that it lies on the Sun's ecliptic position for the required date. Where the rule points on the rim of the mater is the time that star will rise.

Finding setting times is similar, but use the western horizon. A plastic astrolabe can be bought and a kit for building your own astrolabe has been produced (pages 198 – 199).

The astrolabe can be used for measuring star altitudes (Fig. 12). If it is turned sideways so that the mater is sloping, it can be used for measuring azimuths. However, for this you need a stand to keep it stable, while you must also see that the degree scale on the back of the mater is aligned so that the zero points due north (Fig. 12). The altitude and azimuth of stars will give their relative positions on the celestial sphere measured with respect to the horizon, but you will find all tables of star positions are given in right ascension and declination. You can work this out from the altitude and azimuth, but you need to know the the time of your observations and work it out using trigonometry. It is easier to measure right ascension and declination directly, using a stand and a quadrant (Figs. 14 and 15).

First set up the quadrant. The post for supporting it should have a

bracket (Fig. 16) at the top, while the top itself is cut at an angle of co-latitude (90° – your latitude) (Fig. 17). Make sure the post is fixed vertically and that looking through the horizontal hole in the bracket you see the north celestial pole (Pole Star) or, in southern latitudes, σ Octans.

To measure the right ascension of a star, first fix the quadrant through the horizontal hole to the stand (Fig. 14). Choose a star whose position you know; it should be near to the meridian (or south point in the northern hemisphere and north point in the southern hemisphere). Set your sighting arm to the right ascension of this star (see table on page 202). Then keeping the arm fixed, rotate the quadrant until looking through the sights you can see the chosen star, or until the arm is simply pointing in its direction. This fixes the quadrant at the correct position on the celestial equator. Move the sighting arm until it is pointing in the direction of the star whose right ascension you wish to measure, and read off the answer on the scale.

To measure declination the quadrant must be fixed to the stand through the side hole in the bracket so that the plane of the quadrant lies due north-south. Set the arm to the declination of a bright star whose position you know and which is due south (north in the southern hemisphere). Keeping the arm fixed, move the quadrant until you can see the chosen star through the sights. The quadrant is now set up so that the zero on the scale lies in the same direction as the celestial equator. Sight the star whose declination you want to measure and read the answer off the scale.

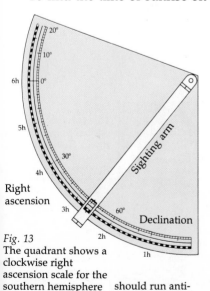

Fig. 13
The quadrant shows a clockwise right ascension scale for the southern hemisphere in which 1 hour = 15°. For the northern hemisphere the scale should run anti-clockwise. The degree scale is for declinations.

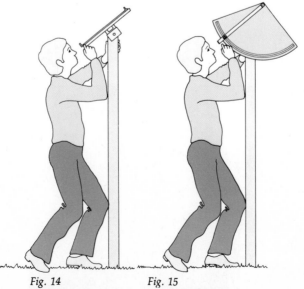

Fig. 14
Measuring the right ascension of a star.

Fig. 15
Measuring the declination of a star.

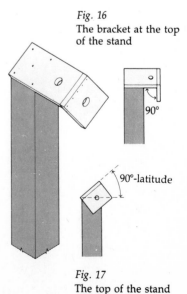

Fig. 16
The bracket at the top of the stand

Fig. 17
The top of the stand cut at the angle of co-latitude.

THE OPTICAL PRINCIPLES OF TELESCOPES AND BINOCULARS

A telescope is the most important, and most expensive piece of equipment required by the practical astronomer. There are two main types of telescope – refractors and reflectors. Binoculars, as their name implies, are *bi*– (two) *oculars* (telescopes) built side by side, one for each eye.

There is now some doubt about who invented the telescope, but we do know that in Italy in 1609 Galileo built his own telescope and that he was the first to publish astronomical discoveries made using one. Galileo built many telescopes and all were refractors. At the front was a lens, or object glass to bend or 'refract' the distant scene, and at the other end of the tube was a lens to magnify the image of this distant scene formed by the light gathered by the front lens. Galileo used a 'diminishing' lens as his eyepiece, so his telescope worked as shown in Fig. 1.

To see how a telescope like Galileo's works take a magnifying glass and hold it at arm's length. It will collect the light rays and refract them so that they bend to end up at a focus, where a tiny image, or picture of a distance object, is formed. This picture is upside down. Now take a diminishing lens – one side of a pair of spectacles worn by someone who is short-sighted will do. Put the diminishing lens close to your eye and line up the magnifying glass with it. Now slowly bring the magnifying glass closer and closer until you see a magnified image of the distant scene. The two lenses together – the larger magnifying lens and the small eye-lens or eyepiece – make a telescope. Your magnifying glass and diminishing lens will not provide a very good image – probably only the centre of the scene will be sharp – but you will see the principle of this kind of telescope.

After he had seen one of Galileo's telescopes, the German astronomer Johannes Kepler designed a slightly different kind of refractor. He replaced the diminishing lens that Galileo had used as an eyepiece with a magnifying lens (Fig. 2). This type of refractor, using two magnifying lenses, gives a larger 'field of view' than Galileo's. Its disadvantage is that it gives an inverted image. To give an upright image as Galileo's telescope did, more lenses are required in the eyepiece. But because every lens absorbs a little light, more lenses mean that less light is available for the final image. Astronomers want every bit of light they can gather, so they have long been content to observe an inverted image. Nor does it really matter since the Moon and planets appear as discs, and stars are points of light, even in a telescope.

Refracting telescopes suffer from two optical defects or 'aberrations'. The first is the failure of a lens to

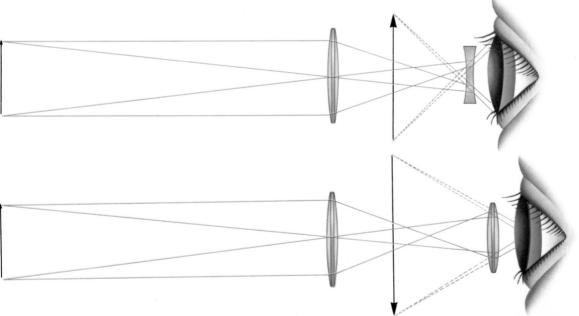

Fig. 1
A Galilean telescope, with a biconvex front lens and a diminishing lens as the eyepiece, gives images the right way up.

Fig. 2
A Keplerian telescope gives inverted images and a wider field of vision than the Galilean.

Fig. 3
This seventeenth-century engraving shows an early telescope being used to project an image of the Sun on a small screen–still the best method for observing sunspots.

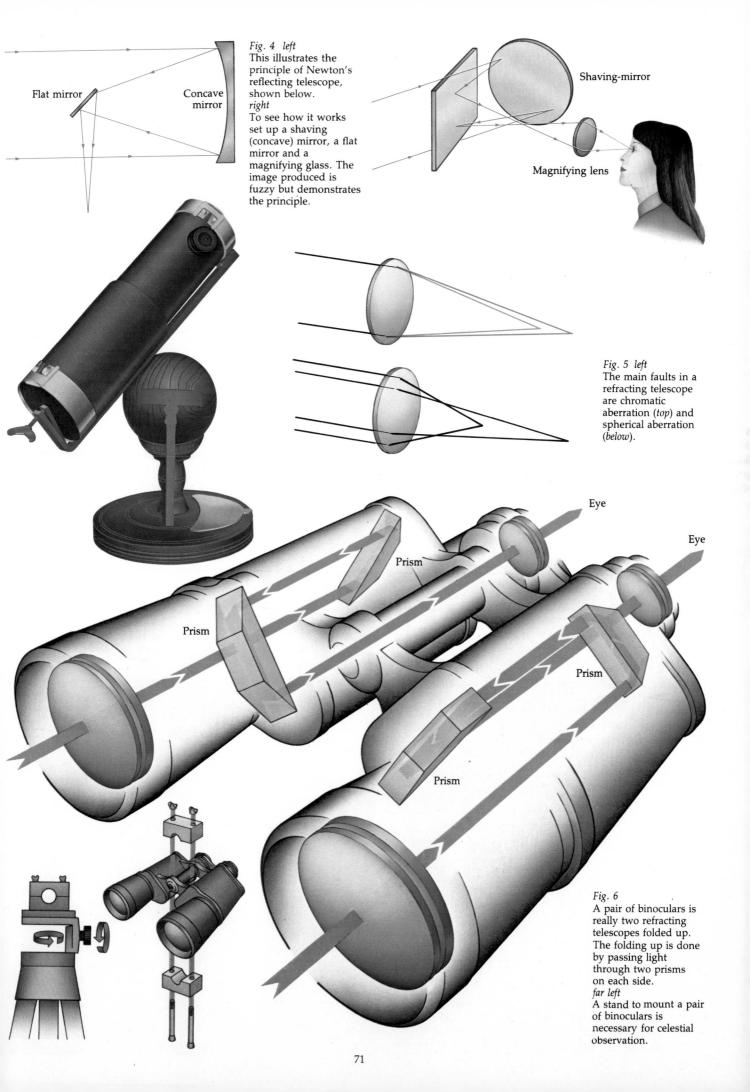

Fig. 4 left
This illustrates the principle of Newton's reflecting telescope, shown below.
right
To see how it works set up a shaving (concave) mirror, a flat mirror and a magnifying glass. The image produced is fuzzy but demonstrates the principle.

Flat mirror

Concave mirror

Shaving-mirror

Magnifying lens

Fig. 5 left
The main faults in a refracting telescope are chromatic aberration (*top*) and spherical aberration (*below*).

Eye

Eye

Prism

Prism

Prism

Prism

Fig. 6
A pair of binoculars is really two refracting telescopes folded up. The folding up is done by passing light through two prisms on each side.
far left
A stand to mount a pair of binoculars is necessary for celestial observation.

71

bring all the different coloured rays to the same focus. The blue rays are brought to a focus closer to the lens than the red ones, for instance (Fig. 5), because the degree to which light is refracted depends on its colour. That is why a prism disperses white light into its separate colours (page 36). The result is that a bright object on a dark background will appear to be surrounded by a coloured ring or halo. For astronomers this is a nuisance.

More serious, however, is the second defect, known as 'spherical aberration', which is the inability of a lens to bring rays from near its edge to focus at the same point as those from near the centre (Fig. 5). Thus if the centre of a scene is in focus, the rest will appear fuzzy. You may not notice this when you use a magnifying glass (because you only look through a small area of it at a time) but it is very noticeable when you look through a telescope. Because of this defect, Galileo used to mask out the edge of the front-lens or object-glass of his telescopes, while astronomers using Kepler's design overcame the worst effects by making the curves of their lenses very gentle so the difference in focus between the edges and centre of the object-glasses was very small. Unfortunately, however this meant that such object-glasses brought the rays to a focus a very long way away – in other words, they had a very long focal length – and telescopes 45 metres long were sometimes constructed. These were unwieldy and difficult to use. It was not until 1745 that both defects could be largely surmounted by the use of an object-glass made of two lenses of different kinds of glass. All refractors and binoculars today have such double-lens or 'achromatic' object-glasses.

Binoculars are really folded up telescopes with prisms inside to turn the light round but so arranged that they do not disperse it into its separate colours. Fig. 6 shows the general scheme and explains why a pair of binoculars is the dumpy shape it is.

In 1670 at Cambridge, England, Isaac Newton built a small reflecting telescope, using a concave mirror instead of an object-glass to gather light from a distant scene and bring it to a focus (Fig. 4). Newton did not invent the reflecting telescope – we do not know for certain who did – but he did make the first one which worked really satisfactorily. You can see the principle of the reflector for

yourself (Fig. 4) using a concave shaving-mirror, a flat mirror and a magnifying lens. You will have to put the flat mirror near the shaving-mirror because the focal length of the shaving mirror, which is designed to help someone shaving, is very short. All the same you can see the principle at work. The light is gathered by the curved mirror and is then bounced back to the flat mirror, which is placed at an angle of 45°. This directs the light to the side of the tube where an image is formed.

Unlike the refractor, though, in Newton's design of reflector the observer looks in through the side of the tube. There are other designs, for example that of the Frenchman Cassegrain, where you look straight through the telescope tube, (Fig. 7), but such designs are optically more complex and difficult to make. The Newtonian design is the type of

reflector most amateur astronomers use because its optics are simple and not too difficult to align inside the tube. A pair of open sights or a sighting telescope are fitted to help align the telescope on to a celestial object. You can of course buy such a telescope, or you can purchase the optics (concave mirror, flat mirror and eyepieces) and build a tube and a mounting to carry the telescope yourself (see pages 198–199).

The mirror of a reflecting telescope is parabolic, not spherical in shape (Fig. 8) and so does not show spherical aberration. Also, the concave mirror is made to reflect light from its surface, not from its back like an ordinary mirror. Since light does not pass through the glass of this mirror or through the flat mirror, neither of these give a chromatic aberration; such as there is comes only from the eyepiece and

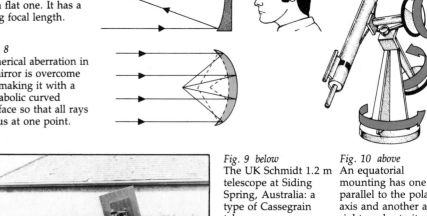

Fig. 7
The Cassegrain telescope uses a convex mirror instead of a flat one. It has a long focal length.

Fig. 8
Spherical aberration in a mirror is overcome by making it with a parabolic curved surface so that all rays focus at one point.

Fig. 11 *above*
An amateur's homemade reflecting telescope on an altazimuth mounting.

Fig. 12 *right*
A German-type equatorially mounted refractor where the telescope is on one side of a bar, which is counterweighted on the other.

Fig. 9 *below*
The UK Schmidt 1.2 m telescope at Siding Spring, Australia: a type of Cassegrain telescope.

Fig. 10 *above*
An equatorial mounting has one axis parallel to the polar axis and another at right angles to it.

that is virtually unnoticeable.

The amount of light a telescope can gather depends on its aperture, that is on the area of its object-glass or concave mirror. Thus a mirror of 30 cm aperture will gather four times as much light as a 15 cm aperture mirror will do (because the area of a circular aperture is πr^2 where r is the radius; the radius of a 15 cm aperture is 7.5, and its area $(7.5)^2\pi = 56.25\pi$; for a 30 cm aperture the area is $(15)^2\pi = 225\pi$ and $225\pi \div 56.25\pi = 4$.) The larger the aperture, the higher the magnifying power you can use, so you will be able to detect more detail and dimmer stars. The actual magnifying power depends on the focal length of your eyepiece: the shorter its focal length, the higher the magnification it gives. (To calculate the magnification, divide the focal length of your mirror or object-glass by the focal length of the eyepiece.

Thus for a 15 cm aperture mirror with a focal length of 1.2 metres, an eyepiece with a focal length of 2.5 cm will give a magnifying power of 120 $\div 2.5 = 48$ and one of 1.25 cm a magnifying power of 96.)

There are various types of astronomical telescopes an amateur can buy. Refractors are expensive, and long compared with their aperture, but a 6.5 cm one can give pleasant views of celestial objects. A reflector is a more economic proposition but one with an aperture of at least 15 cm is required for any serious study of the skies: a smaller aperture than this will probably soon show its limitations. There is another type of telescope, the 'catadioptric' telescope which has both a thin front lens (a single piece of glass) and a concave mirror. Such telescopes, (examples are the 'Maksutov' or the 'Schmidt') give a good field of view

and a very short tube for their aperture. The Maksutov is ideal for visual observation, although for professional photographic work the Schmidt is used. Both types are very expensive. The beginner's best and cheapest buy is a reflector with 15 cm optics and a home-made tube and mounting (as described in Reg Spry's book, mentioned on page 198).

No telescope for astronomical use can be held in the hand: all need a stand or mounting. Just as there are two main types of telescope, so there are two main kinds of mounting, the 'altazimuth' and the 'equatorial'.

An altazimuth mounting is easy to make and comparatively inexpensive to buy. It must be sturdy – a wobbly or shaky mounting is utterly useless – otherwise it presents no great problems. The stars move in a curved path across the sky so, in order to follow them while you observe, you must move the telescope round in azimuth (i.e. round parallel to the horizon) and up or down in altitude as well. The magnification in a telescope is enough to make this movement constantly necessary: if you keep the telescope still you will soon see the star you are observing drift out of your field of view. Nevertheless, you soon get used to this double movement, and for the beginner an altazimuth mounting is quite adequate. If you mount a pair of binoculars on a camera tripod this will be an altazimuth mount.

The equatorial mounting is designed to follow the stars with one movement only. To achieve this, the vertical pivoting axis of azimuth motion in the altazimuth mounting is tilted over until it is parallel to the Earth's polar axis (Fig. 10). The amount of tilt depends on the observer's latitude. A specially designed and built mounting is necessary for this: do not try to tilt an altazimuth mounting over in this way – the whole thing will topple over. The mounting can have a great number of variations as two photographs of amateur telescopes show. The serious amateur will want an equatorial mounting, not least because a motor drive can be installed so that the telescope automatically follows the apparent movement of the stars, and this is necessary for most stellar photography. But for the beginner it is perhaps better to find your way about the sky using a simple altazimuth first. Then, when you decide to continue observing with a telescope, you can think about buying an equatorial.

Fig. 13 above
An altazimuth mounting, moveable in azimuth and altitude.

Fig. 14 right
The 5 m reflecting telescope at Palomar, California, seen inside the open dome in moonlight.

Fig. 15 left
The equatorially mounted 3.9 m Anglo-Australian reflector. The mirror is at the bottom of the framework tube.

Fig. 16 above
The electronic control panel of the Anglo-Australian telescope.

MAGNITUDES OF THE STARS

Gaze up at the sky on a starry night and the fact that some stars are brighter than others is obvious straight away. Does this mean that the brighter stars must be nearer to Earth? Or do stars vary individually in size and brightness so that we cannot judge either size or distance from their brilliance?

In earlier times in our civilization, since the stars were believed to be fixed on the inside of a giant sphere, it was thought that they all lay at the same distance. Brightness might or might not be a measure of size, but it was clearly a measure of importance, and was therefore termed 'magnitude of importance' or 'magnitude' for short. It was the Greek astronomer Hipparchos (often spelled Hipparchus) who decided this about 150 BC, and set out to catalogue the brightness of all the stars he could see. We can follow exactly the same method as Hipparchos used.

To begin, let us find all the brightest stars and write down their positions or, better still, make a drawing (pages 66–67). The planetary plotter (pages 114–115) will be a help to you. These will be stars of first importance or magnitude 1. (For convenience make a chart of only a section of the sky at a time.) Now choose all the stars that seem to be about half as bright as those we have already charted. These we shall call magnitude 2. The next stars to plot are those which are half as dim as those of magnitude 2 (and so 4 times dimmer than magnitude 1). Continue in this way until you have recorded stars of magnitude 6.

Dimmer than magnitude 6, you cannot go with the naked eye, and in fact you may not always be able to see 6th magnitude stars. On a bright moonlit night – that is close to Full Moon – your eyes will not become so dark-adapted with the result that you will not see these stars. Nor will you if there are bright street lights nearby; a slight haze will also hamper visibility, even on a moonless night. With the help of binoculars or a telescope, it is amazing how many more stars one is able to see which cannot be detected with the naked eye.

Modern research has shown that the eye can readily measure the brightness of an object half as bright as something else, and to continue doing this in a series of equal steps. So Hipparchos' method is not as hit-and-miss as it sounds. However, in the 1830s the astronomer John Herschel invented a way of measuring star brightness more precisely and found that most first magnitude stars on Hipparchos' scale

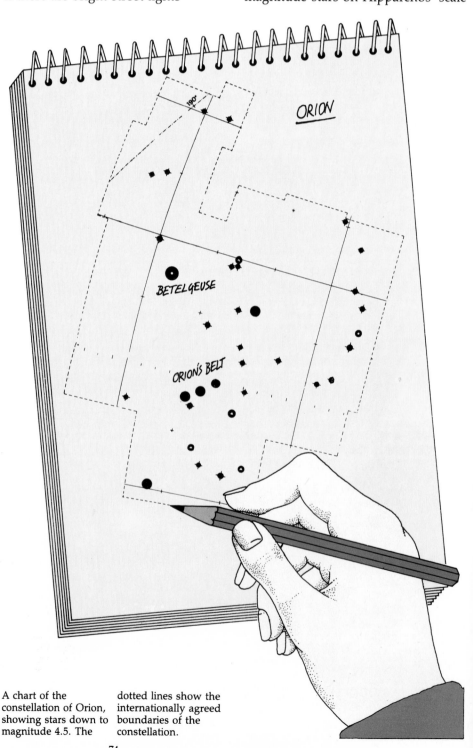

Circumpolar star trails photographed in Arizona. The stars appear as trails, rather than dots, because this is a long exposure photograph and the Earth rotated while it was being taken. The varying brightness and colours of the stars are clearly visible.

A chart of the constellation of Orion, showing stars down to magnitude 4.5. The dotted lines show the internationally agreed boundaries of the constellation.

were 100 times brighter than those that he had classed as 6th magnitude. Two times as bright was actually 2.512 times to be precise (since $2.512^5 = 100$). This is the scale astronomers use today.

John Herschel also discovered that a few stars were brighter than those Hipparchos had called first magnitude, and we now have magnitude 0 (2.512 times brighter than magnitude 1), and even minus magnitude numbers, so that magnitude –1 is 2.512 times brighter than magnitude 0. On this scale the apparent magnitude (i.e. the magnitude we measure looking up into the sky) of Vega is magnitude 0, Sirius magnitude –1.4, the Full Moon –12.5, and the Sun is magnitude –26.8 or 14 thousand million times brighter than Sirius.

But is the Sun really as bright as this? The answer is no; it only seems to be so because it is so close. Sirius is almost 556,638 times further away from us than the Sun. To measure the true or *absolute magnitude* of a star, calculations are made of what brightness it would have at a distance of 32.6 light-years. (This particular distance is chosen because it makes calculations easier for the professional astronomer.) To do this we need to know three things: (a) the apparent magnitude of the star; (b) the star's distance; and (c) how brightness diminishes with distance.

Light diminishes with distance according to an 'inverse square law'. This means that if you move a light twice as far away, its apparent brightness drops to

$$\frac{1}{2 \times 2} \text{ or } \frac{1}{4};$$

three times further away to

$$\frac{1}{3 \times 3} \text{ or } \frac{1}{9};$$

and so on. An experiment to check this is given in the drawing below.

With these three factors in mind, it is found that the absolute magnitude of Vega is +0.5; Sirius +1.4, and the Sun +4.7. We see then that the Sun is really about 21 times dimmer than Sirius, not 14 thousand million times brighter!

A close look at the stars will reveal that they are not all the same colour. With optical aid you can readily notice that Sirius is bluish white, Vega and Rigel white, Aldebaran and Betelgeuse red, and so on. Colours are easier to detect in a telescope or binoculars because more light is transmitted to your eye, which is not so sensitive to colours in dim light. You can prove this for yourself; watch how the colours of surroundings begin to fade as dusk gathers or how difficult it is to pick out colours even by the light of the Full Moon. What is more, the eye is not equally sensitive to light of all colours – it is most receptive to yellow. So our judgement of apparent magnitude is bound to be affected by a star's colour. Professional astronomers have ways of taking this into account, and can actually measure star colours with extreme precison.

The COSMOS high speed automatic scanning and measuring machine. Photographic plates, taken with a large telescope, are scanned by the equipment in the two vertical cylinders. The machine measures the position, brightness and shape of every object photographed so that it can distinguish between stars and other celestial bodies.

By altering the distance of an exposure metre from a torch or flashlight bulb, you can prove that light diminishes with distance according to an 'inverse square law'.

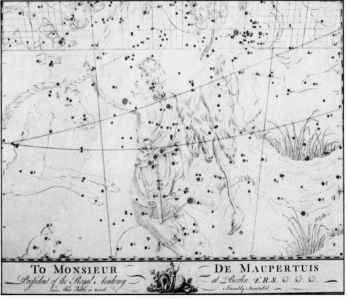

Orion appears as the hunter in John Flamsteed's *Atlas Coelestis* published in London in 1729.

HOW THE STARS SHINE

To investigate how the stars shine means finding out as much as we can about their physical composition and how they produce the vast amount of energy that is needed.

The different brightness and colour of the stars give us some clues. Stars shine by their own light; like the Sun they are great globes of gas, emitting radiation in various colours. Many other substances behave like this when heated, such as coal. A coal fire is black when cold and glows when hot, and as it heats its colour gradually changes from a dull red to a yellowish red. An iron poker heated in a fire will show a similar effect, and the element of an electric fire also goes through the same sequence of colour changes.

These observations tell us that a substance like coal or iron changes colour as it heats and that its colour is determined by its temperature. Materials of this type approximate to what a physicist would call a 'black-body'; that is a body which absorbs all radiation falling on it when cold – and so appears dull black – and then, as it heats, goes through all the colours of the spectrum. Could it be that the stars also approximate to black-bodies and their colour is an indication of temperature?

To pursue this further, let us consider the Sun. On page 36 we used a spectroscope to study the dark lines crossing the Sun's spectrum. By doing this it was possible to identify the chemical elements lying above the Sun's main body or photosphere and to discover the Sun's temperature.

With a telescope of at least 20 cm aperture, it is possible to fit a spectroscope and observe the spectra of the stars. When such spectra are examined, it is found that the lines present vary according to the colour of the star. Such spectra were classified in the 1880s and given the letters, A, B, C etc, but later research showed that some classes were duplicated, and the alphabetical order needed amending. Finally the classification ran O, B, A,F, G, K, M – which English-speaking astronomers memorize by the mnemonic 'Oh Be A Fine Girl Kiss Me!' The O stars are blue, the B stars bluish-white, the A stars white, F slightly yellow, G yellowish-white, K orange and M red. Calculations and a close study of the lines show that OBAFGKM is a scale of temperature where O stars are the hottest and M ones the coolest. The seven spectral classes can be further subdivided into tenths for greater precision, i.e. 00 01 02 03 04 05 06 07 08 09.

We now have information on the colours, spectral classes and temperatures of stars and, for those whose distance we know, the absolute magnitudes. All this information should tell us something, but how can we organize it? Let us chart it, using the details given in Tables 3 and 4 (page 202). Plot out the nearest stars (Table 3) on this scheme. The result will be like that shown on the H-R diagram (page 79). This was drawn up in 1914 by the American astronomer Henry Norris Russell, who used absolute magnitudes derived from measurements of stellar distances by the Danish astronomer Ejnar Hertzsprung. It is still known as a Hertzsprung-Russell or H-R diagram.

It is clear from the H-R diagram that the brighter a star really is (we are using absolute not apparent magnitudes), the bluer and hotter it is, rather like the poker. Russell suggested that stars begin as dim dull objects (lower right), which then shrink and heat up, so that their absolute magnitude increases and the colour moves slowly from the red end of the spectrum towards the blue. They would then cool again to become red stars once more. In brief, the H-R diagram shows stellar development or evolution. This seems an obvious interpretation but further plotting shows that it does not fit all the facts.

Before you insert any more information, however, look again at what is already there. It can tell you something else about the stars. Use your telescope and note down the colours – or better still, with a large telescope – the spectra of the stars. Note too their apparent magnitudes. You can use the diagram, as Ejnar Hertzsprung did, to calculate the distances of the stars. For instance, suppose you observe Sirius. You find its apparent magnitude is –1.4, and an examination of its spectrum shows that it is an A or, more precisely, an A1 star. If we plot it at A1 it should have an absolute magnitude of about +1.4. Knowing both the absolute magnitude and the apparent magnitude, we can work out the distance of Sirius as 2.7 parsecs or 8.8 light-years.

To calculate this we use the

The intensity interferometer at Narrabri, New South Wales used to measure the diameters of hot, bright stars. The mirrors feed a photoelectric cell mounted at the end of a pole so the light signal from the star is changed into an electric current. The distance between the two mirrors can be

varied by moving them along the railway track.

opposite
Composite photograph of Betelgeuse. The patches show different temperatures of gas caused by transfer of heat within the star.

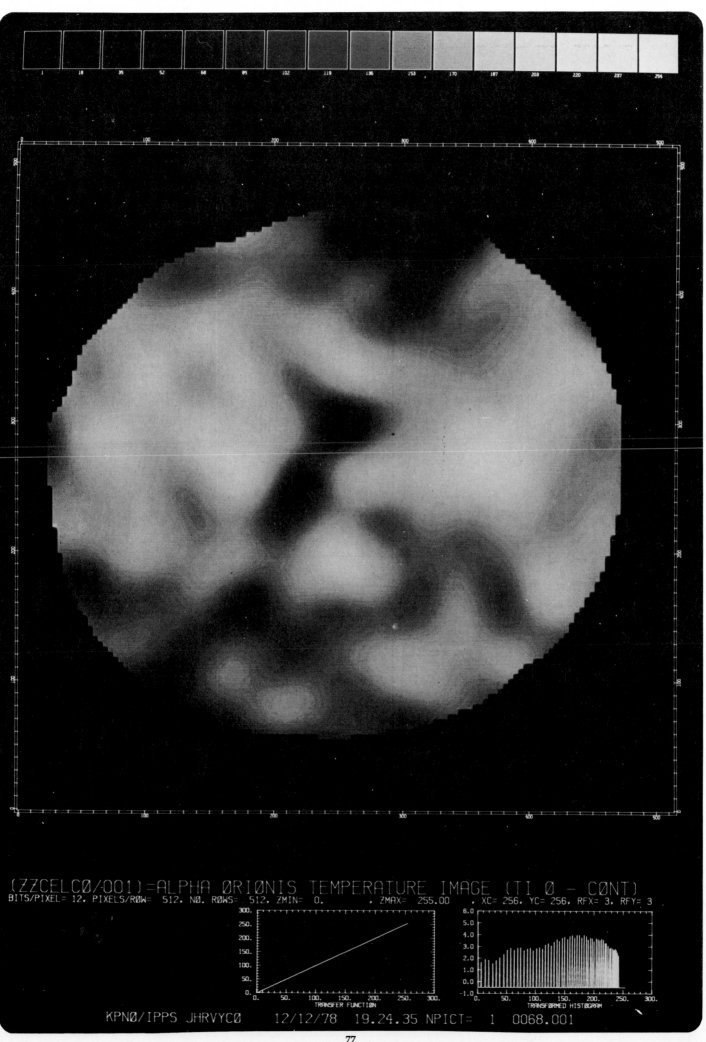

(ZZCELCØ/001)=ALPHA ØRIØNIS TEMPERATURE IMAGE (TI Ø - CØNT)
BITS/PIXEL= 12. PIXELS/RØW= 512. NØ. RØWS= 512. ZMIN= 0.   . ZMAX= 255.00   . XC= 256. YC= 256. RFX= 3. RFY= 3

TRANSFER FUNCTIØN

TRANSFØRMED HISTØGRAM

KPNØ/IPPS JHRVYCØ   12/12/78   19.24.35 NPICT=   1   0068.001

formula: $\log P = \dfrac{m - M + 5}{5}$

P = distance in parsecs, m = apparent magnitude, and M =absolute magnitude.

Now return to the H-R diagram and plot say, twenty of the brightest stars given in Table 4 (page 203). This makes the diagram appear rather different, because some stars do not seem to obey the rules we thought we had found. Betelgeuse is spectral class M2 and one would therefore guess that it has an absolute magnitude of around +12, but is in fact –6. Betelgeuse then is nearly 16 million times brighter than anticipated. Another such star is Aldebaran, spectral class K5 with an absolute magnitude of –0.8 instead of the supposed +7. It seems that there are stars which do not lie along the 'main sequence' we plotted earlier. There are 'red giants' like Aldebaran, and red 'supergiants' like Betelgeuse (the words giant and supergiant originally referred to absolute magnitude, not to size). So it seems that the simple idea of stellar evolution that we – and Henry Norris Russell – worked out cannot be correct in the light of this new evidence.

To explain the H-R diagram in terms of stellar evolution can only be done if we know how stars generate their energy. For centuries this question puzzled astronomers and various answers were suggested, such as burning gas, falling meteorites and shrinkage under gravitation for the production of this energy. However none of these processes would have kept the Sun shining for long enough. Geological evidence had shown the Sun was certainly at least as old as the Earth – about 4,700 million years. It was not until 1905, when Albert Einstein published the first part of his Theory of Relativity, that the riddle at last began to be solved.

In 1907 Einstein announced that one of the consequences of this theory was that mass and energy were interchangeable. This gave rise to the famous equation $E = mc^2$ (E = energy, m = mass and c = the velocity of light). Since c is a very large number, and appears here as a square (i.e. multiplied by itself), obviously the energy generated when some mass – an atom, say – is annihilated, is vast. An atom bomb is an example of this principle multiplied. One of the first to recognize this process as a means of supplying the Sun's energy needs,

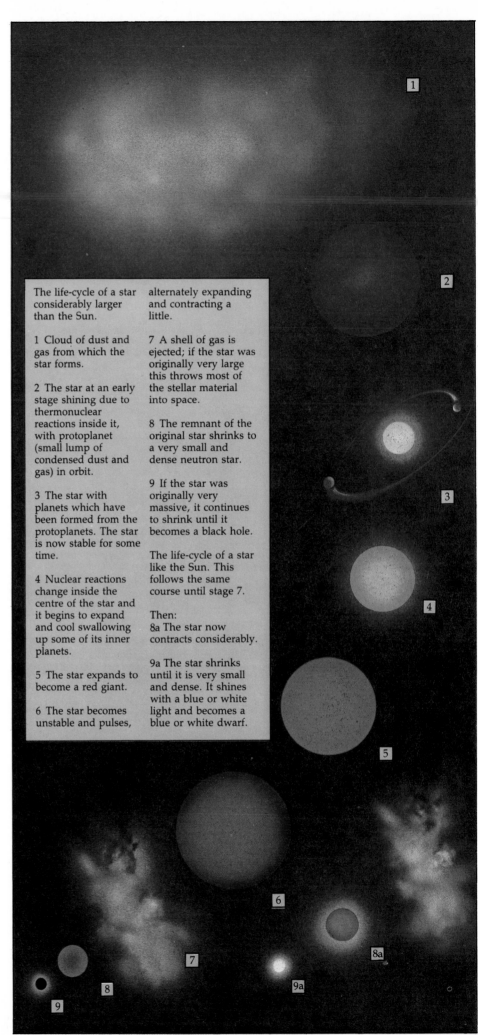

The life-cycle of a star considerably larger than the Sun.

1 Cloud of dust and gas from which the star forms.

2 The star at an early stage shining due to thermonuclear reactions inside it, with protoplanet (small lump of condensed dust and gas) in orbit.

3 The star with planets which have been formed from the protoplanets. The star is now stable for some time.

4 Nuclear reactions change inside the centre of the star and it begins to expand and cool swallowing up some of its inner planets.

5 The star expands to become a red giant.

6 The star becomes unstable and pulses, alternately expanding and contracting a little.

7 A shell of gas is ejected; if the star was originally very large this throws most of the stellar material into space.

8 The remnant of the original star shrinks to a very small and dense neutron star.

9 If the star was originally very massive, it continues to shrink until it becomes a black hole.

The life-cycle of a star like the Sun. This follows the same course until stage 7.

Then:
8a The star now contracts considerably.

9a The star shrinks until it is very small and dense. It shines with a blue or white light and becomes a blue or white dwarf.

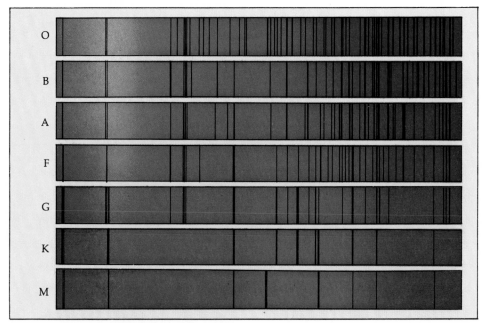

Examples of the principal types of stellar spectra.

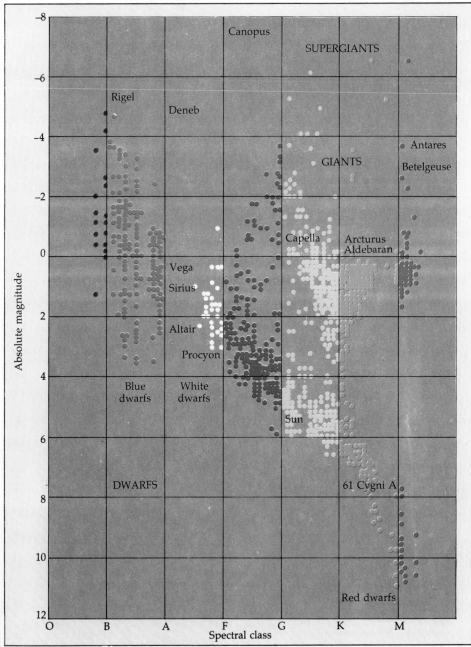

The Hertzsprung-Russell diagram in which stars are plotted according to their absolute magnitudes and their spectral type (temperature). Each dot represents a star.

was an English astronomer Arthur Eddington. In 1924 Eddington calculated results for the Sun, and showed that if atoms were annihilated, then the Sun could keep shining for thousands of millions of years, which fitted in with the geological theory. Eddington applied his idea to all stars, and other astronomers followed his lead.

Stars are composed mainly of hydrogen and in their central regions hydrogen is converted into helium. This is the sort of thermonuclear reaction that takes place in a hydrogen bomb, and it gives out immense amounts of energy. Under certain conditions there is another nuclear reaction which occurs in stars; this involves carbon and nitrogen as well as hydrogen and helium, and emits even more energy. So this is how stars shine; they are giant thermonuclear reactors.

These nuclear reactions make sense of the new more informative H-R diagram we have drawn, and what astronomers think is the life-cycle of stars is as follows. First, stars condense out of dust and gas in space. If they are not too large they start to glow a dull red and then, as nuclear reactions continue, they move up the main sequence from M to G or F. Then after a long time at this stage (which is where our Sun is now), the star expands. At this point the star's outer gases cool, but it is so large it still shines brightly. It has become a red giant. This may last for 100 million years, but eventually all the nuclear energy is exhausted. Under the influence of gravitation it shrinks, contracting into a tiny blue or white star – a 'white dwarf' like 40 Eridani B or van Maanen's star. If the star is initially larger – about twice as large as the Sun or even bigger still – its life-cycle will differ somewhat. It will become a red supergiant instead of a giant, and will end its life explosively (pages 86–87). And there are some large stars which use up their nuclear fuel (hydrogen) very quickly. These are the O, B and A stars which shine very brightly and which appear at the upper end of the main sequence. This modern research has also shown us that the terms giant, supergiant and dwarf are, after all, descriptive of size as well as absolute magnitude.

So you can see that the observations which began with only the magnitude and colours of the stars as they appear in the sky, has brought us nearer to understanding their nature and the way in which their energy is generated.

DOUBLE STARS AND HOW TO OBSERVE THEM

Binaries are very common – perhaps half the stars in space are members of binary systems – and their study is of great importance in astronomy. Some pairs of stars appear double because they lie close together in our line of sight; in true binary systems the two components orbit one another.

It was the late eighteenth-century astronomer William Herschel who first began a systematic study of double stars, using the huge reflectors he built himself, telescopes which were better and larger than any others of his day. To begin with, Herschel thought all pairs of stars were due to line of sight effects, but constant study made it clear to him that some were in orbit about each other. Such a binary is the nearest star to us, α Centauri. Its two components have magnitudes of 0.3 and 1.7; the brighter is yellow and the dimmer red. These separate components can be seen with binoculars but not from the northern hemisphere. In the northern hemisphere there are plenty of stars to choose from, but Castor (α Geminorum) has two components of nearly the same brightness (magnitudes 2.0 and 2.9). Both are white stars but you will need a good telescope to separate them. Mizar (ζ Ursae Majoris) appears a double to the unaided eye, but if you observe it with binoculars you will see that in fact there is a binary and another star. Another beautiful binary is β Cygni whose components are yellow (magnitude 3.2) and blue-white (magnitude 5.4). This is a magnificent sight. Do not expect to see the binaries change much in position: the components of α Centauri take 80 years to complete one orbit and those of Castor 380 years.

A star atlas and certain books list some of the doubles you can see, but some need quite a powerful telescope to show their components separately. But what of the binaries which cannot be separated by any telescope? How do we know they are binaries? The professional astronomer comes to the rescue here by using the spectroscope. As the stars are moving round in orbit, their spectral lines will show a Doppler shift (pages 190–191). When moving away in orbit, the shift will be towards the red; when moving towards us the shift will be towards the blue. Such a pattern of shifts gives the clue that allows a binary to be detected. These very close pairs are known as 'spectroscopic binaries'.

By observing a visual binary the relative orbit of the two components may be determined. The method of doing this is to measure two values or parameters at each observation. One is the 'position angle' – the angle one star makes with the other. The brighter is usually the one considered 'fixed', and the dimmer is the one whose angle is measured. The zero is the line perpendicular to the celestial equator (Fig. 4).

Fig. 1
William Herschel's largest reflecting telescope consisted of a tube 12 m long and a 1.3 m metal mirror on an altazimuth mounting.

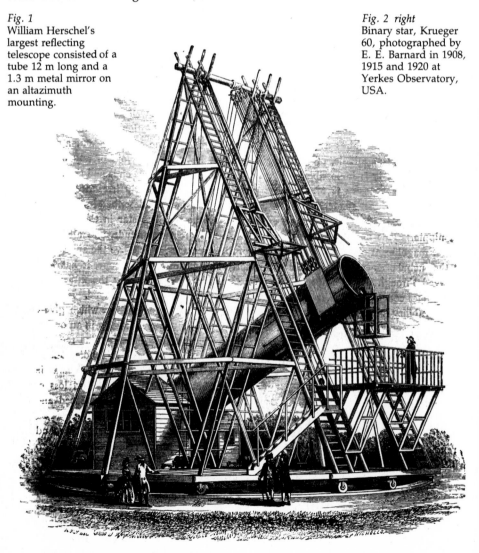

Fig. 2 right
Binary star, Krueger 60, photographed by E. E. Barnard in 1908, 1915 and 1920 at Yerkes Observatory, USA.

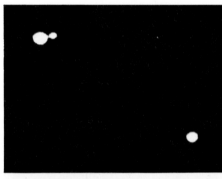

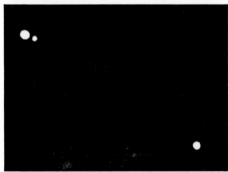

Professionally, photographs are used and accurately measured, but it is possible to make the measures at the eye end of the telescope with a special attachment known as a 'parallel wire micrometer'. Such micrometers are not made now, although a very few amateurs still have them. However, you can always make an estimate of the angle, which you can check making fresh observations some years later.

The separation must also be measured. Again, measuring photographs is the professional way. Visually, the parallel wire micrometer can do the job, and you can also get an idea by timing how long it takes for the second component to follow the first one to the edge of the field, and then doing these calculations. First take the cosine of the position angle and multiply the time in seconds (of time) by this. Now divide your answer by the cosine of the main component's declination. This will give you a time, which you must now multiply by 15 to give you the answer in seconds of arc.

By observing the changes in position and the varying separation of the components of a binary system, and finding their distance, it is possible to compute the masses of each of the stars. If the distance is unknown, then it is still possible to calculate the relative masses of the two components but not the precise mass of each. This ratio of the masses may also be calculated for spectroscopic binaries. The study of binaries thus enables professional astronomers to find the masses of stars of various kinds.

Sometimes we see a binary star system in which the orbits are viewed almost 'edge-on' (Fig. 3). When this happens we see each star crossing in front of the other and eclipsing it. Such an 'eclipsing binary' will vary its light (Fig. 5) and this is how we can recognize it. We can draw a 'light-curve' which will have a special shape because of the eclipses which occur during each orbit. An amateur astronomer can observe these eclipsing binaries without difficulty. The 'Demon' star Algol (β Persei) is the most famous example (Fig. 5). This star was known by Arab astronomers to 'wink' and it was also studied in western Europe where, in 1783, the young amateur astronomer John Goodricke suggested that the winking was caused by a darker star orbiting a brighter one. There are many eclipsing variables and although Algol really needs special instruments to detect the very slight 'secondary minimum' (Fig. 5), there are others where both dips in the curve can be observed. A good example is the star β Lyrae (Fig. 6), which is not far in the sky from Vega. The two components are bright, hot, and very close together and their gravitation causes each star to pull the other out of shape. Indeed the pull is such that some gas is torn out and surrounds both stars in a kind of cloud.

There are also multiple stars, where three or four stars orbit round each other. Their paths are complex. Such a star is ε Lyrae. It looks like a double to the unaided eye, but in a small telescope each of the two components can be seen to be a binary, so this is a multiple system. Castor, too, is a multiple system but a larger telescope is needed to see the six components.

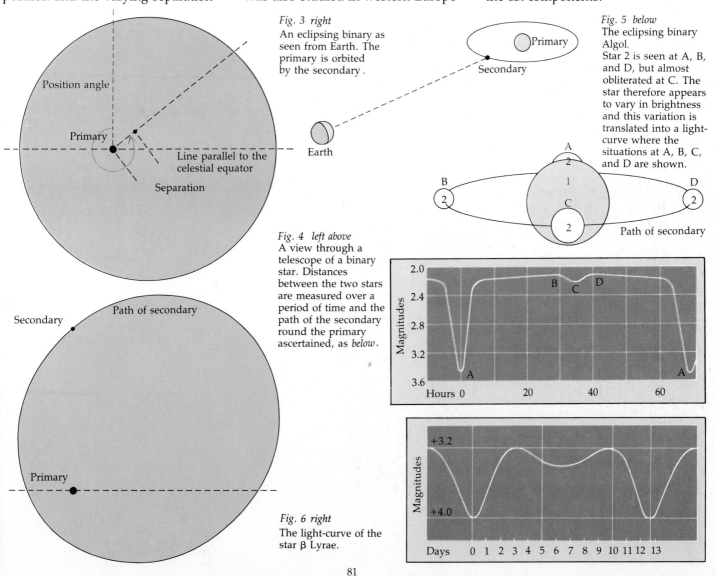

Fig. 3 right
An eclipsing binary as seen from Earth. The primary is orbited by the secondary.

Fig. 5 below
The eclipsing binary Algol.
Star 2 is seen at A, B, and D, but almost obliterated at C. The star therefore appears to vary in brightness and this variation is translated into a light-curve where the situations at A, B, C, and D are shown.

Fig. 4 left above
A view through a telescope of a binary star. Distances between the two stars are measured over a period of time and the path of the secondary round the primary ascertained, as below.

Fig. 6 right
The light-curve of the star β Lyrae.

VARIABLE STARS

Most stars shine with constant brightness, but some, known as variable stars, vary their light periodically. Variable stars are a good subject for the amateur astronomer because on the whole they are not difficult to observe and really valuable results can be obtained.

We have already met with variable stars: some binaries can be classed as variables as their light varies periodically. Their light-curves are characterized by having two dips, or minima, one usually larger than the other, and with equal intervals of time between the maxima (Figs. 7 and 8 on page 81). Such curves show that the light variation is best explained if two stars are orbiting round one another, but with their orbits tilted in such a way that the stars eclipse each other when viewed

from Earth. This explanation is confirmed by observation of binary star systems whose orbits are inclined so as to vary the light but whose components are close enough for their ordinary binary behaviour to be discerned. The majority of variable stars, however, are single stars whose light output varies because of changing conditions inside the stars themselves.

No elaborate equipment is necessary to study variable stars although special instruments can be fitted to the eyepiece of a telescope to measure the amount of light from a particular star. Professional astronomers measure brightness using photographs, which give a permanent record and very precise results, but useful work can nevertheless be done with the telescope estimating brightness by eye. This may sound a haphazard way of making observations but with practice, using nearby stars as a guide, you can learn to make estimates down to one-tenth of a magnitude.

Before you begin to make observations of a variable star you will need a chart of the stars in the

field of view either of your binoculars or your telescope.

To take up variable star observing seriously you will require some help in obtaining comparison star charts and knowing which stars to observe. For this the most convenient way is to join an astronomical association (for details see page 198). But this, of course is only for those who want to take the matter seriously, have a telescope, and know how to use it. To begin with you can use a star atlas. Select at least two stars whose magnitudes lie a little above and below the star you want to observe. As an example let us take the star δ Cephei. Fig. 1 shows where it is in the constellation Cepheus, while Fig. 2 shows a more detailed star field. The next step is to familiarize yourself with the star chosen for observation (δ Cephei) and the nearby companion stars. Once this has been done your actual observations can begin.

There are two chief ways of making estimates of brightness, but one is only really suitable for observers with some experience. We shall consider the simpler of the two, sometimes called the 'Fractional

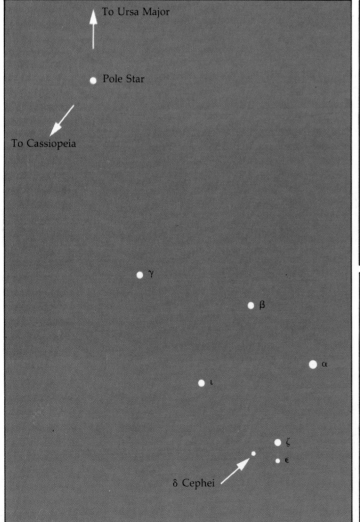

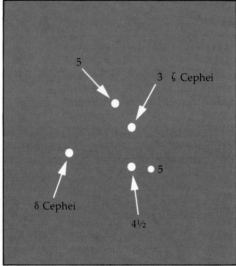

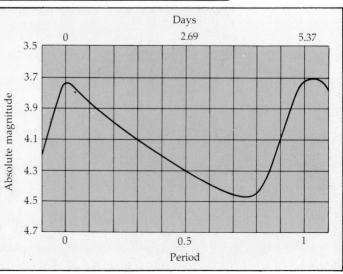

Fig. 1 far left
The position in the sky of δ Cephei.

Fig. 2 left
Close-up view of the star field round δ Cephei. The figures indicate magnitudes.

Fig. 3 below
Light-curve of δ Cephei.

Method'. Here you observe the variable and then, mentally, place it between two companion stars, one above and one below it in brightness. The difference in magnitude between these companion stars should be small: 0.5 magnitude is enough. The difference in this magnitude interval is then divided into fractions, say into fifths. Having done this, mentally compare the variable with each companion star. If you think the variable (V) seems to be three-fifths of the way from a (the brighter of the two companion stars) and two-fifths of the way from b (the dimmer of the two companion stars), then you have made your estimate. You would write this down as $a(3)V(2)b$. Some hours later observe δ Cephei again and make a new estimate. Since this star takes only 5.375 days to complete a cycle from brightest through dimmest and back to brightest again you will have to observe frequently. Note, too, that the total variation from minimum to maximum is only about 0.6 magnitude so you will have to be careful in your estimating. Fig. 3 illustrates the light curve of δ Cephei: to get this you must convert your readings to magnitudes. Take the $a(3)V(2)b$ reading, for example. Suppose the magnitude of a is 3.7 and that of b = 4.2; then the difference $b - a$ is 0.5 magnitude. Therefore a step of one-fifth is 0.1 magnitude. Since V, the variable, is three-fifths dimmer than a, its magnitude number will be greater than that of a by three-fifths of the difference between a and b, i.e. by 0.3 magnitude. Thus when you observed δ Cephei it was 3.7 + 0.3 or 4.0 magnitude.

The star δ Cephei was the first to be discovered of a very important class of variable stars, now known as the Cepheid variables. These are important because they have a very special property: the period a Cepheid takes to complete its cycle from maximum back again to maximum and the luminosity of the star are linked together. The longer the period, the brighter the star actually is. For example, if we take two Cepheids, one having a period of 1 day, say, and another of 10 days, then the Cepheid with the 10-day period is 6.3 times brighter than the Cepheid with the 1-day period – there is, in other words, a 2–

magnitude difference between them. This discovery was made in 1912 by the American astronomer Henrietta Leavitt and it is of immense importance because it provides a new way of measuring distances in space.

Measurements of distance by Cepheids are not hard to understand. Take δ Cephei, for example. It has a variation period of 5.375 days and this means it has an absolute magnitude of –2.5. When we observe it, we find it has an apparent magnitude of 4. This is a difference of 6.5 magnitudes and such a difference is due to the star's distance – if it was nearer it would appear brighter. A difference of 6.5 between the absolute magnitude and that apparent magnitude means that δ Cephei is at a distance of 650 light-years.

Since Miss Leavitt's time more measurements of stars' distances and further studies of the nature of stars themselves have made it clear that there are two kinds of Cepheids. There are those of the type recognized by Miss Leavitt and called 'classical Cepheids'; these have periods ranging from 2.5 days to 40 days and absolute magnitudes from

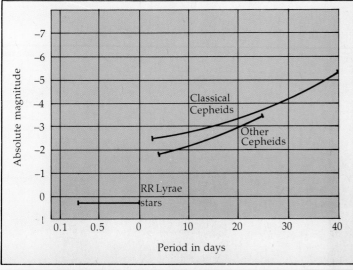

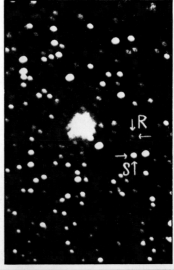

Fig. 4 above left
This diagram shows the varying brightness of two types of Cepheid and the RR Lyrae variables.

Fig. 5 above right
The variables R and S Scorpii. The left photograph shows S very bright, and the right shows S dim.

Fig. 6 left
A double exposure showing in the centre the star WW Cygni, at its maximum on the right and its minimum on the left.

–2.6 to –5.3. These are all whitish-yellow stars. The second type of Cepheids – Type II Cepheids – of which the star ω Virginis is typical, have periods from 4 days to 25 days. They are all whitish stars and have absolute magnitudes between –1.8 and –3.5; they are therefore actually brighter in themselves than the classical Cepheids.

There is also another type of variable very similar to the Cepheid known as the RR Lyrae variable. Named after the star RR Lyrae, stars of this type also have their true brightness linked to their period. They differ from the Cepheid variables in that their periods are very short indeed, ranging from 9.5 hours (0.39 days) to 1 day. They are dimmer stars than the Cepheids, having absolute magnitudes ranging from 0.0 to 0.8, although there is some doubt about the limits: most have an absolute magnitude of 0.6. All three types of 'celestial lighthouses', as they have been called, have been of great help in recent times in measuring distances in space, since the variations in magnitude can be detected at distances far beyond those at which we can measure parallax using the Earth's orbit to act as a baseline (pages 48–51).

Another class of variable star is the RV Tauri type. These are yellowish to reddish in colour and, like the Cepheids, they change colour slightly as they vary in brightness and they have periods measured in tens of days. For instance, RV Tauri itself has a period of about 79 days – sometimes a little more, sometimes a little less – and it has maxima of almost equal brightness but minima which are not equal. Variation is about 1 magnitude. Superimposed on this is a 2 magnitude variation with a period of about 1,300 days.

The 'long-period' variables are stars with periods ranging from about 120 days to a little over 400 days. There are two types here, one of which is named after the red star Mira (o Ceti) and the other just known as long-period variables. The Mira type are regular variables and their periods may be as short as 150 days and as long as 400. They are all red giants and their magnitudes vary by something like 2.5 magnitudes. The stars themselves are bright, their absolute magnitudes ranging from –2.2 to about +0.3. Their true brightness also depends on the period of variation, but in the opposite way to Cepheids, because the longer the period, the dimmer

Double cluster

Fig. 7 *above*
The variable star Algol and the surrounding star-field which includes a double-cluster and the open cluster in Perseus, M34.

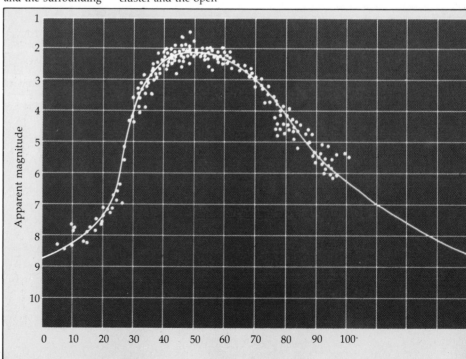

M34

The variable star Algol

the star. Fig. 8 shows the Mira light
curve.
The other type of long-period
variable may have a period as short
as 120 days or as long as 410 days.
These are also red stars but their
variation of magnitude is less than
that of the Mira type. Their absolute
magnitudes range between –2 and
+1 and, as with the Mira type, the
longer their period the dimmer they
will appear.

There are other stars whose
variation is irregular. It is here that
the amateur astronomer can really
come into his own, because he can
watch stars which, because of the
rarity of their outbursts, are not
really suitable material for constant
surveillance at a professional
observatory. There are a number of
such stars, which vary widely in their
colour and in the degree of change
they show; v Geminorum is typical of
this type. They show a large and
rapid increase in brightness and then
a slow decline. Variation covers
about 4 magnitudes, and they have a
maximum lasting from between 3 to
20 days with an average of about 8
days. Periods of inactivity vary
widely from 20 to 200 days. It has
been suggested that such stars as
these are binaries rather than
intrinsically variable stars.

The accepted idea at the present
time is that Cepheids and stars like
them vary their light because they
pulsate, expanding a little and then
contracting a little in a regular
sequence. In an ordinary star the
generation of energy by nuclear
fusion (pages 76–79) gives enough
outward pressure to balance the
gravitational pull inwards of the vast
mass of gas which goes to make up
the star. Any change in this energy
generation process can upset the
delicate balance. If too much energy
is generated the star will expand,
while too little would cause it to
contract. It has been suggested that
variables, which are stars past the
middle of their lives, experience
regular changes in energy generation.
At first the occurrence of a sudden
change in energy generation causes
the star to contract. Then, once this
has occurred, the centre becomes
hotter and more nuclear energy is
emitted than before. As a result the
star expands. As expansion
continues, the central regions become
a little cooler and the hotter nuclear
reactions cease. There is a pause so
the star begins to contract once more
and the cycle is repeated. There are
many details of this process to be
settled by further research, but the
general idea seems to be sound.

Fig. 8 below
Light-curve of Mira
(o Ceti).

The dots show the
positions of
observations.

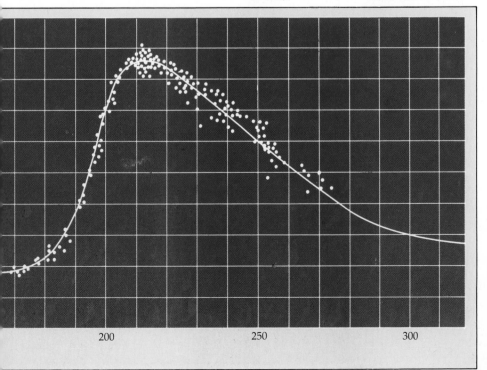

EXPLODING STARS: NOVAE AND SUPERNOVAE

After they have reached middle-age and become red giants, some stars suffer an explosion, ejecting hot gas into space. Such an explosion gives out a vast amount of light for a short time, and a star which is ordinarily too dim to be seen by the naked eye may suddenly become visible. It looks as though a 'nova' or new star has appeared.

In 1572 the Danish nobleman Tycho Brahe was astounded to see an apparently new star in the constellation Cassiopeia. At the time it was generally believed in the Western world that the skies were changeless, and that any changes which did appear were due to events in the 'upper air' (the air nearer to us than the Moon). Tycho Brahe's measurements of the position of the new star in Cassiopeia, and his study of the observations of other astronomers, particularly Thomas Digges in England, made it clear that this star was a long way away. He was unable to measure the exact distance of the star, but he could at least prove that it was further away than the Moon. Clearly, then, changes did occur in the heavens and as we shall see (pages 108–111), within the next 100 years other ancient ideas about the universe were also to be proved wrong.

Tycho's star was bright enough to be seen in daylight, and it is clear to us now that what he had observed was a supernova. No ordinary nova could have been as bright as that. Novae change in brightness by anything between 5 and 15 magnitudes, in other words the star becomes some 100 to 1,000,000 times brighter. Supernovae, on the other hand, change in brightness between 10^8 (100 million) to 10^9 (1,000 million) times, that is they change over a range of 20 to 23 magnitudes.

When a nova occurs the light-curve displays a very rapid rise in brightness, followed by a gradual dimming down again over a long period of time. The initial burst shows us that although a vast amount of energy is emitted, there is always plenty left after a nova explosion, and the same star may erupt more than once. In fact, a number of 'recurrent novae' are known, with periods of between 79 and 32 years. One such star is RS Ophiuchi, whose next outburst is likely to occur in 1993, although it will only be of about magnitude 4 at its brightest (it is now at magnitude 11.6 and so needs a telescope with an aperture of at least 8.75 cm to show it). Brighter will be T Coronae Borealis whose maximum will rise to magnitude 1.9 from its present 10.6 (requiring a 6.25 cm aperture at the moment); this star is not due to erupt until 2025.

Astronomers have compared the

Tycho Brahe observing the supernova in Cassiopeia in 1572.

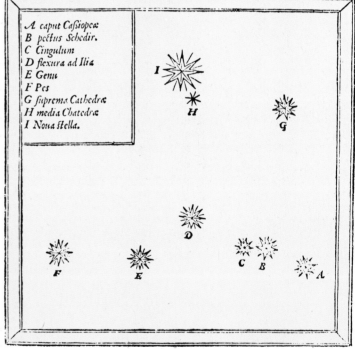

A caput Caſsiopeæ
B pectus Schedir.
C Cingulum
D flexura ad Ilia
E Genu
F Pes
G ſuprema Cathedræ
H media Chatedræ
I Noua ſtella.

Brahe's drawing of the supernova from his *De Nova Stella* 1573.

below
A modern diagram showing the position of Brahe's supernova and the constellation of Cassiopeia.

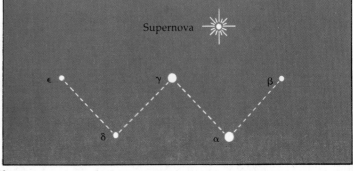

type of spectrum a star has during a nova outburst with the star's normal spectrum. Photographs have also been taken of novae. The result of these studies is that a nova is found to be an explosion of an outer shell of gas from a star, which, having escaped outwards into space, moves very quickly, travelling at something like 100 km per second. Yet space is so vast that we can still see the shell of gas round the star over fifty years later. With a supernova explosion the shell may remain visible for many hundreds of years, as we shall see.

What causes a nova? At the present time astronomers think that most novae are binary systems, where one component is a red giant star and the other a small white dwarf (pages 76–79); in other words one component – the white dwarf – is near the end of its life. It is thought that the gravity of the dense white dwarf might pull off an outer layer of gas from the red giant, whose outer layers would be rather loosely held. Some of this layer of gas would envelop both stars, but some might fall onto the hot white surface of the white dwarf. If this happened then the gas would suddenly be heated and violent nuclear reactions would occur for a short time. These reactions would make the gas glow very brightly and also make it expand outwards at high speed. Sometimes the energy generated by the nuclear reactions is so great that the star radiates X-rays rather than light. Now that X-ray telescopes are in orbit round the Earth, a number of such X-ray novae have been discovered.

A supernova is a very much larger stellar explosion, something like 100 to 1,000 times more energetic than an ordinary nova. Here most of the material of the star explodes into space and what we observe is, in fact, what can be called the death throes of a star. A supernova is a star many times more massive than the Sun, which uses up its energy so quickly that its life cycle is perhaps a thousand times shorter than a less massive star. When it gets to the red giant stage it will use up its hydrogen in nuclear reactions and then go on to 'burn up' the helium, expanding until the helium is consumed. (Helium cannot be burned up in a less massive star.) While this is taking place the star will be very bright – a red supergiant like Antares or Betelgeuse. Sudden changes will then happen in the star's central regions: they heat, expand, contract, causing new nuclear reactions which then get out of control. As a result the star undergoes a giant explosion, pouring most of its material into space. This is a supernova.

The most famous supernova happened in Taurus in AD 1054 and was observed by Chinese astronomers. The remnants of gas from this explosion can *still* be seen, more than 900 years after the event, as the Crab nebula.

Any amateur astronomer can discover a nova – in other words be the first to see one – but to do so you must know your sky very well indeed. The English amateur George Alcock, who has discovered no less than three novae, has expert knowledge of the sky, but it has taken him years to reach this stage.

The shell of gas surrounding Nova Persei 1901.

The Crab Nebula in Taurus, the remains of a supernova explosion.

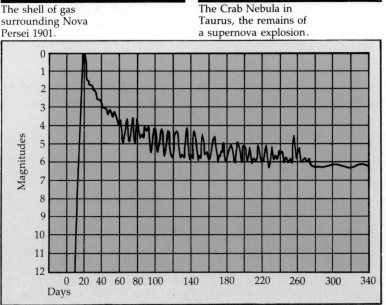

left
Light curve of Nova Persei 1901.

above
Series of photographs showing the eruption

of Nova Cygni in 1975, taken by an amateur.

PULSARS AND BLACK HOLES

Pulsars, which give out very short pulses of energy at a fast regular rate, are thought to be massive stars at the end of their life cycle. Black holes emit no radiation; they are believed to be the collapsed remains of very massive stars.

At the Mullard Radio Astronomy Observatory of Cambridge University in 1967, radio astronomers studying the radio waves emitted by the Sun and other celestial bodies, discovered a source giving rapid radio pulses. There had been much talk at the time about the possibility of other civilizations in space, and the Cambridge radio astronomers wondered for a short time whether, in fact, they were receiving coded messages from somewhere out in the universe. Finally they discovered that there was no doubt where the pulses were coming from: not from some distant civilization but from a star. Since then astronomers have discovered many other similar stars emitting radio pulses; these have been given the name of pulsars. Pulsars can emit light as well as radio waves. The most famous pulsar to do this is in the Crab nebula.

The first pulsar to be discovered had a pulse rate of one every 1.3373011 seconds coming with absolute regularity. Others were found with similar pulses, although in one the interval between pulses was as short as 0.253065 seconds. The Crab pulsar, with an interval of 0.033 seconds has the shortest period known. Its radio and optical pulses occur at the same rate. What could a pulsar be and what causes it to pulse so rapidly?

We have just seen (pages 86–87) that the Crab nebula is the result of a supernova explosion. If we enquire into what is left of the original massive star that exploded we can obtain a clue to the nature of a pulsar. Carbon is formed from the helium in the nuclear reactions of a massive star and then, as a result of the shrinking and heating that takes place in the central regions of the star, reactions occur resulting in the formation of iron. These nuclear reactions would be impossible in a cooler or less massive star. The

temperature inside is so great that the iron atoms begin to break up and the star collapses and then explodes, leaving behind a collection of atomic particles, protons and electrons. These are the building bricks from which all atoms are made, but here

they are crushed together instead of being separated by great spaces as they are in ordinary atoms. Each proton has a positive electric charge, and each electron a negative electric charge. Crushed together they form particles known as neutrons, which

Binary system of which one member is a black hole (right), with material from its companion swirling round it.

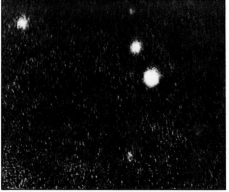

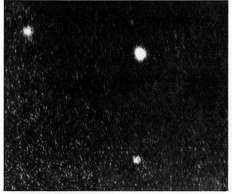

At the centre of the Crab Nebula are the remains of the supernova explosion in 1054 AD. The star itself has become a pulsar: it is visible in the left photograph but not the right.

have no electric charge. The crushed up neutron is very dense: whereas a matchbox full of the dense material of a white dwarf would weigh something like 15 tonnes, the same matchbox filled with neutron star material would weigh 15,000 million tonnes. Before collapse, such a star would have an ordinary 'magnetic field', that is to say it would act like a magnet just as the Earth and the Sun do. But since a neutron star has a diameter of only about 20 km, the magnetic field is concentrated into a tiny space and is thereby made much stronger. Such a star spins very rapidly, twirling its magnetic field around with it at a very high speed. It is thought that the motion of charged particles in the strong magnetic fields of these stars causes a beam of radiation, which on Earth is received as a pulse of radio waves and light, every time the beam strikes us.

It is thought that a black hole is a body which is even denser than a neutron star. According to current theory it is the result of the collapse of a star even larger than the type which makes a neutron star. If the mass of a star is more than two or three times that of the Sun, it will end up as a neutron star, but if it is much more than three times the mass of the Sun, even the neutrons which are formed cannot support the weight and the star collapses. The pull of gravitation of this massive stellar lump is so great that neither light, X-rays, radio waves nor any other radiation can escape, so the star becomes invisible. That is why it is called a *black* hole.

The other part of the name, the word 'hole', is given to the object because of the way it pulls everything near it into its grasp. When we come to talk about the Theory of Relativity (page 182) we shall see that a gravitational pull distorts space. So great a pull as that given by a large collapsed star distorts space so much that nothing near it can move in a straight path; it must slip down into the hole. How close matter must come before this happens depends on the mass of the star that has collapsed.

If one component of a binary star collapsed to become a black hole, then it would draw material off from its companion. As this material whirled round on its way to the black hole, it would be travelling so fast that it would emit many X-rays. Orbiting X-ray observatories have detected such a binary in Scorpius. Known as Sco X-1, it is a binary with one invisible component and emits a great amount of X-rays – just as one would expect if one of the components were in a black hole. So although one cannot see a black hole, it can be detected by its effect on nearby matter.

Although no radiation can escape from a black hole, it seems that a few atomic particles may do so. Thus a black hole may not last for ever, although it will have a life of millions of years; how long depends on how massive it is.

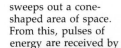

How pulses are received. The pulsar rotates very fast and from its magnetic axis sweeps out a cone-shaped area of space. From this, pulses of energy are received by an observer on Earth every time the magnetic axis sweeps across Earth

The radio telescope with which pulsars were discovered. It consists of a vast array of aerials fitted to posts in a field.

Veil Nebula in Cygnus, part of the visible shell of a supernova explosion.

CHAPTER 3
THE MOON

The Moon is a beautiful sight in the night sky. It is at its best when in a crescent phase, because the sunlight striking it from the side causes the mountains and craters to cast dramatic shadows, emphasizing its rugged surface.

When it is above the horizon, the Full Moon dominates the night sky, shining down on us with a brilliance 2,000 times greater than Venus and 24,00 times that of Sirius. This brightness varies with the Moon's 'phase' or apparent change in shape as the days go by. At Full Moon, when you can see the whole disc, its light is bright enough for you to read a book. Before the days of street lighting people depended on the Moon much more. In England, in 1766, the Lunar Society was formed by a number of eminent scientists, engineers and medical men. They used the name Lunar Society because their monthly meetings were held on the night of the Full Moon, so that they would have enough natural light by which to travel home.

The brightness and changing shape of the Moon made it an ideal timekeeper, and it was for this reason that it was used as the basic guide for the earliest calendars (page 26). The changing shape – the 'phase' of the Moon – is caused by the Moon's orbit and the fact that the Moon has no light of its own. The Moon's surface is dark, and it only reflects about 7% of the light it receives from the Sun; it appears bright to us because it is comparatively near. Orbiting the Earth at an average distance of 384,000 km – a distance equivalent to travelling 9½ times round the Earth's equator – the Moon moves in an elliptical path so that sometimes it is nearer to us than at other times. The difference between its nearest approach and its most distant position is 50,000 km.

How can we measure the distance of the Moon? The ancient Greek astronomers knew this distance and one method of working it out is shown. First, you will want to find the angle p, which is the parallax of the Moon; this is done by measuring the Moon's zenith distance z when the Moon is due south. The easiest way to do this is to measure the Moon's altitude (a), and then subtract the result from 90; this will give you the zenith distance in degrees. Looking at the drawing you can see that in the triangle COM, the angle COM is $180° - z$, and as the angles of a triangle all add up to 180°, the parallax $p = 180° - g - COM = 180° - g - (180° - z) = z - g$. The angle g depends on the latitude of the observer (the angle OCE) and the declination of the Moon (the angle MCE). Knowing your latitude and the Moon's declination (which can be obtained from the *Handbook* of the British Astronomical Association or *The American Ephemeris and Nautical Almanac*), you can then find g (because $g = OCE - MCE$).

To find the Moon's actual distance in kilometres, use the formula $D = 333,577 ÷ p$ where D represents this distance in kilometres and p is the parallax measured in degrees and decimals of a degree.

Make your measurement of the Moon's altitude by sighting on the upper or lower edge of the Moon's disc. It is best to make a number of measurements and then take the average, remembering to measure as precisely as possible and write down the answers correct to a quarter of a degree. Even so your result will not be absolutely correct, partly because you are estimating fractions of a degree and partly because the Earth's atmosphere will distort the Moon's position slightly by making it appear higher than it really is; there is also another factor which is that the Earth is not really round, but oval in shape. Nevertheless you will get a reasonable idea of the distance.

To determine the Moon's distance today, astronomers no longer use the old parallax method. Instead they use radar or ranging by laser beam. In the first case they emit radio pulses to the Moon and time how long it takes for them to reach the Moon and return to Earth. Since radio pulses travel at the speed of light – a speed that is accurately known – the distance of the Moon can be easily calculated. Laser ranging works in a similar way. A laser beam is directed at a mirror left on the Moon's surface by astronauts specially for this work, and pulses of light are sent out to it. The time between the emission of the beam and its return is measured and the Moon's distance determined.

The Apollo 16 Passive Seismic Experiment is in the foreground with four very sensitive moonquake sensors or seismometers. Behind it lies the information receiver and transmitter to send back results to Earth.

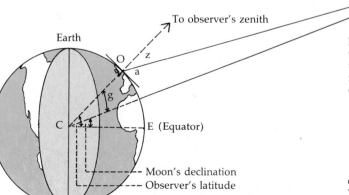

Diagram to show how to find the distance of the Moon by measurement and calculation.

opposite
The Moon in a crescent phase.

STATISTICS AND ORIGINS OF THE MOON

The Moon is the largest satellite in the Solar System in relation to its planet. There is still doubt as to the Moon's origins, but one possible explanation is that the Moon and Earth were formed as a double-planet system.

The Moon is a little over a quarter the diameter of the Earth (3,476 km compared with the Earth's 12,756 km) and its volume is therefore only a fiftieth of the Earth's. In addition Moon rock is only three-fifths as heavy as Earth rock. Together these facts mean that the Moon's gravity is only 0.165 that of the Earth's, and this has had some important effects on the Moon and its history. Above all it has meant that the Moon has lost whatever atmosphere it may have once possessed.

Such a low gravity will not hold on to an atmosphere because the movement of the molecules or particles which compose the gases of such an atmosphere move too fast. For any given pull of gravity by a body, there is a 'velocity of escape.' Objects with a greater velocity than this will be able to get away into space. For the Earth, the velocity of escape is 11.18 km per second; for the Moon it is only 2.37 km per second. The velocity with which the molecules of any gas travel depends on the heaviness of the molecules and the temperature of the gas. Thus for hydrogen gas at 0°C the average speed is between 2 and 3 km per second; for oxygen at the same temperature it is between 0.5 and 0.75 km per second, because oxygen molecules are heavier. As the temperature rises, so the velocity of the molecules increases.

For part of its orbit, the Moon receives just a little more heat from the Sun than the Earth does, because it comes 380,000 km closer to it. Even if it received the same amount, this would be enough to drive off the gases which could have formed the Moon's atmosphere; the molecules would all have passed the velocity of escape. Indeed, even in the case of the more massive Earth, molecules of gases like hydrogen and helium have

above
A lunar landscape near the landing place of the Apollo 14 lunar module, photographed outside the vehicle.

below
The Earth rising above the Moon's horizon, photographed on the Apollo 10 mission.

above
Scientist-astronaut Schmitt by a huge lunar boulder on the Apollo 17 mission.

exceeded our much greater velocity of escape, and are now no longer to be found in the atmosphere.

So the Moon has no atmosphere. Landings by astronauts have confirmed this, but it can be proved by using a pair of binoculars or a telescope to look at the limb (edge) of the Moon just before the Moon eclipses or 'occults' a star – preferably a bright one. Watch it carefully and you will see the light of the star suddenly go out. If the Moon had an atmosphere, then, as the star came closer and closer to the Moon's limb, you would be seeing it through an increasing thickness of that atmosphere. In that case the star would fade and finally flicker out.

How did the Moon become the Earth's companion in space, and what is its origin? Astronomers believe that there are three possible ways in which the Moon could have originated. First, that the Moon was formed elsewhere in the Solar System (the system of planets which orbit the Sun) and was later captured by the Earth; second, that the Moon was created at the same time as the Earth and close to it in space; third, that the Moon was torn out of the Earth a very long time ago, either by a passing star or as a result of the Earth's rotation.

The Moon's average density is similar to the density of the Earth's outer crust, but studies of lunar rock brought back by astronauts has made it clear that the quantities of various chemical elements in the surface rocks of Earth and Moon are quite different. This seems to make it unlikely that the Moon could have been formed from the Earth.

It is more probable that the Moon and Earth were both formed when the other planets were formed. Studies of the Moon's mass and of moonquakes (the lunar equivalents of earthquakes) make it seem likely that the Moon's core is made of iron and so is different from the core of the Earth. In consequence it may be that they formed in different places within the Solar System and that the Moon was captured later. However, we cannot be certain of this; differences between the Moon's rocks and the Earth's rocks are not so great as was once thought. It is therefore possible that the Moon and Earth were both formed near together in the Solar System to make a 'double-planet' system. In brief, then, astronomers have not yet enough evidence to allow them to make a definite decision about how the Moon was formed.

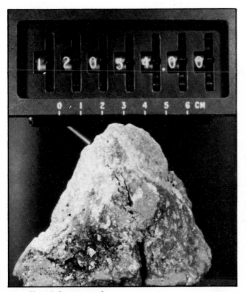

Apollo 12 lunar rock in the receiving laboratory.

The astronaut Aldrin deploying the lunar seismometer during the Apollo 11 mission.

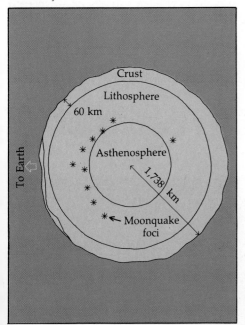

A cross section of the lunar interior.

TABLE OF STATISTICS OF THE MOON	
Average distance from Earth	384,400 km
Greatest distance from Earth (apogee)	406,610 km
Least distance from Earth (perigee)	356,334 km
Average inclination of Moon's orbit to the plane of the Earth's equator	23.4°
Average inclination of Moon's orbit to the ecliptic	5.1°
Average period of Moon with respect to the stars (sidereal period)	27.32 days
Average synodic period (New Moon to New Moon)	29.53 days
Diameter of Moon	3,476 km = 0.27 × diameter of the Earth
Mass of Moon	7.35×10^{22} kg = 0.012 × mass of the Earth
Volume of Moon	2.2×10^{19} cub. metres = 0.02 × the volume of the Earth
Average density of the Moon	3.34 × density of water
Period of rotation of Moon on its axis	27.32 days
Velocity of escape	2.37 km per sec
Surface gravity	0.165 that of the Earth

THE PHASES OF THE MOON

The changing phases of the Moon from New Moon to Full and back again are an endless source of fascination. This is especially true when the Moon is observed through a telescope, because the changing light from one day to the next brings out different features of the Moon's surface.

The Moon shows phases because it shines only by reflecting sunlight. The Moon itself is always half lit by the Sun's light, just as the Earth is, so that one half experiences daylight and one half night. The phases we observe at any time depend on where the Moon is relative to the Sun. To see how this happens you will need models of the Earth and Moon as used in studying eclipses (pages 28–31), and a lamp or torch, or flashlight, on a table (Fig. 1) to represent the Sun. Hold the Earth-Moon system some distance away from the lamp. Then line up the Earth and Moon with the lamp; the Moon being further away from the Sun than the Earth (A). Now, with the main room light off and the Earth-Moon system tilted so that the table lamp lights up the Moon, an observer on the night-side of the Earth will see the full disc of the Moon illuminated – the Full Moon.

Next, move the Earth-Moon system so that the Moon is a quarter way along its orbit round the Earth (B). This is the Moon's position seven days later, and from Earth an observer will see only half the Moon's illuminated disc; the other half is dark. This is the phase of the 'last quarter', the word 'quarter' referring to the Moon's position in its orbit. Now move the Moon another

quarter of its journey round the Earth; it will now lie directly between the Earth and the Sun, but tilted so that it does not eclipse the Sun (C). The dark side of the Moon now faces an observer on Earth, so that it cannot be seen at all. This is the condition of 'New Moon'. Lastly, move the Moon along another quarter of its orbit (D). Once again an observer on Earth can see only one

half of the Moon's disc: This is called the 'first quarter'.

You have now seen how the Moon's phase will change as it orbits the Earth. Take note of its other positions and check your results with the drawing in Fig. 1, so that you can see when the Moon will look gibbous (when more than half but less than the full disc is observed) and when it appears as a crescent.

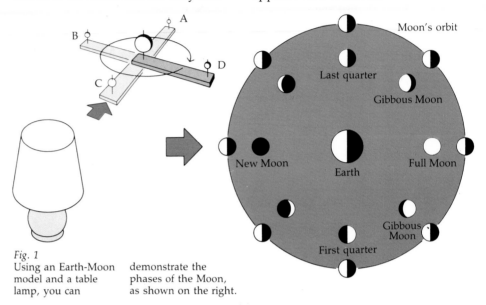

Fig. 1
Using an Earth-Moon model and a table lamp, you can demonstrate the phases of the Moon, as shown on the right.

Fig. 2
The crescent Moon showing Earthshine.

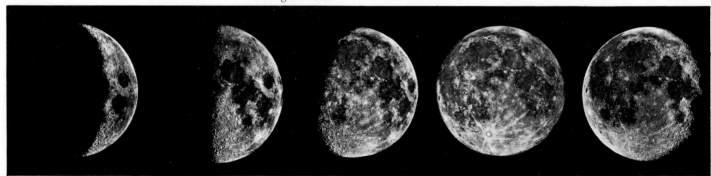

There is another appearance of the Moon which shows when it is a crescent, between New Moon and first quarter or last quarter. This is known as 'Earthshine', or sometimes 'the Old Moon in the New Moon's arms'. Watch the Moon when it appears as a crescent just after New Moon and you will notice that in the dark night sky not only is the crescent visible, but so also is the rest of the Moon's disc. This remainder is not very bright; if it looks a little blue that is because it is lit up by sunlight reflected onto the Moon from the Earth (Fig. 3), and much of this light has passed through the Earth's blue-scattering atmosphere.

The Moon rotates on its axis as it orbits the Earth and yet we can never see 'behind' it: we always see the same face of the Moon. The reason for this is that as it orbits the Earth once, the Moon rotates only once on its axis. Prove this by placing a chair in the centre of a room and walking round it (Fig. 4). When you start you see not only the chair but also one wall of the room, wall A. Now walk round the chair, turning as you do so in order to have the chair still straight in front of you. After you have gone one quarter of the way round you will no longer be facing wall A; you will be facing wall B instead. After another quarter turn, still making sure you are facing the chair, you will find yourself facing wall C; another quarter orbit and wall D will face you. Continue and you will be back where you started, facing the chair and wall A. An observer in the chair will only have seen your face, never your back, during the whole period of the orbit. But you have rotated once, as you have proved by facing each of the four walls, A, B, C and D in turn.

Although the far side of the Moon is never seen from Earth, we get a glimpse of its edge. This is because the Moon's rotation and its orbital motion do not keep absolutely in step and because there is a small angle (6½°) between the Moon's equator and the plane of its orbit. The position of an observer on the rotating Earth also helps in getting these glimpses or 'librations'.

The Moon also seems to change its size. When low down in the sky close to the horizon, it appears much larger than when it is high in the sky. Of course the Moon's apparent size does change a little because sometimes it is nearer and sometimes further off, due to its elliptical orbit. But these changes are small – they amount to no more than 4 minutes of arc – and they do not occur during one night. The effect of largeness near the horizon and smallness higher in the sky is mainly an optical illusion; when the Moon is low down, it looks large when close to trees and houses because there is something with which to compare it. Up high in the sky it appears a small object in a vast empty space.

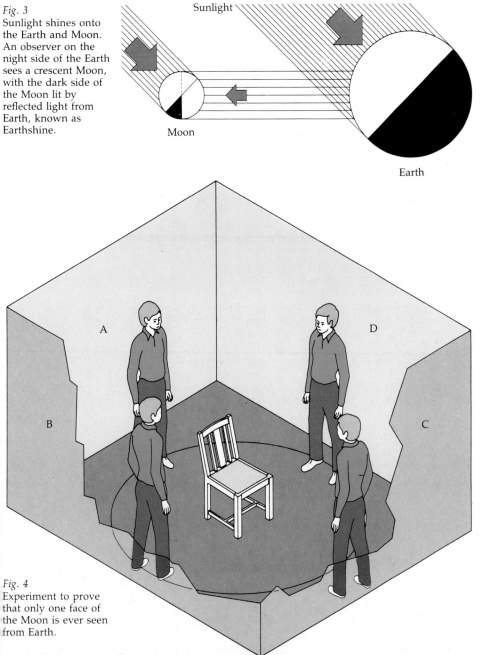

Fig. 3
Sunlight shines onto the Earth and Moon. An observer on the night side of the Earth sees a crescent Moon, with the dark side of the Moon lit by reflected light from Earth, known as Earthshine.

Sunlight

Moon

Earth

Fig. 4
Experiment to prove that only one face of the Moon is ever seen from Earth.

Fig. 5
Photograph showing nine phases of the Moon, from the Lick Observatory.

MAP OF THE MOON

The photograph and a map of the Full Moon are both printed 'upside-down' to show the Moon as it would be seen through an astronomical telescope. These pictures can be compared with the drawing of the Moon by Galileo, made over 370 years ago. The photograph of the far side of the Moon was taken by Moon-orbiting spacecraft; it cannot be seen from Earth.

The Moon's craters are named after famous astronomers. The 'seas' are really large plains; the English translation of their names is given below:

Mare Crisium	Sea of Crises
Mare Foecunditatis	Sea of Fertility
Mare Frigoris	Cold Sea
Mare Humorum	Sea of Humours*
Mare Imbrium	Sea of Showers
Mare Nectaris	Sea of Nectar
Mare Nubium	Sea of Clouds
Mare Serenitatis	Sea of Serenity
Mare Tranquillitatis	Sea of Tranquility
Mare Vaporum	Sea of Vapours
Oceanus Procellarum	Ocean of Storms
Sinus Iridium	Rainbow Bay
Sinus Roris	Bay of Dew
Sinus Medii	Central Bay

* The word 'Humours' refers to the medieval medical and philosophical term for bodily fluids of a special kind which were once believed to exist.

More detailed maps of the Moon may be found in *Norton's Star Atlas* and Patrick Moore's *Guide to the Moon* (page 198).

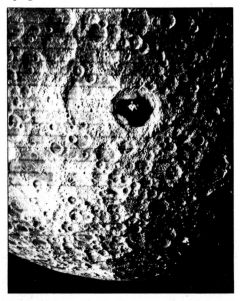

A photograph of the far side of the Moon, which we cannot see from Earth. It has many craters, but few *maria*.

Map of the Moon showing its main features.

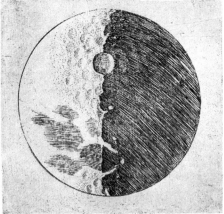

Two of Galileo's drawings of the Moon. The upper one illustrates the uneven nature of the terminator. Also shown are the peaks of the mountains just catching the light. The lower one shows the Moon with a large crater towards the south, dark areas or *maria* and mountains. These drawings have been arranged to have south at the top, although Galileo's telescope did not invert the image and his drawings had north at the top.

Tycho

Mare Humorum

Mare Nubium

Gassendi

Alphonsus

Ptolemaeus

Grimaldi

Copernicus

Kepler

Oceanus Procellarum

Appenine Mountains

Aristarchus

Mare Imbrium

Sinus Iridium

Sinus Roris

Mare Frigoris

The Full Moon taken by Lick Observatory. The large crater Tycho is a notable feature near the southern edge of the Moon.

THE SEAS AND MOUNTAINS OF THE MOON

Looking at the Moon with the unaided eye, we see what seems to be a face – the famous Man in the Moon. This is sculpted on the Moon's surface by its 'seas', mountains and craters. Galileo observed these in 1609 with a telescope he had made, and attempted to calculate the height of the Moon's mountains.

In Galileo's time it was generally believed that the Moon was a smooth body, unblemished by any lumps or spots, but the telescope showed that this was not correct. The dark patches were seen to be flat, and the famous German astronomer Johannes Hevelius, who in 1647 published a map of the Moon (Fig. 1), referred to each of them as a *mare* or 'sea' (plural *maria*). In fact, they are not seas, but huge flat plains created by an outflow of lava from below the Moon's surface, which is thought to have occurred some 3.8 thousand million (3.8×10^9) years ago. Even so, these plains are still called *maria* and astronomers still use the romantic names, like Mare Nectaris (Sea of Nectar) and Mare Crisium (Sea of Crises), given to them by the

Italian astronomer Riccioli in 1651.

The dark *maria* show up well, especially at first and last quarter, and it is worth scanning them with a telescope. The map on the previous two pages provides a guide, and you will see how the plains are scarred with mountains and round craters. The *maria* all seem to be roundish in shape, as can be seen during the Moon's first quarter by looking at the Mare Crisium, Mare Nectaris and Mare Serenitatis. In the last quarter there is the interesting Mare Imbrium to study (Fig. 2). This is an oval *mare* surrounded by mountains, with the large crater Archimedes in it. There is evidence, too, of a boundary or ridge between the Mare Nubium and the Mare Humorum.

The Moon has a great number of mountains and ranges, mostly named after mountain ranges on Earth. Thus, around the Mare Imbrium are the Caucasus Mountains, the Apennines, the Carpathian Mountains, the Jura Mountains and the Alps. Even the Haemus Mountains echo a terrestrial name, for this was what the Balkan mountains were once called.

One of the most striking calculations Galileo carried out at the start of his telescope observing was to try to measure the height of lunar mountains. He watched the Moon each day and noticed when some lunar mountain peaks were just catching the light of the Sun on the line dividing the sunlit and dark side of the Moon, known as the 'terminator'. Galileo compared the

Fig. 1
Map of the Moon showing maria, by Johannes Hevelius, 1647.

Fig. 3
Astronaut Irwin during the Apollo 15 mission, July 1971, with the lunar module and lunar rover. Mount Hadley is in the background.

Fig. 2
The Moon at last quarter (north at top).

distance of these peaks (the distance AC, Fig. 5), with the diameter of the Moon, and so calculated their height by computing the distance AD. For example, Galileo found that AC was equal to about one-twentieth of the Moon's diameter, and worked out the height as 6,700 metres.

We know that the diameter of the Moon (CF, Fig. 5) is 3,476 km or 3.476×10^6 metres. Therefore CE and AE are both equal to half this, that is 1.74×10^6 metres. Note where the terminator lies, by observing with a telescope which crater or other nearby notable feature it passes through when the mountain peaks are just catching the Sun. Observe again a few nights later when the mountains are visible and estimate the distance between these and the feature through which the terminator passed. Your estimate should be in terms of the Moon's diameter. Let us suppose it is like Galileo's, one-twentieth. Then AC will be equal to

$$\frac{1}{20} \times CF = \frac{3.476 \times 10^6}{20}\ m$$
$$= 1.74 \times 10^5\ m.$$

Next consider the line BD. This represents a sunbeam passing across the terminator and striking the mountain peak at D. Since AC is small compared with CE, and since, too, we are only estimating the distance AC, it will be accurate enough if we assume the AC = DC. DC is therefore equal to 1.74×10^5 m. Now in the right-angled triangle DCE, Pythagoras' theorem tells us that $(DE)^2 = (DC)^2 + (CE)^2$. We know the lengths DC and CE, so we can work out DE. [$(DE)^2 = (1.74 \times 10^5)^2 + (1.74 \times 10^6)^2 = 3.06 \times 10^{12}$; therefore $DE = \sqrt{(3.06 \times 10^{12})} = 1.749 \times 10^6$]. We want to find the height of the mountains, so we need to know the length DA, and DA = DE – AE. So in our example DA = $1.749 \times 10^6 - 1.74 \times 10^6 = 9 \times 10^3$ or 9,000 metres.

In measuring mountains on the Moon, we must remember that on the Earth mountains are measured from 'mean sea-level'. On the Moon there is no water and no sea-level, so measuring the mountain heights is equivalent to measuring mountains on Earth from the sea bed, not from sea-level. Galileo's method is not used now for measuring mountain heights because it is impossible to be certain precisely where the line of the terminator is; but shadow lengths measured on photographs and accurate evidence of the precise position of the Sun relative to the Moon allow heights to be determined with extreme accuracy, especially those mountains observed by the lunar orbiting spacecraft.

The highest mountain of the Moon is Mount Huygens, which is in the Mare Imbrium close to the Apennines; it has a height of 5.5 km, and there are many others known at heights of 4.5 km. Nearby, Mount Hadley (Fig. 3) has a height equal to this. (Everest, on Earth, has a height of 8.8 km.) Not all lunar mountains are as high as these. The Carpathian range, which also borders the Mare Imbrium, only rises some 2,000 m, but it is a large range, about 160 km long. Mountains on the Moon are named after famous astronomers.

Fig. 4
The Appenine mountain range on the Moon, 1,000 km long, showing Archimedes, the large ringed plain centre (south at top).

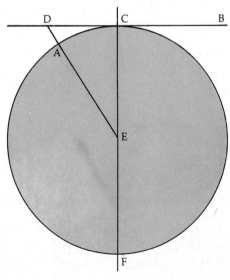

Fig. 5
Galileo's method of estimating the heights of the lunar mountains.

CRATERS OF THE MOON

The Moon's craters are perhaps its most noticeable feature seen through a telescope. They are round circular structures, sometimes with a central mountain peak. They vary widely in size, ranging from some 290 km in diameter down to less than a metre across, and are named after famous astronomers and philosophers.

A crater is surrounded by mountains; if you see one when it is near the terminator – and craters look their most dramatic at this time – then the shadows cast by the mountains round the rim are long, making it appear as a deep pit (Fig. 3). But this is an illusion. In fact, craters are quite different; the mountains do not stick up like sharp walls, but rise gradually out of the crater floor (Fig. 4). Sometimes the crater floor is below the surrounding land, sometimes it is a little above it.

Two of the most notable lunar craters are Copernicus and Tycho. Copernicus, which lies on the edge of the Oceanus Procellarum, is probably about 1,000,000,000 years old. With a diameter of 90 km, it has huge mountainous walls which rise up to some 5 km above the crater floor. There is evidence that there have been great landslides from these walls. Copernicus has a central mountainous area with three masses of peaked rocks. The outer slopes of the surrounding walls are gentle, but on their inner side they show terraces. Copernicus is always worth looking at, but especially when not too far from the terminator.

Tycho lies in a very heavily cratered area south of the Mare Nubium. It is some 87 km in diameter, with high mountainous walls and central peaks. Some other craters near it are larger: Longomontanus (diameter 145 km), Maginus (diameter 178 km) and Clavius, often called a walled plain, which has a diameter of 233 km and walls rising to some 3,658 m. What makes the craters Tycho and Copernicus so exceptional is a system of bright rays which radiate outwards from them (Fig. 5). There are also a few other craters which display a lesser ray system.

Until the landing of spacecraft on the Moon, there was much debate among astronomers as to what the rays were. Now the mystery has been solved: they are formed by debris radiating outwards from or near to these craters, probably the results of crater formation. They are

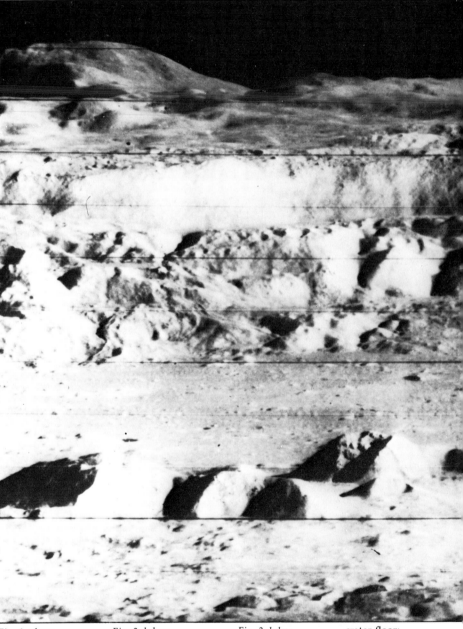

Fig. 1 above
The acclaimed photograph of the interior of Copernicus, taken in 1966 by Lunar Orbiter II.

Fig. 2 below
Copernicus photographed from the Earth using a 2.5 m reflector at Mount Wilson in 1919.

Fig. 3 below
Aristarchus showing erosion of the crater walls and rills in the crater floor; photographed by Orbiter V in 1967.

best seen when the Sun is high above the craters, as at Full Moon. There is still some argument about how the craters were formed, but the general opinion seems to be that although some were caused by the eruption of volcanoes on the Moon, most are the results of bombardment of the Moon by rocks and other material from space, known as meteoric bombardment (pages 146–151). The Earth also shows meteor craters, but these are less in number than those on the Moon, because the Earth's atmosphere gives some protection by burning up a lot of meteoric material before it ever reaches the ground. This would not happen on the Moon, because there is no atmosphere around it.

Another crater worth looking at is Aristarchus in the Oceanus Procellarum; although only 37 km in diameter, it is the brightest object on the lunar surface. There are also many craters which seem to be arranged in chains, and some, like Ptolemæus and Alphonsus, a little south of the Moon's centre, appear to cut into one another.

There are many other surface features on the Moon besides *maria*, mountains and craters, which can be seen by carefully studying the Moon through a telescope and referring to a book describing its surface in detail (pages 200–201). Worth looking out for are the clefts or 'rills' which sometimes look like cracks on the surface of the Moon.

The Moon can also provide some excitement with TLPs or Transient Lunar Phenomena. Observations of these began after the Russian astronomer N. A. Kozyrev had noticed in 1958 that the central peak in the crater Alphonsus appeared as if covered by a reddish mist. Other observations of mist have been seen in Alphonsus, and some glows have been reported from other craters. These reports make it likely that there may sometimes be eruptions of gas from below the lunar surface. Certainly we know from instruments left on the Moon by astronauts that there are internal disturbances or 'moonquakes'. Some professional astronomers are still doubtful about the reality of these 'transient phenomena', but in Britain, for instance, the Lunar Section of the British Astronomical Association has developed special techniques for observing such events and a network of observers for confirming them.

The Moon is thought to have a dense central core, probably about 700 km in diameter, and it is outside this in the 'lithosphere' that the moonquakes occur. The lithosphere is probably some 1,300 km thick and above it lies the lunar crust. The crust is believed, from the evidence of moonquakes, to be some 60 km in thickness. It is this crust that the observer sees, and it is through this that gases may be escaping to create transient lunar phenomena.

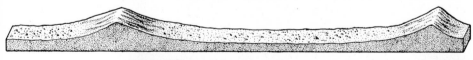

Fig. 4 above
Drawing of a typical lunar crater showing the gradual rise of the mountain walls.

Fig. 5 right
The crater Tycho photographed from the Earth showing rays comprising debris from the impact which originally caused Tycho.

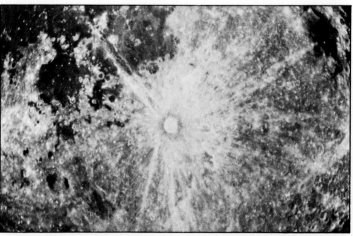

ECLIPSES OF THE MOON

At a lunar eclipse the Moon lies entirely within the Earth's shadow and so the eclipse is visible to all observers on the night side of the Earth. Eclipses of the Moon are seen more frequently than eclipses of the Sun.

The Moon is the brightest object in the night sky. This power that a celestial body has to reflect the radiation it receives is known as its 'albedo' (Latin) meaning 'whiteness'. When it is eclipsed the Moon's albedo is very much reduced. The albedo of a celestial body is calculated by dividing the amount of light reflected by the amount of light falling on the body. The Earth, considered as a planet, has an albedo of 0.36, but the Moon has an albedo of no more than 0.07, or about 5. times less. The Earth's albedo is high because of the white clouds in its atmosphere. All the same, even an albedo of 0.07 is enough for the Moon to look bright in the night sky. Yet there are times when the Moon's albedo drops remarkably: this is during an eclipse of the Moon when direct sunlight can no longer reach it.

To see how an eclipse of the Moon occurs, use the Earth-Moon model (pages 28–31) and a torch

Place the Moon at first quarter in relation to the light beam – that is, at A in Fig. 1, so that an observer will see only the half-lit Moon. Slowly turn the Earth-Moon arm so that the Moon goes into its Full Moon position (B) and the whole of the Moon's disc is illuminated. Next, try the experiment again, starting from first quarter position, and this time tilt the Earth-Moon arm so that the Earth prevents the light beam from reaching the Moon. Instead of having a bright Full Moon facing them, observers on the night side of the Earth will see only a darkened disc. These are the conditions for an eclipse of the Moon, and they occur whenever the Moon moves into the shadow which the Earth casts.

The Moon may be expected to be invisible when it is eclipsed, just as it is at New Moon. However, some sunlight does reach it because a certain amount of sunlight is bent or refracted by the Earth's atmosphere (Fig. 2). Since our atmosphere scatters the blue wavelengths, these do not reach the Moon, but the longer wavelengths do, with the result that during the eclipse the Moon is lit by a reddish orange light.

As with solar eclipses (pages 28–31) we have now to discover why eclipses of the Moon do not occur every time there is a Full Moon. The reason is that the Moon's orbit is tilted with respect to the Earth's orbit, so that sometimes the Moon lies above the Earth's shadow and sometimes below it. Only rarely – not more than three times a year and sometimes not at all – does the Moon

move into the Earth's shadow to give a lunar eclipse. You have seen this for yourself with the Earth-Moon arm at its positions in Fig. 1.

A lunar eclipse is not as exclusive as a solar eclipse. Whereas a total or even a partial eclipse of the Sun can only be observed from a small part of the Earth's surface, a total eclipse of the Moon is visible to any observer on the night side of the Earth. Sometimes, when the Moon is not completely immersed in the Earth's shadow, we get a partial lunar eclipse (Fig. 4).

A lunar eclipse begins with the Earth's shadow slowly moving across the Moon's disc. The shadow is curved and it was this fact which led Pythagoras and his followers in the fifth century BC to conclude that the Earth was a sphere, not flat as previously believed. Gradually, after about one hour, the whole Moon moves into the shadow cast by the Earth, and although still moving through space, the Moon remains covered for about three-quarters of an hour or more. This is quite long compared with the few minutes of totality of a total solar eclipse.

Total eclipses of the Moon will happen in 1982 on January 9, July 6 and December 30 lasting 1.4 hours, 1.7 hours and 1.1 hours respectively, and there will be two in 1985, one on May 4 and the other on October 28; their durations will be 1.2 hours and 0.7 hours respectively. There is no lunar eclipse in 1984, but in 1983 on June 25 there will be a partial eclipse.

The Moon's motion in its orbit means not only that it moves along a curved eastward path among the 'fixed' stars, but also that it rises later each night. This lag in time of moonrise is about 50 minutes. However in autumn in the northern hemisphere, when the declination of the Sun is around zero as it moves from north to south of the celestial equator, the declination of the Full Moon is similar but it is increasing, not decreasing, each day. Changes in declination are at their greatest at the equinoxes, and the effect at the autumnal equinox is that the increase in the Moon's declination goes far to offsetting the lag of the time of moonrise from night to night. This is just because the Moon is moving higher in the sky from one night to the next, and is spending longer above the horizon. At this time of year, the Full Moon rises about the same time each day and gives plenty of light – so helping farmers to gather in the harvest. For this reason, it is often called the 'Harvest Moon'.

A total lunar eclipse showing the surface of the Moon lit by refracted sunlight.

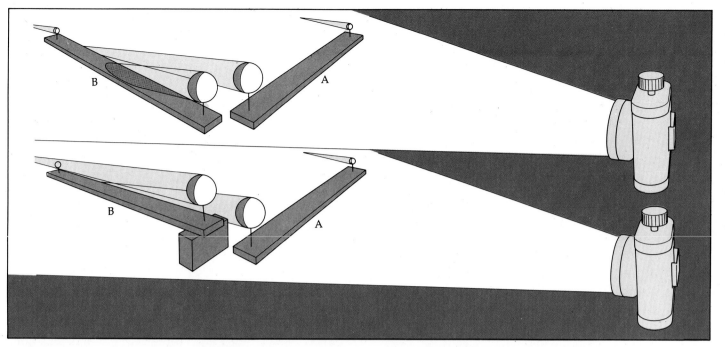

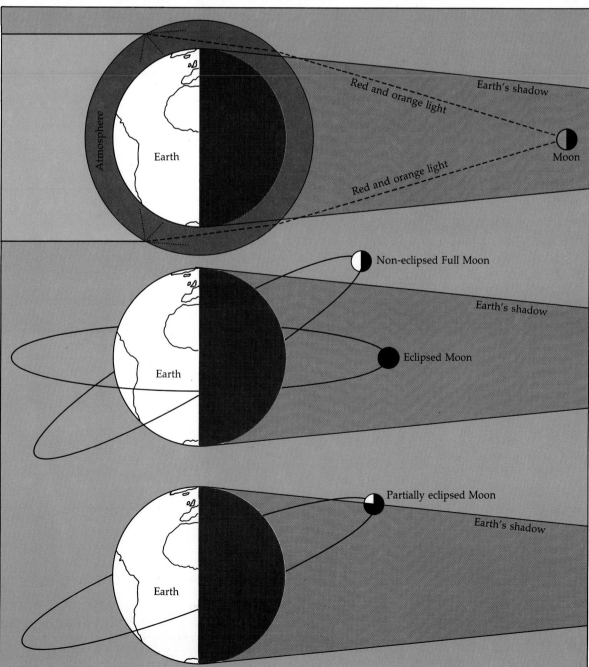

Fig. 1 *above*
An experiment to show how a lunar eclipse occurs when the Moon passes into the Earth's shadow.

Fig. 2
Sunlight is cut off from the Moon by the Earth, but the Earth's atmosphere bends the longer rays which give the Moon a reddish hue.

Fig. 3
Because the Moon's orbit is tilted, sometimes it falls within the Earth's shadow, at others it is above or below it.

Fig. 4
A partial eclipse of the Moon occurs when only part of the disc is in the Earth's shadow.

Earth's shadow

Red and orange light

Red and orange light

Atmosphere

Earth

Moon

Non-eclipsed Full Moon

Earth's shadow

Eclipsed Moon

Earth

Partially eclipsed Moon

Earth's shadow

Earth

OCCULTATIONS BY THE MOON

As the Moon orbits the Earth an observer sees it pass in front of a great number of stars and, occasionally, planets. These eclipses of other celestial bodies are known as 'occultations' because the Moon occults or hides them. Occultations can supply important information about the size and position of celestial objects.

Occultations can be readily observed by the amateur astronomer and are a very useful way of continually checking on the Moon's orbital path.

In spite of Isaac Newton's wonderful work on gravitation over 300 years ago, the Moon's orbital motion is still very difficult to compute precisely because there are many factors affecting it. First there is the pull of the Earth: this varies by a small amount because the Earth is

not exactly round – it bulges at the equator and is a little distorted at the poles. In addition, the Moon itself is not a perfect sphere; it bulges slightly on the side which faces the Earth. The Moon's orbit is also inclined to the Earth's equator and so the gravity effects of the misshapen parts of the Earth vary. What is more the Earth's axis is moving in space due to precession (page 11) and it also has a slight nodding motion caused by the pull of the Moon. These also affect the Moon's path. Then, there are the effects of the Sun and planets. The Moon's orbit is tilted with respect to the ecliptic, so there will be a varying pull because of this. As for the planets, they are continuously

changing their relative positions, so the gravitational pull from them changes with time. All these effects can be calculated but, even so, it means that the Moon's motion is very complex. Moreover the distance between the Earth and Moon is continually changing, mainly because the Moon's orbit is elliptical; and the gravitational or tidal pull between Earth and Moon is affecting the Moon's velocity in orbit, increasing the distance between Earth and Moon as the years go by. Thus it is important continually to check the position of the Moon; this can be done by recording occultations.

The precise moment of an occultation must be timed as exactly

Fig. 1 below
Observing an occultation through a telescope and timing it with a stopwatch.

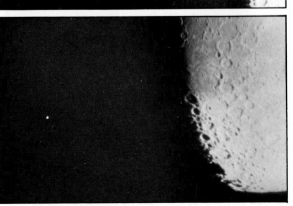

Fig. 2 left
The occultation of a star: in the first photograph are two stars, in the second only one.

as possible. It must be done with an accuracy of one second, although precision to one fifth of a second, as given by a stopwatch, is better. First, one has to know that an occultation is expected, and here a list of future occultations is necessary; this can be found, for instance, in the annual *Handbook* of the British Astronomical Association. However, there are a few very bright stars which lie in the Moon's path, and these can always be watched to see whether it is likely that the Moon will occult one of them. For example, Aldebaran and the Pleiades in Taurus are always possible candidates for occultation.

What the observer is required to do is to watch through a telescope

and note the instant at which the star's light is suddenly extinguished by the forward limb of the Moon as it moves across the starry background. The moment is not difficult to recognize. Because the Moon has no atmosphere there is no momentary fading of the star. One moment it is there, the next moment it has gone, but to time the instant this happens a stopwatch is needed. The moment the star disappears, press the button to start the stopwatch; to find the precise time at which this disappearance occurred go indoors with your stopwatch and look at an electronic clock or watch or dial the telephone number for the speaking clock. At a particular time given by

the clock – the precise moment chosen does not matter – press the button on your stopwatch to stop it. Subtract the interval recorded by the stopwatch from the time given by the electronic clock and you will have the correct time the occultation began.

You should try to time the end of the occultation too. This means knowing whereabouts the star is going to emerge at the other side of the Moon's disc. It is obviously no good simply keeping a lookout and just hoping you spot the star as it emerges; you need to know the instant this happens so that you can record it within one fifth of a second. Tables of occultations give you the 'position angle' (Fig. 4) so that you can be sure precisely where to watch for the emergence. Otherwise you will have to make a plot of the star field and of the Moon's path in the sky so that you can work out your own position angle. In doing so take the Moon's path as a straight line, although in reality it is slightly curved. The difference over so short a distance as half a degree in the sky (which is the Moon's average apparent diameter) will be too small to affect results.

Different observers will note different occultation times (Fig. 5).

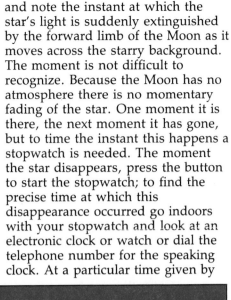

Fig. 3 right
The occultation of a binary system: one star reaches the limb before the other. This momentary diminution of light indicates a binary star.

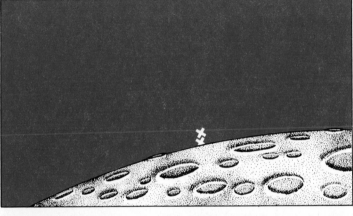

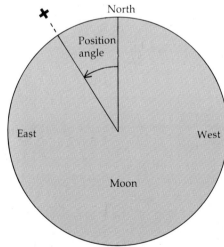

Fig. 4 above
The position angle gives the position of a star's emergence during an occultation.

Fig. 5 left
Observers at different places do not see an occultation at the same time. A will see the Moon at some distance from the star (see diagram A), while B is watching the occultation (see diagram B).

There are two reasons for this, one due to a difference in places from which the observations are made, and the other caused by 'personal equation'. Because the Moon is comparatively near the Earth, observers do not have to be many kilometres apart for their timings to be different. They will differ by a fifth of a second if they are a little over 5½ km apart and, if they live 100 km apart, the difference will amount to more than 3½ seconds. It is therefore very important to know precisely your position and this can be found from an accurate, large scale map, such as one made by the Ordnance Survey or by the U.S. Geological Survey.

A difference in 'personal equation' is due to the fact that everyone suffers a time-lag between the moment they see something and the moment they press a button to record the fact. The amount of this reaction time depends on how you feel, as well as on your general bodily make-up. It is difficult to measure unless you have an electronic stopwatch which will record down to hundredths of a second. Then you can, for example, cover up the display which gives seconds and fractions of a second and watch for a change in the number which records tens of seconds. Watch, in fact, for a change from 19 to 20 seconds; as soon as the number 1 changes to 2, press the button on the stopwatch. What is then recorded will give you your personal equation. Some amateur astronomers who make very precise timings of occultations measure their personal equation every time they make occultation measurements! However, the main thing is that your time-lag should be consistent. The existence of personal equation was not discovered until the early nineteenth century. Previously an observer whose personal equation was large was thought to be failing to pay attention to his observations, and at the Royal Observatory at Greenwich one observer was dismissed for this very reason.

There is yet another problem when observing an occultation and this is the case of the 'fading immersion'. Although the Moon has no atmosphere, there are occasions when a star does seem to fade and lose brightness just before it suddenly disappears. In probably all cases the reason is that the star being occulted is a very close binary system. As the Moon's edge begins to cover the star it first blots out the light from one component of the binary before it reaches the other and blots out the star completely. Although the star cannot be separated visually into two stars in a telescope, nevertheless the Moon's

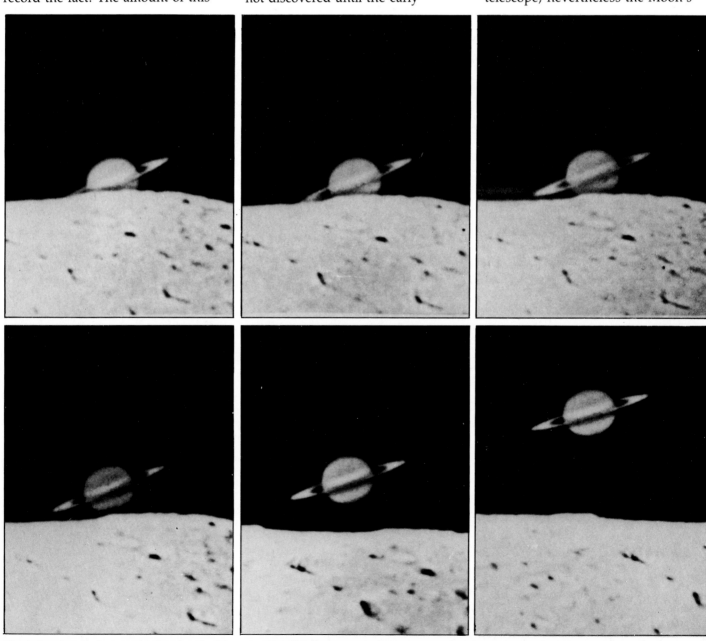

Fig. 6 A series of photographs showing the Moon occulting Saturn.

edge will show up the existence of the two components by causing a slight and very brief dimming.

In addition to occulting stars, the Moon also occults planets. Such an occultation can be a wonderful sight because in a telescope a planet shows a definite disc, and the planet gradually disappears as it becomes covered by the Moon. Tables of occultations always include such planetary disappearances as well as those of stars, and the occultation of minor planets (pages 132–133) are also included. Observations of minor planet occultations are very valuable for checking the positions of these bodies, whose orbits are often much disturbed by the larger planets.

As well as the ordinary type of occultation by the Moon, there is another – the 'grazing occultation'. Here the Moon does not blot out the light by moving across a star or planet, but causes a series of short

occultations as its edge or limb moves across (Fig. 7). Because of the Moon's nearness in the sky such an occultation can only be seen from a small number of places.

A grazing occultation gives a number of short occultations and reappearances of a star because of the ragged edge of the Moon (Fig. 8) formed by the mountains, craters, and other lunar surface features. Such occultations can be very useful because careful records will provide information about the shape of the Moon as well as its motion. Recorded times must be made to an accuracy of at least one second. You need some practice to make them, but some astronomical societies are organized to help their members make worthwhile measurements.

An exciting use of occultations is to measure the diameters of celestial objects. In the early days of radio astronomy, radio telescopes could

not pinpoint the many radio sources they observed. This was because radio telescopes had poor resolution. The power of a telescope to pick out detail (its resolving power) depends not only on the size of its aperture, but also on the wavelength used. Radio waves are ten thousand to one hundred million times larger than light waves, so to give the same resolving power radio telescopes needed to be of vast size. One way to overcome this was to use occultations by the Moon, and see where the Moon was when it cut off the incoming radio waves. In the 1960s this was the only way to measure radio sources which were small in size, and it led to some important discoveries, including that of the first of those strange objects known as quasars (page 194). Some very exciting results also appeared in 1977 from observing the planet Uranus when it occulted a star.

Fig. 7 right
A grazing occultation occurs when the limb of the Moon just touches the star or planet it is occulting.

Fig. 8 centre
A close-up view of the uneven limb of the Moon showing why a star appears to flicker during an occultation.

Fig. 9 below
The Moon occulting a radio source in space, observed by a radio telescope.

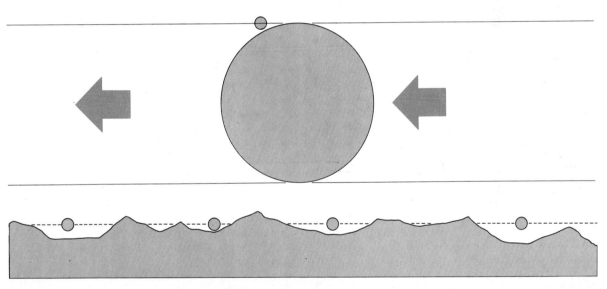

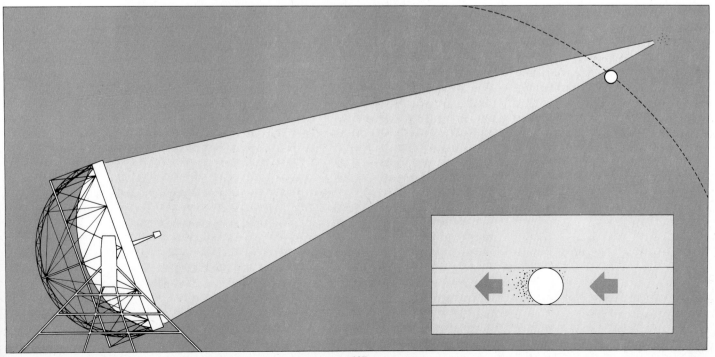

CHAPTER 4
THE PLANETS

Most ancient cultures believed in an Earth-centred universe, and it was not until the sixteenth century that the heliocentric, or Sun-centred, theory was adopted. It was Johannes Kepler who, in 1621, determined the true nature of the planetary orbits in the Solar System.

From the very earliest times observers had been intrigued by the steady brightness of a few wandering 'stars'. These stars, whose positions were seen to change, were in fact the five innermost planets Mercury, Venus, Mars, Jupiter and Saturn. Of the three outer planets Uranus was discovered in 1781, Neptune in 1846 and Pluto not until 1930. It was clear that the planets did not move aimlessly about the heavens, and when the Greek philosophers began to study the question, they tried to recognize some sort of regular pattern in their movements. The philosopher Pythagoras in the sixth century BC claimed that, like the Sun and Moon, all the planets orbited round the Earth. Pythagoras also thought they orbited the Earth in circles because a circle seemed to him to be a perfect shape, having neither beginning nor end. A regular unchanging rate of motion also seemed to be a more elegant kind of motion than one which went at a varying rate, sometimes fast and sometimes slow. These were celestial objects and it seemed only proper that they should behave in a way suited to such exalted bodies.

Pythagoras formed his ideas not only because observational evidence made it seem obvious that the planets did orbit the Earth, but also because they were in accordance with a sense of what seemed beautiful and elegant in the world around him. Some of his followers did suggest that all planets, including the Earth, and the Sun and Moon, orbited round a 'central fire' at the centre of the universe. But because the Earth was so very obviously fixed and immovable and orbiting planets moving in circles appeared much more sensible, this was not accepted

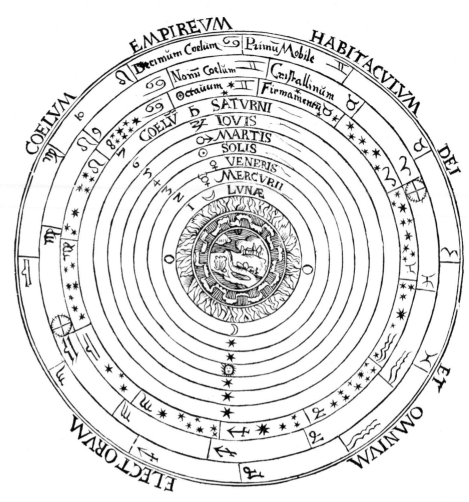

Fig. 1
The geocentric view of the universe: Earth is at the centre, containing earth and water and surrounded by air and fire, and orbiting the Earth are the spheres of the Moon, Sun, planets and stars. From Peter Apian's *Cosmographia*, Antwerp, 1539.

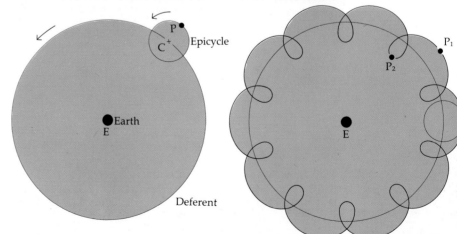

Fig. 2
The loop of a planet in the sky. This is only an apparent motion due to the relative speeds of the planet and Earth as they orbit the Sun.

Fig. 3
To explain loops in the motion of a planet, Greek mathematicians thought that the planet moved in small circles or epicycles while completing a large circle or deferent round the Earth. This theory also accounted for the change in brightness of a planet, depending on its closeness to Earth.

Fig. 4
The paths of Mercury and Venus in the sky.

Being closer to the Sun than Earth, they never appear far from

it and are seen only in the west near sunset and the east before dawn.

by most Greek philosophers, who adopted the geocentric theory, believing the Earth to be quite still at the centre of the whole universe.

This geocentric (or 'Earth-centred') theory dominated all astronomy for the next two thousand years. However, the theory brought all kinds of difficulties to those who wished to work out planetary motions in detail and to calculate or predict where the planets would be in the future. There were two main problems. One was the changing brightness of the planets as they pursued their orbits – a change which is slow but quite noticeable all the same. The other and more obvious problem was the peculiar behaviour of the three planets Mars, Jupiter and Saturn. If you watch any one of these for a number of months you will find that, unlike the Moon, it performs a series of loops as it progresses among the fixed stars (Fig. 2). You need no telescope to detect this motion: it is clear enough if you watch the sky from week to week and follow your chosen planet.

Pythagoras had taught that the planets orbited the Earth in circles at a regular rate. How then could one explain the fact that they sometimes stopped and sometimes went backwards? Mercury and Venus also presented problems. They never appeared in the midnight sky but were only seen in the west around sunset, or in the east around sunrise. Also, their paths seemed mainly to go up and down above the horizon (Fig. 4), which did not seem to fit in with the ideas of Pythagoras either. Yet his theory seemed the only one possible and the problems acted as a challenge to Greek astronomers, who managed to find answers to them. If you were faced with this problem, if you had to use only regular motion in a circle to explain planetary motion, how could you do so?

The Greek astronomers solved the problem by using all their mathematical knowledge, and since Greek mathematics was mainly concerned with geometry, their solution was a geometrical one. They used what have since become known as the 'epicycle', or 'circle', and the 'deferent', or 'carrying circle' (Fig. 3). You can see how it works if you consider the path of a planet P as observed by an astronomer on the Earth, E. As the epicycle rotates around the point C the planet is carried round and round. For an observer on Earth at E, such a planet would appear to perform a loop in the sky about the point C. This is just what happens in the cases of Mercury and Venus. They appear to move in loops about the Sun. But of course, Mercury and Venus move as the Sun moves so we need another motion to account for this, while for the planets Mars, Jupiter and Saturn, the loops are only pauses in a more general motion across the sky. The second motion is caused by rotating the deferent about the Earth at E.

Thus by using two circles and rotating them both at once it *is* possible to account for the observed motion of the planets. What is more the changing brightness of a planet can be accounted for. When the planet is at P_1 (Fig. 2) it is further away from the Earth, E, and therefore dimmer, than when it is at P_2. Full details of the system were written up about 150 AD by the great astronomer Ptolemy.

As the years went by and many more observations were made it became clear that the simple epicycle and deferent system did not quite explain all the planetary motions. Details of the system were altered with the result that the centres of the deferents were placed a little way from the centre of the Earth and more epicycles were used for each planet. But the general scheme of things stayed the same; the Earth was still the centre of the universe.

When, in the sixteenth century, the Polish clergyman, doctor and amateur astronomer Nicholas Copernicus began to read all that the Greeks had written about planetary motion, he found that there were one or two philosophers who had made other suggestions, one at least proposing that the planets orbited round the Sun, not round the Earth.

Copernicus read these opinions at a time when people in Western Europe were questioning old ideas and beliefs, and when the old explanation of planetary motion seemed increasingly unsatisfactory. So Copernicus adopted a heliocentric, or Sun-centred view, and in 1543 he published a book about it, *De Revolutionibus Orbium Coelestium*.

Copernicus still used the epicycle and deferent to explain the planetary motions and he still accepted the Greek idea that the stars were fixed to the inside of a giant sphere. Nevertheless his theory raised a storm of protest, some of it religious (because his idea of the Earth orbiting the Sun seemed contrary to Western religious teaching) and some scientific. You can test one of the scientific arguments for yourself. Hang on the wall of a room two

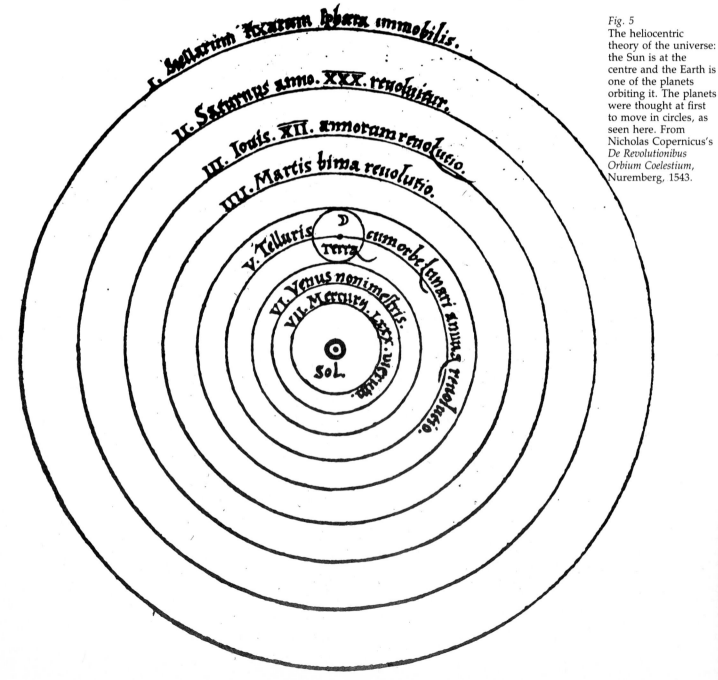

Fig. 5
The heliocentric theory of the universe: the Sun is at the centre and the Earth is one of the planets orbiting it. The planets were thought at first to move in circles, as seen here. From Nicholas Copernicus's *De Revolutionibus Orbium Coelestium*, Nuremberg, 1543.

postcards with a star drawn in the middle of each (Fig. 6). Next place a chair or small table in the centre of the room to represent the Sun. You yourself are to be the Earth and an observer on it. Start near the wall with the star images on it (at A in Fig. 6) and measure the angle between them, using your quadrant (page 68) or some similar device. Now orbit the Sun (the chair). You need not go round in an epicycle but just move to a new position such as B (Fig. 6) so that the stars on the wall can still be seen, but the chair does not interfere with your line of sight. Now measure the angle between the stars once more. You will find that the angle has changed: at B the angle between the stars is smaller than it was when you were at A.

This is the result you might expect, because you are nearer the stars at A than you are at B. Yet observations on the stars themselves did not show any such change. We now know that the stars do show a shift but one too small to be seen with the instruments of the time. Although the heliocentric theory was viewed with some suspicion, many astronomers nonetheless thought it was mathematically superior.

The situation changed again after the work of the Danish astronomer Tycho Brahe. He built much more accurate instruments, which were like the quadrant but far more precise, and he devised specially efficient ways of using them. Between 1576 and 1601 he made the most precise determinations of planetary positions to date. The German mathematical astronomer Johannes Kepler, who was working with him, found that Tycho's observations would not fit in with the old geocentric theory. But they would not fit in with the theory of Copernicus either and finally, by 1621, Kepler found that Pythagoras had been totally wrong. The planets do not orbit the Earth in circles at a regular rate. Instead they orbit the Sun in ellipses (Fig. 7), moving at a varying rate, fastest when they are nearest to the Sun and slowest when they are furthest from it.

Kepler worked out precise laws to express exactly how the planets orbited the Sun, but it was not for another 66 years that anyone could explain why they moved in such paths. Then, in 1687, Isaac Newton published his famous theory of gravitation (page 170) and at last astronomers came to an accurate understanding of what we now call the Solar System.

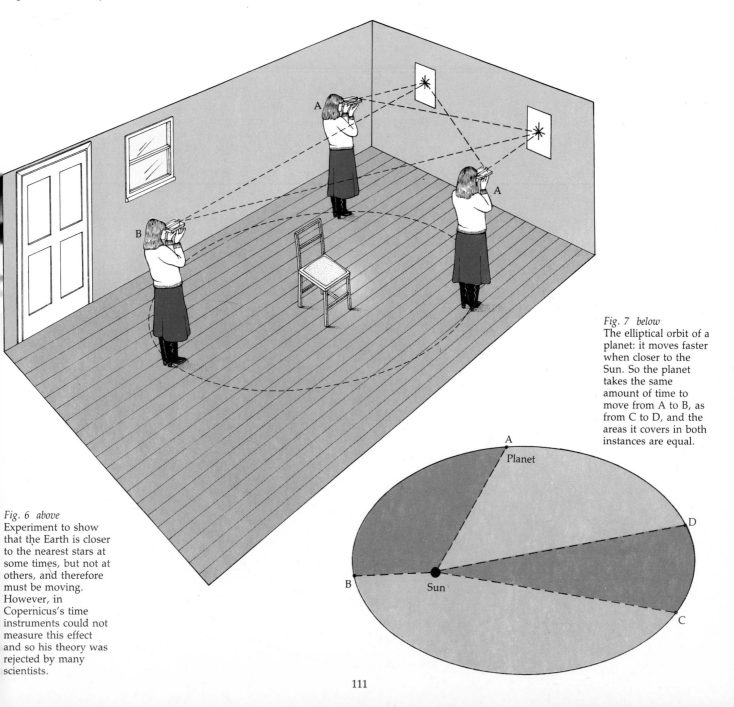

Fig. 7 below
The elliptical orbit of a planet: it moves faster when closer to the Sun. So the planet takes the same amount of time to move from A to B, as from C to D, and the areas it covers in both instances are equal.

Fig. 6 above
Experiment to show that the Earth is closer to the nearest stars at some times, but not at others, and therefore must be moving. However, in Copernicus's time instruments could not measure this effect and so his theory was rejected by many scientists.

PLAN OF THE SOLAR SYSTEM

The Solar System contains nine major planets and vast numbers of smaller ones. All the planets move in almost the same plane, but at different speeds. In addition, all move in elliptical orbits, but these vary widely in 'eccentricity'.

The ellipses of some planets, the Earth and Venus for example, are hardly eccentric at all and it is hard to distinguish them from circles. Others, such as Mercury and Pluto, have rather eccentric orbits and so their ellipses are considerably more elongated. The most eccentric orbits are those of certain comets (pages 140 – 141).

The drawing in Fig. 1 shows the orbits of the major planets and the main area where most (but not all) of the minor planets (page 130) are to be found. This drawing is not to scale because a scale plan would not fit on the page. You can, however,

make a scale plan for yourself. Measure out a distance of 3 metres, and let this represent the distance Sun to Pluto. Make up some 'flags' with sticky labels and large pins, one for each planet, one for the minor planets, and one for the Sun. Put the Sun's flag in the floor near one corner of the room and Pluto's flag in 3 m away. Now put in a flag for Neptune at 2½ m and one at 1½ m for Uranus. A flag at 70 cm will represent Saturn, one at 40 cm will mark the position of Jupiter, and the minor planets will come at 19 cm. Mars lies at 11 cm from the Sun, our Earth at 7½ cm, Venus at 5½ cm and Mercury at 3 cm. These positions are only approximately correct but they will show you how the planets near the Sun look fairly close together whereas the spaces between Jupiter and the planets beyond become larger and larger.

The speeds at which the planets move in their orbits round the Sun differ a great deal. All move fastest when closest to the Sun and slowest when furthest away, and those closer to the Sun move faster than the more distant ones. Mercury takes only 88 days to complete an orbit and Venus 225 days. The Earth, of course, takes 1 year, Mars 1.9 years, Jupiter 11.9

years, Saturn 29.5 years, Uranus 84 years, Neptune 165 years and Pluto 248 years.

The sizes of bodies in the Solar System vary widely too. Jupiter is very large, with a diameter 11 times greater than the Earth's, yet even it is only a tenth the diameter of the Sun, which is vast. If you take a pin-head as being equal to the size of a fairly large minor planet, then the other planets in the Solar System could be represented as follows: Mercury would be the diameter of a shirt-button, Venus and Earth about as big as a walnut, and Mars a man's jacket button. For the larger planets, which are not solid bodies like the smaller ones, but solid 'cores' surrounded by a thick cloudy and gaseous atmosphere, we need much larger objects. Jupiter would be a large beach ball and Saturn also would be a beach ball about 5 cm smaller, Uranus and Neptune would need really large cooking apples to represent them, but Pluto would only require the head of a paper fastener. If you make a collection of such objects you will gain a fair idea of the relative sizes of the planets. For the Sun you would need a ball as big in diameter as the height from floor to ceiling of the average bedroom!

Planet	Equatorial diameter (km)	Average distance from Sun (millions of km)	Orbital period (planet's year)	Period of rotation (planet's day)	Mass (Earth = 1)	Eccentricity of orbit taking Venus as the unit**
Sun	1,392,530	—	—	25.4 days	332,948.34	—
Mercury	4,878	58	88 days	58.6 days	0.06	30
Venus	12,104	108	225 days	243 days	0.81	1
Earth	12,756	150	1 year	1 day	1.00	2.5
Mars	6,794	228	1.9 years	24.6 hours	0.11	13.8
Jupiter	142,800	778	11.9 years	9.8 hours	317.89	7.1
Saturn	120,000	1,427	29.5 years	10.2 hours	95.14	8.2
Uranus	52,000	2,870	84.0 years	16–28 hours*	14.52	7.0
Neptune	48,400	4,497	164.8 years	18–20 hours*	17.25	1.3
Pluto	3,000	5,899	247.7 years	6.3 days	0.10	37.4

* These are uncertain values

** Venus has an almost circular orbit, therefore on this scale 1 represents a circle or zero eccentricity.

Sun Mercury Venus Earth Mars Jupiter Saturn Uranus Neptune Pluto

top
The view of the planets
orbiting the Sun

bottom
Drawing to scale of
the comparative sizes

of the planets in
relation to the Sun at
the bottom of the picture.

PLANETARY POSITIONS

The planets are not always visible in the night sky. Whether or not they can be seen depends on their positions in their orbits and on the Earth's own position in its orbital path. It is not difficult to follow the paths of the planets across the sky; plotting these paths will make it clear to you how the planets travel in relation to the Earth.

There are two ways in which you can plot the positions of the planets: one is simply to make a chart of the part of the sky surrounding a planet's position, and then to plot in the planet's place every three or four days, using your quadrant to measure its position with respect to nearby bright stars (page 69). The other is to make a planetary plotter which enables you to chart the sky without making measurements. Fig. 2 shows the idea; you will see that what you have is a wooden frame with a piece of glass in it and a foresight. All you need to do is to hold up the plotter and mark on some bright stars with a wax pencil which will write on glass – a 'Chinagraph' pencil, for instance. Once you have marked the stars you can then mark in the planet, using a different coloured wax pencil.

Your charts will show loops in the planetary paths for Mars, Jupiter and Saturn. The reason for these becomes clear when we realize that the further away from the Sun a planet lies, the slower it travels in its orbit. If we plot out the movement of Mars and the Earth we can see very clearly what happens. The Earth takes a year to complete an orbit but Mars takes nearly two; in other words Mars only moves about half as fast as the Earth. In Fig. 1, successive positions for Mars and the Earth are plotted, and the appearance of Mars in the sky against the background of stars is shown. You can see that after the Earth reaches position 4, it overtakes Mars, and this gives the loop as shown in the drawing. A similar effect happens with Jupiter, Saturn, Uranus, Neptune and Pluto because all these planets orbit more slowly than the Earth does.

From Fig. 3, which once again shows Mars and the Earth, you will see that there is a time – while the Earth is between B and A – when the Sun is in the way and Mars will not be visible in the night sky. The same kind of thing happens for the other more distant or 'superior' planets. Indeed, to guide observers, astronomers have devised names for the various relative positions of the Earth and the superior planets. These are given in Fig. 4. For Mercury and Venus, which lie closer to the Sun than the Earth and are therefore called the 'inferior' planets, there is also a series of named positions (Fig. 5). These two planets also are not

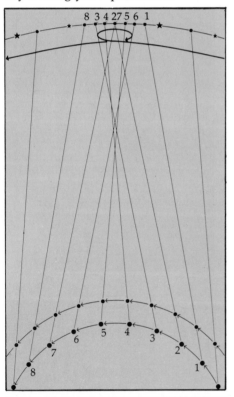

Fig. 1 left
Various positions of the Earth on its orbit round the Sun are numbered, as are positions of Mars in orbit. If lines joining the positions of Earth to those of Mars are projected to the stars (as indicated by the numbers on the skyline), a loop seems to appear in Mars's path across the sky. This is because Earth moves faster and overtakes Mars in orbit.

Inclination of Planetary Orbit to the Ecliptic	
Mars:	1.85°
Jupiter:	1.3°
Saturn:	2.5°

Velocities of Planets		Opposition of Planet	
		1981	1982
Earth	1	—	—
Mars	0.5	—	March 31
Jupiter	0.08	March 26	April 25
Saturn	0.03	March 27	April 8

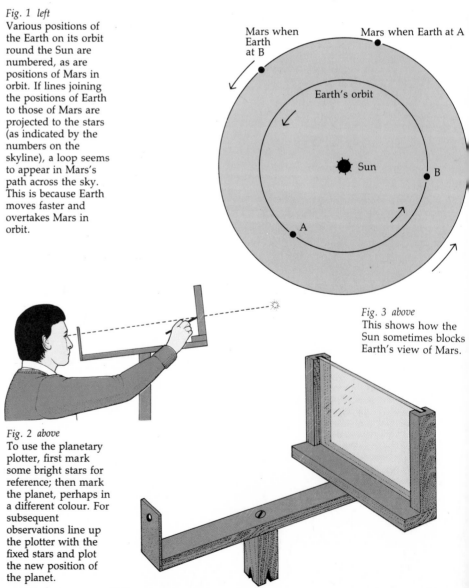

Fig. 2 above
To use the planetary plotter, first mark some bright stars for reference; then mark the planet, perhaps in a different colour. For subsequent observations line up the plotter with the fixed stars and plot the new position of the planet.

Fig. 3 above
This shows how the Sun sometimes blocks Earth's view of Mars.

always visible, although Venus is an unmistakable sight when it does appear above the horizon.

You will want to know when the different planets are visible, and there are various ways you can find out. Some reference books give this information (page 200) and some newspapers print monthly star charts. The positions of the planets can also be worked out using a small electronic calculator which can do trigonometry, but this is more complicated. (You can find instructions in Peter Duffet-Smith's *Practical Astronomy with Your Calculator*.) You can also do some plotting of paths, which can be interesting. The table on page 113 shows that the planets each take a different time to orbit. From this you can work out how fast each planet orbits the Sun and how many degrees it moves each day; on p. 114 is a table of the speeds of the planets compared with the Earth. With this information, together with the following details about oppositions, you can get an idea of the future

visibility of Mars, Jupiter and Saturn.

You can draw a chart of future positions (Fig. 6). Draw a circle to represent the Earth's orbit and mark this out with one year's positions for the Earth. Next draw another circle to represent the orbit of your chosen superior planet (Saturn in this case). Point A is the opposition point for 1981. Now since Saturn orbits only 0.03 times as fast as the Earth, when the Earth has gone 90° (from A to B), Saturn will only have moved 0.03 × 90 = 2.7°, that is from *a* to *b*. When the Earth has moved 360° and is back at A, Saturn has only moved 0.03 × 360 = 10.8°, so its position in 1982 will be rather similar to its position in 1981. You can work out similar diagrams for Mars and Jupiter, although you will see that Mars will not be in opposition in 1981.

Such a diagram does not give you the full picture, however, since it does not tell you anything about how high or low in the sky the planet will be. The orbit of each of the superior planets is inclined a certain amount to the ecliptic; the precise amount for

each of those visible to the unaided eye is given below. You will see that, roughly speaking, they all lie so close to the ecliptic that we need not worry about variations from it. But we do need to be concerned about the ecliptic itself. For Saturn, in 1981, at opposition on March 27, the planet is near the autumnal equinox (Fig. 7). This means it has a very small declination and can be thought of as on the celestial equator. Jupiter, with opposition on March 26, is further along the ecliptic; its declination will change more because it moves more quickly than Saturn. Mars was in opposition in 1980 but does not reach opposition again until March 27, 1982. Its declination will not be too far from the ecliptic then, but it will alter soon after because it moves quite rapidly round the ecliptic (at half the speed of the Earth). Mars will not be very favourably placed for observing because of its distance: it was at its furthest from the Earth in 1980, and will return only slowly to reach its next closest approach in 1988.

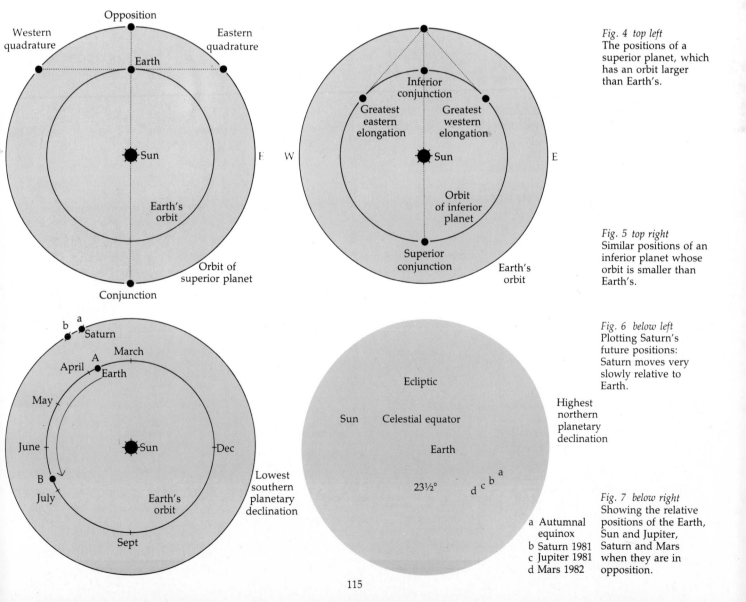

Fig. 4 *top left*
The positions of a superior planet, which has an orbit larger than Earth's.

Fig. 5 *top right*
Similar positions of an inferior planet whose orbit is smaller than Earth's.

Fig. 6 *below left*
Plotting Saturn's future positions: Saturn moves very slowly relative to Earth.

Fig. 7 *below right*
Showing the relative positions of the Earth, Sun and Jupiter, Saturn and Mars when they are in opposition.

a Autumnal equinox
b Saturn 1981
c Jupiter 1981
d Mars 1982

JUPITER

Jupiter, the largest planet of the Solar System, is a magnificent sight when seen through binoculars or, better still, a telescope. In the seventeenth century Galileo's discovery of its four brightest moons helped to challenge contemporary theories about the universe. Today, as a result of the Voyager missions, we know more about the physical nature of the planet than ever before.

Babylonian and Greek astronomers charted the movement of Jupiter against the background of the stars. You can do this too; all you need is a sheet of paper and a pencil, or you could use the planetary plotter mentioned on page 114. Jupiter is not visible every night of the year, and sometimes it can be seen only well after midnight; you will recognize it by its steady whitish light. First plot the brighter stars near Jupiter in the sky, and then put in the planet's position every few nights. To follow Jupiter right round the sky will take a little over 13 months, but plotting for only a few consecutive months will prove that Jupiter is a moving planet.

During January and February 1610, Galileo Galilei, became the first man to look at Jupiter through the recently invented telescope. He was amazed at what was shown by his instrument, which he had made himself. You can use binoculars to see what so astounded him, although they will produce an optical quality superior to that of Galileo's telescope. Jupiter appears as a disc, quite different from the nearby stars, and there are four star-like bodies which accompany the planet. If you observe these every night, you will see that they keep changing their positions. Gradually you will realize, like Galileo, that these 'stars' are really satellites or moons orbiting round Jupiter. To observe them now is endlessly fascinating, but in the seventeenth century their discovery revolutionized astronomical thinking.

At that time most educated people thought of the Earth as fixed in the centre of the universe. On this theory it was claimed that if the

left
Pages from Galileo's *Sidereus Nuncius* 1610, in which he published descriptions of his discoveries with the telescope. The drawings show accurately the changing position of the satellites around Jupiter. Galileo realized that, because these moons orbited round the planet, the Earth could not be the centre of all orbital movement.

below
Binoculars clearly reveal Jupiter to be a planet accompanied by four bright moons. It appears as a small circle with the moons as brilliant dots.

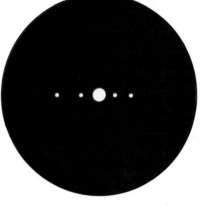

above
With a small telescope you can distinguish the compression of Jupiter's poles. A few bands are also visible, and possibly the Great Red Spot.

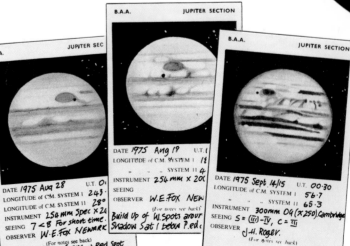

left
Three drawings of Jupiter as seen through a serious amateur's telescope. Good records like these are very important for the practical astronomer. It is also a good idea to contact an organization of amateur observers for advice.

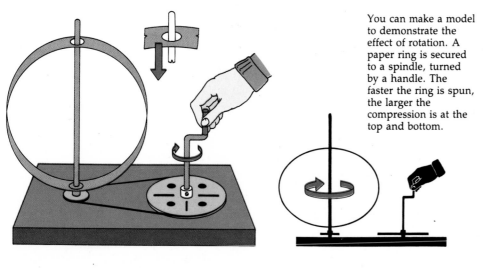

You can make a model to demonstrate the effect of rotation. A paper ring is secured to a spindle, turned by a handle. The faster the ring is spun, the larger the compression is at the top and bottom.

Earth really did orbit the Sun, then it would leave the Moon behind. The fixed Earth supporters believed that Jupiter orbited around the Earth, while Galileo and others like him thought it orbited the Sun. As soon as Galileo saw that Jupiter had four orbiting satellites he realized that here was definite proof that an orbiting body did not leave its moon behind. (Jupiter has nine other moons besides these four, but all are too small and dim to see without a large telescope.) Galileo's discovery did not prove that the Earth was a planet in motion but provided evidence that this was a real possibility.

There are two telescope observations of the satellites which you can make. The first is to determine the orbital period of each of the four. To do this, time how long it takes each one to move round Jupiter from a given point (almost touching the planet's disc, for example) back to the same position. You will find, as you would expect, that the more distant the satellite from Jupiter, the longer the period.

Secondly, watch Jupiter's eclipses of the satellites, which disappear as they move into the shadow which the planet casts into space. With a good telescope you can also detect the shadows of the satellites as they cross in front of Jupiter's disc. Satellite periods may be used to determine how massive Jupiter is (page 118), while timing the intervals between eclipses can give us a measure of the speed of light (page 178).

There are two other very noticeable things about Jupiter, when seen through binoculars, or preferably, a telescope – its shape and the series of belts that cross the planet. Jupiter is not exactly spherical, it is compressed at its poles and bulges at its equator. The Earth also bulges at the equator, and in the seventeenth century the English scientist Isaac Newton proved that this bulge was caused by the comparatively high speed of the Earth's rotation. (A point of the Earth's equator moves round at a speed of 1,670 kph.) Now since Jupiter is 11 times the Earth in diameter and rotates about 2½ times faster, it should show a very much greater bulge, if Newton were correct. Seen through a telescope Jupiter's equatorial bulge is indeed very large, and is actually some 23 times greater than that of the Earth.

Jupiter's belts, which need a telescope to reveal them properly, are

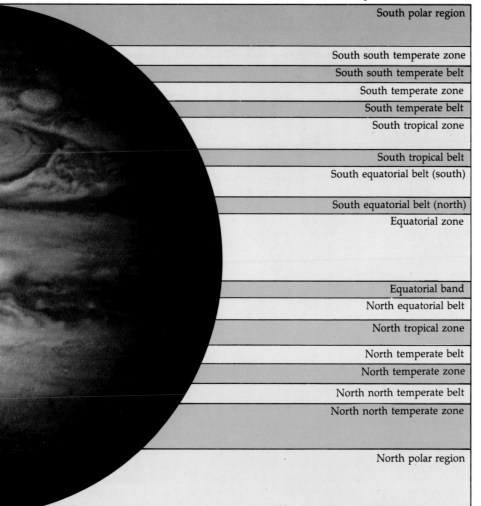

Jupiter's Zones and Belts

| South polar region |
| South south temperate zone |
| South south temperate belt |
| South temperate zone |
| South temperate belt |
| South tropical zone |
| South tropical belt |
| South equatorial belt (south) |
| South equatorial belt (north) |
| Equatorial zone |
| Equatorial band |
| North equatorial belt |
| North tropical zone |
| North temperate belt |
| North temperate zone |
| North north temperate belt |
| North north temperate zone |
| North polar region |

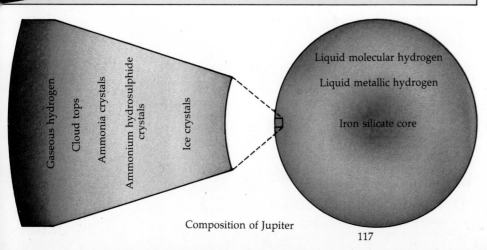

Gaseous hydrogen
Cloud tops
Ammonia crystals
Ammonium hydrosulphide crystals
Ice crystals

Liquid molecular hydrogen
Liquid metallic hydrogen
Iron silicate core

Composition of Jupiter

part of the planet's atmosphere. This atmosphere – which is what we see when we look at the planet – is very thick, but how thick is unknown. If we watch Jupiter's zones and belts for several nights, two observations can be made. The atmosphere changes all the time and the material near the equator rotates faster than the rest.

The rotation period of the equatorial material, known as System I, is nearly ten hours. North and south of these regions the material, known as System II, has a period some five minutes longer. You could try to measure exactly how long each System takes to rotate.

The most conspicuous feature in Jupiter's cloudy atmosphere seems first to have been recorded in 1664 by the English scientist Robert Hooke. This is the Great Red Spot, which is oval in shape and lies south of Jupiter's equator. It varies considerably in both intensity and colour, sometimes it is a strong red and very noticeable indeed, and on other occasions it pales into insignificance. In 1873 it was easily recognizable and has been carefully studied ever since, although during some years, such as 1968, it has become almost invisible. You can check the appearance of the Great Red Spot as it is today.

At first the Great Red Spot was thought to be a giant mountain peak or plateau sticking up above the clouds, but since it has been seen to move almost a third of the way round Jupiter's disc, this idea has been abandoned. It is cooler than the surrounding clouds and one possible explanation is that it may be a tropical hurricane. If this is correct, then it has a storm centre that almost baffles the imagination, not only because it lasts year in and year out, but also because of its immense size. For the Great Red Spot is so big that the whole Earth could be swallowed up in it some 2½ times.

By all standards Jupiter is a giant planet. It is also the most massive planet in the Solar System: its mass is 19 hundred thousand million million tonnes (i.e. 1.9×10^{24} tonnes), and so is 2½ times more massive than all the other planets in the Solar System put together.

But how do we know Jupiter's mass? We cannot take a balance into space and weigh the planet. The answer lies in Newton's theory of gravitation. By measuring the time taken for one body to orbit round another at a given distance, we can work out the ratio of their masses.

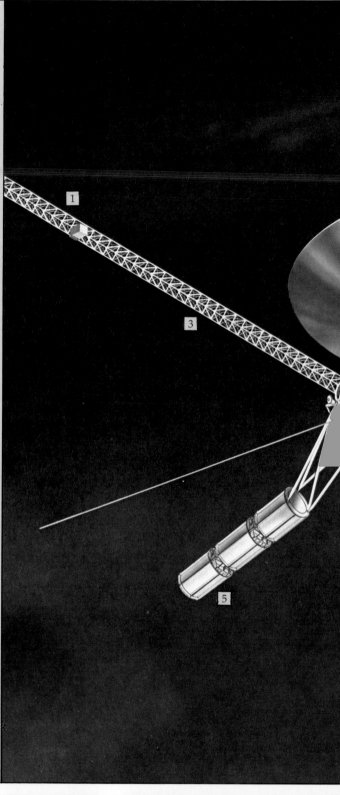

A Voyager spacecraft approaching Jupiter.

1 Magnetometer
One of 4 instruments for measuring the magnetic field of a planet.

2 Electronic compartments
Inside are contained the electronics and radio transmitters which send the observations made by Voyager back to Earth.

3 Extendible boom
Magnetic detection equipment to probe the environment is carried on this boom, as far away as possible from the spacecraft.

4 High-gain directional antenna
Dish-shaped radio antenna for directing transmissions of observations to Earth.

5 Radioisotope thermoelectric generators (3)
Nuclear power generation equipment for supplying electricity to the spacecraft. This is the sole power source on Voyager.

6 Propulsion fuel tank
Fuel tank for feeding the thruster jets.

7 Cosmic ray detector
Device for measuring the intensity of high-speed atomic particles near a planet.

8 Plasma detector
Instrument to detect electrified gases.

9 Photopolarimeter
The degree of polarization of radiation (the plane in which the waves of radiation are emitted) is measured by this instrument.

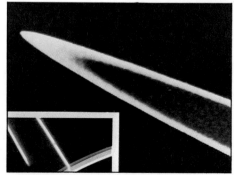

Jupiter's ring as seen by Voyager 2 from 1,488,000 km. Inset is another view of the ring and the planet's limb (the coloured band).

Voyager 1 view of Jupiter showing the Satellite Io and Europa.

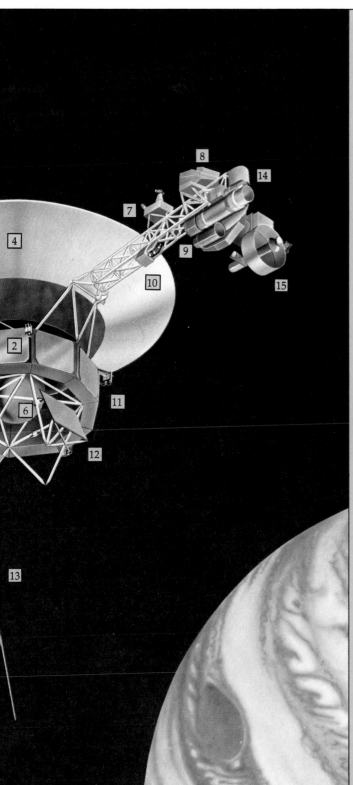

10 Low-energy charged particles
A detector for low-energy charged particles not 'seen' by the cosmic ray detector.

11 Thrusters
16 thruster jets provide the only steering mechanism on the spacecraft; they are used to adjust the alignment of Voyager.

12 Instrument calibration panel and shunt radiator
Here the radiation received is assessed so that the sensitivity of the scientific instruments is adjusted correctly. The shunt radiator reflects away unwanted radiation.

13 Planetary radio astronomy and plasma wave antenna
One of two antennae (radio aerials) for detecting radio waves and waves emitted by hot electrified gases.

14 Wide-angle and narrow-angle TV cameras
TV cameras are used because their images can be radioed back direct using TV electronics. The narrow-angle camera on Voyager 1 discovered the ring of material around Jupiter.

15 Ultraviolet spectrometer, infrared interferometer, spectrometer and radiometer
These instruments examine the ultraviolet, infrared and radiation at other wavelengths from Jupiter.

Gravitation theory gives us the formula $\dfrac{P}{S} = \dfrac{a^3 T^2}{A^3 t^2}$

P = the planet's mass, S = the Sun's mass, and a = the average distance between Jupiter and one of its satellites (see table on page 133). A is the average distance between the Earth and the Sun; T is the time the Earth takes to orbit the Sun (in days) and t is the time (in days) a satellite (the one for which a is given) takes to orbit Jupiter – this is one of the values you may have measured from your observations of Jupiter's satellites. Knowing that the Sun is 332,946 times the mass of the Earth, you can readily work out the mass of Jupiter in terms of the Earth's mass.

Dividing Jupiter's mass by its volume gives its density. Oddly, the average density of Jupiter is little more than the density of water, whereas a planet like the Earth has a density some 5½ times that of water. This means that, piece for piece, Jupiter is much lighter than the Earth. It must, then, be mainly gaseous, and its solid core (if it has one) must be comparatively small.

The American Voyager space probes have taken superb close-up photographs of Jupiter and made exciting discoveries about the four Galilean moons. Voyager 1 has also found that there is a ring of material around Jupiter. This is no more than 30 km thick, but at least 9,000 km wide; it lies with its outer edge 57,000 km above the top of the planet's cloudy atmosphere. Voyager 1 has also confirmed that Jupiter is hotter than was expected; it emits twice the heat it receives from the Sun. This is probably due to heat coming from the core deep in Jupiter's central regions, just as heat comes from deep down in the Earth's core, as is proved by the way the temperature rises at the bottom of a deep mineshaft.

In 1955, radio astronomers found that Jupiter emits radio waves, which is most unusual for a planet. Unfortunately all are too short in wavelength and too weak for you to receive on an ordinary radio. They tell us that Jupiter has radiation belts which are apparently similar to those which surround our Earth (page 160), but are about 10,000 times more intense. It seems unlikely that any manned space flight could ever travel close to the planet because of this powerful radiation. However our knowledge will increase as information from the Voyagers continues to be studied.

Compare the similarity of the Voyager 1 close-up of the Great Red Spot with the satellite photograph of a hurricane on Earth.

SATURN

Looked at through a telescope, Saturn, with its system of rings, is the most beautiful of all the planets. The rings are a permanent feature, but their tilt towards us is continually altering.

It was thought that Saturn – the 'ringed planet' – was unique in this respect, but recent research has shown that both Uranus and Jupiter possess rings also. Jupiter's rings can only be observed by a spacecraft close to the planet and the rings of Uranus cannot be seen directly in a telescope from Earth, so from an observer's point of view Saturn is still the only ringed planet!

Saturn's rings change their appearance because they lie around the planet's equator, and as Saturn's axis of rotation is tilted over more than 26° to its orbit, the rings too are inclined. As a result we on Earth sometimes see the rings from above, sometimes from below, and sometimes we view them edge-on (Fig. 2). The rings contain hundreds of individual ringlets; and although the rings have a diameter of more than 274,000 km, they are only about 5 km thick. So when seen edge-on even through a large telescope, they are unobservable, which is one of the reasons why it was difficult for observers to discover them.

The first person to record Saturn's appearance through a telescope was Galileo. He made his first observations in July 1610, when the rings were 'open', as at G in Fig. 2. Galileo's earliest telescopes were not able to show the rings for what they were, and all he could see was that Saturn seemed to have a blob either side of it (Fig. 1). He thought it might be a triple planet – a planet orbited by two large moon-like bodies very close to it. When he next looked, in 1612, Saturn's rings were edge-on and Galileo found that the planet's 'companion stars' had vanished. Since he was sometimes taunted with the criticism that what he observed through his telescope was merely an illusion, he must have found this very disturbing. However, by 1613, the planet's 'triple' nature was visible again.

You will get an idea of what Galileo saw if you use a pair of not too powerful binoculars. You will not be able to see the rings very clearly and the planet will look oval. When the rings are 'opened' (G in Fig. 2) you can well see why Galileo thought Saturn was a triple planet. However, if you look through a telescope (the larger the better) you will see the rings more clearly and, with careful observing, you will be able to see their more obvious divisions. Before you do this look at Fig. 2 to see how open the rings are when you look at the planet.

In 1656 the Dutch astronomer Christiaan Huygens was the first to see the rings clearly, but it was not until 1875, more than two centuries later, that it was discovered that they are made of millions of tiny lumps or particles – probably lumps of frozen gas. The rings could have originated from pieces of a moon which were torn away by Saturn's gravity; but a more likely possibility is that they formed from material which did not collect into a moon when the planet and its many moons evolved.

Fig. 1
Drawing of Saturn by Galileo whose telescope was not precise enough to enable him to see the rings as rings.

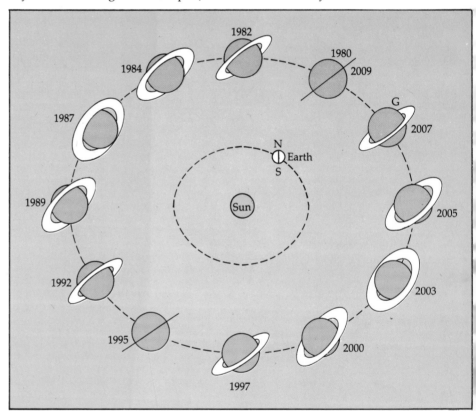

Fig. 2 above
This shows Saturn in orbit and how the angle at which we view the rings changes as the relative positions of the Earth and Saturn alter.

Fig. 3 below
Shadow of Saturn's globe on its rings.

There are many concentric rings around Saturn, but four main sections are visible from Earth. These are an outer ring A, a bright ring B, faint ring C – called the Crêpe Ring – and ring D which lies close to the planet's equator and is difficult to observe. The largest gap in the ring structure is between rings A and B and is called Cassini's division after the Italian astronomer Gian Domenico Cassini who, in 1675, was the first person to observe it. The divisions in the rings are probably caused by the gravitational forces of Saturn's satellites (page 131).

Saturn is one of the large outer planets and although it is smaller than Jupiter it is still very large, being 9.4 times bigger in diameter than the Earth. Like Jupiter it is oblate – that is to say its globe is flattened, its diameter from pole to pole being only 108,000 km compared with its equatorial diameter of 120,000 km. This is a flattening only one-sixth as much as that shown by Jupiter, even though Saturn rotates on its axis at almost the same speed (Saturn 10 hours 14 minutes; Jupiter 9 hours 51 minutes). Because it is not as massive as Jupiter, the velocity at which a body could escape from Saturn is only 32.26 km per second, compared with Jupiter's 60.22 km per second. All the same Saturn is believed to be very like Jupiter in construction, with a dense solid core surrounded by a thick cloudy atmosphere. But Saturn has the lowest density of all the planets in the Solar System; its average density – core plus atmosphere – is 0.7 times that of water (Jupiter 1.3, Earth 5.5). So theoretically this giant planet could float in water! Saturn's clouds are a shade whiter than those of Jupiter, and its albedo is 0.76 while Jupiter's is 0.73. Like Jupiter, Saturn emits more heat than it receives from the Sun, so it too must have a source of heat, probably in the core.

As a planet Saturn is, then, very similar to Jupiter. But through a telescope it looks much smaller because, of course, it is almost twice as far from the Sun, and a further 649 million km from us. So whereas Jupiter gives an image almost an arc minute across when at its nearest (actual size 50 arc seconds), Saturn never appears larger than two-fifths of this (21 arc seconds). All the same it is a bright object in the sky and, at its nearest, shines with a magnitude of -0.3. Of the fixed stars, only Canopus and Sirius are brighter.

When you look at Saturn's disc with a telescope you will see that its cloudy atmosphere is crossed by bands, rather like those on Jupiter. Amateur astronomers can study changes in these bands just as in the case of Jupiter although, as Saturn is so much further away, you need a larger telescope to do any useful observing. A 15 cm reflector is probably the smallest aperture that can be successfully used for this kind of work. But Saturn is always a fascinating, as well as a beautiful sight, well worth looking at through a smaller telescope or even a good pair of binoculars.

The Voyager 1 visit to Saturn in November 1980 revealed fascinating new information. A Red Spot, only one-eighth as large as Jupiter's, was detected. A thin outer braided ring, F, (Fig. 3) was discovered and there are possibly two more: one, E, outside the A ring and another, G, lying far beyond the F ring. The rings displayed 'spokes' caused perhaps by electrified particles. Some new satellites were also discovered by the space probe.

Fig. 4 above
A Pioneer space probe photograph of Saturn in 1979, showing its disc and rings and satellite, Rhea.

Fig. 5 left
Saturn's rings as seen from underneath by Voyager 1 on November 12 1980, when the space probe was at a distance of 740,000 km from the planet. Seen from this angle the rings look dramatically different from the view of their sunlit side. For example the bright B ring appears dark (it has been tinted magenta by processing), while the normally dark Cassini's division is the brightest feature. The thin F ring is clearly visible at the outer edge. In some places the F ring consists not of a single strand, but three which are apparently braided. It is thought that a pair of satellites orbiting on either side of the F ring forces its particles into a narrow band.

MARS

Mars is not a very large planet, but when near opposition it can approach quite close to the Earth. It has always been considered one of the most exciting planets since it has not seemed hostile to life. However, now that spacecraft have orbited and landed on Mars, some of the earlier ideas about the planet have been disproved.

Mars has a very red colour in the sky and when you look at it through a telescope it only shows a very small disc. At best, when Mars is nearest to us, its diameter appears a mere 25.7 arc seconds. It was at its furthest point from the Earth in 1980 and will not be close to us again until 1988. It will therefore be some years before it can be satisfactorily studied with a small telescope. All the same it is perhaps possible to distinguish a white patch at one pole – one of its 'polar caps' – and to detect a triangular-shaped dark patch, known as Syrtis Major, on its red surface (Fig. 1). For these features alone it is certainly worth looking at.

Galileo observed Mars but his telescope showed no detail on its surface and the first true marking to be detected with a telescope was Syrtis Major, which Christiaan Huygens observed in 1659. The difficulty in seeing detail on Mars led some astronomers to believe they had observed some features which were not really there at all. You can see for yourself how this happens if you take a drawing like Fig. 2 and look at it from a distance. If you set it up 2.5 metres away you will get some idea of what you would see in a telescope. If you then make a drawing of what it looks like (*not* what you think it ought to look like!) you could get a result like that shown in Fig. 3. It was a long series of results like Fig. 3, seen in slightly unsteady images due to our Earth's atmosphere, that led the Italian astronomer Giovanni Schiaparelli in 1877 to record many straight lines or channels. The Italian for 'channels' is *canali*, but Schiaparelli's were soon translated as 'canals', which made people think of artificial waterways built by intelligent creatures. This idea was taken up very keenly by the American astronomer Percival Lowell, who in the 1890s set up an observatory in Flagstaff, Arizona, primarily to study Mars.

Space probe close-ups of Mars, and landings on it by the Viking spacecraft, have made it clear that there are no canals on Mars. All the same this does not mean that terrestrial observing is useless. Mars has great dust storms and these can

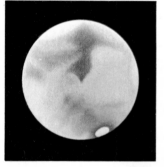

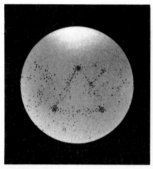

Figs. 2 and 3 left
A drawing of Mars showing dark patches which appear to connect when seen from afar. The figure on the right shows how these may be misinterpreted as canals on Mars.

Fig. 5 below
These drawings, made using a 115 mm refractor, show the changing north polar cap on Mars during the first quarter of 1980: top, 15 February, then 13 and 21 March.

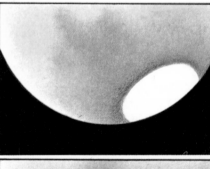

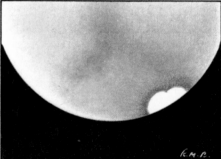

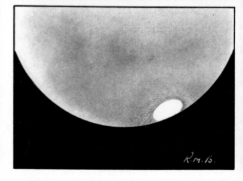

Fig. 1 above
Mars as seen from Earth, drawn by Richard Baum using a 115 mm refractor. The image is inverted with the north polar cap at the bottom appearing small. The central dark area is Syrtis Major.

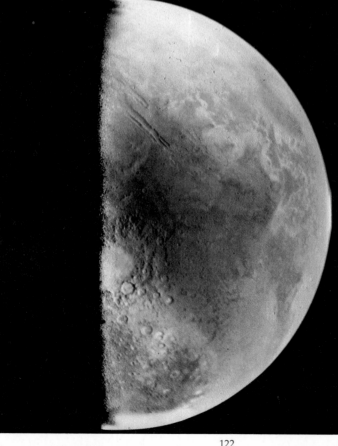
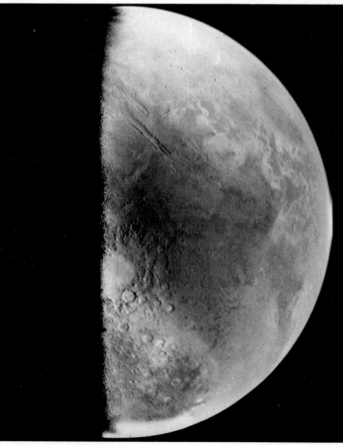

Fig. 4
Mars as seen by the approaching Viking 1 spacecraft at a distance of 322,000 km.

be observed from Earth: noting when they occur, how long they last and how widespread they are can be useful. But you need at least a 15 cm or, better, a 21 cm, reflecting telescope for this kind of work. With a smaller telescope, though, you can detect changes in the polar caps of Mars. The axis of rotation of Mars, like the Earth's, is tilted over with respect to its orbit (Mars 25.2°, Earth 23.4°), and so it also experiences seasonal changes (page 20). In the Martian northern summer, the northern polar cap shrinks, and in the southern summer, the southern polar cap shrinks (Fig. 5). The caps, as we now know, are made of ice with a covering of carbon dioxide gas in solid form. Their changes can be fascinating to observe, especially as the melting and shrinking of a polar cap is accompanied by a darkening of the dark areas below it.

Observations of changes in the dark areas led some astronomers to suggest that perhaps these patches, which appear to have a dark greenish-blue colouring in contrast to the generally red surface of the rest of Mars, were regions of vegetation. The red areas were assumed to be desert. The Viking landings on the surface of Mars, and the spacecraft which have orbited it, have made it clear that there is no vegetation in these dark areas. The apparent change of colouring is due to water from the ice-caps causing rocks to discolour. Nevertheless Mars seems to have conditions so like the Earth – an atmosphere, seasonal changes, and a day (more properly called a 'sol') of 24.623 hours (Earth =23.934 hours) – that to suggest there was some kind of life on Mars seemed sensible enough. Admittedly, Mars is colder than the Earth, because it is one and a half times further from the Sun, but even so life of some kind would be possible, and even when the Viking spacecraft landed in June and August 1977, the question remained unanswered.

Space probes either orbiting or landing on Mars have greatly increased our knowledge of the planet and have given us some marvellous pictures. Look at the map of Mars drawn from the evidence given by orbiting spacecraft. You can see that Mars has large plains and mountainous areas. The dark area Syrtis Major is in fact a giant depressed plain. Some other dark patches like the Aurorae Planum (once called Aurorae Sinus) and the Solis Planum (the one-time Solis Lacus) are huge plateaus.

The mountainous areas are extensive and the south polar region is entirely mountainous and cratered. In some of the valleys there are clearly the dried-up beds of streams, suggesting that there was once water on Mars. Perhaps the most striking evidence of this is shown in a photograph of the Chryse region. Here there are three large craters, Gold, Bok and Lod, which have land shaped like tear-drops around them.

Fig. 6
A preliminary chart of Mars which includes the North and South polar regions. North at the top of the lower chart. Turn this chart upside down to check observations in a telescope, which inverts the image.

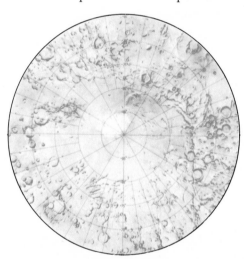

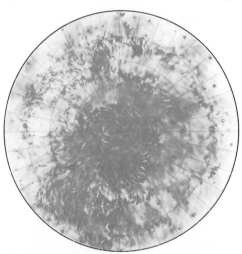

Such land shows that the ground has been eroded or worn away by something flowing past the craters. No similar evidence of erosion is to be found on the Moon, which we know has always been without water. This gives even more weight to such features on Mars as evidence of rivers some time in the past.

Besides valleys on Mars, there are some large canyons, the biggest of which is the vast Valles Marineris. This is 5,000 km long and up to 200 km wide in places, while its depth in some places measures as much as 6 km. The Grand Canyon in Arizona is a vast impressive canyon to us: yet it is only 150 km long, 2 km wide at the most and less than 2.2 km deep, and pales to insignificance beside its Martian counterpart.

The craters on Mars are numbered in their hundreds. Two observers on Earth saw craters years ago – the American astronomer E.E. Barnard in 1892, using the giant 91 cm refractor at Lick Observatory, and another American J.J. Mellish, using the even larger 1 metre refractor at Yerkes Observatory twenty-five years later – but neither published his results, probably because they would have been doubted. Not until 1975 were they seen and photographed by a spacecraft. The craters are, presumably, due to bombardment by meteorites (page 148), which would not find such resistance on Mars as on Earth, because the atmosphere is thinner. We should remember, though, that they would fall with less force, since the gravitational attraction of Mars is only 0.38 that of the Earth.

Mars also has a considerable number of volcanoes. There are four huge ones in the Tharsis region, near the Martian equator, and the largest of these is enormous, dwarfing any volcano on Earth. It is called Olympus Mons (Olympus Mountain), and is in the position that Earth observers used to call Nix Olympica (the Snow of Olympus). The base of Olympus Mons is well over 500 km across and it is about 25 km high. The Earth's highest volcano is Mauna Kea in Hawaii but its height, even if measured from its base well below the surface of the Pacific Ocean, is only 9 km. The crater at the top of Olympus Mons is 65 km in diameter. From the way volcanic craters are spread over the surface of Mars, one planetary expert has suggested that volcanic activity has not yet reached all over Mars.

What about the most exciting question of all: is there life on Mars?

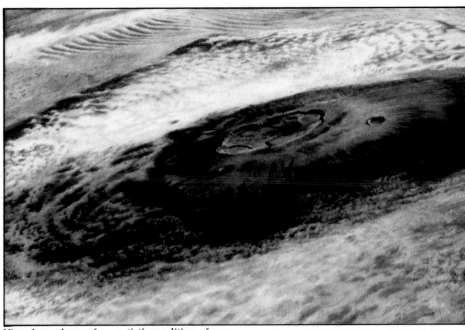

View from above of the giant Olympus Mons on Mars: an artist's rendition of a scene taken by a Viking lander.

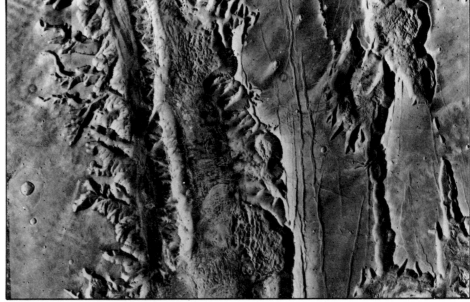

above
A close-up composite photograph showing the Valles Marineris, which is about 5,000 km long.

left
Clouds around the canyons of Noctis Labyrinthus, a high plateau region of Mars, as seen from Viking 1.

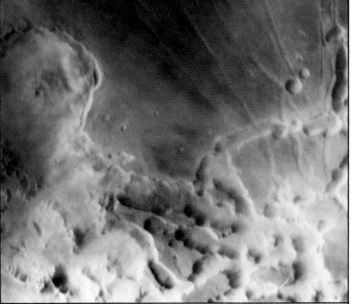

A panoramic view of the Martian surface taken in late afternoon by the Viking 1 lander. The horizon is 3 km away, the nearest large rock 8 m away from the craft.

The temperature range on Mars is not too wide to support life, nor is it too cold. At the Martian equator at midday, the temperature can rise to 10°C, which is like a not-very-warm day on Earth, but this is exceptional, and at many places on Mars it never rises above freezing (0°C), even at noon on a summer's day. When Viking 1 landed in June 1976 in the Chryse Plain at a latitude of 17°, it found the dawn temperature only −86°C, and even at midday it reached only −31°C. Some creatures or microscopic organisms could, however, survive these conditions.

Mars has a very thin atmosphere; its pressure is only one-hundredth that of our own atmosphere. What is more it is mainly carbon dioxide, although there is a little oxygen, some nitrogen and some water vapour. This too could support life.

The purpose of the Viking spacecraft which landed on Mars was to investigate whether or not there was life there, by digging up a sample of Martian earth and then testing it in miniature automatic laboratories built into the spacecraft. The results were radioed to Earth.

One laboratory looked for traces in the soil of organic compounds, that is the sort of complex chemicals remaining in soil when living creatures have existed there. This test was negative. The result could mean that there is no life on Mars or, of course, that forms of life on Mars are more efficient and able to consume all the debris of their predecessors. Another laboratory studied the soil to see if there was any sign of living organisms – examining it to detect any evidence of the chemical changes that occur when such organisms are present. The third laboratory tested for the kind of evidence left by organisms breathing. The results of these were uncertain because, although they did give some evidence which could be explained as due to organisms, their results could also be explained as purely chemical changes happening for quite other reasons. Since no organic material was found, the ambiguous results of the remaining two tests should probably be considered as negative.

Viking 2, which landed in Utopia Plain at a northern latitude of 35°, thought to be a more favourable place for life, produced similar results. Life on Mars does not therefore seem to be very likely, but until other spacecraft carrying different tests land there, no one can be absolutely certain.

above
Martian landscape taken by two cameras on the Viking 1 lander at noon in July 1976.

right
A close-up of the ground on Mars, showing Viking's collector arm displacing a rock to get a soil sample from beneath it.

MERCURY AND VENUS

The two innermost planets Mercury and Venus are always seen close to the Sun in the sky. Although these planets are our near neighbours in the Solar System their conditions are very inhospitable to life.

Venus is bright enough sometimes to be seen in daylight, but even so it is never far from the Sun in the sky. To see it you must know precisely where to look and this means using tables of positions for the Sun and Venus such as those in the *Handbook* of the British Astronomical Association. What you must *never* do is to use a pair of binoculars to sweep round the sky; it is dangerous because you may sweep the Sun into your field of view by mistake and that can blind you. A telescope with an equatorial mounting set on the right point in the sky is the only safe way of making daylight observations of Venus.

Since Mercury and Venus are closer to the Sun than the Earth, they show phases rather like the Moon. Fig. 1 shows you why this is so. When either of the planets is at greatest elongation, east or west, we can see half the illuminated disc, so in a telescope, which inverts them, they look like the Moon at first quarter when they are at greatest western elongation and as it looks at last quarter when they are at greatest eastern elongation. As they move from western elongation towards superior conjunction and from superior conjunction to greatest eastern elongation, they exhibit a gibbous phase (this is the bulgy shape between quarter and full). But we never see the equivalent of Full Moon because when they are at superior conjunction they lie beyond and behind the Sun and cannot be seen at all. We cannot usually see the planets when they are at inferior conjunction either, because their dark sides are turned towards us. However, they do show as crescents when between greatest elongation and inferior conjunction.

Galileo was the first person to see the phases of Mercury and Venus. He observed the phases of Venus late in 1610, and it was this observation which convinced him that the heliocentric theory was correct. The planets, he realized, must orbit the Sun not the Earth because only by orbiting the Sun would they show the phases. You, too, can see the phases if you use a good pair of binoculars or a telescope. It is best to observe at twilight when the Sun has gone down, or just before it has risen, when the sky is not dark enough for the planet to shine too glaringly.

Sometimes, although not often, when they are at inferior conjunction, both Mercury and Venus appear to cross the face of the Sun. Because of the tilts of their

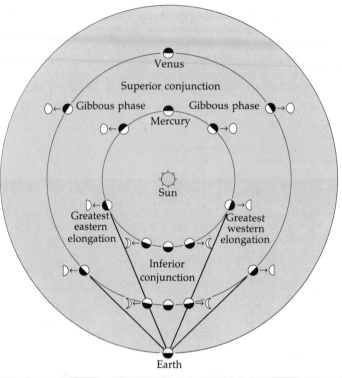

Fig. 1
The phases of Mercury and Venus as they orbit the Sun, as seen by an observer on Earth.

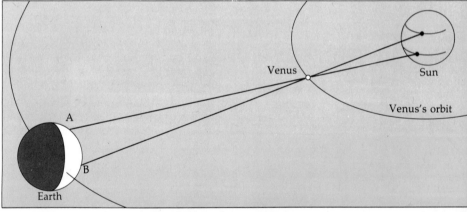

Fig. 2 below
A transit of Venus across the Sun's disc, observed from A and B on Earth. By knowing the distance AB and timing the transit, the distance from Earth to Venus and to the Sun can be obtained.

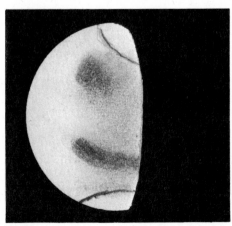
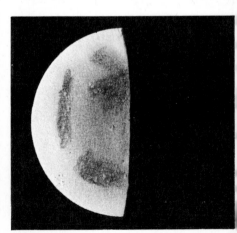

Fig. 3
Venus, observed in daylight, some detail can be seen. Drawings by amateur astronomer J. Hedley Robinson, using a 260 mm reflector, March 1980.

orbits (7° for Mercury and 3.4° for Venus) such 'transits' are rare. For Venus they occur in pairs with eight years between transits and a gap of some 105 to 120 years between pairs: the last one was in 1882 and the next will not be until 2004. Transits of Mercury are more frequent: there will be one in 1986, one in 1993 and another in 1999. In the past, transits of Venus were an important way of determining the Sun's distance. The English astronomer Edmond Halley pointed this out in 1691 and 1761 and in 1769 after Halley was dead, measurements were made. The principle is shown in Fig. 2. Timings of the transit are made from widely separated places, and from the differences and the known distance between observers (i.e. the distance AB) the distance of Venus may be found. Using the laws of planetary orbits discovered by Kepler in the seventeenth century, the distance of the Sun can be accurately calculated.

Fig. 4
Venus photographed by the Russian space probe, Venera 9.

Fig. 5 *above*
A photograph of Venus in ultraviolet light by space probe Mariner 10 in 1974. Cloud belts are shown in great detail.

Fig. 6 *right*
The cratered surface of Mercury photographed at a distance of 200,000 km from Mariner 10.

Even with the largest telescopes it is not possible to see any real detail on either Mercury or Venus. However, hazy patches can be seen on Venus (Fig. 3) which is almost the same size as the Earth, and these can help in determining the rotation of the uppermost cloud layer, for Venus is covered by a dense atmosphere extending from 35 to 65 km above the surface. The upper clouds are very cold (-50°C) but spacecraft have shown that the planet's surface (Fig. 5) is immensely hot (475° C) while the pressure of the atmosphere at ground level is 90 times that on Earth. The atmosphere is unbreathable, being mostly carbon dioxide and there are droplets of sulphuric acid which fall to the ground like rain. The atmosphere of Venus rotates in about four days but the solid planet itself rotates in a retrograde direction, the only planet to do so, once every 243 days.

Recent research makes it seem likely that the surface of Venus is fairly smooth compared with the Earth or Mars or even the Moon. The surface of Mercury on the other hand is very like the Moon. Although you cannot see details of Mercury's surface because it is always too close to the Sun for good optical observation, the Mariner 10 spacecraft has taken many close-up photographs of it. These show that it is covered with craters and that there are highlands and plains. The surface can get very hot, as high as 500°C, because Mercury is two and a half times nearer the Sun than Earth, and twice as close as Venus. But as Mercury has no atmosphere it cannot capture heat as Venus can and during Mercury's night the temperature drops to below -200°C. It rotates on its axis once every 58.65 days and takes 88 days to complete an orbit of the Sun. Venus being further away, takes longer; its year is 225 days.

Mercury and Venus are beautiful objects in the evening or morning sky and are interesting because they show phases. They are well worth a look from time to time. However, for any serious observation of Venus, you will need some experience and then guidance from an astronomical association.

Fig. 7
The phases of Venus. When Venus is full the disc is very small as Venus is close to the Sun and on the opposite side of the Sun to Earth. When Venus is close to Earth, only a portion of it is lit, so we see a thin crescent.

URANUS, NEPTUNE AND PLUTO

Uranus, Neptune and Pluto are the outermost planets of the Solar System. Only Uranus can be seen with the naked eye – the others are too dim. These cold planets take a long time to circle the Sun; Pluto, the one furthest away, takes 248 years.

The discovery of Uranus is an exciting story, for it was the first planet to be found since those observed in ancient times. In 1757 the professional musician, William Herschel from Hanover, settled in England. Ten years later he moved to Bath and became one of the leaders of the musical life of what was then a very fashionable city; he also became very keen on astronomy and in due course built his own reflecting telescopes. These were exceptionally good instruments and with them he began to survey the sky. In March 1781, while he was charting the stars in one part of the sky using a 15 cm reflector, he observed an object which seemed to have a tiny disc. Watching it on subsequent nights, he saw that it moved across the background of the fixed stars and came to the conclusion that it was a comet. This is an understandable mistake because a comet does sometimes appear as a tiny disc through a telescope (pages 138–143). However, as the months passed, it became clear that the path of this object was not the elongated orbit of a comet, but more like the orbit of a planet. Once it was realized that another planet had been discovered, there was great excitement. Herschel wanted to call it Georgium Sidus (George's Star) in honour of King George III, who was a Hanoverian too. However, international opinion wanted to use the name of a classical god or goddess as for the other planets, and Herschel was overruled. The planet was named Uranus.

Uranus has a magnitude of 5.5 at opposition, but of course it gets dimmer than this. It can be seen with the unaided eye, but looks just like an insignificant star and, in fact, no one seems to have paid any attention at all to it until after Herschel's

discovery. Its disc is very small – only 3.9 arc seconds at the most – so it is impossible to see any surface detail. Uranus appears small because it is so far away – never closer than 2,500 million km to Earth – although its actual diameter is 52,000 km or 4 times larger than the Earth's. In 1981 it will be in the constellation Libra, beginning the year near κ Librae.

Some years after Uranus had been discovered, astronomers found that it was not moving along its orbit as it should. It moved slowly, taking 84 years to orbit the Sun once, but even so, it was deviating enough to make some think that there must be the gravitational pull of another

Fig. 1
Uranus with its rings, which were discovered in 1977. They are round the equator, of the planet whose axis of rotation is tilted at more than 90°.

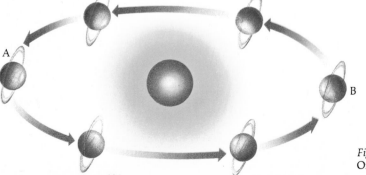

Fig. 2
Orbit of Uranus.

planet affecting its motion. Two astronomers were convinced of this – John Couch Adams in England and Urbain Le Verrier in France – and they decided to calculate where such a planet might be. This was not easy: they did not know how massive it was nor its orbit and they had to make some assumptions before they started. (Before electronic computers there was no way of quickly testing a wide variety of results.) Both worked independently, but both came up with the same answers. However, they had a difficult job in convincing other astronomers that they had succeeded in what everyone thought was an impossible task. Finally, at the Berlin Observatory in September 1846, Johann Galle and Heinrich d'Arrest saw the planet in the predicted position. It was named Neptune, had an apparent diameter of about 2.5 arc seconds, a real diameter of 49,500 km, and was so far away – some 4,308 million km when nearest to the Earth – that it took 165 years to complete an orbit. At best it has an apparent magnitude of 7.7 and in 1981 will be in Ophiuchus (close to ξ Ophiuchi).

Neptune also showed some distortions in its path, and astronomers began to seek yet another planet further out. In 1930 a careful search by Clyde Tombaugh revealed Pluto, although this was some distance from the computed position. Pluto is very small compared with Uranus and Neptune, having a diameter of only 3,000 km. Its orbit is the most eccentric in the Solar System: sometimes it comes closer to us than Neptune and it is highly inclined to the orbits of the other planets. It takes 248 years to complete one circuit of the Sun. A very difficult object to see, its magnitude is only about 14 and it is no more than 0.2 arc seconds in diameter. However, its period of rotation has been found: it is 6.39 days.

Uranus and Neptune seem to be similar in construction to Jupiter and Saturn. They each have a small solid core surrounded by vast cloudy atmospheres mainly composed of frozen or liquid hydrogen, for both are very cold, being so far from the Sun (Uranus –216°C, Neptune –228°C). Pluto is a solid body and also very cold. Uranus is unique among the planets of the Solar System in having its axis of rotation tilted over at an angle of 98°. As it orbits the Sun first one pole and then the other receives sunlight (Fig. 2); at these times (positions A and B) the equator will be the coldest part of the planet. Although no detail has been observed on Uranus, Neptune or Pluto, we do know that Uranus has rings. These were discovered in March 1977 when Uranus occulted the 8.8 magnitude star SAO 158687. The occultation ought to have been instantaneous, but instead it flickered out five times before its real occultation, which lasted half an hour. The star then reappeared and blinked five more times. This was quite unexpected and showed that Uranus does indeed have rings. This discovery emphasized again the importance of observing occultations (pages 104–107).

Fig. 3
Pluto (indicated by arrows) was discovered in 1930 at the Lowell Observatory where these two photographs were taken.

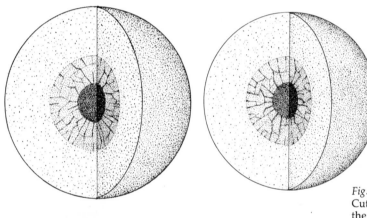
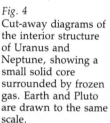

Fig. 4
Cut-away diagrams of the interior structure of Uranus and Neptune, showing a small solid core surrounded by frozen gas. Earth and Pluto are drawn to the same scale.

Fig. 5
William Herschel's 15 cm reflecting telescope on a simple altazimuth stand. With a similar telescope he discovered Uranus.

PLANETARY SATELLITES AND ASTEROIDS

Except for Mercury and Venus, all the planets have orbiting satellites. Some planetary satellites are very small, but they vary greatly in their composition and appearance. The other small bodies in the Solar System are the host of minor planets or 'asteroids' which orbit the Sun.

The two satellites of Mars – Phobos and Deimos – are hard to see because they are very small. Phobos is only 23 km across and has a magnitude of 11.6; Deimos is only 16 km in diameter and its magnitude is 12.8. They were discovered in 1877 by Asaph Hall in Washington, USA, using a 66 cm refractor, then the largest telescope in the world. Phobos orbits Mars at an average distance of 5,873 km above the surface, moving in a retrograde (west to east) direction over 7½ hours; Deimos orbits in the normal way at a distance above the surface of 20,000 km, taking 1¼ days. Both bodies are irregularly shaped and pitted with craters. The Viking spacecraft to Mars have taken close-up photographs of them.

An interesting fact about the two satellites of Mars is that although they were not discovered until 1877, the authors Jonathan Swift and Voltaire wrote about them, Swift in 1727 and Voltaire in 1750! However, this was nothing more than guesswork, made because at the time it was generally thought that as the Earth had one satellite and Jupiter had four, Mars could well be expected to possess two!

Galileo discovered the four largest satellites of Jupiter, all of which are easy to observe with a pair of binoculars. It is fascinating to watch their changing positions and their eclipses when they move into Jupiter's shadow and the movements of their own shadows across Jupiter's disc, although a telescope is needed to show these. Jupiter also has ten other moons, discovered between 1892 and 1975; they are all very dim and only one can be seen visually in a telescope, the rest have to be observed photographically. The

fourteenth satellite is unnamed and even its orbit is at present uncertain. Details of satellites I to XIV, are on page 132, they are numbered in order of discovery, but in the table are listed by increasing distance from Jupiter. The four Galilean satellites Io, Europa, Ganymede and Callisto can be readily observed by an amateur.

The Voyager spacecraft which have flown close to Jupiter have given us all sorts of details of the satellites which simply could not be

obtained by observers back on Earth. They have photographed Amalthea, but their main pictures and data have concerned the four large Galilean satellites. Amalthea is a small rocky body, but the other four satellites show considerable differences in detail. Perhaps the most exciting discovery was that Io, the innermost Galilean satellite, is volcanically active. It also has an atmosphere, while sodium vapour and hydrogen are present in clouds around its orbit

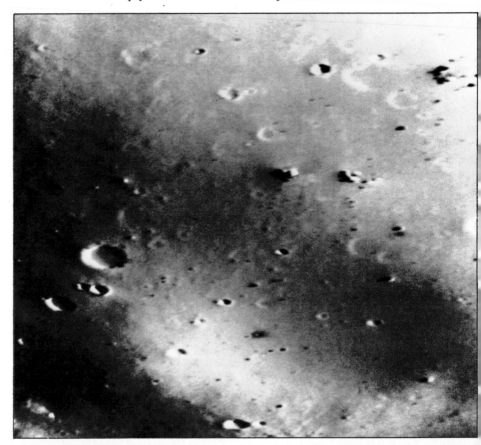

The Martian satellites, Deimos and Phobos, photographed by Viking spacecraft in 1976 and 1977.

130

and are especially concentrated near the satellite. Amalthea, Europa and Io are about the same as our Moon in density, but Europa seems to be covered with ice, probably about 100 km thick. Its surface is therefore very smooth although crossed by many thin cracks. Ganymede and Callisto are less dense than our Moon, but a little larger in diameter. Ganymede has a darkish surface and is heavily cratered; it also has some large 'faults' which give it rifts and

escarpments. Callisto is peppered with craters – indeed it may be the most cratered body in the Solar System. These Voyager observations have provided scientists with evidence about the geological history of Amalthea, Io, Europa, Ganymede and Callisto.

Saturn has sixteen or seventeen satellites, one of which, Titan, is the biggest in the Solar System – 1½ times larger than the Moon. But Titan has a very dense atmosphere

which Voyager 1 discovered to be composed mainly of nitrogen. Voyager 1 photographs show many craters on Dione, craters and wispy, white streaks on Rhea, a gigantic crater 100 km across on Mimas and an enormous trough on Tethys. Saturn has no very small satellite as has Jupiter, but all, including Titan, need a telescope to detect them; even then Hyperion and Phoebe are really too faint for anyone but the professional to examine.

Uranus, Neptune and Pluto each have one or more satellites. They are not really objects for the amateur astronomer to observe, although two of those of Uranus can be seen without too large a telescope. Their details are given on page 133.

The tables show that, except for some of Jupiter's, the satellites are all substantial bodies, never less than 200 km in diameter. Indeed, Pluto's satellite is so large compared with Pluto itself (Charon is about 1,200 km diameter, Pluto about 3,000 km) that it has been suggested that Pluto-Charon is virtually a double-planet system. Jupiter, however, has eight, possibly nine, satellites under 200 km in diameter and at least six are tiny bodies between 20 and 30 km in size. Jupiter is very massive and so has a strong gravitational pull, and some astronomers think it likely that these small satellites may, in fact, be captured asteroids.

The asteroids or minor planets are all small bodies that look starlike, hence the name 'asteroid' given them by John Herschel soon after the discovery of the first ones, although minor planets is really a more correct term for them. Their discovery is an intriguing story. In 1756 the German scientist Johann Titius stated a 'law' about the distances of the planets, but he did so only as a footnote in a book on general science that he had translated, and it might never have become well known. This law was an attempt to describe a mathematical relationship between the planets themselves and the Sun. However, in 1772, Johann Bode publicized this mathematical relationship which can be simply described as follows: take the numbers 0, 3, 6, 12 etc where each subsequent number is twice the previous one, and add 4 to each. We then get a series of numbers 4, 7, 10, 16, 28, 52, 100, 196. Now, if we take the distance of Sun to Earth as 10, then on the same scale, we have the following average distances for the planets in the same sequence: Sun to Mercury 3.9, to Venus 7.2, to Mars 15.2, to Jupiter 52, and to Saturn

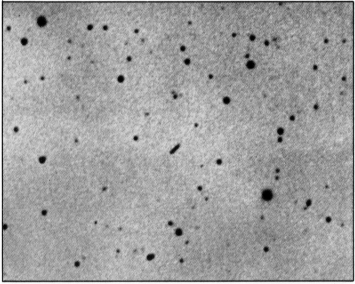

The discovery of the minor planet, Sappho, by Max Wolf, Heidelberg, 1892. Whereas all the stars appear as dots, the minor planet, which was orbiting, shows as a small line.

Jupiter's largest satellite, Ganymede: the bright spots on the surface are relatively recent impact craters.

95.4. When Uranus was discovered, its average distance on this scale came to 192. So the Titius-Bode numbers indicate approximately the position of each planet in relation to the Sun. However, many astronomers now believe that this law is purely a mathematical coincidence without any real significance. Nevertheless, notice one thing: 16 represents the distance Sun to Mars, and 52 is exactly correct for Jupiter, yet what does 28 represent? There is no planet in that position.

Astronomers found this disturbing, and in 1800 some organized themselves as 'celestial police' to track down the missing planet which they believed must be there. They scanned the ecliptic with their telescopes for almost a year without success. Then on 1 January 1801, a Sicilian astronomer Giuseppi Piazzi, who was not one of the team, discovered the first minor planet by chance while compiling a catalogue of stars. The minor planet was named Ceres and lay at an average

distance of 27.7 on the Titius-Bode scale. Its size turned out to be 1,003 km. After Piazzi's discovery other similar but smaller objects were discovered and by 1807 a total of four were known.

Since 1807, hundreds upon hundreds of minor planets have been discovered, most of them by photography, and the total for which orbits are known amounts to about 2,000. Many orbit in the gap, often known as the 'asteroid belt', between Mars and Jupiter, but there is a

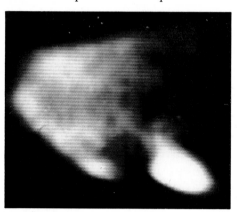

Jupiter's satellite Amalthea, as seen from Voyager 2.

No.	Name	Distance from centre of Jupiter (km)	Orbital period	Diameter (km)	Magnitude	Discovery
V	Amalthea	181,000	12 hours	150	13.0	Barnard 1892
I	Io	422,000	1.77 days	3,640	4.8	Galileo 1610
II	Europa	671,000	3.55 days	3,050	5.2	Galileo 1610
III	Ganymede	1,070,400	7.15 days	5,220	4.5	Galileo 1610
IV	Callisto	1,882,700	16.69 days	4,890	5.5	Galileo 1610
XIII	Leda	11,110,000	240 days	16	20.0	Kowal 1974
VI	Himalia	11,478,000	251 days	100	13.7	Perrine 1904
X	Lysithea	11,720,000	259 days	20	18.6	Nicholson 1938
VII	Elara	11,735,000	259½ days	30	16.0	Perrine 1905
XII	Ananke	21,243,000	1.7 years	20	18.8	Nicholson 1951
XI	Carme	22,589,000	1.9 years	20	18.1	Nicholson 1938
VIII	Pasiphae	23,487,000	2.0 years	20	18.8	Melotte 1908
IX	Sinope	23,637,000	2.1 years	20	18.3	Nicholson 1914
XIV					21	Kowal 1975

SATELLITES OF JUPITER

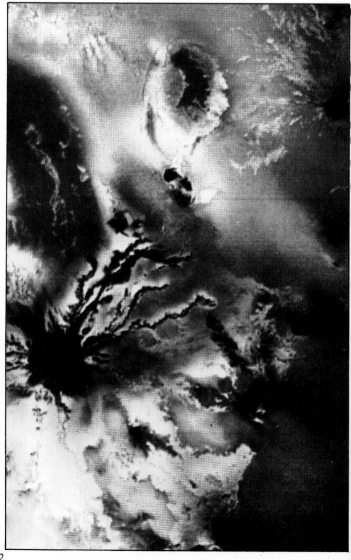

above
The first extra-terrestrial volcanic eruption was discovered in this Voyager 1 photograph of Io, when the faint plume from a volcano on the planet's limb was detected. Another volcanic eruption is visible on the terminator.

right
A close-up of Io: the dark spot with a radiating pattern near the bottom may be a volcano with lava flows.

group which goes around the Sun in the same orbit as Jupiter. They never collide with Jupiter because they all lie about 60° from it, some to the east and the others to the west: they keep their distance due to gravitational forces. They are called the Trojan group and all have Greek or Trojan names from the Trojan War.

Many minor planets have very eccentric orbits and some come close to the Earth from time to time. In 1931 one, Eros, came within about 23 million km and was used for determining the distance of the Sun, using the same basic technique as was used with transits of Venus (page 126), although the distance of Eros was measured directly, not with the Sun as background since it never transits the Sun.

There was once an idea that the minor planets were the remains of a broken-up planet, but recent research has shown that there just is not enough material in the lot of them put together to make up a full-sized planet. They are probably bits of material that condensed when the planets were formed, but into small pieces not large lumps. Those in the asteroid belt are found to orbit in groups with gaps between, almost forming an equivalent of Saturn's rings, but around the Sun instead.

You can see some of the brighter asteroids with a telescope and the annual *Handbook* of the British Astronomical Association and *The American Ephemeris and Nautical Almanac* give details of those which are observable during the year.

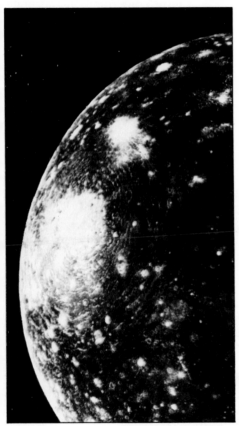

above
The outermost Galilean satellite, Callisto, has been heavily bombarded by meteors and is covered with craters.

right
Saturn and six satellites in April 1980.
1 Mimas 2 Enceladus
3 Tethys 4 Dione
5 Rhea 6 Titan

SATELLITES OF SATURN (provisional list)						
No.	Name	Distance from centre of Saturn (km)	Orbital period	Diameter (km)	Magnitude	Discovery
Outer edge of A ring		137,400				
S 28	–	138,200	?	100*	?	Voyager 1 1980
S 27	–	139,400	?	200*	?	Voyager 1 1980
F ring		140,600				
S 26	–	141,700	?	250*	?	Voyager 1 1980
G ring		150,000				
S 3	–	151,400	?	200*	?	Voyager 1 1980
S 1	–	151,450	?	140*	?	Voyager 1 1980
X	Janus	168,700	18 hours	200	14	Dollfus 1966
I	Mimas	185,500	22½ hours	500	12.1	Herschel 1789
II	Enceladus	238,000	1.4 days	600	11.8	Herschel 1789
S 13	–	289,600	?	?	?	Voyager 1 1980
III	Tethys	294,700	1.9 days	1,040	10.3	Cassini 1684
S 6	–	377,400	?	80*	?	Voyager 1 1980
IV	Dione	377,400	2.7 days	820	10.4	Cassini 1684
V	Rhea	527,000	4.5 days	1,580	9.8	Cassini 1672
VI	Titan	1,222,000	15.9 days	5,800	8.4	Huygens 1655
VII	Hyperion	1,481,000	21.3 days	500	14.2	Bond 1848
VIII	Iapetus	3,560,000	79.3 days	1,600	11.0	Cassini 1671
IX	Phoebe	12,930,000	1½ years	200	16.5	Pickering 1898
*approximate						

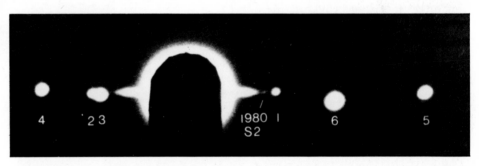

Uranus and three of its five satellites, photographed by the Lick Observatory.

SATELLITES OF URANUS, NEPTUNE AND PLUTO						
No.	Name	Distance from parent planet (km)	Orbital period	Diameter (km)	Magnitude	Discovery
Uranus						
V	Miranda	130,400	1.4 days	300	16.5	Kuiper 1948
I	Ariel	191,700	2.5 days	800	14.4	Lassell 1851
II	Umbriel	267,100	4.1 days	600	15.3	Lassell 1851
III	Titania	438,300	8.7 days	1,100	14.0	Herschel 1787
IV	Oberon	586,200	13.5 days	1,000	14.2	Herschel 1787
Neptune						
I	Triton	355,200	5.9 days	3,700	13.5	Lassell 1846
II	Nereid	5,562,000	360 days	300	18.7	Kuiper 1949
Pluto						
	Charon	17,000*	6.4 days	1,200*	15 to 16	Christy 1978
* means that the data is provisional						
Uranus, Neptune and Pluto each have one or more satellites. They are not really objects for the amateur astronomer to observe, although two of Uranus's can be seen without too large a telescope.						

THE EARTH AS A PLANET

When astronomers realized that the Earth was not fixed at the centre of the universe, but orbited round the Sun, they saw that it must be a planet. It resembled the other planets which orbited the Sun, obeying the same laws of motion.

As a planet, Earth is not very different from Mercury, Venus and Mars. It is a solid body, approximately spherical in shape. Its surface features are very slight compared with the size of the planet. Mountains and canyons and the depths of the oceans appear huge to us, but if a beach ball was taken to represent the Earth, the height of Mount Everest would only be one quarter of a tenth of a millimetre. If the beach ball was covered with a sheet of air mail writing paper, that would represent the entire thickness of Earth's outer layer, from the bottom of the deepest ocean to the top of Everest. So the Earth is really a very smooth planet.

Photographs from space show the vast amount of cloud covering the Earth. The atmosphere is thickest close to the Earth's surface and becomes progressively thinner, extending in a very rarified form up to some 2,000 km above the surface.

The uppermost parts of the atmosphere absorb the gamma-rays, X-rays and short ultraviolet radiation from the Sun and from space. A little ultraviolet radiation does penetrate the atmosphere and that is why people get suntanned; the skin manufactures a colouring substance (melanin) as a protection against the harmful ultraviolet rays.

Astronomers gradually came to accept the idea that the Earth was a planet orbiting the Sun. After Newton's theory of gravitation, which explained mathematically the movements of the Solar System, had been published in 1687, they felt certain it was true. But how could it be proved? Astronomers puzzled

over this for a long time, but proof did not come until 1726, almost forty years after Newton's theory and more than 180 years after Copernicus had suggested that the Earth was a planet. The observations were made by James Bradley and William Molyneux in Kew near London. They involved some very delicate measurements which are very difficult for an amateur astronomer to repeat, requiring special equipment.

Bradley and Molyneux had not set out to measure the Earth's motion in space, but to determine the distance of some nearer stars. They knew the measurements would have to be very accurate and therefore used a telescope of long focal length.

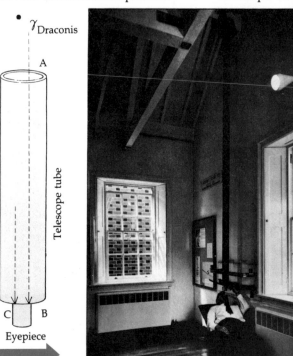

Fig. 1
Diagram of Bradley's experiment to prove the orbital motion of the Earth. Light from γ Draconis enters the telescope at A; if the Earth were stationary, the light would exit at B, but in fact it exits at C. Bradley's zenith telescope (*left*), with which he observed.

Fig. 2.
Diagram to explain stellar aberration. The direction in which the rain is seen to fall by a moving observer.

Fig. 3 opposite
The Earth photographed from space by Apollo 17, showing heavy cloud cover over the southern hemisphere.

Although this had a very narrow field of view, enabling them to see only a small area of the sky at any one time, it meant that any apparent shift of a star across the background of more distant stars would be easily visible. However, there was a problem: a long telescope tube would bend enough to spoil their very delicate measurements. They therefore chose to measure the distance of a close star, which appeared nearly overhead at Kew – the star γ Draconis: the tube would bend less because it was almost vertical and under less strain.

A change was observed in the position of γ Draconis – a total change of 80 arc seconds – but it was not the sort of change that should have happened if the movement was due to the star's distance. It was not a shift caused by parallax (pages 48–51). Bradley puzzled for two years over what could cause this shift. In 1728 he hit on the answer: the shift was due to the Earth's motion in space. This is illustrated in Fig. 1. Starlight was coming through space to Bradley's telescope and entering the tube at A. Bradley knew that light travels at a certain speed because, in 1675, the Danish astronomer, Ole Römer, had shown how the velocity of light affected the timing of eclipses of Jupiter's satellites (page 178). So Bradley realized that the light would take a certain time to pass down the tube to the eyepiece. It would not take long – about 100 millionth of a second – but while this was happening the Earth had moved through space in its orbit. The Earth's motion would move the telescope tube sideways so that the light ray would come out at C instead of at B. The distance C to B was small – only a fraction of a millimetre – but it was big enough to be detected. Thus Bradley proved the Earth was moving in space and, indeed, was able to measure the speed. Alternatively, working out the Earth's velocity from the size of the Earth's orbit and the length of the year, his measurements could give a new value for the velocity of light.

Although Bradley's observation cannot be successfully repeated without very special equipment, you can see the principle for yourself. Looking again at Fig. 1, you will see that the change, or 'aberration of starlight' as it is called, moved the light from B to C. This is the distance Bradley measured.

The Earth's shape is not exactly a sphere but an 'oblate ellipsoid'; in other words, it bulges at the equator. This bulge is not as great as Jupiter's, but it does mean that the diameter through the equator (12,756 km) is greater than the polar diameter (12,714 km) by 0.3% (the difference for Jupiter is 6.4%). Artificial satellites in orbit round the Earth have also shown that there is a very slight bulge at the north pole. Thus the Earth has sometimes been described as 'pear-shaped', but this is really an exaggeration as photographs of the Earth from space show.

Fig. 4
Tiros, a weather satellite, which is surrounded by solar cells and carries two camera lenses and infrared equipment to observe from space climatic conditions on Earth.

NAVIGATION ON EARTH

Finding a route across the oceans was a hazard for mariners until it became possible, almost 250 years ago, to determine longitude at sea with certainty. Both longitude and the tides depend on the fact that the Earth is a rotating planet with the Moon orbiting round it.

As we saw earlier in the book (pages 8–9), positions are given by co-ordinates. In the sky we use right ascension and declination to fix star positions; on Earth we use their equivalent, known as latitude and longitude. The poles are at the points where the knitting needle sticks out of the ball, and the equator is the 'great circle' mid-way between them.

(A 'great circle' is a specific term referring to a circle drawn round the surface of a ball or sphere with a diameter equal to that of the ball or sphere.) Fig. 1 shows that latitude runs north or south of the equator: it is measured in degrees and fractions of a degree (usually arc minutes and even arc seconds).

It is not difficult for a mariner to obtain his latitude at sea. All he has to do is to measure the altitude of the midday Sun or the altitude of a star when it is due south (Fig. 2). This does not necessarily mean having a clock because at midday the Sun is at its highest in the sky, and so is any star when it is due south – or due north if the ship is sailing in the southern hemisphere. Once the altitude is measured, the navigator looks up the declination of the Sun or the star, in special nautical tables. Then, as Fig. 2 shows, he can work out the latitude of the ship (90° − altitude of star + declination of star). You can prove this by the following equation:

$$l = 90 - [90 - (\delta - l)] + \delta$$
$$= 90 - 90 - \delta + l + \delta = l$$

Mariners had known how to work out latitude in this way since ancient times, but they took care not to look directly at the Sun. You could make a simple 'back-staff' for measuring the Sun's altitude (Fig. 4). With this device the Sun casts a sharp shadow which is lined up with the horizon – a particularly ingenious and safe way of taking noonday altitudes.

Finding longitude is a quite different matter: it is much more difficult and was impossible to do accurately in early times. Ships had, therefore, to hug the coasts or risk being lost for months once they had moved out of sight of land. At best they could only guess where they were from calculating how far they had sailed.

The reason for this difficulty is shown in Fig. 3. When the Sun, which rises in the east, is highest in the sky, it is noon at A, but it is not noon at B; from B it is only beginning to rise on a summer morning. As the Earth rotates so the Sun will begin to set when viewed from A, when it is noon at B. So it is clear that local noon occurs at

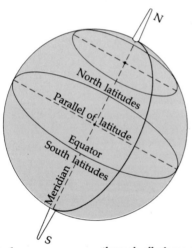

Fig. 1
Drawing of the Earth showing the equator, a parallel of latitude (a line, parallel to the equator, going through all places of the same latitude), a small circle and a meridian (a line stretching from north to south pole).

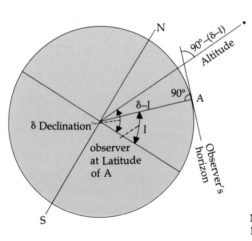

Fig. 2
Diagram to prove that latitude =
90° − altitude
+ declination of a star.

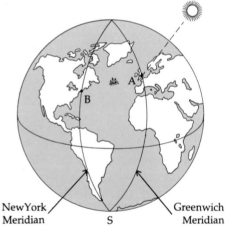

Fig. 3
Local noon occurs at different times at different places on the Earth's surface. While it is noon at A, the Sun is just rising at B.

Fig. 4
The back-staff: the shadow vane casts a shadow from the Sun onto the horizon vane. Align the shadow with the horizon seen through one of the two holes in the horizon vane. Then, looking through the sight vane, move it until you see the horizon at the top of the hole in the horizon vane. Read off the angles of the shadow vane and sight vane which when added together will give you the altitude of the Sun. The latitude can then be determined.

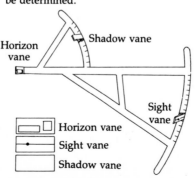

Horizon vane
Sight vane
Shadow vane

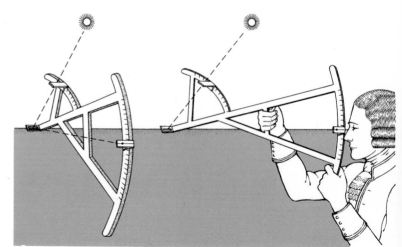

different times at different places on the Earth's surface.

The Sun moves 15° across the sky every hour (because it covers 360° in 24 hours, and 360 ÷ 24 = 15). So if we divide up the Earth into 180° longitude west and 180° longitude east of Greenwich we shall cover the whole globe. If, when it is noon at B, we know how long it is since the Sun was at noon at A, then we know the longitude of B from A. Before the invention of radio or even of accurate clocks or chronometers, finding the time difference between A and B was very difficult. In the seventeenth century, when France and England were becoming great maritime powers, both countries tried to tackle this problem by using the Moon's position among the stars as a timekeeper. The basic idea, in fact, was to use the Moon as a clock-hand and the stars as a clock-dial. If a mariner could measure how far the Moon was from certain bright or 'clock' stars, then by consulting tables of the Moon's position in the sky at different times measured with respect to particular stars, he could

determine the time at A. He could compare this time with his local time at B determined from Sun or stars, and so calculate the difference. This difference gave him his longitude.

To achieve the accuracy required for finding a position at sea to within a few kilometres, both the positions of the stars and the positions of the Moon had to be known more precisely than they were at this time. New observations had to be made and, as a result, King Louis XIV of France set up the Paris Observatory in 1667, and King Charles II established the Greenwich Observatory in 1675. The appropriate observations were made and tables were compiled, but, by the time they were ready, John Harrison had invented the marine chronometer, the first clock capable of keeping accurate time at sea. This was in 1762, when his fourth marine timekeeper had an error of no more than 5 seconds after a voyage from England to Jamaica, equivalent to an error of only 1¼ arc minutes of longitude or 2.2 km. Today the method of sighting Moon and stars is

a useful standby but, of course, radio and electronic detection methods have superseded the old astronomical system of navigation.

The tides are important to mariners coming in to berth or setting off on a voyage. They change each day, but why do they do so, and by how much? At the seaside, the tides can be observed and the interval between one high tide and the next can be timed. Provided there are not too many local irregularities in the coastline or unusual local currents, the interval should be about 12 hours 25 minutes. This period is half the time it takes for the Moon to complete a circuit of the Earth: it is the time from one moonrise to the next. This correlation, then, shows us that the Moon and the tides are intimately connected.

The truth is that the Moon is our main tide-raising force, although the Sun also has an influence. Fig. 6 explains this: it shows how the Moon pulls the tides directly under it, and by causing a lowering at the poles, effects a bulge on the opposite side of the Earth as well.

Fig. 5
Harrison's chronometer no. 4 which allowed accurate time-keeping at sea and solved the problem of determining longitude; it could be held in the hand.

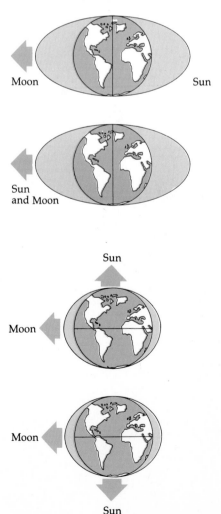

Fig. 6 right
Two drawings showing that spring tides occur when the Sun and Moon are pulling in opposite directions or in the same direction, which causes the greatest tide.

Fig. 7 above
Two drawings showing that neap tides (the smallest)

occur when the Sun and Moon are pulling at right angles to one another.

CHAPTER 5
COMETS AND METEORS

Comets and meteors are not permanent features of the night sky. Comets appear for a few weeks or months, while meteors are seen for about a second or even less. Before the nature of comets was understood, these brilliant objects were thought to be evil omens.

In the time of the early Greeks, comets and meteors were considered as 'things of the upper air', which is the origin of the word 'meteor'. The Greeks believed the heavens were eternal and unchanging; in consequence anything which appeared only for a time and then vanished could not be celestial. The clouds, the wind and the rain came and went, and so, they thought, did comets and meteors. They were wrong about comets but right, to some extent, about meteors as will be seen (pages 146–147).

Of the two, comets are the more spectacular, with their bright heads and long tails stretching out far into

space, visible every night in the sky for perhaps weeks on end. The most famous of all comets is Halley's (pages 144–145). In early times Halley's and all other comets were looked on with dread: this was because people believed that the heavens foretold the future, and a comet became an evil omen. There was, however, a 'scientific' reason too. With their long, bright, somewhat fuzzy tails and their

shining heads, they looked like flames of hot vapours. People therefore expected them to be followed by hot dry conditions and, in days before efficient hygiene and public health arrangements, such conditions often ended in a plague or epidemic of some kind.

In November 1577 a comet appeared which caused a lot of interest because of its great brightness and extremely long tail.

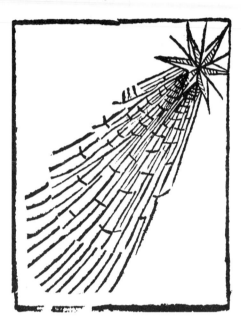

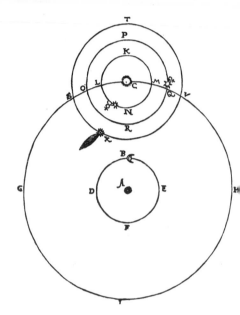

The drawing of a comet from the *Nuremberg Chronicle*, 1493, which gave illustrations of many comets, but they were all stylized like this one.

Tycho Brahe's planetary system, showing the comet of 1577 at X, beyond the sphere of the Moon.

From Tycho Brahe's *De Mundo Aetherei Recentioribus Phaenomensis*, 1588.

Comet Arend-Roland. This shows an unusual feature, a spike of material stretching from the comet's head towards the Sun.

The circumpolar stars round the north celestial pole taken on a time exposure. The line is a meteor, which varies in brightness along its path.

Pamphlets about it, and especially about what its arrival heralded, flooded the cities of Western Europe. One of those to see it was Tycho Brahe, who carefully observed its position with his accurate instruments from November to January 1578, when it became so dim and small as to be hardly recognizable. He noticed that its tail always pointed away from the Sun and, casting aside old theories about cometary tails, he suggested that they were caused by sunlight streaming through a comet's head and out into space behind. Next, after the comet's disappearance, Brahe collated observations made by other astronomers, and notably those of Thomas Digges in England. When he studied them he found that together they showed that the comet had no parallax (pages 48–49).

The fact that the comet had no parallax did not, of course, mean that the comet was an infinite distance away, as Brahe realized. After all, a star's parallax could not be measured at that time either. But what this did mean was that the comet was further off than a body which did have a measurable parallax, like the Moon. This was a tremendously important discovery, because the old idea that comets were a phenomenon occurring in the upper air was proved to be wrong. According to old beliefs the upper air extended from above the ground as far as the Moon but no further. But if the comet were further away than the Moon, it must be a truly celestial body, not a meteorological one. Knowledge of precisely what a comet was had to wait until more modern times, although even now there remain some unsolved problems.

Meteors last for so short a time and are so much less spectacular than comets that they have never had such a popular appeal, nor have they caused panic or fear to anywhere near the same degree. Usually meteors fall singly but sometimes they appear as showers. Then literally hundreds, or even thousands, of meteors are seen per hour flashing through the sky. As meteors are in the upper air and so close to the Earth, when observed, they can only be seen from certain areas, not from all over the night side of the Earth, as with a comet.

above
The brilliant comet of 1811 seen over Paris.

From Paul Lacroix's *Directoire, Consulat et Empire*, Paris, 1884.

below
Two photographs of Morehouse's Comet,

1908, showing changes in the tail.

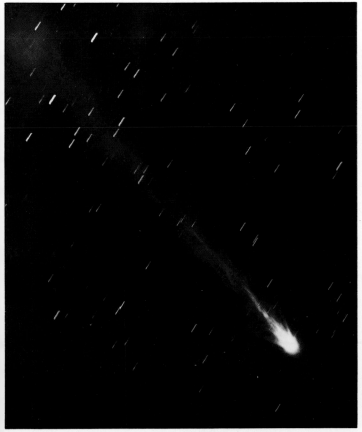

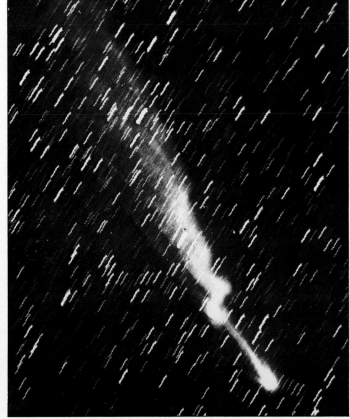

COMETS IN SPACE

Comets travel round the Sun in very long elliptical orbits. As a comet nears the Sun its appearance can become spectacular, with a bright head and a tail streaming millions of kilometres into space.

In early times astronomers concentrated on the shape of a comet's tail and classified various types as 'short and pointed', a 'burning torch' or a 'horse's mane'. Those which appeared with little or no tail were likened to a 'fleece surrounded by nebulosity', and those with what seemed like a spike at the front were referred to as 'bearded'. Although these are not scientific descriptions, they are very graphic ones and help us understand what a comet looks like. Unfortunately, bright comets visible to the unaided eye are rare; and the interval

between one bright one and the next may be many years.

A comet seems to have two main parts – a head and a tail. A closer examination of the head will show that it has a very bright central region or 'nucleus', which is only 10 km or so across, and a larger, less bright and cloudy surrounding patch known as the 'coma' or hairy portion (Fig. 1). A bright comet may or may not have a spike, but most probably will not. The comet's tail may extend millions of kilometres into space. It is never still and often changes shape, always pointing away from the Sun and sometimes quite noticeably curved in shape.

There are two main theories about comets. One, the 'dirty snowball' theory, is perhaps the more widely accepted. According to this, a comet's nucleus is believed to be rock covered with vast amounts of frozen gases. The coma comes into existence when the comet is near enough to the Sun for the Sun's radiation to vaporize some of the frozen gases. The alternative theory claims that a comet is a vast cloud of

particles of dust and frozen gases moving around the Sun, and explains very well some events in the life of a comet. Whichever theory is correct, observations made from Skylab, the orbiting space observatory, show that the coma of a comet is surrounded by a huge cloud of hydrogen shining with ultraviolet light which is invisible from Earth.

A comet is not a massive body. Its mass can be calculated from the way it moves around the Sun, and although comets vary in size, they never seem to exceed a millionth of the mass of the Moon. This means that no single comet can have any noticeable effect on the orbits or behaviour of other members of the Solar System. However we do know that Jupiter and Saturn have often attracted comets and changed their paths in space.

Comets orbit the Sun in very long narrow paths – in other words in orbits of high eccentricity (Fig. 2), far more so than any planetary orbit. Even Pluto's eccentric orbit pales into insignificance compared with a comet which, when in orbit close to the

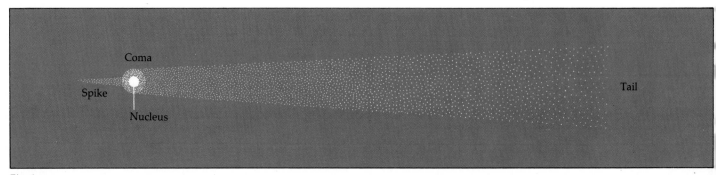

Fig. 1
The constituent parts of a comet.

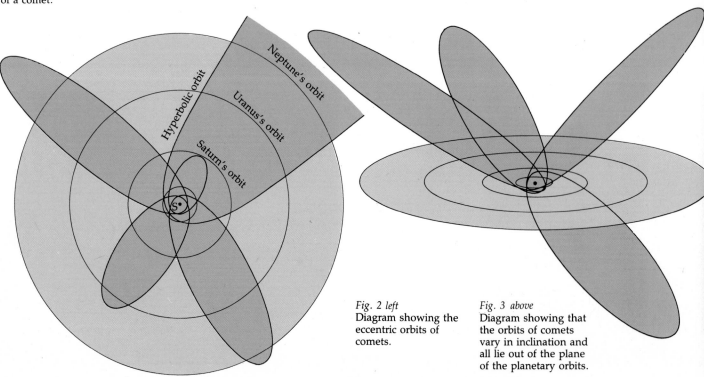

Fig. 2 left
Diagram showing the eccentric orbits of comets.

Fig. 3 above
Diagram showing that the orbits of comets vary in inclination and all lie out of the plane of the planetary orbits.

Sun, may come within less than a million kilometres, whereas at the other end of the orbit, will be at a distance of thousands of millions of kilometres from the Sun. Fig. 2 shows the orbits of several different comets whose periodic returns are well known and their very elongated shape is clearly illustrated: all except one of those shown have periods of return of less than 200 years, although some comets are known whose calculated periods of return lie between 1,000 and 10,000 years. A comet can be much disturbed when it passes close to Jupiter or Saturn and may even be thrown into a 'hyperbolic' orbit, so that it moves right out of the Solar System.

Another thing about cometary orbits is that they are all tilted noticeably out of the plane of the Solar System in which the orbits of the planets lie. Indeed some of them are so inclined that their orbits are turned over (Fig. 3) so that it looks as though they travel in a backwards or retrograde direction: Halley's comet is one of these. Comets are named after the persons who discovered

them or who have made extensive calculations of their orbits and they also have numbers and letters attached to them. P/Halley signifies that the comet was discovered to be periodic by Halley (the P stands for periodic), who calculated its orbit. While Comet West 1975 n means that the comet was discovered by West in 1975, the letter 'n' denoting the fact that it was the fourteenth to be discovered that year. The number and letter change after the comet has passed perihelion (closest approach to the Sun); as Comet West reached perihelion in February 1976, it became Comet West 1976 VI because it was the sixth comet to reach perihelion in that year.

Perihelion passage is important because it is only when close to perihelion that a comet becomes visible, even in a telescope. This is due to the Sun's radiation vaporizing some of the frozen gases which sets them glowing. As the comet comes closer to the Sun, so the Sun's effect increases, becoming four times as strong when the comet is twice as near. The closer the comet comes to

perihelion, the greater the light and other radiation emitted, and the larger the comet's tail. Sometimes a comet does not 'grow' a tail, either because at its perihelion approach it is still too far away for this to happen, or because the amount of spare gaseous material is insufficient.

Most comets do have a tail – usually two tails, in fact. One is composed of glowing cometary gas ionized (electrified) by the stream of particles continually shot out from the Sun, known as the 'solar wind' (pages 156–159). This tail is pushed away by the solar wind. The other is a tail of ionized gas particles which are driven away by the power of the light and other electromagnetic radiation coming from the Sun. This tail is often bent, echoing something of the comet's changing path which becomes more sharply curved as the comet approaches perihelion. It shines by reflected sunlight. On rare occasions, when a comet does come very close to the Sun – a 'Sun-grazing comet' – the tail is large, long and straight because the gases are pushed away with great velocity.

Fig. 4
Comet West
discovered late in 1975

by Richard West at the
European Southern
Observatory.

Fig. 5
Comet Ikeya-Seki in
1975.

Fig. 6
A comet with two tails:
Comet Bennett in 1969.

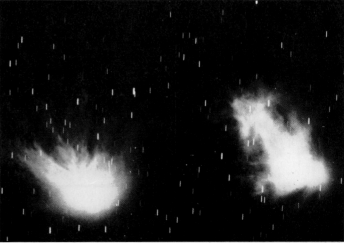

Fig. 7
Comet Humason in
1962. A strange-

looking comet with an
irregular coma: on 6
Aug (left) it had a

number of tails which
had almost disappeared
by 8 Aug (right).

THE APPEARANCE AND DISCOVERY OF COMETS

Many amateur astronomers have discovered comets. Although sometimes there is an element of luck in identifying one, it usually requires great perseverance and a thorough knowledge of the skies.

Today, it is unlikely that a bright comet will suddenly arrive in the sky complete with bright coma and long tail. Careful observers who spend some of their time watching out for comets in their early stages of development, when the coma is just beginning to glow, will already have detected any new comet with their telescopes, and followed its gradual growth into an impressive object: it will be expected. It may not be visible from both hemispheres, depending on the angle of its orbit to the plane of the Solar System.

There are times when a telescopic comet shows promise of becoming a great spectacle, but it turns out to be a disappointment. Such a comet was Kohoutek 1973 f, discovered by Lubos Kohoutek at Hamburg Observatory. A number of photographs were taken of what was then a dim comet – it was some 770 million km from the Sun – and an orbit calculated for it. The orbit showed that the comet should reach perihelion about December and pass within 21 million km of the Sun, so it was expected to be bright. Yet, in the event, though it did become visible to the naked eye, it never reached a brightness equal to Venus, as had been hoped. However, three astronauts in the Skylab orbiting observatory were able to study it during the entire period of its perihelion approach, as Earth-based observers could not because of the closeness of the Sun, and it was from here that they detected the hydrogen cloud round the coma. (Such clouds had been detected from other spacecraft for two other comets.) Comet Kohoutek also had a spike at the front; this pointed directly towards the Sun and was composed of particles about 1 mm across, larger than the particles which formed the comet's tail.

A comet may have a tail which cannot be seen. This can happen when its angle of approach to the Sun and the angle from which we on Earth view it are such that we see the comet 'head-on' (Fig. 1). On the other hand, the comet of 1843 had what must be the longest tail in recorded history. It stretched for some 320 million km into space, or more than half the distance between the Earth and Jupiter, and appeared perfectly straight, lying across half the entire sky. But a comet's tail is an insubstantial thing, and when, in 1861, the Earth passed through the tail of Tebbutt's comet no effects of any importance were noticed. Surprisingly enough, a comet's tail may go ahead of the comet some time before or after perihelion (this depends on whether the comet is moving in the normal anti-clockwise direction when viewed 'from above', or in a clockwise, or retrograde, direction), because of the Sun's

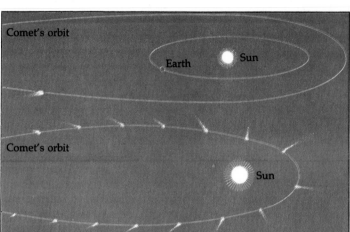

Comet's orbit

Earth   Sun

Comet's orbit

Sun

Fig. 1
Diagram to show how a comet may approach the Earth at such an angle that its tail cannot be seen.

Fig. 2
The path of a comet round the Sun showing how the comet's tail always points away from the Sun.

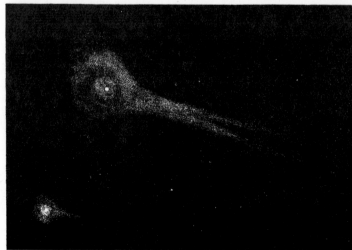

Fig. 3 above
Comet Alcock, 1959, had a very bright head and coma with a wispy tail.

Fig. 4 left
Biela's comet was discovered in 1826 and reappeared in 1845 split in two (*above*). It was the first comet to be observed which broke up between its first appearance and return. Amedée Guillemin's *Le Ciel*, Paris, 1870.

action on the gases coming away from the coma (Fig. 2).

Comets have been known to break into pieces, and the most notable of these was Comet Biela. This was a short periodic comet discovered in 1826 which orbited the Sun once every 6¾ years. It was missed on one return, but when it came back in 1845, it had split into two pieces. Then it continued to orbit in this way for at least one more circuit, but after its 1852 appearance it has never been seen again. Later, in 1872, when it should, theoretically, have appeared again, it was replaced by a great shower of meteors (page 146). Recently the nucleus of Comet West broke into at least four pieces.

Studies with a spectroscope of the light from comets show that they contain atoms grouped together to form molecules and many compounds containing hydrogen and carbon, such as hydrogen cyanide (HCN) and methyl cyanide (CH_3CN); Comet Kohoutek, and possibly others, also contain water (H_2O). Comets are therefore cool objects, as would be expected if they were largely composed of frozen gases. Each time they orbit and come to perihelion, streaming out a tail, some of their material is used up and, since some is usually deposited along their orbits as well, comets may, like Beila's comet, disappear after a number of returns. Indeed, no less than 11 periodic comets observed this century have failed to reappear. Not all these disappearances may be due to the comets wearing away or breaking up – Jupiter or Saturn may have sent some on paths taking them out of the Solar System, or at least out of a short-period orbit; but the number is significant.

Discovering a comet is a wonderful thing. Some observers have been lucky: for instance, Lubos Kohoutek was photographing the stars for quite another reason when he found the comet which has his name, but many comet searchers like George Alcock, who has discovered four, as well as some novae, have done so with knowledge and perseverance, sweeping given areas of the sky regularly, night after night. Knowledge of the night sky takes time to acquire, because it is not just a matter of knowing the constellations, as most amateurs do, but knowing all the stars in the star-fields normally observed through a powerful pair of binoculars. The other skill is an ability to recognize an object which seems to have a disc; and then continue to observe it on subsequent nights. If it moves, it is probably a comet or, possibly, an asteroid. Further observations of its path will help decide which it is. Incidentally, it was to help him in his comet-hunting that the French astronomer, Charles Messier, compiled his catalogue of nebulae (page 166–167) and published it in 1774. He was not really interested in the nebulous objects he saw in space through his telescope, but wanted to make sure he did not confuse them with comets in early stages of their approach to perihelion.

Each year a number of telescopic comets are scheduled to return and it is worth having a look for these, once you have learned to find your way about the sky. The *Handbook* of the British Astronomical Association and *The American Ephemeris and Nautical Almanac* always list details of them for the current year.

Fig. 5
The great comet of 1843 passing over Paris. It passed close to the Sun at perihelion, thereby showing a very long straight tail. From Camille Flammarion's *Astronomie Populaire*, Paris, 1881.

Fig. 6 *above*
Comet Kohoutek, 1973, photographed at the Hale Observatories.

Fig. 7 *right*
The same comet photographed from Skylab showing the comet surrounded by a cloud of hydrogen gas which could not be seen from Earth.

HALLEY'S COMET

Halley's Comet is the most famous of them all. It was the first to have its return predicted – by the man after whom it was named. Its appearances have been traced further back in history than those of any comet. It is due to return in 1986.

The idea that a comet could return and would do so on a specific date was put forward by Edmond Halley, who, in 1720, became Britain's second Astronomer Royal. Halley (whose name in his own day seems to have been pronounced 'Hawley') was a friend of Isaac Newton, and it was he who persuaded Newton to write a book on his (Newton's) new theory of gravitation. Halley saw to the whole business of having the book printed and published; thus it was due to him that Newton's famous *Principia* saw the light of day. Newton showed why the planets orbit the Sun in ellipses, and changed the whole face of astronomy. It was Halley's intimate knowledge of Newton's ideas which led him to consider the idea that comets, too, orbited the Sun.

Before Halley's time, there had been some argument about how comets moved in space. This was a difficult subject because comets were only seen for a short time in the sky and only a part of their paths could be charted. The great astronomer Hevelius thought they travelled in straight lines and many agreed with him. When the *Principia* came out in 1687, it contained nothing definite about cometary paths, although Newton clearly favoured a parabola (Fig. 1). If observations far out into space away from the Sun had been available, the matter would have been solved, and a definite choice between one curve in preference to another could have been made. Such evidence as there was in the seventeenth century meant that paths could not be traced further out than A or B on the diagram.

Halley discovered that the comets which had appeared in 1682, 1607 and 1531 had been observed in positions in the sky which seemed to indicate that they were all re-appearances of the same comet. If this were so, then the comet must have been moving in an elliptical orbit; when he calculated this elliptical orbit, Halley found it fitted well. He also tried a parabolic orbit for each appearance and noted some very small differences for which his elliptical orbit seemed to account. In the end he took his courage in both hands and, on the basis of an elliptical orbit, worked out when the comet should return. He followed this with a public announcement. The return date he predicted was Christmas 1758, which allowed for a delay caused by the attraction of both Jupiter and Saturn. Since he did not expect to be alive in 1758 (he would have been 102), he appealed to a

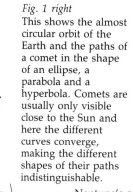

Fig. 1 right
This shows the almost circular orbit of the Earth and the paths of a comet in the shape of an ellipse, a parabola and a hyperbola. Comets are usually only visible close to the Sun and here the different curves converge, making the different shapes of their paths indistinguishable.

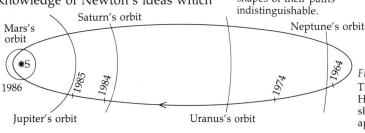

Fig. 2 left
The elliptical path of Halley's Comet showing its perihelion approach for 1986.

Fig. 3 below
Halley's Comet's path through the stars to its perihelion approach in 1986.

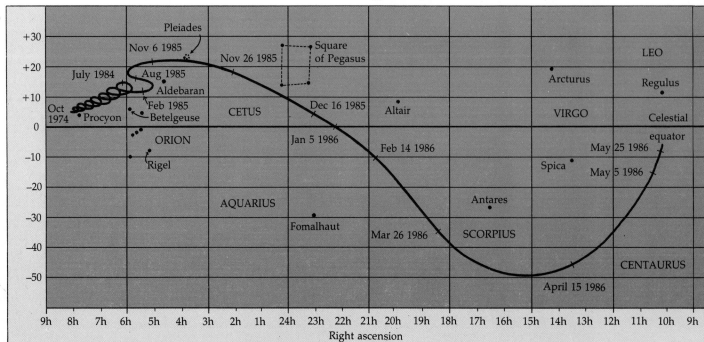

subsequent generation of astronomers to watch out for it, asking them '. . . to acknowledge that this [the predicted return] was first observed by an Englishman'. In 1758 the comet returned on Christmas Night, delayed a little more than he had expected. Halley's achievement was acknowledged by naming the comet after him.

The most important thing about Halley's successful prediction was not that it told everyone where to look, but that it was an independent proof of the correctness of Newton's theory of gravitation. After the *Principia* had been published there were still scientists who remained unconvinced, but Halley showed that the theory could be used to predict the return of a comet, a body which had hitherto been an object of mystery, not of scientific study.

Once Halley's Comet was recognized as having an elliptical orbit, which was completed once every 76 years, astronomers and historians began to look back in early records to see whether they could find evidence of its appearances. Since it is the only really bright short-period comet, plenty of reports of sightings have been found. The oldest surviving accounts come from China, where astronomical observation was developed at a very early date. They have an observation recorded in 467 BC which may have been of Halley's Comet, but their observation of 240 BC leaves no doubt. The next appearance is missing, that of 163 BC doubtful, but from 87 BC every arrival has been recorded. The comet appeared in 1066, some seven months before the Battle of Hastings, and is depicted on the Bayeux Tapestry, and in 1910 it arrived one month before the death of King Edward VII. This was its last appearance, but those elderly people still alive who saw it when they were children often confuse it with another much brighter comet which also appeared in the same year.

Halley's Comet is to appear again in 1986. At present it is well on its way and Figs. 2 and 3 show its orbit with dates indicating its position at various times and a chart of where it will be in the sky when close to us. Charts similar to Figs. 2 and 3, marking in the comet's changing position, can be made nearer the time, while astronomers will be watching the area north of Orion, hoping to detect Halley's Comet when it is still a tiny telescopic object so that they can follow its complete development. The ellipses early on in its path are due to the slow motion of the comet compared with the quicker orbiting of the Earth: later the comet moves more quickly, its speed increasing all the way to perihelion.

It was hoped that the United States National Aeronautics and Space Administration would be launching a spacecraft to make a rendezvous with Comet Halley in 1985–86, but this does not now seem likely, and we may have to be content with a fly-by. This is a pity because the 1985–86 appearance of Halley's Comet is a golden opportunity to discover more about the true nature of a comet.

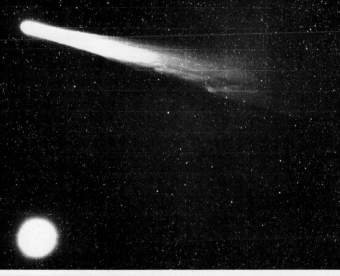

left
Halley's Comet and Venus photographed in 1910 in Johannesburg, S. Africa.

right
Halley's Comet over Jerusalem in 66 AD. From Stanislaus de Lubienietski *Historia Universalis Omulum Cometarum*, Amsterdam, 1666.

Halley's Comet also appeared in 1066 and is shown in the Bayeux Tapestry. The drawing of its 1456 appearance (*right*) is from Conrad Lycosthenes *Prodigiorum ac Ostentorum Chronicon*, Basle, 1557.

METEORS

Meteors appear as a streak of light in the sky for only a second or less. Meteors are often called 'shooting stars'; in fact they are not stars at all, but small particles of material which burn up in the Earth's atmosphere. They appear both singly and in streams or showers.

Most pictures and descriptions of meteors are of bright ones – brilliant streaks of light across the sky. The majority, however, are rather dim, having the brightness of a third, fourth or even fifth magnitude star. You will probably see a number of them if you go outdoors at night when there is no Moon to give a glare. If you go out before midnight you should look in the west and south-west fairly high up in the sky, but if you go out after midnight – a

better time to observe them – then look towards the east and south-east, near to the zenith. In either case, after five or ten minutes you will probably see a faint streak across the sky. It will not have a very long trail – probably no more than 5° of arc and will last for only a second or less. Very occasionally you will see a spectacular meteor – also very brief in duration, but a memorable sight.

The word 'meteor' usually refers to the visible effect produced when a particle of interplanetary material or 'meteoroid' enters the Earth's atmosphere and burns up. Most meteors are extremely small; generally they are no larger than a grain of sand. When a meteoroid enters our atmosphere it is travelling quite fast, typically at a speed of 30 km per second. Because it is travelling so fast, the metallic rocky material of which it is made becomes heated by friction with the atmosphere. The heat causes it to glow and vaporize, and this incandescence makes the meteor visible to the naked eye despite its small size and great distance (usually 80 km or more) above the Earth. As

it is heated the meteor also electrifies (ionizes) the air through which it moves, and its path or trail therefore glows for a very short time, while the meteor itself journeys to extinction.

Some meteoroids (the interplanetary fragments) travel through space in the same direction as the Earth, and some in the opposite direction. This explains why after midnight, you are likely to see more meteors because you are on the side of the Earth which is then facing the incoming meteoroids.

Meteors which appear on their own are called 'sporadic'. Other meteors occur in streams or 'showers'; when these occur you should have absolutely no difficulty in seeing them, provided the sky is not cloudy. Showers have differing rates but as a general rule meteors can be expected to appear at a rate of one every couple of minutes or as often as one every 30 seconds, although greater frequencies are not uncommon. When you watch a meteor shower you will find that the meteors all seem to be radiating from a particular point in the sky. This is a purely optical effect due to

left
Illustration of a very heavy fall of Leonid meteors seen off Cape Florida in 1799.

above
In November 1966 another Leonid meteor shower was photographed at Kitt Peak Observatory. The meteor tails are clearly seen against a background of stars, some of them very faint.

perspective, as illustrated.

Being on the Earth watching a meteor shower is rather like standing on a bridge over a straight section of a motorway or highway. When you look along the road its edges appear to get closer together as they go into the distance until, at the horizon, they appear to join together. Of course this is simply an optical illusion, and so it is with a meteor shower: as you see the stream of meteors coming down to Earth, they all seem to be coming from a convergent point or 'radiant'.

Meteor streams are usually named after the constellation in which the radiant appears. The table gives some details of the most important showers. (For further details of all showers, major and minor, consult the *Handbook* of the British Astronomical Association or *The American Ephemeris and Nautical Almanac*, a yearly publication of the U.S. Government Printing Office.)

As these meteor showers usually appear each year on, or nearly on, the same date, it is clear that the streams, like the Earth, are following regular orbits round the Sun and that these orbits intersect with our own at fixed points. The orbits are similar to those of comets, and at least ten of the showers have been shown to follow orbits similar to those of certain comets. For example, the η Aquarids may be associated with Halley's Comet. The Lyrids are definitely associated with the great comet of 1801 and the Perseids with one of 1862. What seems to have happened in the case of every shower is that material from the comet has gradually become dispersed along the cometary orbit. When the Earth crosses the orbit it meets some of this material and we observe a meteor shower.

Name	Constellation in which radiant lies	Usual date of maximum	Duration of shower	Number of meteors per hour
Quadrantids	Boötes	January 4	1 day	110 or more
Lyrids	Lyra/Hercules boundary	April 22	2 days	12 (usually bright)
η Aquarids	Aquarius	May 5	3 days	20
δ Aquarids	Aquarius	July 27	under 24 hrs	35
Perseids	Perseus	August 12	5 days	68 (usually a good sight)
Orionids	Orion	October 20	2 days	30
Taurids	Taurus	November 7	under 24 hrs	12 (a bright shower)
Leonids	Leo	November 17	under 24 hrs	10
Geminids	Gemini	December 12	3 days	58 (very brilliant shower)

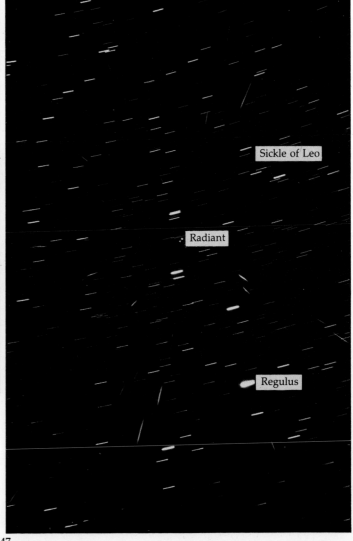

Sickle of Leo

Radiant

Regulus

above
Leonid meteors across a background of coloured star trails are shown in this extraordinary photograph. Note how the meteors vary in brightness as they travel through the atmosphere.

right
Leonid meteors photographed in the sickle of the constellation Leo, coming from one apparent point in space – the radiant. Over 100 meteors a minute were recorded, and at the height of the shower over 1,000 arrived in a period of 40 minutes.

METEORITES AND FIREBALLS

The brightest meteors can appear more brilliant than the Full Moon and are known as 'fireballs'. Meteorites are fragments of interplanetary materials which survive their journey through the Earth's atmosphere to hit the ground. It is thought that meteorites can provide information about the origin of the Solar System.

Meteors vary widely in size. Most weigh no more than a few milligrams and when they enter the Earth's atmosphere they soon vaporize and are burned out even before they come to within 80 km of the ground. But some of them are larger and take longer to burn up, so that they come much nearer the ground. Such a meteor, which will have a negative magnitude, can shine very brightly indeed, lighting up the surrounding countryside; it is then called a 'fireball'. As a fireball burns it will give off hot gases, which sometimes, in escaping, cause the fireball to explode into pieces, which then fall to the ground. The final moments of a fireball, whether it explodes or not, are often accompanied by a loud report. Fireballs are rare, but if you are fortunate enough to see one, it is a sight you will long remember. A really large one will leave a trail that remains in the sky for some time; one such trail from a fireball in 1896 was recorded as lasting 5½ hours.

Meteorites (as meteroid fragments are called once they reach

Earth) also vary a great deal in size. They may be no larger than a small stone; very rarely they are quite large, weighing several hundred kilograms. When a large meteorite lands, the hot gases it carries will cause it to gouge out a crater many times larger than itself. The most famous crater of this kind is the Barringer Crater near Winslow, in Arizona. This was formed probably some 20,000 years ago and is 1.2 km in diameter. Its rim rises some 50 metres above the surrounding plain and its depth, measured from the top of the rim, is 170 metres. The bulk of the meteorite, called the 'primary body', lies buried below the surface of the crater, but searches in a wide area surrounding the crater have

revealed a number of meteoritic fragments ranging from the size of gravel up to a lump weighing 635 kg. Two other very large meteorite craters are known: one in Antarctica and the other at Hudson's Bay in Canada. In recorded history there have been no reports of the falling of huge meteorites such as those which formed these craters, although in 1908 a large one fell near the Tunguska River in Siberia, flattening the forest for some 30 km around the point where it fell. There are reports of another fall in 1947, also in an uninhabited area of Siberia northeast of Vladivostock. But such large falls are rare and the chance of even a small meteorite hitting your home is so unlikely as to be discounted.

The Barringer Crater in Arizona was discovered in 1891. Its age has been estimated between 5,000 and 50,000 years.

left
The Strathpepper fireball. This fell near Dundee, Scotland on 14 December 1974 and is thought to be one of the densest meteoric bodies ever to have entered the Earth's atmosphere.

above
Fragment of the Barwell meteorite which fell in Barwell, Leicestershire, on Christmas Eve, 1965. The pieces totalled 50 kg and it was a stony meteorite. The dark area shows where melting took place during the fall.

Fragments of meteorites showing pitted surfaces.

Meteorites are sporadic; they never arrive with meteor showers, which consist of very small meteoroids.

It is worthwhile visiting a geological museum to see pieces of meteoritic material. Samples that have been recovered have pitted surfaces showing where material has been vaporized during the meteorite's fall. Most meteorites are made of rock. Such 'stony meteorites' are often hard to distinguish from ordinary stones, but when a fall is actually witnessed, meteoritic material can often be recovered from that area without doubt about its origin. Many stony meteorites (about 80 per cent) are what are known as 'chondrites' (from the Greek *chondros* meaning 'a grain') because they contain small round particles called 'chondrules'. Stony meteorites without these chondrules are known as 'achondrites'. All chondrites contain some iron and nickel, and some – the 'carbonaceous chondrites' – also possess some hydrocarbon compounds. The other main type of meteorite is the iron meteorite; these are composed of many minerals, notably kamacite or taenite (both alloys of iron and nickel) but also include smaller amounts of germanium and gallium.

One of the most famous meteorites to be recovered was the Orgueil meteorite, which fell at Montauban, France, in 1864. This broke up into some 20 stones of the carbonaceous chondrite type and has recently been the subject of considerable argument because some investigators claim that some of the stones contain microscopic fossils and chemical compounds which are evidence of living things. The problem relates not so much to the evidence itself as to its origin: is the evidence the result of contamination after landing on Earth – after all, the meteorite fell over a century ago – or was it present in the meteorite originally? If the meteorite brought the evidence with it then, clearly, it is an important argument for there being life elsewhere in the universe.

Recently it has become clear that the bodies we see as meteors and those we call meteorites probably differ in their structure and origin, whereas previously they were considered to be the same kind of body, differing only in size. Meteoroids, both the sporadic ones and those in showers, are probably the debris of comets. Indeed, many scientists think the 'Tunguska meteorite' was no meteorite at all but the head of a small comet. This would account for the lack of meteoritic fragments in the area. Studies of meteorites show that they were formed soon after the planets were formed, and it may be that they are pieces of planetary material, probably from asteroids that later collided with each other.

If you see a meteorite fall, you should report it so that the fall can be checked. (The British Astronomical Association has a service for dealing with such reports from its members.) Should you come across what you think may be a stony meteorite or an iron one (such an object is called a 'find', as contrasted with a 'fall', whose descent is observed), take it to a geological museum for identification. It is important that meteorites be professionally examined, so that we may eventually succeed in determining precisely what their origin is.

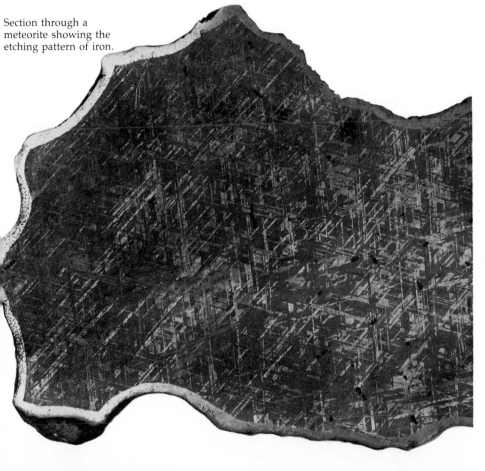

Section through a meteorite showing the etching pattern of iron.

Impact crater of a piece of the Barwell meteorite.

Close-up of Barwell meteorite crater.

Fragment of the meteorite which fell on Orgueil, France, in May 1864.

OBSERVING METEORS AND FIREBALLS

Although you can often see meteors through casual observation, you will not learn much from them unless you apply a little organization to your meteor-watching. You can then chart a meteor's course and estimate its height.

First of all, as with all astronomical observations, you must note down the date and time of the observation; and it is also advisable to make a note of the viewing conditions. It is a clear night? Are the stars shining brightly? How much moonlight is there? You must also determine your position precisely – use a large scale Ordnance Survey or U.S. Geological Survey map for this.

First, let us consider sporadic meteors. What you need to know is the meteor's path, but this is not easy since its trail is visible for only a very short time. It is also useful to estimate the meteor's brightness, which you can do by comparing it with nearby stars. Make a note, or a quick sketch, of your comparison stars and estimate the brightness of the meteor relative to them. Later you can check up the actual brightness of your comparison stars and adjust your estimate of brightness for the meteor, if necessary. Use an electric torch, or flashlight, with a red transparent cover to light your note pad.

As for the meteor's trail, you will really need to know your stars pretty well in order to locate it. You can then say that the trail extends from such-and-such a star down to some other star you recognize. If you are not sure, make a sketch of the star field and draw in the trail. Some people find it useful to have handy a length (about 1 m) of thick white thread or fine string; as soon as you see a meteor, hold this up along the path of the meteor, placing your fingers at the path's beginning and end. You can then transfer this line to your rough star map and later on identify the stars lying close to it.

You cannot, of course, make all your observations at once, desirable though it would be if you could. So first make a mental estimate of

brightness (don't stop to write it down) and quickly locate the meteor trail, using the string if you find this helpful. If you pause to make a note of the estimated brightness, you will find it difficult to recollect where the trail was. Obviously practice is important in learning to do this. You also need to determine the time of the meteor's appearance. If you look at your watch when the meteor first

appears you will lose valuable observation time. Ideally, you should have a stopwatch which you set going the moment the meteor appears. Leave it running. Then when you have made your estimate of brightness and located the trail and have made a note of these, take your stopwatch to an accurate clock or watch and stop it when the clock indicates an exact time. Subtract the

Illustration of a fireball by the amateur astronomer Paul Doherty.

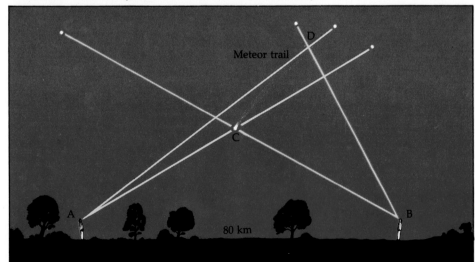

Fig. 1
The observers at A and B see C and D (the start and finish of the meteor trail) against a background of stars. By knowing the altitudes of the stars they can calculate the angles CAB, CBA, DAB and DBA. The distance between A and B is known, so by using trigonometry the height of the start and finish of the trail can be determined.

time on the stopwatch from the clock time and you have the time the meteor appeared. If, however, you have no stopwatch, you had better try to estimate how much time elapses between the meteor's first appearance and the time you look at your watch. After all, you are not making an occultation observation (page 104) and do not need the time so very precisely. All you need is enough accuracy so that another observer can verify whether the meteor he or she observed is the same one that you saw.

Another way to observe meteors is to photograph them. Of course, since you do not know when a meteor is going to appear – except in the case of a shower – it is no good just taking out a camera and hoping to get a snapshot. The best thing is to set up your camera pointing in the direction in which you expect to see a meteor – near the zenith, either westwards or eastwards depending on the time (page 146) – and leave the camera shutter open. If your camera has a T (time) setting, use this, but if it has not you must use the B (bulb) setting and a cable release with a lock to keep it pressed down. Should your camera have a wide angle lens, so much the better, because this will encompass a wider area of the sky. Photographic observing makes things easier, for it records the brightness and trail positions for you, so that all you need to make a note of is the time. When the meteor has vanished, close the camera shutter, wind on the film and open the shutter for the next exposure. You need, of course, to use a film from which prints can be made – a black and white film is best. One point to remember: make sure there are no street lights to fog your film, since by opening the shutter and leaving it open you are over-exposing your surroundings.

Obtaining the trail of a meteor, whether by eye or with a camera, is important, because it can help determine the meteor's height. You cannot obtain the height from one person's observation alone; you will need an observation from someone else positioned some distance away – a distance of 80 km or more is desirable. Then the meteor's height can be worked out by comparing the observations and doing a little trigonometry (Fig. 1). Should you be observing a meteor shower, then things are easier because the observations required are the meteor radiant (which you can judge by looking), meteor brightness and, most important, the hourly rate at which the meteors are appearing.

In the late 1940s and early 1950s Sir Bernard Lovell and his colleagues at Jodrell Bank near Manchester made observations on sporadic meteors using radar. In these experiments (Fig. 2) they shot out radio pulses and timed how long it took the pulse to reach the ionized meteor trail and return. Knowing the speed of the radio pulses – they travel at the same speed as light – the radio astronomers were able to determine meteor trail heights and velocities directly. They were also able to do something no camera or visual observer could do: they could detect meteors in daylight and so discover, for example, some meteor showers not previously known because they were invisible.

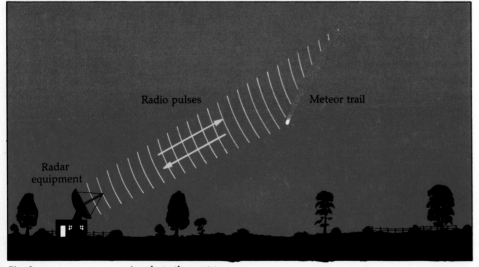

Fig. 2
Radar observations of a meteor trail are made by shooting short-wave radio signals to the meteor where they are reflected by ionized gases in the meteor trail and returned to Earth.

151

CHAPTER 6
ATMOSPHERIC ASTRONOMY

The Earth's atmosphere affects our observations of the universe because the light of all celestial bodies passes through it to reach our telescopes. But some celestial bodies also affect the atmosphere so that we see phenomena like rainbows and the aurora.

The most obvious effect of the Earth's atmosphere on our observations of the heavens is the twinkling of the stars. This twinkling is caused by currents of air at different temperatures. The warmer air is, the less densely its particles (molecules) are packed together, and the smaller the angle through which it refracts light. As light from the stars passes through layers of the atmosphere which are at different temperatures, so it is refracted by slightly different amounts (Fig. 1). The layers of air move about relative to each other, with the result that the light beam from a star will move about slightly (Fig. 2). Because the star is so far away, its light appears a mere pinpoint, and when this narrow beam is, for an instant, deflected away from the observer's eye and then, an instant later, deflected back again so that it can be seen once more, the effect perceived is that the star twinkles.

When a star is low in the sky its light strikes the layers of atmosphere at an oblique angle. As a result the layers act rather like a prism and disperse the starlight into a spectrum. The spread of the spectrum is small, but it is there nevertheless, as you can see by looking at a very bright star like Sirius when it is not far above the horizon. Not only will you see it twinkle, but you will also see that it seems to change colour at the same time. This is because the beam of starlight is split into colours and these different colours appear and disappear as they are refracted differently by the layers of air.

Another spectroscopic effect caused by the Earth's atmosphere is the 'Green Flash'. This phenomenon occurs at sunrise or sunset and is a patch of green light refracted towards the observer as he faces the distorted and reddened Sun. It is very hard to see, lasts only a fraction of a second, and is only visible when the Sun is almost sunk into the horizon; also, you need to be able to see the horizon distinctly, as at the seaside, in the mountains or on a plain.

Unlike stars, planets do not twinkle in the night sky, but shine with a steady light – indeed, that is one way of recognizing them. This is because a planet is much closer than a star; seen through a telescope it appears as a tiny disc, whereas a star is only a pinpoint of light, even under the strongest magnification. As a beam of light from one point on the planet's surface is refracted away from the eye by the atmosphere, another beam from some other point on the surface takes its place. The observer therefore sees a steady

Fig. 1
The solid line is light from a star reaching an observer on Earth. As the light is bent by the Earth's atmosphere, the observer thinks he is seeing the star in the higher position indicated by the dotted line. Astronomers allow for this apparent shift in their calculations.

Fig. 2
Stars twinkle because, as a light beam travels from the tiny point source to Earth, it is shifted by the moving layers of air around the Earth. This means that sometimes the light will strike the eye of an observer and sometimes it will not.

Fig. 3 right
The layers of the Earth's atmosphere, showing aurorae, etc.

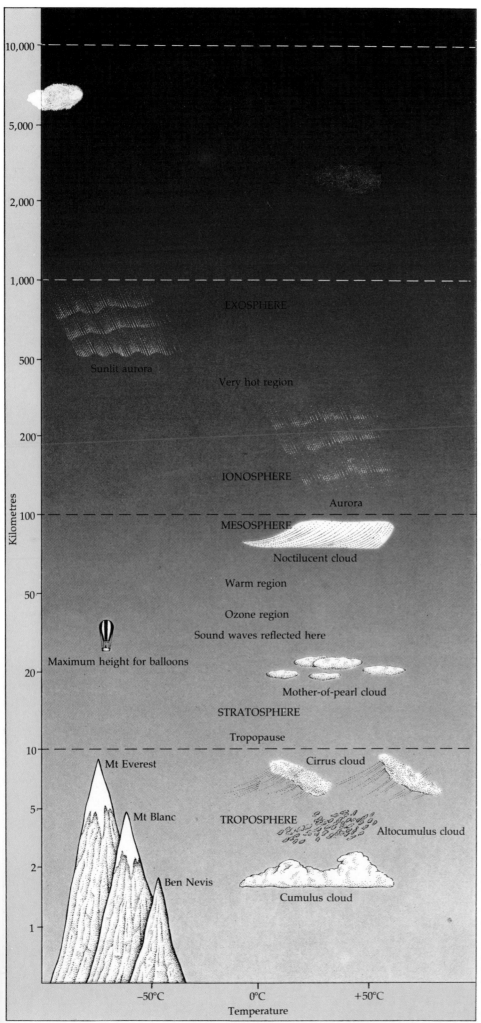

10,000

5,000

2,000

1,000

EXOSPHERE

Sunlit aurora

500

Very hot region

200

IONOSPHERE

Aurora

100

MESOSPHERE

Noctilucent cloud

Warm region

50

Ozone region

Sound waves reflected here

Maximum height for balloons

20

Mother-of-pearl cloud

STRATOSPHERE

Tropopause

10

Mt Everest

Cirrus cloud

5

Mt Blanc

TROPOSPHERE

Altocumulus cloud

2

Ben Nevis

Cumulus cloud

1

−50°C   0°C   +50°C

Temperature

Kilometres

beam of light from a planet, even when it is fairly low in the sky and thus subject to more refraction by the Earth's atmosphere.

As we have seen (pages 40–41) the Earth's atmosphere acts like a filter, preventing some dangerous radiation – gamma rays, x-rays and short ultraviolet radiation – from reaching us on the ground. It also reflects some of the radio waves emitted by celestial bodies, although others – wavelengths between 1 mm and 30 metres – do reach the Earth and can be detected by radio telescopes. Fig. 3 shows the different regions of the atmosphere. The part in which we live is the troposphere, which varies in depth but averages about 14 km deep and gets colder the higher up one goes. Next comes the tropopause, a transitional layer about 4 km thick, which separates the troposphere from the stratosphere. In its upper regions, the stratosphere, which is some 30 km deep, contains the ozone layer. The ozone molecule contains three oxygen atoms, and it is this layer which absorbs the shorter wavelengths of ultraviolet radiation. The absorption of solar radiation produces energy, which causes the increase in temperature found in the ozone layer. The temperature drops as one moves upwards through the next layer, the mesosphere, which is about 40 km deep. Above it lies the ionosphere, where a great many of the atoms are ionized, producing several layers of electrically charged particles. These particles or electrons can reflect very long wavelength radio signals. In the ionosphere the gamma-rays and x-rays are absorbed, which causes the temperature to rise again. The aurorae (pages 156–159) also occur in the ionosphere, which is some 300 km deep. Beyond the ionosphere is a very thin atmosphere, the exosphere, which is composed mainly of hydrogen and helium. At about 970 km above the Earth the exosphere gives way to an even thinner atmosphere of hydrogen, which is the magnetosphere where fast-moving atomic particles are trapped in the Earth's magnetic field. At a distance of something like 9,500 km above the Earth this merges into the interplanetary gas – the very tenuous gas which lies between the planets. Whereas the temperature of the atmosphere fluctuates, the density drops uniformly: at a height of 15 km above the Earth it is only one-tenth as dense as it is at ground level, at 30 km it is only one-tenth as dense as it was at 15 km, and so on.

RAINBOWS, HALOES AND MOCK SUNS

The interaction between our atmosphere and the Sun and Moon produces a number of striking optical effects including lunar and solar haloes, mock suns and rainbows.

A rainbow is a spectacular confirmation of Newton's discovery that sunlight is composed of light of all colours. You are likely to see one when the Sun is opposite in the sky to the direction in which rain is falling. If you have a garden hose, however, you can make an artificial rainbow, provided the Sun is shining. All you need to do is to stand with your back to the Sun and let the water spray outwards from the hose so that it falls like rain (Fig. 1). You will see a rainbow in front of you.

This is because the raindrops act like prisms and disperse the rays of sunlight into the colours of the spectrum while at the same time reflecting these colours by the phenomenon of 'total reflection' which is sometimes called the 'shop-window' effect. It is caused when a light ray reaches an interface between one transparent medium and another

at a certain angle. At most angles a light ray will be refracted at the interface, but as the drawing shows (Fig. 2) there are some angles at which the light ray does not pass through but is reflected. You get this effect with a shop-window, where light from the street goes through the glass and helps to light the display. But, as you will have noticed, not all the light from the street goes through the window; some of it is reflected and prevents your seeing in. Whether it is reflected or goes through depends on the angle at which it meets the window. The same thing happens with a rainbow. Sunlight goes into raindrops (Fig. 3) and as it enters it is refracted and dispersed, just as in a prism, then

totally reflected back at a specific angle. Each colour emerges at a different angle, and the colour you see emerging from a particular drop at a particular instant depends on your position relative to it. The rainbow you see is caused by thousands of raindrops, each one reflecting one colour back to your eyes. This is why a rainbow always moves away as you move towards it: the angle between your eyes and the raindrops must stay the same and so you can never walk right up to a rainbow.

Sometimes it is possible to see a secondary rainbow as well. This lies outside the main or primary rainbow and its colours are reversed, with red on the inside and violet on the

Fig. 1
Stand with your back towards the Sun, holding a spraying hose and the droplets will split the Sun's light into a spectrum. Make sure your shadow does not get in the way.

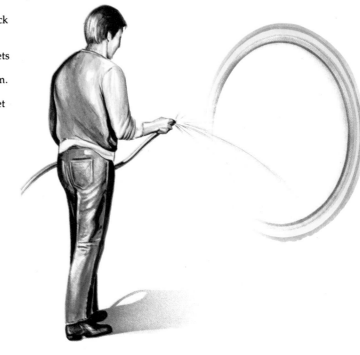

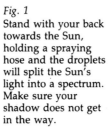

Fig. 2
The 'shop-window' effect. Some light rays pass through the window, while others do not and are reflected outwards again.

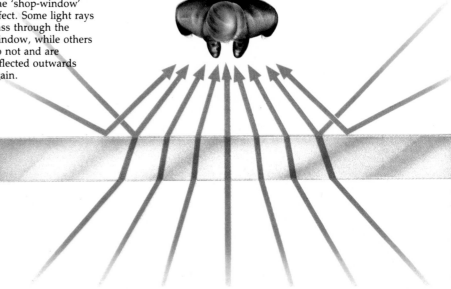

Mock suns observed in 1740, from Charles Blunt *The Beauty of the Heavens*, 1845.

A lunar rainbow photographed by William Sager on the Pacific island of Maui.

outside. It is also dimmer than the primary bow. The secondary bow is caused by raindrops in which the light undergoes a second reflection inside, and it is this second reflection which reverses the colours.

On rare occasions the Moon casts a rainbow like the Sun. The explanation for this is the same as for a rainbow formed by sunlight, and on a very bright night of Full Moon, you can use your hose to make a 'moonbow'.

When you look up at the Full Moon, especially when it is fairly high in the sky, you will sometimes see it surrounded by a ring of light. This 'halo' can appear red on the inside with yellow and blue on the outside, but at other times the colour is faint and the halo appears whitish. Some people regard a halo as a sign of impending rain, but this is not necessarily so, although the ring does indicate the presence of thin cirrostratus clouds in the upper troposphere which, under some circumstances, will produce rain. The halo is caused by moonlight being refracted by the ice crystals of which the clouds are composed.

Haloes are also seen around the Sun when thin cirrostratus clouds are present. More rarely, these conditions will produce the phenomenon of 'mock suns' or *parhelia*. These are spots of light which occur on either side of the Sun at the same elevation and are caused by the refraction of sunlight through vertical ice crystals. When the Sun is on the horizon, the parhelia lie on the halo, but when the Sun is high in the sky they are positioned a little outside the halo. Parhelia are whitish in colour with a red tinge on the side nearest the Sun.

The Sun also plays a part in the appearance of noctilucent clouds, which, as their name indicates, are luminous at night. These lie in the upper part of the mesosphere and may be partly caused by the very low temperature there (around -80°C). They lie between 75 and 90 km above the Earth and are visible only in the summer, most frequently between latitudes of 55° and 64° – for example in Scotland, Denmark, Russia (Moscow and further north), Alaska and northern Canada. The clouds which are silvery or bluish-white, can be seen during summer nights when the Sun is between 13° and 15° below the horizon – their great height enabling them still to catch its light. There is still some doubt about their nature; they could be composed of dust or of ice crystals. The rockets sent up to these heights have shown that the clouds appear only when it is very cold, but also that much more dust is present than when there are no such clouds. The dust seems to be composed mainly of iron and nickel and may be meteoritic dust. The clouds themselves often have a tenuous wavy pattern, which indicates the presence of strong winds in this high region of the atmosphere.

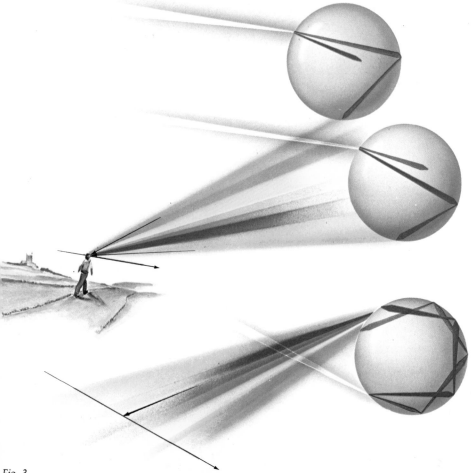

Fig. 3
Raindrops act as prisms, splitting sunlight into spectra. They also act as mirrors reflecting light. An ordinary rainbow is made by light reflected and dispersed by a number of raindrops. In a secondary rainbow light travels in a more complex path inside the raindrop and the lower drawing shows how it gives a coloured spectrum in the reverse order.

Primary and secondary rainbows photographed at Newport, Wales, in 1975.

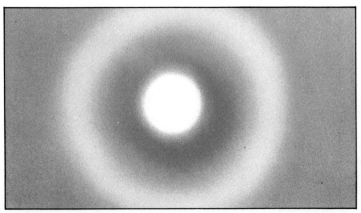

A rainbow-coloured ring or corona around the Sun, caused by diffraction through water droplets in the clouds.

A noctilucent cloud photographed at 5 am, July 1971, at Newton Stewart, Scotland.

THE AURORA

Near the Earth's poles a magnificent spectacle of shimmering coloured light can sometimes be seen – the aurora. This phenomenon is connected with solar activity.

The aurora is called the *aurora borealis* (northern lights) and the *aurora australis* (southern lights); it can appear as bright as Full Moon. The aurora usually appears near the Earth's poles, and the more northerly (or southerly) your latitude, the more impressive the displays you will see. If you live in Scotland or Alaska, for example, you may have seen some spectacular manifestations of the aurora. Sometimes it is accompanied by a swishing or rustling noise, which prompted an old superstition that an auroral display was a battle in the sky – some observers even claiming that they could hear the clashing of swords. Aurorae can take various shapes, and we shall look at these more closely in a moment, but first we must consider the causes of the aurora: the 'solar wind' and the Earth's magnetic field.

The Sun continuously emits electrified atomic particles – protons, which have a positive electric charge, and electrons, which have a negative charge. These particles normally travel at a speed of about 400 km per second near the Earth. This stream of particles takes about four days to reach the Earth and is known as the solar wind. The emission of the particles varies; there are more on some occasions than on others, the number depending on the Sun's activity. At sunspot minimum (pages 32–33) the solar wind is at its lowest intensity, but at sunspot maximum it is more active, and this activity becomes even greater whenever there is a solar flare. A solar flare appears visually as flashes of light, but being an explosive release of energy from the Sun, it radiates at nearly all wavelengths, from x-rays to radio waves. The Sun's emission of atomic particles also increases, and these rush towards the Earth at a speed of over 2 million km per hour, reaching us in about two days. The x-rays accompanying a flare reach the Earth more quickly, taking only 8.3 minutes, because they travel at the speed of light.

The x-rays affect the electrified

air layers that together form the ionosphere. Ordinarily the ionosphere makes possible short-wave broadcasting over long distances, the ionized layers acting like a mirror in the sky. But when there is an intense x-ray burst from a solar flare the ionosphere becomes transparent to the short-waves and they pass through into space. As a result radio operators experience a short-wave fade-out. To see what effects are caused by slower-travelling atomic particles, we must first look at the Earth and its magnetic field.

In addition to its geographical north and south poles, the Earth has two magnetic poles, each located about 1,900 km from the corresponding geographical pole. Thus, the Earth acts like a giant bar magnet – a fact that can easily be verified with a compass. If you have not got a compass, you can make one (Fig. 3). You will find that the eye of the needle in your home-made compass – like the point of the

An aurora accompanied by sounds was thought to be the clash of weapons of celestial armies. From Conrad Lycosthenes *Prodigiorum ac Ostentorum Chronicon*, Basle, 1557.

needle in a manufactured one – points north. Or, rather, it points to the north magnetic pole. You can check this from the observations you made of the south line with a gnomon (pages 20–21). William Gilbert, one of Queen Elizabeth I's physicians, wrote a book about the Earth's magnetism in 1600, and ever since then an increasing number of studies have been made of the Earth as a magnet. Now, with the discoveries made by high-flying balloons and by artificial satellites, we know that the Earth is surrounded by a vast area containing electrons and protons moving at great speed back and forth within the Earth's magnetic field. It is this region – called the magnetosphere – with which the particles forming the solar wind react.

The magnetosphere extends for tens of thousands of kilometres into space around the Earth. It is not, however, shaped like a sphere, because it is distorted by the solar wind. The solar wind, travelling as it

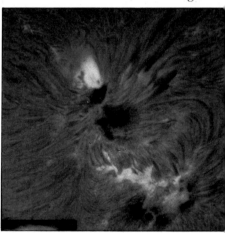

A solar flare photographed in 1971 at the Big Bear Solar Laboratory, California.

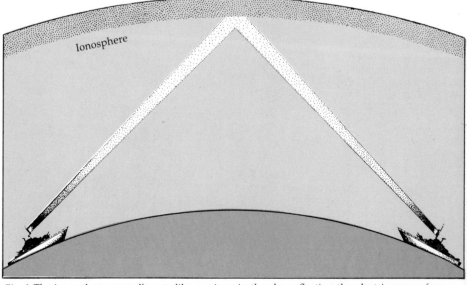

Fig. 1 The ionosphere normally acts like a mirror in the sky, reflecting the electric waves from a radio transmitter and sending them back to Earth.

does at an average of 400 km per second, gives a slap or shock wave to the Earth's magnetosphere and causes it to spread out away from the Sun and the solar wind to form a magnetic tail stretching far out into space (Fig. 4) beyond the Moon's orbit. The magnetosphere is bounded by the 'magnetopause', an area in which the magnetic activity ceases; and the outer edge of this area, where the solar wind strikes it, is called the 'magnetosheath'.

Within the Earth's magnetosphere are some concentrated areas known as the Van Allen radiation belts, named after the American scientist who directed the experiments on Explorer I, an early artificial satellite launched in 1958, which discovered them. Shaped rather like doughnut rings, these are areas in which protons and electrons are spiralling about in great numbers between the Earth's magnetic poles (Fig. 5). The inner belt is some 1,000 km above the Earth and extends to over 5,000 km, while the outer belt

stretches from approximately 15,000 km to 25,000 km.

When a solar flare causes the number of protons and electrons in the solar wind to increase greatly, many of those in the solar wind break through the magnetosheath and are captured in the Van Allen belts. The belts are unable to retain so many particles and some spill over at the ends of the belts near the north and south magnetic poles. The spill-over occurs in thin 'sheets' within an area known as the 'auroral oval'. Under fairly quiet, normal conditions, when the spill-over is small, the oval extends down to about latitude 59° on the night-side of the Earth and only 69° on the sunlit side. But during magnetic storm conditions when a solar flare is active, the oval expands, reaching 59° on the sunlit side of the Earth and 39° on the dark side. So when there is a magnetic storm, and protons and electrons spill over in large quantities from the Van Allen belts, aurorae are visible from many places which are

usually too far south for an aurora to be seen (or too far north for the aurorae in the southern hemisphere).

As the electrified atomic particles spill over, they move with immense velocities of between 50,000 km and 100,000 km per second. They have therefore a great amount of energy and they crash into the air molecules of the ionosphere and ionize them. The electrons knocked off these air molecules recombine with them, and this recombination causes the molecules to emit radiation, which appears as the aurora.

The aurora can take a great many forms, and no two displays are ever exactly the same. To see the aurora clearly you need to be away from the glow of city lights and the lights of motorways, out in the country. A moonless night is ideal. If you ever travel say, to the north of Scotland or Alaska, or to the south of the South Island, New Zealand, it is worthwhile keeping a watch out for it. If you travel there at the time of a sunspot maximum, you are likely to see some spectacular displays.

When you see an aurora you should make a note of the date and the time and also the observing conditions – the amount of moonlight, if any, the presence of any clouds and the temperature. Most important of all, naturally, is a clear description of the aurora itself. To help you do this, here is a list of the main kinds of aurorae you can see:

Quiet arcs: these arcs, curving upwards in the sky like a rainbow, may be either broad or narrow. They may be uniformly bright or bright only in patches. However, the upper edge is usually fuzzy and the lower edge sharp, and there may seem to be a dark band in between. In some displays the lower edge is regular, rather as a rainbow is regular, but in other displays it is irregular, and then often very luminous. This kind of arc may turn into rays (see below) at any time.

Sometimes you will see more than one arc at once, each arc extending down to the horizon and parallel to the one next to it. The arcs may merge together, and sometimes the upper arc turns round at one end (at the eastern end in the northern hemisphere) and continues back as a lower arc. The colours of quiet arcs vary, but usually they are greenish-yellow and sometimes white. You should, of course, write down the colours and the extent of the arcs in degrees, both sideways in azimuth and vertically in altitude.

North geomagnetic pole

North pole (geographical)

Fig. 2 right
The Earth is like a giant bar magnet, but its magnetic poles do not coincide with its geographical poles.

Fig. 3 below
To make a magnetic compass, first take a needle and stroke it with a magnet as shown; the eye will then have a north-seeking polarity. Push the needle through a cork and float the cork in a bowl of water. The needle, which is free to spin round, will line up with the Earth's magnetic field, pointing north and south.

South geomagnetic pole

South pole (geographical)

Pulsating Arcs: these are often alone in the sky and are usually bluish-green in colour. Either the whole arc or part of it flashes up in a sort of pulsating movement and disappears, at regular intervals of a few seconds.

Bands: these have not got the regular shape of arcs. The lower edge is usually sharp but uneven and sometimes the band is curved like part of a semi-circle or part of an ellipse. If it is broad, a band may be made up of rays. Bands never stay completely still but move about, sometimes quite rapidly.

Curtains: a curtain aurora is really a variation of a band aurora but it can be so spectacular that it deserves an entry to itself. In this case the bands are crossed vertically by dark areas like shadows, so that they look like vast, heavy curtains hanging down from somewhere high up in the sky. As with all aurorae the actual sight is hard to describe, but anyone who has experienced the beauty of these giant greenish-bluish-white curtains glowing in the night sky and slowly moving as if in a breeze is unlikely ever to forget it.

Rays: these look like giant searchlights shining up into the sky. They may be thin or thick, long or short, and may appear separately or gathered together in great bundles. They seem to converge towards a point high in the sky, just as if they were radiating from an invisible point; clearly this is a perspective effect. Usually they are greenish-yellow but sometimes red, and often they do not appear alone but in conjunction with other auroral effects. Sometimes an arc will be built up of rays, as occasionally will auroral bands. At other times long rays make up what seems to be a curtain, which may sometimes appear pulled into the shape of a fan.

Luminous surfaces: these usually appear after an intense auroral display of curtains or rays. They are patches which are a pale violet, rose

A painting of an aurora by an amateur astronomer.

An aurora in August 1978, photographed from the Glacier National Park, Montana.

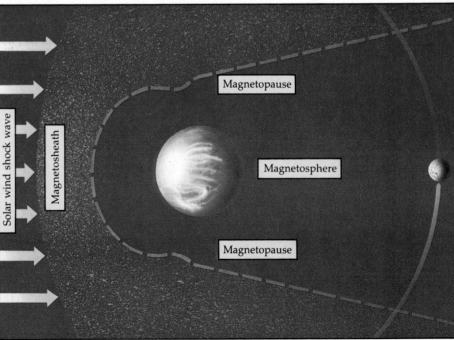

Fig. 4 Solar wind affects the shape of the Earth's magnetosphere.

158

or red, and they look rather like coloured clouds.

Pulsating surfaces: these are diffuse patches like clouds which appear and disappear rhythmically at any frequency between about one second and one minute, while apparently retaining their shape and position. They are often seen with flaming aurora.

Flaming aurora: this often appears after an intense display of rays or curtains and is frequently followed by a corona (see below). It often takes the form of strong arc-shaped waves of light moving quickly upwards one after the other; at other times the waves remain invisible until they illuminate broad rays and patches as they pass through them, making them seem to appear and disappear rhythmically.

Corona: not to be confused with the solar corona (page 31), this is an auroral display composed of rays or bands which all seem to converge to one point in the sky.

Auroral displays vary in altitude, but as the drawing on page 152 shows, they generally lie between 100 and 350 km above the Earth.

The aurora is an ideal subject for the amateur astronomer because no telescope or any other optical apparatus is needed for observing it. It also makes a good subject for anyone who can draw or paint, and some beautiful paintings of auroral displays have been done by amateur artists. The aurora can also be photographed, but as it is moving and not very bright by daylight standards, you need a very fast colour film; you may be able to have it 'pushed' during processing, so that the film speed is artificially increased. (First ask your local processing service about this; if they can do it, you will give the film a shorter exposure time than it would otherwise require.) It is also advisable to use a wide-angle lens if possible, unless the display covers only a small area of the sky.

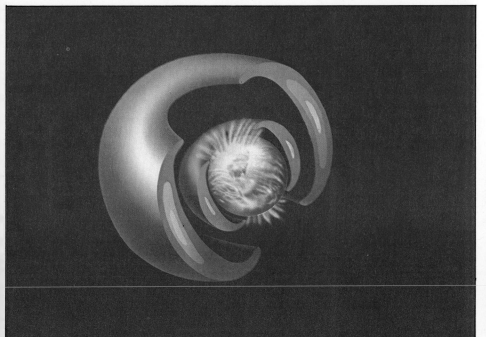

Fig. 5 The Van Allen belts are concentrated regions of electrified particles in the magnetosphere.

A photograph of an aurora taken by Gustav Lamprecht in Alaska.

THE ZODIACAL LIGHT

The Zodiacal Light which appears as a faint glow in the sky just before dawn or just after sunset has been recognized for centuries. It is now known that this phenomenon is caused by sunlight reflected by interplanetary dust.

Eight hundred years ago, in Persia, there lived a mathematician and an astronomer al-Khayyami, who was also a poet and is better known to most people as Omar Khayyam. In the famous set of poems attributed to him and called the *Rubaiyat* there is a verse which runs:

Before the phantom of False Morning died,

Methought a Voice within the Tavern cried,
 'When all the Temple is prepared within,
 'Why nods the drowsy Worshipper outside?'

This eleventh century reference to a 'False Morning' is probably the earliest literary reference to the Zodiacal Light, also called the 'False Dawn'. If you go out on a clear, moonless night before the twilight which heralds the dawn and look eastwards you can see a faint cone-shaped light spreading over some 15° to 20° of the horizon and tapering upwards towards the zenith. If you want to avoid getting up before dawn, you can see the Zodiacal Light in the west after sunset. As it is very dim, you will need to be far away from artificial lights, and that is not so easy to achieve these days. The best time of the year to see it from temperate regions of the Earth is either spring or autumn.

If you travel to the tropics you have a better chance of seeing the Zodiacal Light. This is not only because you will get clearer skies but also because the cone of the Zodiacal Light rises more vertically above the horizon so that more of it is shining through the thinner air found in the slightly higher altitude.

The Zodiacal Light is notoriously difficult to photograph, because although it is about two or three times as bright as the Milky Way (as seen by the naked eye), it will not – like the Milky Way – yield interesting detail on being magnified. A fast film may succeed in capturing it, particularly in southern latitudes.

Omar Khayyam may have observed the Zodiacal Light, but he could not have known its cause. Indeed it is only fairly recently, since the launching of artificial satellites, that astronomers have been able to verify the modern theory that the Light is caused by sunlight reflected from interplanetary dust. Myriads of dust particles lie in the plane of the Solar System and this, as Fig. 2 shows, is why the Light is the conical

Fig. 1 Zodiacal Light as seen from the tropics.

shape it is. This also explains why it is best observed in spring and autumn (i.e. near the time of the equinoxes), because the plane of the Solar System lies along the line of the Sun's equator and so the Zodiacal Light is at its most vertical, observed from temperate latitudes, at these times. The drawing also shows that the Zodiacal Light is most easily seen from the tropics.

The dust grains which form the Zodiacal Light are small – probably between 1 micron (i.e. one thousandth of a millimetre) and 0.1 micron. They cause the Light by scattering sunlight and, following solar flares, the Light is brighter.

It was probably the seventeenth-century astronomer Domenico Cassini, the first director of the Paris Observatory, who used the name Zodiacal Light, but it was known before this time by Kepler and other astronomers. It is not, however, the only faint glow to be observed in the night sky. It has a counterpart known as the *Gegenschein* or Counterglow, described by a Danish astronomer Theodor Brorsen nearly 130 years ago. This is a very faint, elliptically-shaped patch of light situated on the ecliptic on the opposite side from the Sun; it spreads over an area of something like 20° by 10° or more, depending on the observer's position and the clarity of the sky. Like the Zodiacal Light, it is best seen from the tropics. Sometimes there seems to be a hazy light either connecting the Zodiacal Light with the Counterglow or just as an extension of either of them; this is known as the 'Zodiacal Band'. The Counterglow and Zodiacal Band are also caused by interplanetary dust in the Solar System reflecting sunlight.

Another faint glow is the actual glowing of the night sky itself and known, simply, as the 'nightglow' or 'airglow'. This is caused by chemical reactions taking place among the molecules of the upper air and emitting some visible light. It is very faint indeed and you cannot observe it with the naked eye, but it is important to astronomers taking very long exposure photographs – perhaps extending over more than one night – for its presence limits the length of any exposure; after some time the glow of the air will fog the photograph and obliterate the images of extremely faint objects. But the airglow is only troublesome at visual wavelengths; it does not appear at radio wavelengths. Thus to radio astronomers, the sky is always 'black'. The airglow does not affect their data, nor does the scattering of sunlight that gives us our blue daylight sky. This means that radio astronomers can observe the universe by day as well as by night, an obvious advantage.

Optical astronomers have also found that in the plane of the Milky Way there is an additional very faint glow caused by the starlight from the many stars in the plane of the galaxy which are too dim to be seen separately. This is yet another factor limiting exposure time when photographing this region of the sky.

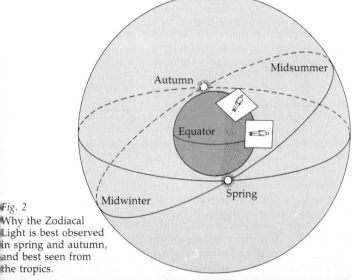

Fig. 2 Why the Zodiacal Light is best observed in spring and autumn, and best seen from the tropics.

Fig. 3 How the Zodiacal Light appears in relation to the Sun.

The Zodiacal Light and Comet Ikeya-Seki photographed at 5.07 am on 26 October 1965 in the Catalina Mountains near Tucson, Arizona, with a 25-second exposure.

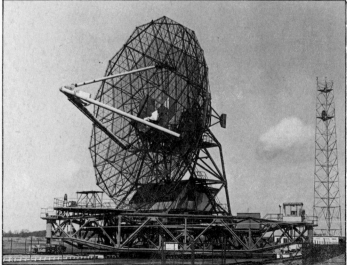

The 25 m radio telescope at Defford, England, which forms a part of a network of radio telescopes con - nected to Jodrell Bank.

CHAPTER 7
THE MILKY WAY, STAR CLUSTERS AND NEBULAE

The Sun and the planets are part of a giant star island, the Milky Way system. The distribution of stars in the Milky Way varies and in interstellar space there are vast clouds of dust and gas – the nebulae.

The Milky Way can be seen from everywhere on Earth because it spreads across the entire sky, a hazy band of light which will be examined in more detail on pages 168 and 169. It is part of a star island of which our Sun is a member star.

In our star island only a few thousand stars are visible to the unaided eye. Through binoculars many thousands more can be seen, and with a telescope the number increases according to the aperture of the telescope. The question is whether you could go on doing this for ever. If a very large telescope was used – one like the Anglo-Australian 3.9 metre, for instance – and then one double that in size, and then one twice as large as that, would more and more stars be seen, or is there an end? And if there is an end, what would then be seen: nothing at all? Some of these questions are answered from page 186 onwards but a start can be made here.

The first thing to ask is whether the stars are equally distributed over the entire sky. Are there the same number in any direction, or are some places more heavily populated than others? To get some sort of an answer to this, not even a telescope is needed; anyone can simply go out on a starry night and look at the sky. Some parts of the sky look as if they are almost empty, whereas others seem to be full of stars. Look, for

Region around the Square of Pegasus. There are few stars in this part of the sky.

above
The constellation of Orion: there are many stars in and around Orion.

right
The beautiful open cluster, the Pleiades. Clouds of gas surround the brighter stars.

instance, at constellations like Taurus, or Gemini, or Orion. They seem to be in parts of the sky which are simply seething with stars. On the other hand, if you look at the great square of Pegasus, you will see that except for the stars which form the square (α, β and γ Pegasi and α Andromedae), there are not many others in that region of the sky.

The stars, therefore, are not equally distributed over the sky. This was one of the facts that intrigued

and puzzled William Herschel in the eighteenth century when he began to make surveys of the skies. He counted the number of stars he could see in different areas, and also noted down other objects that did not look like stars or planets, or even comets, but were hazy patches of light. They looked, in fact, like glowing clouds, and he called them 'nebulae' from the Latin word for 'clouds'. Herschel was not the first to observe them, but he was the first to catalogue them,

although his catalogue contained some objects we should not call nebulae today. He was also careful to note down all clusters of stars and did not confuse them with the separate stars he was counting.

You can do a similar kind of observation yourself, but a vast number of observations will be needed if you are to gain a proper idea of how the stars are distributed, because only a small area of the sky can be observed at a time. Herschel used to count stars in a small area of sky, and then repeat this ten times in order to get an average which was likely to be more correct than just one single count. He made thousands of observations, using his favourite 48 cm telescope, which was over 6 metres long. Herschel assumed that the more stars he could see, the further they were stretching into space, and in the end he came up with the idea that the stars were distributed in a kind of long box-like shape. He believed that the Sun and the Solar System were in the centre. Herschel published his idea in 1784, and although we now know that he was not quite correct, he was certainly thinking along the right lines with this theory.

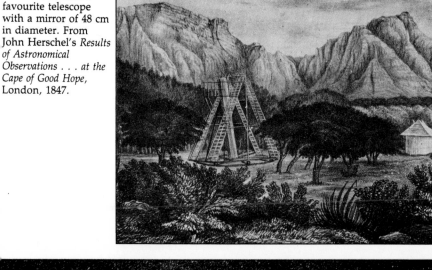

William Herschel's favourite telescope with a mirror of 48 cm in diameter. From John Herschel's *Results of Astronomical Observations . . . at the Cape of Good Hope*, London, 1847.

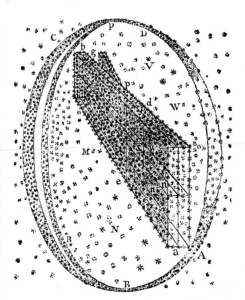

above
William Herschel believed that the stars were distributed in space in the form of a box. From *Encyclopedia Londiniensis*, London, *c* 1810.

left
Part of the Milky Way near Cygnus containing a number of gaseous nebulae.

STAR CLUSTERS

In the sky there are some lovely star clusters to be observed. They are groups in which the stars seem close to each other. Some of the stars can be seen with the naked eye, but the true beauty of a cluster can only be appreciated through a telescope or binoculars.

The most noticeable and beautiful of all the star clusters in the sky is without doubt the Pleiades. It can be found in the winter constellation of Taurus, and Fig. 1 shows where it lies. With the unaided eye, Galileo saw only six stars in this cluster, despite the clear skies of seventeenth-century Florence, yet there are more than this. The name Pleiades comes from Greek legend: they were seven sisters – Alcyone, Celaeno, Electra, Maia, Merope, Sterope, and Taygete – daughters of Atlas, who supported the 'pillars of heaven'. The seven sisters suggest that there are seven bright stars in the cluster, not six, and some observers have seen seven, or even more stars. Michael Maestlin, who was observing about 1580, some 30 years before the first use of the telescope in astronomy, plotted eleven stars, but this was exceptional. Yet as the cluster was known as the 'seven sisters' it may be that one of them was once brighter than it is now. Certainly, looking at old records of the Pleiades, it seems that the members of the cluster have varied in brightness. Alcyone, now the brightest, was not catalogued by Ptolemy in AD 145 and must have been dimmer, while another, known as Pleione, has erupted and thrown off shells of gas from time to time which makes it temporarily brighter. The last time this happened was in 1970.

In a telescope many more than seven stars can be seen. Galileo observed thirty-six, and in modern times photographs taken through professionals' telescopes have shown that the cluster contains 120 stars or more. The brighter members are surrounded by clouds of gas. Taurus has another lovely 'open cluster' of stars known as the Hyades. The name is Greek and means 'the rainers' because the cluster set in the evenings and rose in morning

twilight at rainy times of the year. The Hyades spread across 8° of sky due mainly to the fact that they are the nearest cluster to us, lying at 150 light-years, compared with 400 light-years for the Pleiades. Twenty-seven stars can be seen with the naked eye, and binoculars will show more.

Another group well worth observing with binoculars or

telescope is the 'double' cluster in Perseus. Visible to the unaided eye as a couple of hazy patches lying very close together between Cassiopeia and Perseus, they are magnificent when observed through an optical instrument. The one to the west has a red star at its centre. These two clusters lie about 7,100 light-years away from us.

Two other open clusters that are

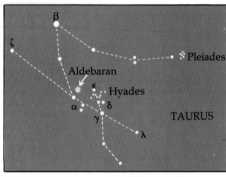

Fig. 1 above
The constellation of Taurus showing the positions of the Hyades and Pleiades clusters.

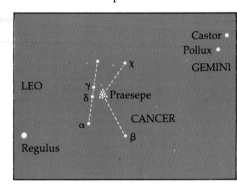

Fig. 2 above
The beautiful beehive cluster of Praesepe in Cancer with surrounding stars to help locate it.

Fig. 3 below
The double cluster in Perseus round the stars h and χ Persei.

Fig. 4 above
The Jewel box cluster, only visible from the southern hemisphere, has stars of many different colours.

delightful to see in a telescope are Praesepe and the 'Jewel box' cluster. Praesepe is a bright object in Cancer which looks fuzzy to the unaided eye (Fig. 2). Situated at a distance of 500 light-years, it is a widely spread out cluster with more than 200 members, although binoculars will show only about forty. The name Praesepe means 'manger' in Latin; the cluster is so-called because it lies between the two stars γ and δ Cancri which have the Latin names Asellus Borealis (Northern Ass) and Asellus Australis (Southern Ass).

The 'Jewel box' is only visible to southern hemisphere observers. It is in the constellation Crux, the Cross, the star κ Crucis, which is a brilliant red, providing a great contrast with the other stars. William Herschel's son, John Herschel, gave it the name 'Jewel box' and with a telescope more than 100 stars can be seen in spite of the fact it is 7,800 light-years from the Earth.

Open clusters are only one type of star group: another is the globular cluster. These are not as beautiful as open clusters, but they are astonishing since they contain hundreds of thousands, or even millions, of stars packed comparatively close together: they look in a photograph (Fig. 5) as though they are touching one another. This is not so; towards the centre of such a cluster, where the stars are most densely packed, there are still only about one or two stars per cubic light-year.

The largest and most readily observable globular cluster in the northern hemisphere is one in Hercules (Fig. 5), catalogued by the French astronomer Charles Messier in the eighteenth century, and now known as Messier 13 or, more usually, M13. It can be seen with the unaided eye as a hazy patch of about 6th magnitude, but through a telescope (preferably 15 cm or more) you will see it as a blob of light surrounded by hundreds of stars. It is about 25,000 light-years distant, and contains about 100,000 stars. Its diameter is about 170 light-years.

Another globular cluster visible with a small telescope is M4 in Scorpius, near Antares. Like M13 this has a magnitude of about 6 and you can see it without optical aid on a clear night. In a small telescope it is a hazy circular patch, brighter in the centre than at the edge. Its distance is some 5,700 light years, making it the nearest of all the globular clusters, and it contains stars equal in mass to some 60,000 Suns.

Lastly, there are two wonderful globular clusters visible to observers in the southern hemisphere. One is 47 Tucanae in the constellation Tucana (the Toucan), a fifth magnitude object some 13,000 light-years from us: the other is ω Centauri, probably the finest of all the globular clusters to see. It is magnitude 3.6, so is readily visible with the unaided eye, and on photographs it shows well the characteristic structure of a globular cluster. Its distance is 16,500 light-years and it is gigantic with a diameter of 620 light-years.

There are, of course, many more clusters than those described here, and reference books will give details of these (see book list on page 200). How they fit into the scheme of the galaxy is explained on pages 168–169.

Fig. 5 above
The globular cluster M13 in the constellation of Hercules is the largest in the northern sky.

Fig. 6 below
The globular cluster ω Centauri, visible in the southern skies, is the largest in our galaxy with a diameter of more than 600 light-years.

NEBULAE

Nebulae are great clouds of gas and dust spread over large areas of the sky. They appear either bright or dark, and are best observed through a telescope. A photograph, however, will often reveal parts of a nebula that cannot otherwise be seen.

The bright nebulae are clouds of gas which are usually set glowing by stars embedded in them. The brightest nebula in the sky is M42, the Great Nebula in Orion. Fig. 1 shows where it can be found in Orion, lying in Orion's sword, between the stars σ and ι, with the multiple star θ in it. Discovered in 1610 by Nicholas Peiresc, it is a truly magnificent sight: long-exposure colour photographs show it at its best because they bring out the colour and show up parts of the nebula which the observer never sees, because the light is too dim, even through a telescope, to stimulate the colour receptors in our eyes.

The Orion nebula is a bright 'emission' nebula, shining because of the hot stars in it, which emit ultraviolet light. This light ionizes the hydrogen atoms in the gas, and as the particles (electrons and protons) of these atoms combine once again,

the atoms emit radiation, mainly pinkish in colour. It lies at a distance of 1,300 light-years. Right inside the nebula, which has a diameter of about 30 light-years, new stars are condensing out of the dust and gas.

There are hundreds of other emission nebulae in the sky, many of them worth observing, although you must not expect any of them to look as good in a telescope as they do in photographs, even black and white ones. The reason is simple enough; photographs show up parts of the nebula which are too dim to affect your eye, but which will gradually build up an image on a photograph. So do not be disappointed.

Another emission nebula is the Lagoon nebula (M8) in Sagittarius, a constellation which straddles the Milky Way. Binoculars will show the great spread of this nebula, which covers 1° × ½° of the sky, and a telescope will, of course, give more detail. Fig. 2 shows where to find the Lagoon and another famous nebula, the Trifid. There is a small cluster of stars in the middle of the Lagoon nebula, which shows dark patches and spots. In the spots new stars are believed to be forming. The nebula lies at a distance of 4,500 light-years and its pink colour is due to glowing hydrogen. About 1⅓ arc minutes north of the Lagoon lies the Trifid

A photograph of the Great Nebula

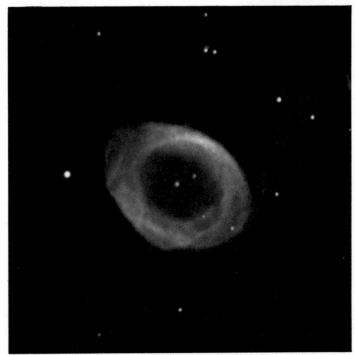

above
The Ring Nebula M57 in Lyra. This ring of gas was thrown off by a star in a late stage of evolution.

above
The Horse's Head Nebula in Orion is a dust cloud against a region of glowing hydrogen.

nebula. This is only of 9th magnitude and is not a very special sight in a telescope. Yet a colour photograph in a large telescope shows it to be very beautiful, with a glowing hydrogen colour; it appears to be split in three pieces – hence its name – but the dark parts are due to dust. Just above the Trifid, and looking almost part of it, there is a blue nebula. This is a cloud of gas lit up by the light of a star inside it. The star is not hot enough to set the gas glowing, so the nebula merely scatters the light from the star inside it, and looks blue just as the sky looks blue because it is scattering the light of our nearby star, the Sun. Such a 'reflection'

nebula is the other type of bright nebula.

If you look with a telescope in the constellation Lyra, in between the stars β and γ, you will see what looks like a round patch of light that appears like a planetary disc. Indeed, its discoverer, Antoine Darquier, who came across it in 1779 with his 7½ cm refractor, described it as 'A very dull nebula . . . as large as Jupiter and looks like a fading planet'. In Messier's catalogue it has the number 57 and so is often known as M57. It is not a planet, but is typical of yet another kind of celestial object – a sphere of gas thrown out from a star, most probably a white dwarf. A

'planetary nebula', then, is a small spherical nebula with several colours in it because different gases are set glowing by the ultraviolet light from the star at the centre. Oxygen and nitrogen give a green glow close to the star, but further out the energy is only sufficient to make hydrogen glow. A star atlas or star catalogue gives other examples of this kind of nebula.

The Trifid nebula is sliced in three by dark lanes of dust, and dark dust clouds exist in space. They can be detected by radio telescopes, but in optical telescopes they can only be seen when they blot out light from nearby stars or nebulae. In Orion near ζ Orionis there is a famous dark nebula known as the 'Horse's Head' for a reason easily seen from the picture. The bright emission nebula is shining in pink hydrogen light, and the dark dust cloud with the 'Horse's Head' projecting into it lies nearer to us. The blue nebula on the left is nearer still. The dark material is dust, and the Horse's Head itself is made of dust particles which in due course will break away from the main mass of dark material. The Horse's Head will then disintegrate into particles and these may form the central parts of new stars, as gas collects around them. This wonderful dark nebula is not visible in binoculars or even in a amateur's small telescope. But if you look at the star ζ Orionis, you will see it seems to lie in an almost totally empty space. That is because there is a vast dust cloud behind it, the Horse's Head nebula.

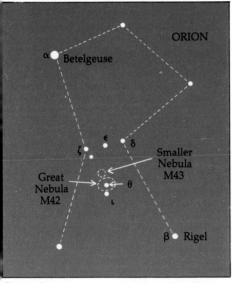

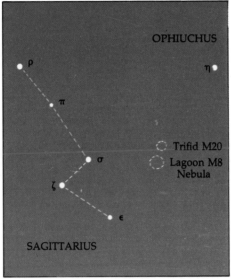

Fig. 1 above
The constellation of Orion showing the
location of the Great Nebula M42 and the smaller nebula M43.

Fig. 2 above
The constellation of Sagittarius showing the Lagoon Nebula M8 and the Trifid M20.

below
Photographs of the Lagoon and Trifid Nebulae, pink from glowing hydrogen.

THE MILKY WAY

The band of hazy light which extends across the night sky is known as the Milky Way. This is part of our galaxy and is composed of billions of separate stars.

When Galileo turned his telescope to the Milky Way he recorded that 'all the disputes which have tormented philosophers through so many ages are exploded at once by the irrefragable evidence of our eyes.' The Milky Way, he said, ' . . . is nothing else but a mass of innumerable stars planted together in clusters'. Look at it yourself through binoculars or, better still, a telescope and you will see that this is true enough. The Milky Way *is* a collection of stars, but why are they all concentrated together in a small band across the entire sky?

William Herschel's star counting led him to suggest that the universe of stars was like a kind of flattish box in shape (page 163). If this were so and if the stars were concentrated more in one section of the box than anywhere else, and if, in addition, the Sun was in the centre as he suggested, then an observer on any one of the Sun's planets would see something very like the Milky Way. All around us would be a layer of stars and they would only spread over a certain band of the sky. Look

at a photograph of the whole sky, or observe it on a clear moonless night. Either will show that this is what the Milky Way does. Does this then mean that the universe of stars is box-shaped?

The answer is 'not quite'. Studies of the Milky Way, its brightness, the number of stars in various parts of it, and the width of the band of sky which it covers, made with optical and radio telescopes, show us that our island of stars and nebulous gas is disc-shaped and not like a box. It is rather like two soup plates placed face to face – in other words, a disc with a central bulge (Fig. 1).

Because the galaxy is soup-plate

shaped, when we look up in the sky away from the central layer of stars, we would expect to see many fewer stars and this is what happens in most of the sky we look at. We are observing in a direction at right-angles to the soup-plates, and so observing far fewer stars. We are looking in the directions A, B, C and D Only in directions E, F, G and H do we see the Milky Way and the main concentration of stars.

The size of this star island or galaxy (so named because *galaxias* is the Greek word for 'milky') is vast. Even the central bulge is almost 10,000 light-years thick and the diameter of the whole galaxy is

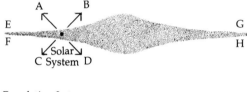

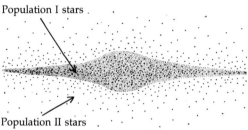

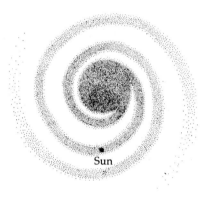

Fig. 1 top
A section through our galaxy showing its shape and the position of the Sun and stars.

Fig. 2 above
The distribution of Population I and Population II stars in the Milky Way.

Fig. 3 above right
Our galaxy seen from above is a spiral of dust, gas and stars, with the Sun in one of its arms.

Fig. 4 below
This is a photographic map of the entire Milky Way showing the concentration of stars, dust and gas in the central plane of our galaxy.

nearly 100,000 light-years. Herschel was wrong, though, when he thought the Sun was in the centre: in fact, it lies some 32,000 light-years away from the centre.

The greatest concentration of stars in the Milky Way occurs in that part which lies to the west side of Sagittarius. It is in this direction that the centre of the galaxy lies. But there is an observation problem, as there is much dark obscuring matter in this area. Between Sagittarius and Ophiuchus there seem to be separate bits of the Milky Way, and great dark patches where there are very few stars.

Radio telescopes can penetrate some of this dust, and confirm that this is the direction of the centre of the galaxy. But both they and optical telescopes make it clear that we cannot see to the centre of the galaxy from our position. One thing, however, that radio astronomers have been able to discover is that the stars, dust and gas in the plane of the galaxy (i.e. in the layer EGHF of Fig. 1) are arranged in a spiral (Fig. 2).

It is in the plane of the galaxy, or close to it, that we find a lot of the dust and gas clouds – the nebulae – and the open clusters. One thing not to be found there, however, are any globular clusters. Globular clusters are always found away from the plane of the galaxy, never close to it. From this evidence, and much more besides, all of it concerned with the way stars develop throughout their lifetimes, the American astronomer Walter Baade, in the 1940s, classified stars into two groups or 'populations'. Population I comprises the kind of stars found in the spiral arms which lie in the plane of the galaxy. These are comparatively young stars, and, as we have seen when looking at the Great Nebula in Orion, there are dark globules where it appears new stars are being born. Population II stars are old ones and they are found in the central regions of the galaxy and in the 'galactic halo' formed by the globular clusters. The layout is, in fact, rather like that shown in Fig. 1. Of course, this separation into two groups gives rather a simplified picture. In practice, there seem to be some stars and some globular clusters which are intermediate in age between Population I and Population II, but the fact remains that most globular clusters contain old stars.

By looking at nebulae and star clusters we can see different stages in the life-cycle of a star (pages 76–79). Open clusters, such as the Pleiades and Hyades, are made up of fairly youngish stars. The Orion nebula or the Lagoon nebula are places where stars are coming into being. On the other hand, globular clusters consist of ageing stars and stars that are very old; and a planetary nebula is in fact a star at the white dwarf stage, close to the end of its life.

Fig. 4 above
A dark nebula in Sagittarius showing up clearly against the background of bright stars and nebulae.

Fig. 5 below
The Milky Way in the region of Scorpius.

CHAPTER 8 GRAVITY AND SPACE

What keeps the planets in our Solar System continually in orbit? Why do objects on Earth always fall to the ground? Astronomers today give the answer as gravity, but the ancient world had its own theory.

When you visualize the Earth and other celestial bodies moving about in space, you may wonder what supports them. Why don't they fall? And where would they fall *to*? What keeps the Moon orbiting the Earth, month after month, and the Earth orbiting the Sun, year after year? Today we know that gravity is the force that keeps the planets in their orbits around the Sun. But in earlier times, when people believed that the Earth was at the centre of the universe – in other words, the universe was geocentric – there was a totally different explanation.

This old explanation was one given by the Greek philosophers of antiquity, notably Aristotle, and was based on the idea that everything in the universe had its natural place. The Earth was at the centre; around it was the air and above it the spheres which carried the Moon, the Sun, the planets and the stars. Everything around us on Earth was made of the four elements – earth, air, fire and water. The difference between one substance and another was simply the varying proportions of these elements contained in the

substance. For instance, a piece of wood was composed of the elements earth, water and a little air; a lump of lead, which was heavier, contained more earth than anything else, to account for its weight: It felt heavy because the natural place for the element earth lay at the centre of our planet Earth, the centre of the universe. The earth element was constantly seeking its natural place, and so any object containing it would

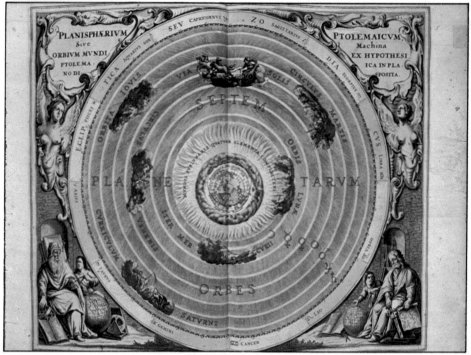

The Ptolemaic system of the universe, showing Earth at the centre surrounded by water, air and fire. From Andreas Cellarius *Harmonia Macrocosmica*, Amsterdam, 1708.

This picture of a crescent-shaped Earth and Moon – the first of its kind taken by a spacecraft – was recorded in September 1977 by Voyager 1.

fall towards the centre of the Earth when it was dropped. Because lead contained more of the earth element than did a piece of wood, it pulled itself towards the centre of the Earth more strongly, so it was said to be heavier. On the other hand, a flame was pure fire, and the natural place of the fire element was a sphere above the Earth; that is why a flame always burned upwards. And if you spilled a cup of water, it would run out all over the ground because the natural place of the element water was around the surface of the Earth.

The Greek concept of the elements was plausible when the universe was thought to be geocentric, but once Copernicus's heliocentric theory had been accepted and the Sun placed at the centre of the known universe, there were problems. It no longer seemed so logical, for example, that objects containing the element earth should fall to the Earth, because the Earth was no longer at the centre of the universe. Another problem lay in the idea – conceived by the Greeks – that all celestial bodies, from the Moon outwards, were made of a fifth element or essence – the 'quintessence' – whose natural place was the heavens. It was an incorruptible essence, which was why the heavenly bodies never showed any change. Yet once the Earth itself was acknowledged to be a celestial body, the existence of such an essence became doubtful.

When Kepler proved that the planets do not orbit in circles, as previously thought, but in ellipses, many astronomers believed that the whole scheme of the universe needed some radical rethinking. What could be the cause of such eccentric motion? Why did a planet remain in orbit? The word 'gravity' was being talked of, and some scientifically minded people had come to the conclusion that as the planets were all in orbit around the Sun, there must be some force operating on the Sun and each planet. They called this gravity, but giving it a name was not enough. They had to explain precisely how such a force could work, and the mathematics needed was beyond them. This is where Newton triumphed with his detailed mathematical explanation of the forces of gravitation.

Astronaut Edward White floating outside his space capsule during the Gemini-Titan 4 flight. He is actually in orbit round the Earth, which prevents him from falling back to Earth.

The heliocentric universe depicted by an eighteenth-century orrery made by Edward Troughton. The Sun is the central brass globe with two white globes, Mercury and Venus, near it. The Earth shows the inclined orbit of the Moon around it.

GRAVITY AND THE PLANETS

In the early 1600s Johannes Kepler had described the elliptical orbits of the planets. It remained for a later generation of scientists – notably Sir Isaac Newton – to discover the force governing these orbits and to define it in mathematical terms. This work also entailed challenging Aristotle's concept of motion.

When Newton began to study the orbits of the planets, Kepler had already formulated laws describing their motion. These laws gave precise mathematical relationships between the rate of movement of a planet and its ever-changing distance from the Sun and also explained how the average speed of one planet was related to another planet in a nearer or more distant orbit. To express all this mathematically was certainly difficult in the seventeenth century because, in considering the forces acting on a planet in an elliptical orbit, one had to deal with a distance between Sun and planet that was continuously changing. If the strength of a force acting on the Sun and a planet depended on the distance between the two – and this seemed logical – a mathematics was needed which would deal with continuously changing quantities. No such mathematics was available, and it is a mark of Newton's genius that he was able to invent one, which we now call calculus. A contemporary of Newton's, the German Gottfried Leibniz, also, quite independently, invented the calculus.

Newton began by considering the motion of the Moon round the Earth. He knew that if you whirl something round on a string and then suddenly let go, it will fly off into space (along MA in Fig. 1). Try it when you are outside (and no one is standing nearby), using a weight of some sort firmly tied to the end of a string. Whirl the string round and the weight will orbit round your hand. Let go suddenly and the weight will fly off into 'space', taking the string with it.

There is a story that while Newton was sitting under an apple

tree in the garden of his family home at Woolsthorpe, in Lincolnshire, an apple dropped at his feet. This set him wondering whether the force that pulled the apple to the ground was the same as the force which pulled the Moon towards the Earth. There is a force thrusting the Moon

along in the direction MA (Fig. 2), which is the direction in which the Moon would move if there were no pull from the Earth. In order for the Moon to travel in an orbit, the force along MA has continually to be balanced by another force, a pull in the direction ME towards the centre

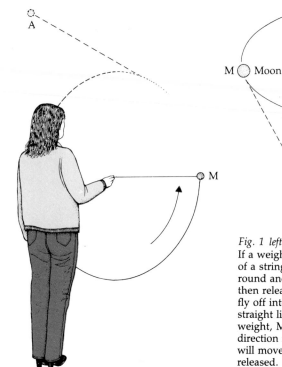

Fig. 1 left
If a weight at the end of a string is swung round and round and then released, it will fly off into space in a straight line. M is the weight, MA the direction in which it will move when released.

Fig. 2 above
The Earth's gravity keeps the Moon where it is. If it should ever vanish, the Moon would move off into space in a straight line.

Fig. 3
Aristotle believed that no body could undertake more than one motion at a time, so a projectile had to move forwards in one straight line and then fall to Earth in another.

Santbech's *Problematum Astronomicorum*, Basle, 1561.

172

of the Earth. The force along ME is the force of gravity, which the scientific community of Newton's time were discussing. It was generally thought that gravity was an 'inverse square' force, meaning that it diminishes according to the square of the distance between the bodies concerned; thus, if the bodies are moved twice as far away, the force is diminished by $2 \times 2 = 4$ times; if they are moved three times as far apart, it is diminished by $3 \times 3 = 9$ times, and so on. What Newton was able to do with his new mathematics was to prove the truth of this theory.

Newton could also answer the question about the apple. It fell to the ground at a speed which was just what it should be if the Earth pulled it with the same force as it pulled the Moon. And when he calculated the effect of the force on all the planets, he found that their calculated orbits corresponded exactly to their actual orbits. Newton called the new force 'universal gravitation' because it operated everywhere: it applied not only to the apple and to other objects on Earth but to every body in the universe. In brief, it stated that every body – celestial or otherwise – attracts every other body with a force which is proportional to the inverse square of the distance between them.

In his work on gravitation, Newton also had to consider the question of motion. Aristotle and other Greek philosophers had talked of 'natural motion'. A body falling downwards towards the centre of the Earth was, in their view, undergoing natural motion. A planet going round in orbit was performing its natural motion, which was motion in a circle. A body moving along the ground – a cart being pulled by oxen, for instance – was not undergoing natural motion; its movement was 'violent' motion, caused by the action of the oxen in pulling.

In late medieval times many people had become dissatisfied with this theory. Its inadequacy was apparent, for example, in the case of an arrow shot from a bow. The arrow begins its motion because the string of the bow pushes it, but once it has left the bow, it must, in Aristotle's view, be pushed by something all the time it is flying through the air (because this is 'violent' motion). So he said that the arrow parts the air as it moves and then the air closes in again, pulling the arrow forward as it does so. But this was not satisfactory.

To explain the motion of arrows and cannon balls they conceived the idea of *impetus*: when you gave something a push, according to this notion, it moved on for a while because of the impetus given to it by the push. Gradually this impetus became used up, and the arrow or cannon ball fell to the ground. This idea was also applied to ordinary moving bodies on the ground, and you can test it for yourself. Put a large coin on the edge of a smooth table so that part of the coin hangs over the edge. Now give it a shove with your hand: it will move across the table and then stop. According to the impetus theory, it stops because the impetus is used up.

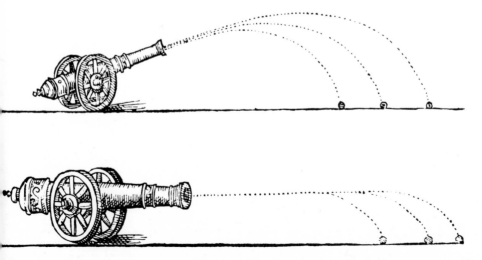

Fig. 4
An early eighteenth-century sketch of Woolsthorpe Manor, Lincolnshire, Newton's family home.

Fig. 5
The trajectory of a cannon ball shown as a parabolic path rather than a circular arc, reflecting the work of Galileo and, later, Newton on the paths of projectiles. From Robert Fludd's *Utriusque cosmi historia*, Oppenheim, 1617–19.

AN INVESTIGATION INTO FALLING BODIES

Scientists of the late Renaissance began to investigate the motion of bodies. Chief among these was Galileo, whose discoveries paved the way for Newton's work on planetary motion.

Galileo Galilei was born in 1594. At the age of twenty-five he was appointed professor of mathematics at the University of Pisa, and it was while he was there that Galileo made some important experiments about moving bodies. The most famous of these was his experiment with falling bodies – that is, bodies moving under gravity.

Galileo is supposed to have dropped a heavy and a light weight made of the same material from the Leaning Tower of Pisa and to have noted that they landed at the same time. He was not the first to do such an experiment. The Flemish scientist Simon Stevin had done such an experiment in 1586, a few years earlier. What was important was that the experiment demonstrated an error in Aristotle's view of the motion of bodies, at a time when these views were generally thought to be absolutely correct.

Aristotle believed that the heavier a body was, the more earthy material it contained; and the more earthy material it contained, the greater its attraction for its natural place, the centre of the Earth. In simple terms, this means that a heavier body will fall faster to the ground than a lighter one. Galileo and Stevin showed that Aristotle was wrong: all bodies, whether they are light or heavy, fall at the same speed.

It is not easy to demonstrate this exactly because one has to be careful that the light body is not slowed down by air resistance and that both objects start falling at precisely the same instant. But if you take, for example, a nail and a bundle of three nails tied together, and drop these at the same moment, you will find that they will both land together. Of course, if you drop one nail and one postage stamp the nail will land first. This is because the weight of the stamp is insufficient for it to cleave its way quickly through the air; it only floats gently to the floor. But they would fall at the same speed if there were no air. At the Science Museum in London this fact is demonstrated by a tube with no air in it containing a feather and a coin; the tube can be turned over and the coin and feather can be seen to land at exactly the same time.

Although bodies fall at an equal speed, regardless of weight, they do not fall at a constant speed; on Earth, falling bodies accelerate by 9.75 metres per second for every second of their fall, so moving faster and faster as they descend. In the first second of fall they reach a speed of 9.75 metres per second (22 miles per hour); at the end of the next second their speed is 19.5 metres per second (almost 44 miles per hour); at the end

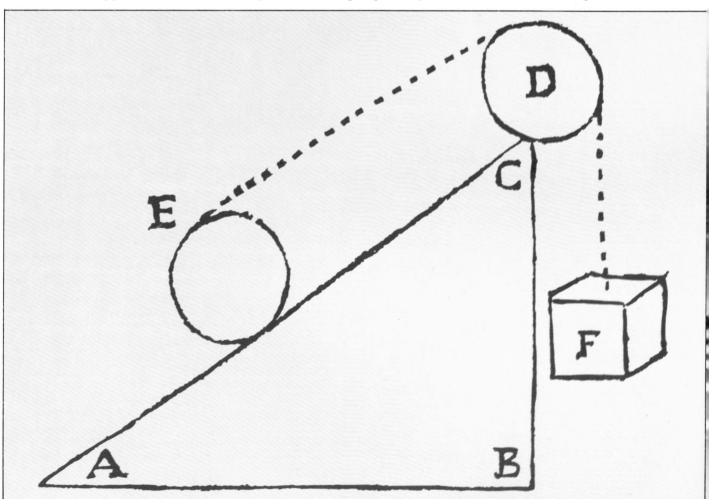

Fig. 1
Galileo's experiment to measure the force of a ball rolled down an inclined plane. From *Operere Galileo Galilei*, Bologna, 1665–66.

of the third second 29.25 metres per second (about 66 miles per hour), and so on. You can investigate this acceleration by building a simple machine out of a construction set (Fig. 2). Place it on a mantel or shelf at eye level. Put equal weights in the pans and then put an additional small weight in pan A. Pan A will now begin to descend. Note where it is on the scale after one second and then after two seconds. If you make the weights nearly equal, so that pan A falls relatively slowly, you may be able to measure the position after 3 seconds. You will find that the falling pan A moves at an increasing velocity as time passes – as does the upward-moving pan B, the motion of which is governed by the descent of the other pan.

Galileo also disproved Aristotle's idea of natural and violent motion in an experiment in which he allowed balls to roll down inclined planes. You can construct a similar experiment. Make two V-shaped troughs (Fig. 3), using either wood, polystyrene sheet like Plastikard, or stiff cardboard. Make them as long as you conveniently can; one metre is

satisfactory. Fix one trough at an angle of about 30°. Now set up your second trough at the same angle. Mark the first trough at a point about halfway along it. Take up a marble, hold it at this point and then release it. You will find that it will climb a certain way up the second trough. Next, lower the angle of the second trough to 15°. You will see that if you start the marble from the same point on the first trough, it will run further up the second. Now, if you lower the second trough a little more, the marble will run even further up it before stopping. You can now try starting with the marble only a quarter of the way up the first trough (marking this position before you release the marble). Again, as you lower the other trough more and more, so the marble climbs further and further before it stops. If the second trough is lying flat the marble should, in theory, run on indefinitely. In fact it does not do so, but we shall look into this question of why this is so in a moment.

After making his own experiments, Galileo came to the conclusion that 'any velocity once

imparted will be rigidly maintained as long as the external causes of acceleration or retardation are removed, a condition which is found only on horizontal planes. . . .' In other words, as later amplified by Newton to cover all motion – not only motion in a horizontal plane – the law states: 'Every body continues in its state of rest, or of uniform motion in a straight line, unless it is compelled to change that state by forces impressed on it'. This first law of motion was totally different from Aristotle's long accepted conception and is the law which governs motion throughout the universe.

When you pushed your coin across the table (page 173), it stopped moving after a while. According to Newton's first law of motion, the coin should go on moving if left alone; since it stops it must be acted on by some other force or forces. In this case the force is friction between the two surfaces. This force will also, eventually, bring the marble to a stop, even on a flat surface. We find that gravity and friction give a better account of the world than Aristotle's ideas were able to do.

Fig. 2
A simple machine made from a construction set to find out the speeds of falling bodies, with a side view of the wheel at the top.

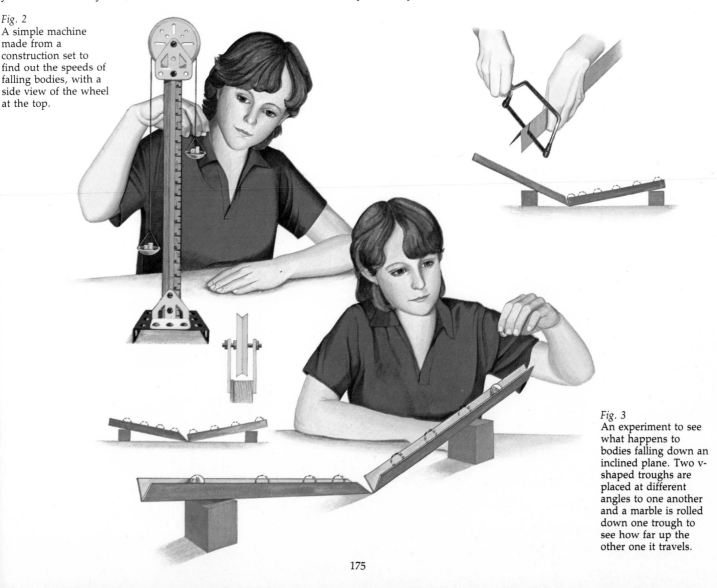

Fig. 3
An experiment to see what happens to bodies falling down an inclined plane. Two v-shaped troughs are placed at different angles to one another and a marble is rolled down one trough to see how far up the other one it travels.

GRAVITY AND SPACECRAFT

Much astronomical observation is carried out from spacecraft which are put in orbit around the Earth or Moon, or even around the Sun. The launchings and the orbits are all governed by the laws of gravity.

Newton's law of universal gravitation states that every body in the universe attracts every other body with a force which depends on the masses of the bodies and, inversely, on the square of the distance between them. This force is the force of gravity. (In mathematical shorthand you can write the law as $F \propto \frac{m_1 m_2}{d^2}$, where m_1 and m_2 are the masses of the bodies, d is the distance between them, F is the force and the sign $\propto$

means 'is proportional to.') In other words, the more massive the bodies, the stronger the force between them; and the closer they are together (the smaller d becomes), the stronger the force between them.

To launch a rocket, it must reach a certain velocity before it will go out into space. When it reaches this critical velocity, known as the 'velocity of escape', then the rocket will have enough energy to overcome the backward pull of gravity and will go into orbit. This velocity of escape is 11.18 km per sec for the Earth; for Jupiter, which is many times more massive, the velocity is 59.6 km per sec. Newton realized this principle, and in a book published after his death, based on part of his famous *Principia*, a diagram appeared showing how, if a body goes fast enough, it will escape from Earth. The drawing shows the body thrown from a mountain top, but the principle applies wherever the launching-pad may be.

Launching a rocket to reach escape velocity is not easy because chemical

fuels can only generate a limited amount of thrust per kilogram of fuel burned. Rocket engineers have to consider what they call the *mass ratio*, that is the ratio of the mass of the rocket when filled with fuel to the mass of the rocket when empty. It has been calculated that if the mass ratio is 2.72, then a rocket will reach a final speed equal to the speed at which the burning gases shoot out of its rear. If the ratio is 2.72 x 2.72, that is 7.4, then the rocket will reach twice the velocity of its exhaust gases. The maximum velocity of exhaust gases provided by chemical fuels is 4 km per sec, but to reach escape velocity from Earth the rocket needs a velocity three times this, and therefore a mass ratio of 7.4 is inadequate. A mass ratio of 20 would do the trick, giving us 12 km per sec, but this is not possible in practice because a rocket with such a mass ratio cannot be made strong enough to work safely and carry a load of instruments or astronauts into orbit.

The answer found by rocket engineers is to make a multi-stage

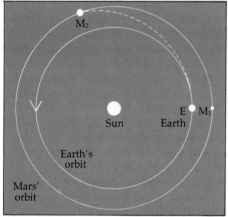

Fig. 1
Diagram to show how a spacecraft is launched from Earth. It travels in direction EM₂ because it can then use the momentum of Earth's orbit. The rocket would use more energy going to EM₁, although it is shorter.

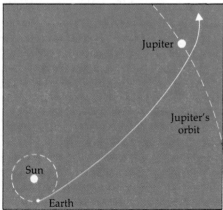

Fig. 2
Diagram to show how a spacecraft can escape from our Solar System. Here a spacecraft flies by Jupiter whose gravitational pull takes it out of orbit and gives extra impetus so that it can accelerate out of the Solar System.

Fig. 3
The Apollo/Saturn V spacecraft leaving its launching pad, 1969, on the first manned lunar landing mission.

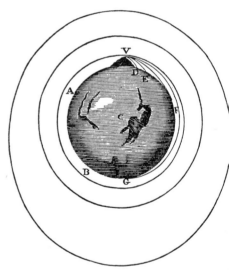

Fig. 4 above
A projectile is ejected at different velocities until it is travelling fast enough to go into orbit round the Earth. From an English translation of Newton's *System of the World*, London, 1728.

Fig. 5 opposite
Stages in the launch of a three-stage rocket. First, the rocket leaves the launching-pad. Then, when the fuel in the lower part is used up, the lower part falls away and the next stage of the rocket fires. Lastly, the second stage drops away and the third stage fires. The rocket has now reached the appropriate speed to go into orbit round the Earth or go out into space.

rocket. This consists of a series of rockets, one on top of another. One rocket fires and carries itself and the other rockets upwards until its fuel is all burned, then the empty rocket shell drops off and the next rocket fires. This already has a certain velocity so that it will reach a speed higher than that of its exhaust gases, even if its mass ratio is only 2.72. Only by using multi-stage rockets has it been possible to exceed escape velocity and put astronauts and instruments into space.

The reason why rockets are used is that they are the only kind of vehicle which will operate out in space. An aircraft flying through the air is prevented from falling to the ground because the air flowing under its wings presses upwards and keeps it aloft. If the aircraft stops moving, it will fall because it needs a forward motion to keep the air pressing up under the wings. This is demonstrated by a model aircraft or a paper dart. They continue to fly only while they are moving; if they are simply left in mid-air, they will fall.

Out in space there is no air, so all aircraft would be useless: there is nothing on which the wings can float to support the craft.

A rocket works on the principle of Newton's third law of motion: this states that when one object exerts a force on a second object, the second object exerts an equal force on the first. So if the rocket gases stream out of the rear of the rocket with a particular thrust, then the rocket is forced forward with the same thrust. And this works equally well out in space, because the rocket gases need no air to push on; they merely push on the rocket as they escape out at the back. Indeed, a rocket works more efficiently in space than it does in the Earth's atmosphere.

Once a rocket has been launched and its empty stages have been dropped off, the capsule containing the 'payload' (instruments, or astronauts, or both) is placed in the correct 'attitude' so that it is travelling at the correct speed in the right direction. Since the Earth is orbiting in space at about 29 km per

sec, satellites are always launched in the direction of the Earth's motion so that they can make use of this velocity instead of wasting energy opposing it. So when the Voyager probes were launched to Mars they followed the path shown by EM_2 in Fig. 2. No-one tried to send them by a path like EM_1 because that would have used more energy even though it is shorter, for, once launched in orbit, the spacecraft will carry on unless something stops it (Newton's first law of motion).

Once a spacecraft has left the Earth and is moving in interplanetary space, it is not on its own; it has only added an orbit round the Earth to its existing orbit (as an object on Earth) round the Sun. But if a spacecraft reaches the outer parts of the Solar System and is pulled to a faster speed by one of the larger planets (Fig. 2), it may exceed the escape velocity for the Solar System. It will then move out into interstellar space and orbit round the galaxy, this is what happened to the American space probe Pioneer 10 in December 1973.

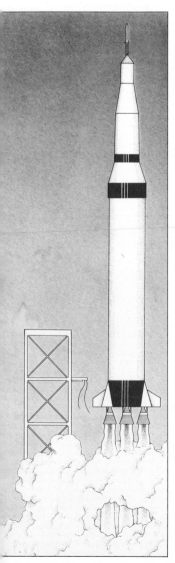

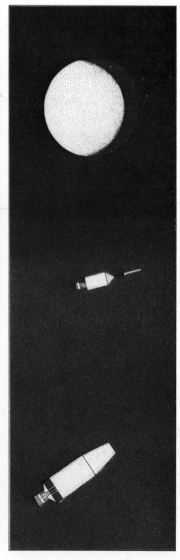

THE SPEED OF LIGHT

The speed of light is very important to astronomy, but because light travels so fast, it is difficult to measure. Observations of Jupiter's satellites are one way of determining its speed. Investigations into the speed of light pinpointed problems which were only solved later by the Theory of Relativity.

If you have ever been present at a ceremony at which cannons are fired you may have noticed that from a distance the flash appears before you hear the bang. During a thunderstorm, too, you may see a flash of lightning seconds before you hear the accompanying rumble of thunder. In each case you are experiencing the basic fact that light travels much faster than sound.

People have been well aware of this difference for a long time. Measuring the speed of sound posed few problems for scientists, but the speed of light seemed to be too great to be measured accurately. Galileo

tried and failed, and it was not until the middle of the nineteenth century that the speed of light was successfully measured in a laboratory. However, in 1676 the Danish astronomer, Ole Römer, had come close to calculating its speed as a result of observing a peculiar effect in connection with eclipses of Jupiter's satellite, Io. It is an effect which you can observe too, provided you make regular observations with a telescope – quite a small one will do – or with a pair of binoculars.

Io is the innermost of the four largest satellites of Jupiter and it takes 1.769138 days to orbit the planet. Viewed from Earth this period is just a little longer because both Jupiter and the Earth move in their orbits round the Sun, and so our viewpoint changes slightly. From Earth this period – the 'synodic' period of the satellite – is 1.76986 days or 1 day 18 hours 28 minutes 35.9 seconds. If, then, you observe Jupiter's satellites, you should see Io go into eclipse as it passes into Jupiter's shadow (Fig. 1) once every 1.76986 days. Unfortunately this is not a very convenient period for observation, for if an eclipse occurs at 19.00 hours one evening, then the next eclipse will occur some time after 1.0 pm two days later, when Jupiter will be invisible, as it will be daylight. However, four synodic periods come to a total of

7.07944 days or 7 days 1 hour 54 minutes 23.6 seconds; you can observe, therefore, every fourth eclipse at night over a period of several weeks. First you will have to find when Io is being eclipsed, but a careful watch of Jupiter for a few nights, paying special attention to Io's motion, will show you when an eclipse is due. (Or you can get this information direct from the current *Handbook* of the British Astronomical Association or from *The American Ephemeris and Nautical Almanac*).

To make your observations, first note the exact instant that Io is eclipsed. If you are using a large telescope and can see Io as a disc, then time the moment half Io's disc is covered by shadow; otherwise record the moment Io disappears as it goes into the shadow. You can do this by looking at your watch the moment it happens, or setting a stopwatch at that moment and then comparing the elapsed time later with an accurate clock or a telephone time signal, as in the case of an occultation (pages 104–107). Once you have done this you must wait a week and then make another observation of an eclipse, again noting down the time. Also note the time interval between the first observation and the second one. As the weeks go by, continue making a note of the observed times of eclipse; you will find that they change.

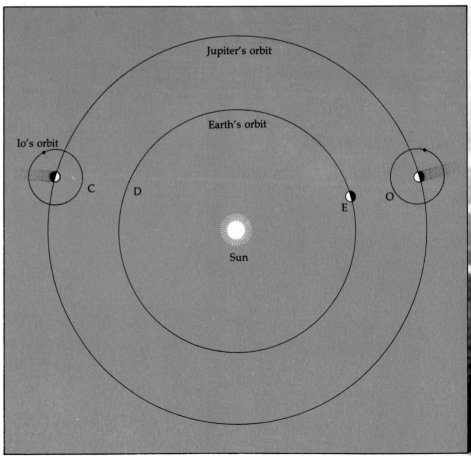

Fig. 1
The Jovian satellite, Io, moving into Jupiter's shadow during orbit.

Fig. 2
Römer's method of measuring the speed of light by eclipses of Jupiter's satellites.

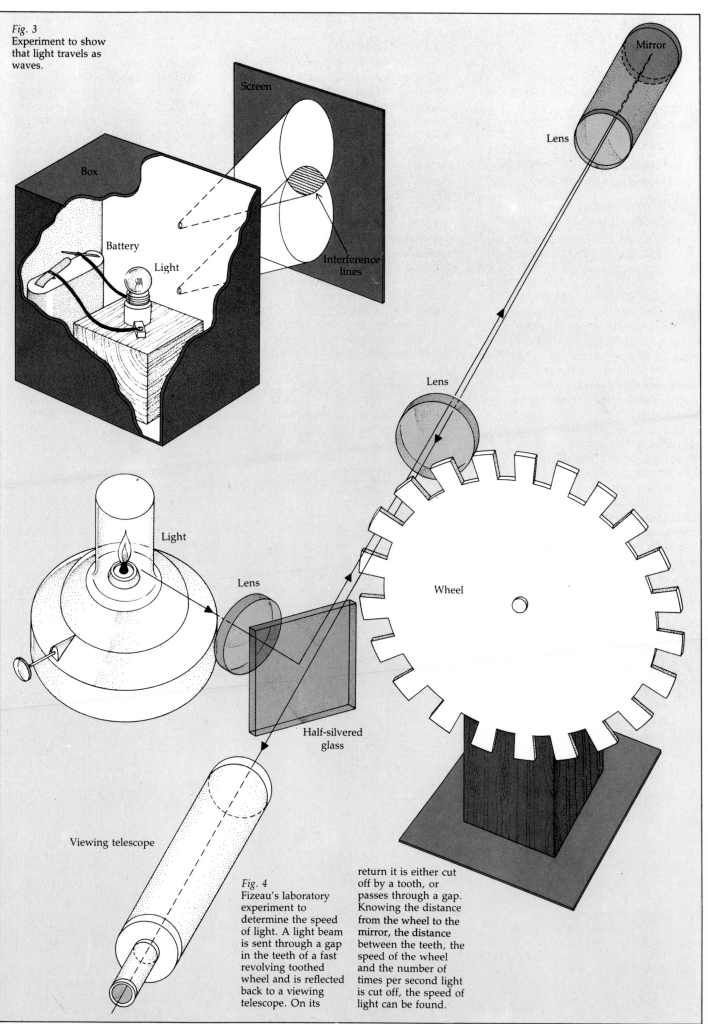

Fig. 3
Experiment to show that light travels as waves.

Mirror

Lens

Screen

Box

Battery

Light

Interference lines

Lens

Light

Wheel

Lens

Half-silvered glass

Viewing telescope

Fig. 4
Fizeau's laboratory experiment to determine the speed of light. A light beam is sent through a gap in the teeth of a fast revolving toothed wheel and is reflected back to a viewing telescope. On its return it is either cut off by a tooth, or passes through a gap. Knowing the distance from the wheel to the mirror, the distance between the teeth, the speed of the wheel and the number of times per second light is cut off, the speed of light can be found.

Depending on the relative positions of Jupiter and the Earth when you started observing, the intervals between eclipses will either increase or decrease. After some time, this trend will reverse, so that the increasing intervals begin to decrease, or vice versa. There may be a break in your observations because Jupiter is not visible for a time, but you will notice that the change in interval continues to occur.

This change in the interval between one eclipse of Io and a later one was what Römer noticed. He had been making measurements of the longitudes of places on Earth and had been using the movements of Jupiter's satellites as a celestial clock. If he used eclipses of Io – or any other satellite – he found the clock changed its rate, sometimes running slower, sometimes getting faster again. The greatest difference seemed to him to be about $16\frac{1}{2}$ minutes. What could be the cause of this?

On working out the relative positions of the Earth and Jupiter, Römer was able to see what caused the difference. To understand his discovery, look at Fig. 2. When Jupiter is in opposition (at O) the interval between eclipses is at its lowest value. On the other hand, when the Earth and Jupiter are further apart (Earth at E and Jupiter at C), the light from Jupiter (and Io) has to travel an additional distance (the distance ED) to reach an observer on Earth, and so requires more time. The additional distance is almost as large as the diameter of the Earth's orbit. (The proportion is about 0.97, although it looks less in Fig. 2 because the drawing is not to scale.) So, taking 0.97 x the diameter of the Earth's orbit and dividing this by the greatest difference between eclipse intervals for Io will give the speed of light.

Römer, using clocks which were poor by today's standards and a seventeenth-century value for the distance from the Earth to the Sun (which was not quite correct), obtained a value of 225,000 km per second for the velocity of light. This compares quite well with the modern value of 299,792 km per sec. To make your own calculation, take your greatest difference in time intervals and use a value of 290,224,000 km as the distance (ED) across the Earth's orbit, and see what value you get for the speed of light. Because this is so important in astronomy it is worthwhile making the effort to measure it. If you want to cut down the work, make some observations

close to the time of opposition and then as close as you can to conjunction (Jupiter at C). Then do your arithmetic to obtain the speed of light, (which is usually referred to in scientific formulae by the letter c).

Römer's measurement needed confirming, but it was not until nearly 200 years later, in 1849, that the French physicist Hippolyte Fizeau did so in a laboratory experiment, using a fast-moving toothed wheel and mirrors (Fig. 4). Some thirteen years later another Frenchman, Léon Foucault, (whose pendulum is described on pages 14–15) made measurements using a rotating mirror to reflect light back and got a velocity very close to the true one.

The nineteenth century also saw the triumph of the wave theory of light, in which light was believed to travel in waves and not particles, as Newton thought. One of the chief

architects of this new theory was Thomas Young. He did a famous experiment to prove the theory – one that you can easily duplicate (Fig. 3). Fit a small light bulb inside a box and pierce one end of the box with two holes. Place a sheet of white cardboard, or something similar, so that the light from the two holes falls on it. You will see two round patches of light. Turn out the room lights and you will see that where the two beams mix, there is not just a simple patch of light – instead there are alternate bands of light and dark. This is caused by the waves of light from the two holes overlapping so that sometimes both waves coincide and sometimes they cancel each other. Where they coincide there is light and where they cancel there is a dark line. The phenomenon of *interference* between beams of light can only be explained in terms of

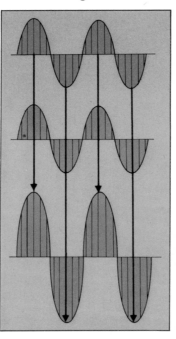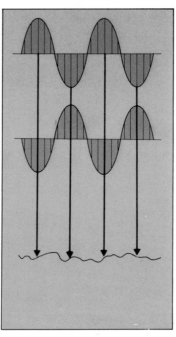

Fig. 5
Diagram to show that light waves in step reinforce each other; out of step they cancel each other out to give no light at all.

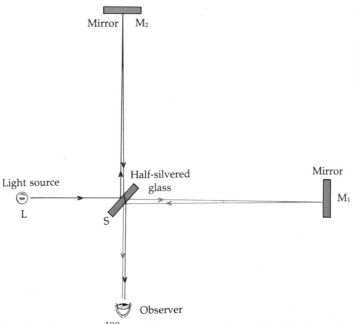

Mirror | M₂

Light source

Half-silvered glass

Mirror

M₁

L

S

Observer

Fig. 6
The Michelson-Morley experiment which showed that the Earth's motion did not affect the speed of light.

light moving in waves.

The wave theory of light had important implications. Among other things it stimulated a very famous experiment which showed that the universe is even stranger than it appears. This experiment, first made by the American Albert Michelson and then repeated by him with the help of another American, Edward Morley, in 1887, was to have the most profound effect on physics and on astronomy. The basic thinking behind the experiment was simple enough. If light was made of waves, then these waves had to travel in some substance because you cannot have waves by themselves. They must be waves in something – in the sea, or in a wind-blown field of grain for instance. It was known that there was no air in interstellar space, and yet light waves travel through space; that is how we see the stars. It was

therefore believed that there must be something out in space which carried the light, and this something was called the 'aether'. It could be neither weighed nor seen, nor did it offer any resistance to the motions of the planets as they orbited the Sun. What Michelson decided to do was to try to detect this aether by an experiment measuring the movement of Earth through it.

Michelson argued that since the Earth was moving through the aether as it orbited the Sun, it should be possible to measure changes in the speed of light depending on whether light was moving in the same direction as the Earth or perpendicular to it. The relationship between the light beam and aether might be compared to that of a swimmer and the current. Swimming with the current, he gains speed; swimming against it he loses speed.

And if he swims across the river and back, he finds no difference in his speed in either direction: the current affects him to the same degree in both directions.

Michelson used an instrument he had invented – an interferometer – which allowed two beams of light to interfere (Fig. 6). Suppose the Earth is moving from left to right, the apparatus will also travel in that direction. A beam of light goes from the light L to a sheet of lightly silvered glass S. Some of the light passes through the glass and back into the aether. It moves with the Earth to the mirror M_1, and is then reflected back, moving against the motion of the Earth to S. Here it is reflected to the observer at O. The rest of the light is reflected by S up to the mirror M_2: it moves across the Earth's motion at right-angles and is then reflected back, once more at right-angles to the Earth's motion. On arriving at S, the light goes through to join the other beam and interfere with it. Thus the observer at O will be watching two interfering beams and will see light and dark interference patches. (The distances SM_1 and SM_2 are the same.)

If you work on the assumption that light travels through aether, then taking the analogy of the swimmer and the current you would expect the speed of light travelling in the direction of the Earth's orbit to differ from that of light travelling perpendicular to this direction. Thus, when Michelson rotated his apparatus through 90°, so that SM_2 lay in line with the Earth's motion and SM_1 at right-angles to it, he expected the speeds in the two directions to change over, thus causing a shift in the pattern of light and dark interference patches. But no change in the pattern occurred.

When Michelson first performed the experiment, in 1881, he observed no shift at all. He and Morley, therefore, made the apparatus more sensitive and repeated the experiment in 1887; again there was no shift. The experiment was repeated when the Earth was moving in the opposite direction, but still no shift was seen. Yet the result did not make sense. It seemed incredible that the speed of light was not affected by the Earth's motion and remained constant. The scientific world searched for an explanation, but it was not until 1905, when a young German called Albert Einstein published a paper, that one was found. It was called the Special Theory of Relativity.

Fig. 7
Fighter planes with jet streams. Fast-flying aircraft are seen before they are heard because light travels much faster than sound.

THE THEORY OF RELATIVITY

In 1697 Isaac Newton published his *Principia* and lent a new dimension to the world of astronomy with his gravitational theory and laws of motion. Between 1905 and 1916 Albert Einstein published his Theory of Relativity. This modified Newton's ideas and provided scientists with a more accurate method of interpreting gravitation and problems posed by space and time in the universe.

Newton's theory of gravitation is concerned with expressing the behaviour of the world around us using the basic dimensions we can measure – mass, length and time. In working out his theory, Newton took for granted that in measuring something, you could rely on that measurement to be the same always. This seemed like common sense. If a brick was 21 cm long, it stayed 21 cm long, no matter who measured it. In Newton's universe everything remained fixed and absolute.

The starting point of Einstein's Theory of Relativity is that there is no fixed still point in the universe, but that everything is moving relative to something else. This affects measurement, as the speed of both the observer and observed is involved. We usually measure motion with reference to the Earth, but this is only relative as the Earth is moving in orbit round the Sun. Yet if we measure motion with reference to the Sun, that will only be relative because the Sun is in orbit round the centre of the galaxy. But the galaxy itself is not fixed in space; wherever we look we see bodies in motion relative to each other.

This is very important because it affects our laws of motion. For example, Newton's first law of motion begins: 'Every body continues in its state of rest, or of uniform motion in a straight line, unless . . .', but if we have no fixed point in the universe, we can have no absolute state of rest such as Newton visualized. Continue with his second law of motion: 'The change in motion is proportional to the motive force

impressed . . . .' Here again change in motion is relative; it depends what we are taking as fixed – the Earth, the Sun, the galaxy or whatever. And if change of motion is relative so, too, is force, according to Newton's definition. For physics, the implications of a relativity viewpoint are immense.

Einstein was not the first to realize that there was nothing fixed in the universe, but he was the first to tackle its implications and to work out its consequences in detail. He began first to consider only bodies in

uniform motion relative to one another, ignoring any changes of speed; so to start with he did not deal with falling bodies, or gravity. The first theory was therefore called the Special Theory of Relativity, because it dealt with special kinds of motion: it was published in 1905. After this Einstein worked on the next stage, which incorporated changes in velocity, or acceleration, including falling bodies under gravity and, indeed, the whole question of gravitation. The new and broader General Theory of Relativity was

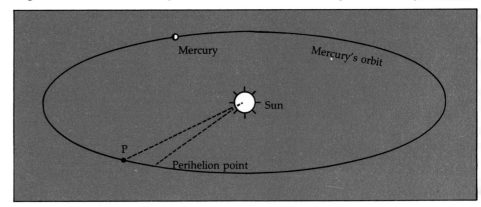

Fig. 1
Diagram showing the effect of gravitational pull on the perihelion point in Mercury's orbit.

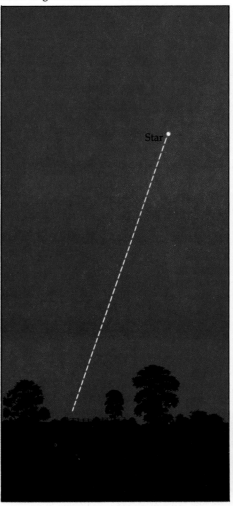
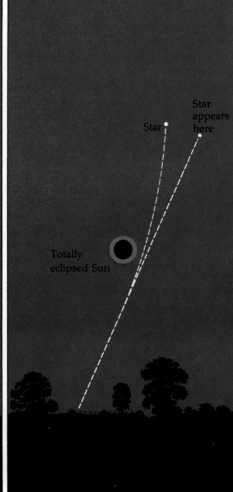

Fig. 2
During a total eclipse of the Sun the stars can be seen, but the positions of those near the Sun are distorted because the Sun curves the space—and therefore the light.

published in 1916.

In working out his Special Theory of Relativity, Einstein noted the results of the Michelson-Morley experiment (page 181) and especially the interpretation of it by two physicists, the Irishman George Fitzgerald and the Dutchman Hendrik Lorentz. They had argued that mass, length and time were different for a moving body compared with a stationary one. More precisely, Lorentz showed that the mass of a moving body should increase with speed, length should shorten, and time should slow down. Yet all Lorentz's equations expressing these changes were nullified as soon as a body reached the speed of light. When Einstein examined them, he realized that the speed of light was crucial in these calculations.

Common sense would suggest that if you literally ran towards a ray of light, you would see it approach you faster than if you were standing still. Yet the Michelson-Morley experiment showed that if you added any other speed to the speed of light, you would still end up with the speed of light, since nothing travels faster than light. Einstein therefore built this into his Theory of Relativity. It may have set aside commonsense notions, but was remarkable in giving a much more accurate description of the universe than Newton's laws.

An increase of mass with speed may also sound improbable, but we now have practical proof that it is true. When physicists accelerate atomic particles in an atom-smashing machine until they are travelling very fast indeed – at speeds half the speed of light or more – and measure the mass of the particles, they get a strange result. The fast-moving particles weigh more than they did when they were standing still. Their mass has increased.

The Theory of Relativity explains that this increase of mass happens to every moving body. When you throw a ball, its mass increases while it is moving relative to you. When astronauts travel to the Moon, their masses measured by someone back on Earth are greater while they are actually moving in orbit than when they are stationary. The astronauts themselves notice no change because they are not moving relative to each other; they are sitting still in their moving spacecraft.

Although relativity claims that the mass of a moving body is greater than its mass when standing still, the difference is tiny unless the body is moving very quickly. For most bodies on Earth this difference is too small for us to notice. For instance, if you throw a ball as fast as you can, its change in mass will only be 2,000 millionths greater than its mass when at rest. This is too small to be measurable and is why the results of relativity seem to go against commonsense experience. In astronomy, however, where we deal with speeds which are very large, the changes do show up.

Relativity states that not only mass, but length and time alter too. So if we observe a spacecraft going out into space then, because it is moving relative to us, while its mass increases, its length decreases. If you had a super-powerful telescope and could see inside the fast-moving spacecraft, you would see things become shorter in length. And, even more surprising, if you watched a clock on the wall of the spacecraft, you would see it running slower than an equivalent clock on Earth.

The General Theory of Relativity is more complicated than the special one, but one thing that becomes

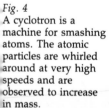

Fig. 3
Hinkley Point nuclear power station, Somerset, England, showing the machine control platform and upper magazine.

Fig. 4
A cyclotron is a machine for smashing atoms. The atomic particles are whirled around at very high speeds and are observed to increase in mass.

evident in both is that the universe is made up of something more than three-dimensional space. Imagine a brick 21 cm long, 10 cm deep and 10 cm wide. Does it exist only in these three dimensions? In reality, the brick is undergoing chemical changes from moment to moment until it eventually crumbles to dust. To describe the brick fully, we must not only say where it is and how big it is, but we must also say *when* it is. Einstein developed this idea to show that the universe exists in four dimensions: the three dimensions of space and the fourth of time. This amalgam is called 'space-time'.

Einstein also showed that space-time is curved and its curvature increases wherever an object having mass is present. The effect of this curve is to make objects in the universe move along particular paths. For example, the way in which space curves round the Sun makes the planets orbit in the way they do. So the force of gravity which Newton 'discovered' and saw as a force reaching out from objects across space to attract others was no more than a basic property of space-time itself. As Einstein once said: 'Space tells mass how to behave and mass tells space how to behave'.

In Newton's theory the gravitational force between two bodies depends on the masses of the bodies and the distance between them; in relativity masses and distances vary with speed so even the force of universal gravitation is not fixed. Because of this there is no way of measuring whether a body is being acted upon by gravity or whether it is simply accelerating away. The fact that one cannot distinguish between movement under gravity or a simple acceleration is called the principle of equivalence. It is very important for all studies of the basic quantities in physics – mass, motion and acceleration.

To illustrate this, imagine you are put into a large box without any windows, and you drop a coin. What will happen? The coin will land on the floor. Now suppose that your box is out in space, right away from the Earth's (and the Sun's) gravitational field, and it suddenly begins to accelerate 'upwards', i.e. in a direction straight above your head. Now you drop another coin. What happens this time? There is no gravitational field to pull it down, so will it just stay in your hand? The answer is 'yes and no'. It will remain at the point where your hand was because there is no gravity to make it

fall, but your hand will not stay in the same place. As the box is moving upwards, so its floor moves upwards, carrying you with it and away from the coin. In due course, though, the floor will have moved up enough to hit the coin. But what will you experience? As the box is moving upwards you will get just the same feelings as if you were in a gravitational field. You would also see the coin leave your fingers and apparently drop to the floor. You could not tell whether you were in a gravitational field or just accelerating.

This, too, is what happens to astronauts in orbit round the Earth. They are moving forwards and also falling down in a gravitational field – this is why they orbit. Gravity pulls them downwards, but their mass keeps them moving forwards so they stay where they are, experiencing 'free-fall' conditions, always falling towards the Earth, but never reaching it because of their forward motion. These 'free-fall' conditions are sometimes described as 'zero gravity' conditions, but this description must not be taken

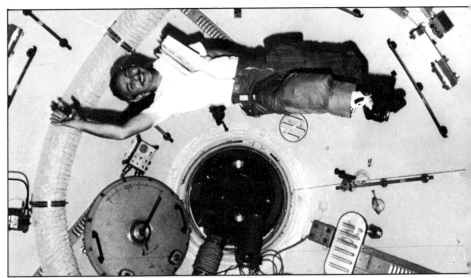

Fig. 5
Zero-gravity conditions in Skylab. Here the Earth's gravity is nullified by a thrust in another direction, so that the astronaut experiences no gravitational pull and floats near the dome.

Fig. 6
Reactor operators use a small crane to remove a fuel element from the High Flux Isotope Reactor at the Oak Ridge National Laboratory, USA.

literally: gravity *is* there, otherwise the spacecraft and astronauts would zoom off into space.

In astronomy, scientists deal with very large volumes of space in which gravitational fields are not everywhere the same. So to overcome this, Einstein had to link space and gravitation in a particular relationship. Near the Earth Newton's theory explains things very well, but in the larger spaces of the universe it begins to break down. This can be seen in studies of the orbit of the planet Mercury. As it orbits the Sun the whole orbit itself rotates (Fig. 1). According to Newton's theory of gravitation this motion of Mercury's orbit should be such that the perihelion point P moves round 9 minutes of arc per century. On the other hand observations show that the perihelion moves faster than this, at a rate of 9.57 minutes per century. Why is there this difference? People suggested that there was another planet still closer to the Sun – they even gave it a name, Vulcan – but it has never been seen. Einstein's General Theory of Relativity clears up the difficulty, however. According to his theory, gravitational pulls by the planets should cause the rate to be 9.57 minutes, just what is observed. According to relativity, the presence of a body curves the space close to it.

Evidence to support this comes from total eclipses of the Sun (page 28). At that time the stars are visible in the sky although it is daytime, and relativity theory predicted that when this happened, the positions of the stars would appear to be shifted due to space being distorted near the Sun because of the Sun's mass. So a beam of starlight, which would ordinarily travel in a straight line, will move in a curve near the Sun (Fig. 2). This will give us the impression that the star is further from the Sun in the sky than is really so.

This is difficult to prove for yourself because evidence is available only if there is a total solar eclipse and you must have photographs of the sky during eclipse and at some other time when the Sun is not in that area of the sky. You must also measure these with the most delicate equipment. But to demonstrate the principle, make the following model. You will need a simple wooden frame on short legs. Next take a rubber sheet and draw a line across its middle to represent a beam of starlight. Now stretch the sheet lightly over the frame and fix it in place with drawing-pins. You now want something to represent the Sun: a marble will do (provided you have not stretched the rubber sheet too tightly). Put the marble near the centre of the sheet and you will see it 'distorts' space as represented by the rubber sheet. Now look at the line of starlight: it has curved round the Sun.

In the total solar eclipse of 1919, measurements confirmed Einstein's theory, and observations made at subsequent total eclipses have done the same. There are also other observations, all of which confirm that we live in a 'relativistic' universe, not just a Newtonian one.

Another consequence of the Theory of Relativity is that mass and energy are interchangeable. Einstein expressed this in his famous equation $E = mc^2$, which tells us that a vast amount of energy (E) will be released when a quite small amount of mass (m) is annihilated (because m is multiplied by the square of the speed of light, c, and this is a very large number). This vast release of energy occurs in nuclear explosions, in nuclear power stations and, above all, in the Sun and stars.

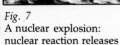

Fig. 7
A nuclear explosion: nuclear reaction releases vast amounts of energy, as predicted in Einstein's equation $E=mc^2$.

CHAPTER 9
THE DEPTHS OF SPACE

Our galaxy is a vast conglomeration of planets, stars, dust and gas, whirling round in space. One of the most astounding facts of modern astronomy is that we now know that our galaxy is only one out of millions of galaxies extending into space as far as the largest telescopes can see.

When William Herschel began to study the stars in the eighteenth century, using his powerful home-made telescopes, he discovered that a few of the nebulae were really collections of stars. This caused him to wonder whether perhaps all nebulae were clusters of stars, and only appeared hazy because of limitations in his telescopes. Even with his famous 'forty-foot telescope', completed in 1789 and containing a mirror 1.2m in diameter, he still found that while he could resolve more nebulae, there were still many which could not be resolved into separate stars; they remained as cloudy patches of light.

Would a still larger telescope be successful in resolving all of them? The third Earl of Rosse, who lived at Parsonstown, Ireland, certainly thought it might. He started a vast enterprise aimed at constructing a telescope with a mirror of 1.8 m diameter and a resolving power at least one and a half times better than Herschel's largest instrument, and after many difficulties he succeeded. The new giant telescope was finished

in 1845, and with it the Earl of Rosse began to examine nebulae. He found that many, although not all, of the nebulae could be resolved, and that some, like the nebula M51 in the Canes Venatici (the Hunting Dogs) constellation (Fig. 2), seemed to have a spiral structure, similar to a pin-wheel firework.

For some years astronomers argued the question of whether all nebulae were stars or whether some were genuine gas clouds. The problem was

solved in 1864 by the amateur astronomer William Huggins, who observed the spectrum of a nebula. Huggins saw a spectrum of bright lines on a dark background and this (pages 38–39) was certain evidence for a cloud of glowing gas. Other unresolved nebulae also showed such spectra (Fig. 3). So the question was answered: some nebulae were clouds of gas, but others were certainly collections of stars and had star-like spectra.

Fig. 1 left
Lord Rosse's giant 1.8 m reflector at Birr Castle. It could move only in a north-south direction, but the Earth's rotation allowed movement in an east-west direction. From Flammarion's *Astronomie Populaire*, Paris, 1881.

Fig. 2 below
Engraving of Lord Rosse's drawing of the spiral galaxy in Canes Venatici. From *Philosophical Transactions* London 1850.

Fig. 5
The barred spiral galaxy in Pegasus NGC 7479.

Fig. 6
The spiral galaxy M81 in Ursa Major.

Fig. 7 above
A close-up view of the elliptical galaxy NGC 147 in Cassiopeia.

Fig. 8 opposite
The Great Galaxy in Andromeda M31.

The discovery of what, for a time, were called the 'spiral nebulae' posed a new puzzle for astronomers: were they part of our own galaxy or did they lie outside it? At the turn of the century, no one could decide for certain because the size of our own galaxy was not known precisely and the distance of even one spiral nebula was not known even approximately. Arguments raged until, in 1922 and 1923, the Cepheid variable stars were discovered (pages 82–85) within some spiral nebulae, and their apparent magnitudes measured. These showed that the distances of such spiral nebulae were to be measured in millions of light-years, not merely in thousands. It was at last clear that they were not part of our own galaxy, but star-islands or galaxies in their own right. Later the name 'spiral nebulae' was dropped completely and they were called 'galaxies'.

Not all galaxies are spirals; some show no spiral structure although they are often elliptical in shape, and are, therefore, known as 'ellipticals'. Obviously there is a real difference between an elliptical galaxy and a spiral one, but before trying to discover what this difference is, it is necessary to classify galaxies in rather more detail. Elliptical and spiral are the two main types – although the spirals are themselves classified into two different kinds: the ordinary spiral and the barred spiral, which is a spiral with a bar of material across the centre. The ordinary spirals are designated by the letter S, the barred type by SB. They are further subdivided according to other variations in their structure (pages 188–189), while the ellipticals are classified according to the degree of ovalness in their shapes, on a scale of 0 to 7 – the higher numbers indicating greater ellipticity. The initial M, which appears before the number of some galaxies, stands for Messier, the eighteenth-century French astronomer who catalogued some 100 nebulae, many of which were later identified as galaxies. More recently discovered galaxies are catalogued using various other systems.

Galaxies are not easy to see with an amateur's telescope, although some advanced amateurs have taken photographs of them, using long exposure to build up a detailed image. But this will not result in the kind of picture that you find in most modern books on astronomy, including this one; those are taken through very large professional telescopes with apertures of 1.5 m or more. All the same, a look through a small telescope may be rewarding. The spiral in Andromeda, M31, is relatively easy to see (Fig. 4 gives details of its location); so is the one in Canes Venatici (M51) that Rosse saw as a spiral (Fig. 2), now classified as an Sc with a magnitude of 8. Others are given below, with their positions in Fig. 4.

Fig. 3 right
Photograph of the spectrum of the Dumb-bell Nebula with comparison spectra of iron above and below, taken by Max Wolf.

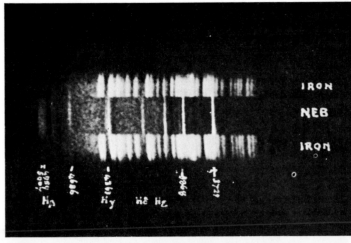

Fig. 4 below
Positions of various galaxies which the amateur can observe.

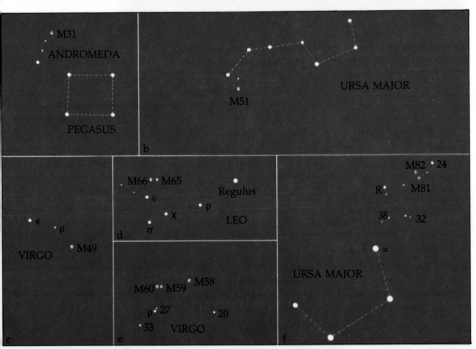

Number	Type	Area of sky covered by galaxy (' = arc minutes)	Magnitude	Position in Fig. 4
M49	E4	3' x 2'	8	4c
M65	Sa	8' x 1½'	9	4d
M66	Sb	8' x 2½'	5.5	4d
M81	Sb	16' x 10'	7.9	4f
M82	Irreg	7' x 1½'	8.8	4f
M89	E0	1½' diam.	9.5	

GALAXIES

Galaxies are noticeably different in shape. Sometimes the variation is caused only by the angle at which they are seen from Earth, but often it is due to the actual shape of the galaxy itself. Some galaxies contain clouds of gas, others nothing but stars.

As we have seen (pages 186–187), the elliptical galaxies are classified from 0 to 7, according to their degree of 'ellipticity'. Spiral galaxies are grouped not only into ordinary spirals and barred spirals, but also by means of a lettering system from 'a' to 'c', which denotes the shapes of their arms and centres. Sa galaxies are spirals with a bright central region and rather closely wound arms. Sc galaxies are those whose arms are more loosely wound with a much less bright inner region, while Sb galaxies lie between these two extremes. The barred spirals have a similar classification, SBa, SBb and SBc. Between the E7 galaxy and the Sa or SBa is the SO galaxy, which looks like a spiral with a bright nucleus but virtually no spiral arms. There are also irregular galaxies.

Most of these types of galaxy can be seen with an ordinary telescope, but do not expect them to present a spectacular sight. Galaxies are really objects for large professional telescopes. This is especially true of Seyfert galaxies (named after the American astronomer who discovered them in 1943), which have small but very bright nuclei and seem to be extremely active, emitting much radiation in ultraviolet and other short wavelengths. Probably 1% of all spiral galaxies are of this type.

Most galaxies like our own, which is probably an Sb type, are reasonably stable objects, although not as lethargic and peaceful as astronomers once believed. But some are very active indeed. Among these are radio galaxies, so-called because they emit an enormous amount of radio energy; visually they attract no attention from optical astronomers, because they are relatively inconspicuous. Radio galaxies often show two sources of radio waves from either side of the visible galaxy. These sources are now taken as evidence of some explosion inside the nucleus of the galaxy, after which, it is thought, great masses of gas and atomic particles were expelled. These lumps of material do not emit much light, if any, but they do give out considerable radio energy. Some radio galaxies interact with one another; and professional telescopes have shown some dramatic examples in which two

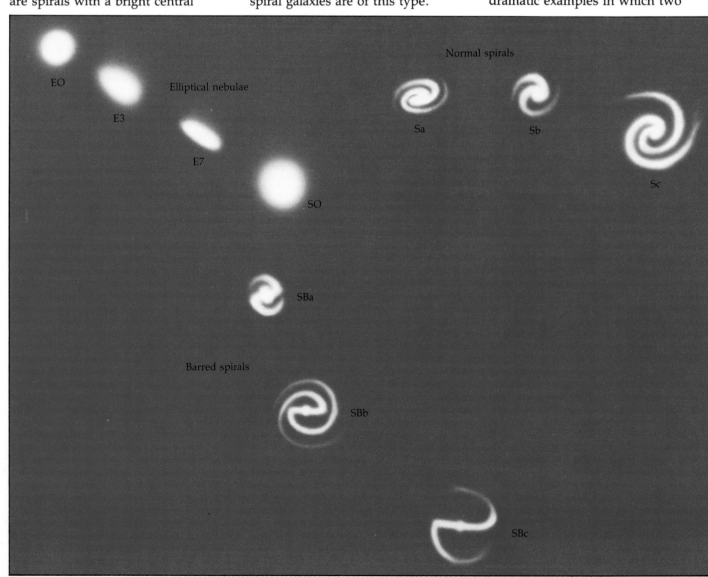

Fig 1
The classification of galaxies as originally devised by Edwin Hubble.

spiral galaxies look as if they are colliding – or perhaps splitting apart – and photographs have also been taken which make it clear that material appears to be flowing from one galaxy to the other. So it now seems certain that quite a lot of interactions really are occurring between galaxies as well as within galaxies themselves.

The differences between the galaxies expressed by the main classification EO to Sc and SBc were worked out by Edwin Hubble, the American astronomer who first proved in 1924 that 'spiral nebulae' were galaxies which lay beyond our own galaxy. In arranging the galaxies in the order he did, Hubble believed that he might be looking at some evolutionary sequence, beginning with the EO ellipticals and ending with the open spirals – although he acknowledged that this was merely a hypothesis. Today, astronomers have discarded this evolutionary theory;

nevertheless Hubble's classification scheme has much to commend it and has formed the basis of some more elaborate schemes devised by other astronomers who spend their time on galactic research.

The elliptical galaxies contain little or no gas or dust, whereas the spirals, contain considerable amounts of dust and gas, as well as stars. Our own galaxy is a case in point; M51 is another. Look at the photograph of it and you will be able to pick out dark lanes of dust in the spiral structure. Another notable example is the Sombrero Galaxy M104. We see this galaxy edge-on, and the photograph shows how it is crossed by a layer of dusty absorbing material. This galaxy has a magnitude of 8, spreads over 6 arc minutes in width, and is located between the Virgo and Corvus constellations (Fig. 2), although you will have to look at it carefully to make out the band of dust.

The evolution or development of

galaxies is linked with the way in which scientists believe the universe began (page 196). The current view is that before galaxies formed, space contained clouds of gas and dust, which contracted under the force of gravity. Where the density was high enough, they contracted to form stars. This process continued for millions of years.

The next stage in the development of a galaxy would have varied from one case to another. Giant nuclear explosions in the centre of a young galaxy would have driven out the gas and dust, leaving an elliptical galaxy. In another case, the dust and gas remained trapped in the galaxy and in due course became part of the rotating spiral into which the galaxy collapsed (Fig. 4). But this is only a very rough picture: astronomers still have many details to work out. One very important clue to the formation of galaxies may lie in those peculiar objects, the quasars (page 194).

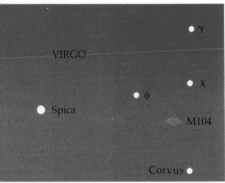

Fig. 2 above
Diagram showing the position of the Sombrero Galaxy M104 in Virgo.

Fig. 3 right
The Sombrero Galaxy M104; note the dark dense band of matter across the central plane of the galaxy.

Fig. 4 left
The spiral galaxy NGC 5194 in Canes Venatici and a companion galaxy; compare this with Lord Rosse's drawing on page 186.

Fig. 5 above
The radio source Cygnus A is a powerful emitter of radio waves, but when viewed optically appears to be two galaxies close together, or one splitting apart.

189

THE EXPANDING UNIVERSE

When astronomers started studying the spectra of various galaxies, they discovered that the galaxies are moving away from our own and each other at an ever-increasing speed. The whole universe is, in fact, expanding.

Galaxies are collections of stars (with or without dust and gas) which show dark line spectra. In the early 1900s, the American astronomer Vesto Slipher measured the positions of the lines in the spectra of fourteen spiral galaxies and discovered a strange fact: all showed a large shift of the lines towards the red end of their spectra. This meant that they were all moving away from the Earth at high speed.

The method used by Slipher and other astronomers studying this redshift was to photograph the spectrum of a spiral galaxy and, on the same photographic plate, just before this exposure and just after, to photograph the spectrum of iron. Iron was used because its lines fall throughout the spectrum thus providing an effective comparison with the galaxy's spectrum. A spark was passed between the tips of two iron rods, and its light split by a spectroscope and photographed. When the plate was developed, it showed three spectra (Fig. 3): one of the iron spark before the exposure of the galaxy, the spectrum of the galaxy itself, and finally, the iron

spark spectrum again. This allowed the positions of the lines on the galaxy spectrum to be measured accurately, and the second photograph of the iron spectrum served as a control: any shift in its lines, when compared with the first photograph, would show up minute changes in the spectroscope during the exposure time – changes due to the contraction of its metal parts, for instance.

The reason for this redshift is the 'Doppler effect'. In the mid-nineteenth century, the Austrian physicist Christian Doppler had discovered that sound waves are compressed as they approach the listener, but are stretched as they move away. A similar thing happens

to light waves, as illustrated by Fig. 4. In Fig. 4a we see a certain wavelength reaching the eye of an observer. Because this wavelength is travelling at the speed of light c, and the wave-crests are a certain distance (d_1) apart, wave-crests will reach the observer's eye at a certain frequency (f). (Mathematically $f = c/d_1$). If the source is moving away (Fig. 4b) then the time between one wave-crest and the next reaching the observer will be longer, because the second wave-crest has a little further to travel, and it can only go at the same speed c. So the observer sees a lower frequency, which means that the light appears to have a longer distance (d_2) between crests. A longer distance between crests – i.e. a longer

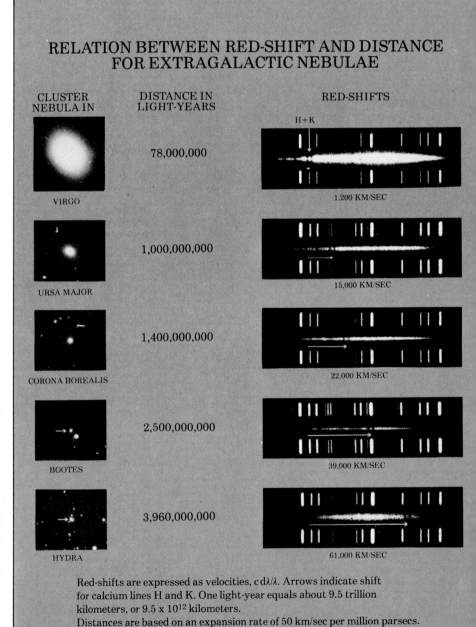

RELATION BETWEEN RED-SHIFT AND DISTANCE FOR EXTRAGALACTIC NEBULAE

CLUSTER NEBULA IN	DISTANCE IN LIGHT-YEARS	RED-SHIFTS
VIRGO	78,000,000	1,200 KM/SEC
URSA MAJOR	1,000,000,000	15,000 KM/SEC
CORONA BOREALIS	1,400,000,000	22,000 KM/SEC
BOOTES	2,500,000,000	39,000 KM/SEC
HYDRA	3,960,000,000	61,000 KM/SEC

Red-shifts are expressed as velocities, $c\,d\lambda/\lambda$. Arrows indicate shift for calcium lines H and K. One light-year equals about 9.5 trillion kilometers, or 9.5×10^{12} kilometers.

Distances are based on an expansion rate of 50 km/sec per million parsecs.

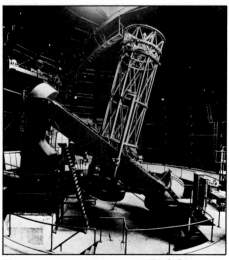

Fig. 1
The 2½ m reflector at Mt Wilson which was used by Hubble. It is on an 'English' equatorial mount, i.e. with a polar axis supported at each end.

Fig. 2
These are spectra of various galaxies compared with iron spectra. They show that the further the galaxy is from us, the larger its redshift. The arrows indicate the shift for calcium lines H and K.

wavelength – gives a shift of the spectral lines towards the red end of the spectrum. (A shorter wavelength shifts them in the direction of the blue).

Since almost all galaxies display a redshift it seems they are moving away from us. But this is not the whole story. Edwin Hubble, in 1929, found that for the galaxies whose distance he could measure, the further off in space a galaxy was, the faster the speed at which it was receding (Fig. 2). Distances of galaxies are hard to determine because they are so far away; even the nearest spiral lies more than 2 million light-years away. Their distances were determined by the presence in them of Cepheid

variables (pages 82–85) or by the appearance of supernovae whose apparent light output can be compared with what a supernova actually gives out. Hubble's law, as originally formulated, states that the velocity of a distant galaxy increases by approximately 100 km per second for every 3¼ million light-years or every megaparsec (1 million parsecs) it travels. Today, astronomers think it more likely that the increase is nearer 50 km per second than 100, but the basic principle remains valid.

Hubble's law is important in calculating the distances of very remote galaxies. When dealing with galaxies further than about 32½ million light-years from Earth, it is impossible to measure their distances

by Cepheid variables or even supernovae. However, it can be done by first measuring the redshift, then calculating the speed and, finally, using Hubble's law to obtain the distance for that particular velocity.

If all galaxies are moving away from us, does this mean that we are in the centre of the universe? The answer is 'no', and a simple experiment will demonstrate why not. Inflate a round balloon just enough so that you can write on the surface with a felt pen. Draw some dots on the surface to represent galaxies; make them 1 cm apart and mark three of them A, B and C (Fig. 5). Next blow up the balloon so it is larger, and then measure the distances of other galaxies from A. You will find that they have all increased. So if you imagine yourself on galaxy A, you would see the distances between your galaxy and other galaxies all increase with time. But equally well, if you were in galaxy B, the other galaxies A and C would appear to have moved away from you; and the same observation applies to galaxy C. So wherever you are, on whatever galaxy, you would observe the same effect: all galaxies would seem to move away from you.

The obvious conclusion is that the universe is expanding. As time goes on, so the distances between galaxies increase. Our galaxy is not the centre of things: it is just one of myriads of other galaxies which are all moving away from each other, all taking part in this universal expansion. How long will this expansion continue and how far can the universe expand – in other words, is there a limit to space? These are questions which we feel the need to answer. But in order to do so, we must take a relativity or 'space-time' view of the universe.

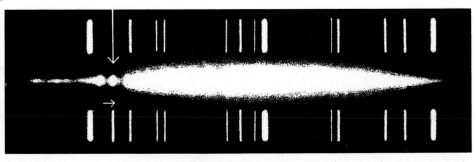

Fig. 3 above
The spectrum of a cluster of galaxies in Virgo shown between two iron spectra. A comparison between the lines of each spectrum can show up a redshift, as indicated by the arrows.

Fig. 4 right
Light with wavelength d_1 travels towards an observer A. As the light source moves away, light still travels to A, but it takes longer to reach him (wavelength d_2).

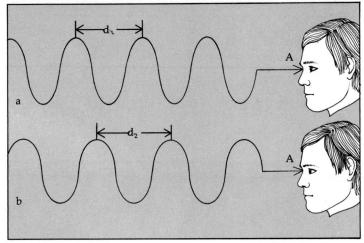

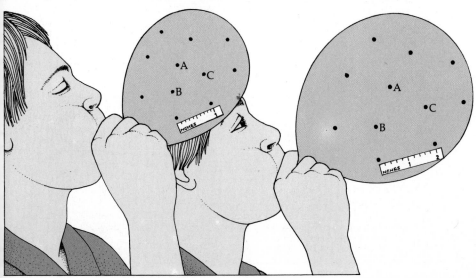

Fig. 5
Experiment to demonstrate the principle of an expanding universe.

Fig. 6
The barred spiral galaxy NGC 3992.

THE EDGE OF THE UNIVERSE

Many galaxies, including our own, are grouped together in clusters, in which individual members may be very far apart. Clusters extend as far as telescopes can see and although there seems to be no visible edge to the universe, this need not mean that the universe is infinite.

When you look at a galaxy like the large one in Andromeda (M31) or the lovely spiral in Canes Venatici (M51), it is easy to get the impression that galaxies are all separate objects, each a star island in its own region of space. Our own galaxy, for instance, seems to be isolated, with M31 a very long way off; after all, they are

separated by more than 2 million light-years. Yet a closer look at M31 and M51 will show that neither is isolated. M51 has a companion galaxy, NGC 5195 (which is quite separate although it looks as if it is attached to a spiral arm), and M31 has two companion galaxies: M32, an elliptical, and NGC 205, another small elliptical, both in orbit around M31. So there is evidence that some galaxies are in fact double or even triple systems.

More evidence of the grouping of galaxies can be seen in the southern hemisphere, where the night sky contains two large luminous clouds. These are named after the explorer Ferdinand Magellan, who sailed round the world between 1519 and 1521, and are known as the Large Magellanic Cloud (LMC) and Small Magellanic Cloud (SMC). The LMC is in the constellation Dorado and the SMC in Tucana. Both look like detached portions of the Milky Way, but both are, in fact, companion galaxies of our own galaxy. The LMC is 169,000 light-years away and the SMC just a little further, at 205,000

light-years; the SMC is classified as an irregular, the LMC is classified by some as an irregular and by others as a barred spiral.

Our galaxy is a member of a group of galaxies called the Local Group, of which the brighter members are four spirals, four ellipticals and an irregular, (if the LMC is classed as a spiral). There are some dwarf galaxies as well. The Local Group consists of three 'sub-clusters'. Our galaxy, the two Magellanic Clouds and some dwarf galaxies form one sub-cluster; another, about 2 million light-years away, contains the Andromeda galaxy (M31) and its two companion galaxies, the beautiful spiral M33 in Triangulum and some small ellipticals; a third group is composed of small ellipticals in the constellations Fornax (The Furnace) and Sculptor, as well as some other dwarf galaxies.

The Local Group contains a comparatively small number of galaxies – nine large bright ones, and some dwarfs – numbering no more than 30 or so. Other groups of galaxies can include hundreds or

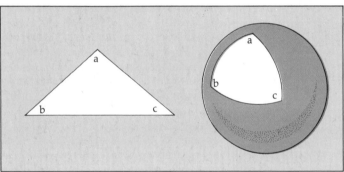

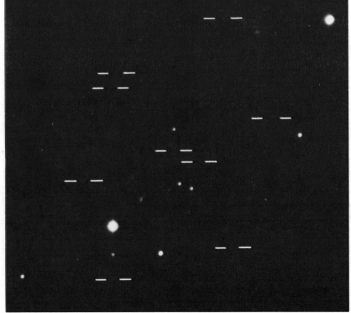

Fig. 1 above
The geometry of curved space: a triangle on a flat plane has angles which add up to 180°. Transfer it to the surface of a sphere and the angles add up to more than 180°.

Fig. 2 below
A field of faint galaxies in Coma Berenices, some of which are indicated by pairs of lines.

Fig. 3
The Large Magellanic Cloud which is a

companion galaxy to our own visible in the southern hemisphere.

even thousands. The nearest rich cluster is the one in Virgo. It covers an area of some 6° of sky, and when you realize that it lies at a distance of 65 million light-years, you have some idea of the vast region of space it occupies. It is probably about 6½ million light-years across, and contains literally thousands of galaxies. Another rich cluster is to be found in Coma Berenices. This seems to be shaped like a sphere with more galaxies concentrated towards the centre than dispersed through the outer regions: it is rather like a globular star cluster, but with galaxies instead of stars. It lies about 450 million light-years away and contains something like 800 galaxies, with two notable radio galaxies near the centre. There is also a cluster in Perseus which contains both radio and optical galaxies; it seems to be shrouded in gas clouds, which have been detected by radio astronomers, and which appear to stretch for hundreds of thousands of light-years.

Astronomers are now beginning to recognize what they call 'superclusters' of galaxies, – that is,

clusters of clusters. One such includes the Virgo cluster and our Local Group, as well as about 100 smaller clusters. The distance from one end to the other measures 300 or more million light-years.

The study of galaxies and groups of galaxies takes us deeper and deeper into space; some galaxies have been detected at distances of more than a thousand million light-years – indeed there is one radio galaxy that has been found at what appears to be 10,000 million light-years. Is this the limit of our universe or does it continue further into space? It seems certain that this is not the limit for quasars (page 194) have been found which appear to be even more distant. But the answer to the question of whether the universe goes on for ever seems to be 'no'. Yet there does not appear to be an edge to the universe!

The problem in understanding this is that we are accustomed to thinking in terms of Euclid's geometry when we think of objects in space. But space is curved, and curved space is different from Euclid's flat space. To

understand the difference, first think of a triangle and draw it on a sheet of paper (Fig. 1a). When you measure the internal angles (angles a, b and c), you will find that all add up to 180°. Next, take a large ball and draw a triangle on that (Fig. 1b). On measuring the inside angles of this triangle you will find they come to more than 180°. This curved triangle is different from the flat one and there is no way you can flatten it out without distortion. (Mapmakers flatten out maps of the world as you did a map of the heavens in making an astrolabe, but to do this you have to squash up some areas and stretch out others; in other words, you get distortions.)

Mariners and airmen have to navigate using a curved surface and take account of the way triangles and other geometrical figures on it differ from their equivalents on a flat plane. So it is with space. It is curved, but it is not just a curved surface, as you get on the Earth or on a ball. It is a curved *space* and impossible to draw. Yet astronomers have evidence that this is what space is like.

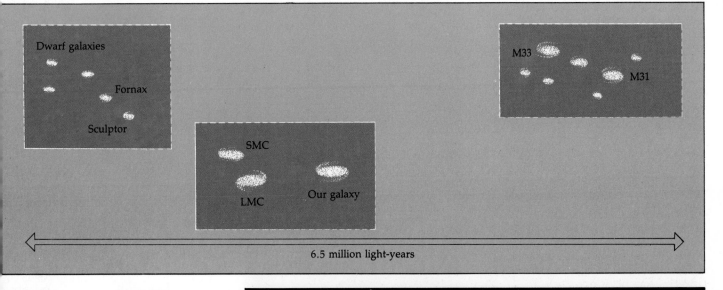

Dwarf galaxies

Fornax

Sculptor

SMC

LMC

Our galaxy

M33

M31

6.5 million light-years

Fig. 4 above
Drawing to show the three sub-groups of galaxies which form our local group of galaxies.

Fig. 5 below
M51, seen partly from the side, showing that the companion galaxy NGC 5195 is not part of M51 as it appears to be when seen from Earth.

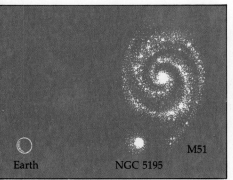

Earth

NGC 5195

M51

Fig. 6
Part of a cluster of galaxies, showing different types, in Coma Berenices. As they are 400 million light-years away, this does not show them as they are now.

QUASARS

Quasi-stellar radio sources, or quasars, were discovered in the 1950s by radio astronomers. Because they seem relatively small and yet emit radiation many times that of a galaxy, they have caused much speculation. They could contain a clue to the origins of the universe.

From 1950 onwards, Sir Martin Ryle and his team of radio astronomers at Cambridge University made detailed catalogues of all radio objects they could observe in the sky. As their equipment and techniques improved, so did their catalogues, including dimmer and dimmer radio sources charted with increasing accuracy. In 1957, a British optical astronomer took the third and latest Cambridge University radio catalogue of the sky to the Hale Observatories in California, to compare it with a photographic atlas of optical objects. He was able to identify only 21 out of a total of 450 objects in the Cambridge. However, three years later, two radio astronomers working at the California Institute of Technology identified one radio object – 3C 48 – in the third Cambridge catalogue (whose objects are denoted by the prefix 3C) with a dim blue star. This aroused little interest or excitement. It was merely a star, and the only curious thing about it was that it emitted strong enough radio waves to be detected: stars did not usually do that, and all other identified radio sources appeared as hazy patches. Subsequently, two more radio objects were identified with blue stars.

In Australia, near Sydney, there was another active team of radio astronomers making surveys of the sky. In 1963, one of them, Cyril Hazard, watched the object 3C 273 while it was occulted by the Moon and was able, therefore, to fix its position very accurately. It turned out not to be a double radio source as had been thought, but a single optical one, whose position was known well enough for there to be no doubt about it. A Dutch optical astronomer, Maarten Schmidt, who was working at the Hale Observatories in the United States, photographed its spectrum and

found a curious pattern of bright emission lines. Although he could make no sense of these results, Schmidt decided to publish them to see if other astronomers could.

It was while Schmidt was preparing these results that he saw the solution. The reason why he had been unable to recognize any line in the spectrum became obvious. All the lines in the quasar spectrum were a

set of hydrogen lines which usually lay in the ultraviolet part of the spectrum and were not visible under normal circumstances. They had appeared only because this object had an enormous redshift – a redshift large enough to push the whole invisible short-wavelength spectrum into the visible range. As soon as Schmidt's discovery was announced, a similar redshift was found in the

far left
The first quasar to be discovered, 3C 48, photographed with the Palomar 5 m reflector. This discovery confirmed that a quasar resembles a galaxy and is not a star.

left
The elliptical galaxy M87: this photograph shows a jet of material from the galaxy, probably due to an internal explosion.

A night view of the 64 m diameter radio telescope at Parkes, Australia: it has measured the position of a distant radio source using Moon occultations.

194

spectrum of the quasar 3C 48.

The nature of these strange bodies was unknown. They looked like stars, but clearly were not: stars do not show bright emission lines nor do they emit radio waves as strongly as these objects did. They were therefore given the name 'quasi-stellar radio sources' or 'quasars' for short. They still remain something of a mystery, not only because of their appearance and spectra, but also because of their distance. No quasar is near enough to have its distance measured directly by triangulation (pages 48–51) and the only indirect method available is to measure their redshifts and apply Hubble's law, which tells us that a redshift increases with distance. The redshifts of quasars are so immense that they appear to be more distant than any other objects in the universe. Their distances are measured in millions of light-years; indeed the most distant quasar lies some 16,000 million light-years away. The fact that we can pick up its radiation on Earth, clearly indicates that the amount of energy it is emitting is vast.

Despite this enormous energy, quasars are apparently relatively small. Astronomers are able to estimate their size by observing the variation in their radiation, which can change within a period of less than a year. With this information, astronomers can calculate that they must measure less than one light-year across. And yet, astonishingly, one of these relatively small objects may emit anything up to 10,000 times the energy of a whole galaxy, like the one in Andromeda (M31) which contains about 100,000 million stars.

Ever since their discovery, quasars have been the subject of argument and speculation among astronomers. Some quasars, 3C 273 for example, have been found to be associated with clusters of galaxies displaying comparable redshifts. The general opinion among astronomers is that they are the centres of intense activity inside galaxies, which seems to accord well with the distances implied by Hubble's law. However, quasars may not be as distant as they seem: some astronomers think they may be material from explosions in nearby galaxies, and their redshifts due only to extreme speeds caused by the explosion. Yet if this is correct, we should see big blueshifts too as quasars move towards us, but none has been observed. Although various theories have been offered, the active galaxy explanation is the favoured one, because it fits in well with the very active nature of the world of galaxies shown in recent years by radio telescopes, and by X-ray and ultraviolet telescopes put into orbit around the Earth.

Astronomers now know that there are huge masses of gas moving about among clusters of galaxies, and that galaxies interact with one another, sometimes violently, and often experience terrific explosions within themselves. The elliptical galaxy M87 is a case in point, its jet showing evidence of an eruption. Perhaps, then, quasars are evidence of the explosive nature of the universe in the past, for if they really are as far away as they seem then they are showing us events which occurred many, many millions of years ago.

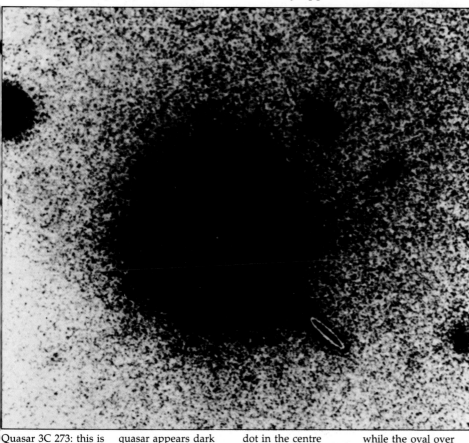

Quasar 3C 273: this is a negative picture where the bright quasar appears dark so that more detail can be seen. The white dot in the centre marks one component of the radio source while the oval over the jet marks the second component.

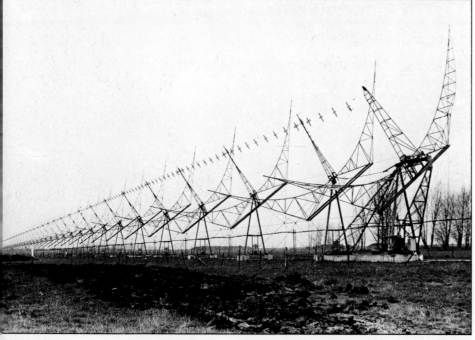

Fixed radio interferometer aerial at Cambridge used by Martin Ryle and colleagues to make their early catalogues of radio sources which led to the discovery of quasars.

THE BEGINNING AND END OF THE UNIVERSE

Cosmology – the study of the origin and evolution of the universe – is a subject which has intrigued astronomers throughout history. Today we know many facts about the universe which most astronomers take as evidence that the universe began with a giant explosion or 'big bang'. How it will end is not so clear.

We have said that the universe is expanding. Evidence for this lies in the redshifts of quasars and distant galaxies, but this cannot be observed by the amateur astronomer as the largest optical and radio telescopes are required. Much of this type of astronomical data must be taken on trust by an amateur, but this does not stop him legitimately questioning conclusions drawn from it. Is the redshift really caused by a movement away from us, or is there some other, quite different explanation?

Einstein's General Theory of Relativity states that the spectrum of every massive body will display a redshift caused by the body's gravitation. Galaxies – even dwarf ones – are indeed massive objects, so could the Einstein redshift account for what is observed? The answer is

quite definitely 'no'. The redshift is too great to be accounted for by relativity theory. A small part of the shift may be due to this cause, but not the whole of it. It has, however, been suggested that in travelling through the vast distances of space that separate the galaxies from us, light may become 'tired'; in other words, it loses energy, which shows up as a redshift. Yet even this does not seem to be really satisfactory on detailed examination; if it were correct, then the galaxies would never appear sharp but always fuzzy, even in the largest telescopes, and this does not happen. Moreover, precisely why the energy loss should occur is not easy to explain and no one seems satisfied with the explanations which have been given. So, when all is said and done, there appears to be no satisfactory alternative to accepting the redshift of galaxies, and probably those of quasars, as due to recession.

Having reached this conclusion,

what can we infer from this regarding the beginning of the universe? Obviously if we take an expanding universe as our premise and go back in time, we shall find that in earlier times everything was closer together than it is now. If we extend this argument, and go back far enough, we might come to one giant black hole and that would be that. However, we have to remember that space-time and matter are intimately linked. In fact, cosmologists believe that there was no single point from which the universe began, but that matter and space-time started together in an almightly explosion, 10,000–20,000 million years ago. This caused matter and space to be 'everywhere' at once, not just in one single place; the problem of a giant black hole does not, therefore, arise.

What happened before this vast explosion, this 'big bang', is not clear: indeed the very question may have no meaning because if time,

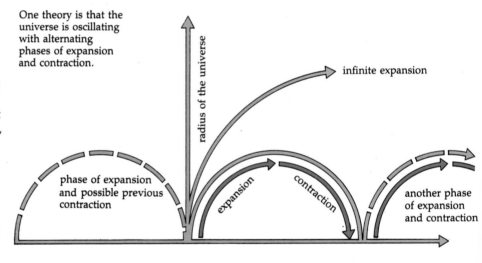

One theory is that the universe is oscillating with alternating phases of expansion and contraction.

radius of the universe

infinite expansion

phase of expansion and possible previous contraction

expansion

contraction

another phase of expansion and contraction

Diagram to show the possible stages of the beginning of the universe.
a The creation of space, time and matter at the moment of the big bang.
b The universe at a very high temperature was dense and opaque; in it hydrogen started to form.

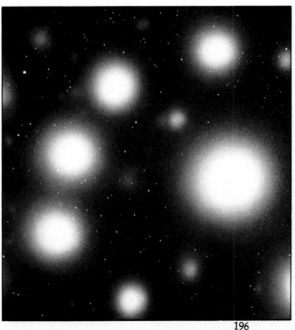

space and matter all began at the 'big bang', then before the 'big bang' time did not exist. Calculations have been made of the first fractions of a second after the explosion, using the laws of nuclear physics now known to us, and it is found that about 0.0002 seconds later the temperature was 1 million million degrees Kelvin (0°K= -273.16°C) with many electrons and muons (atomic particles like electrons but about 207 times more massive). Then the temperature fell, and when it had dropped to 4,000 million degrees K the protons and neutrons present formed hydrogen and its isotopes (atoms with the same chemical properties, but with heavier centres or nuclei). These were the gases deuterium and tritium. After about quarter of an hour the universe began to radiate strongly: it was still hot – around 500 million degrees K – but as time went on the temperature went on dropping, and at around 1 million degrees K other elements were formed. All the time there were lots of electrons around, still unattached to atoms, and these scattered the radiation, so at these stages the universe was opaque, not transparent. When the temperature had sunk to 3,000°K, the electrons combined with atomic nuclei, the universe became transparent, and proto-galaxies began to form. Later galaxies with stars within them formed, and the universe acquired the structure we know today.

Could the universe have originated this way? The answer is, probably, 'yes'. That the universe was once extremely hot seems to be supported by the fact that radio astronomers have discovered a very faint but uniform background of radio radiation all over the sky. The temperature of this scattered radiation is only 3°K, so it is very cold, but its presence does give strong confirmation of the hot 'big bang' theory. It is the remnant of the original very hot gas.

What about the end of the universe? Will all the galaxies continue moving apart until they are all so far away from each other and travelling so fast that no observer in any one galaxy can see any other galaxy? The observers in each galaxy would then consider themselves alone in space, and their view of the universe would be very different from ours. Is this what will happen? It is a possibility, but not the only one.

There may be enough material in the galaxies and between them for their gravitational pull to be slowing down the expansion of the universe. At the present time, observations make it apparent that there is not sufficient material to exert so strong a pull, but new techniques of observation are continually making it possible for astronomers to detect fainter and fainter traces of matter in space, such as the gas that exists between galaxies in a cluster. Perhaps, then, enough gas will be found to make it certain that the expansion will cease.

Once expansion has stopped, the gravitational force will cause contraction to occur. Space-time will shrink either until the universe collapses altogether – possibly into a giant black hole – or perhaps only until the material is very compressed, when nuclear forces will set the entire universe expanding again. Indeed, it is just possible that our universe is an oscillating one, and has always been like this, going through alternate phases of expanding and contracting. Only future observations will give us the answer, but this very question, as well as others still awaiting further research, helps to make astronomy one of the most exciting of all frontiers of knowledge.

The horn antenna at Crawford Hill, USA; originally designed for radio communication work, it was a key element in discovering background radio radiation in the universe.

c At 3,000°K the universe became transparent and proto-galaxies formed.
d The expanding universe of galaxies we see today.
(after Rees and Silk)

ADVANCED PROJECTS AND EQUIPMENT

With the aid of even a modest-sized telescope and possibly a camera as well, you can study such phenomena as stellar spectra and solar activity. Simple radio astronomy too is within the scope of the amateur.

Most advanced projects can be done only if you have a fair-sized telescope. What 'fair-sized' means depends on the project, but as a guide you cannot really do much useful telescope work with a reflector which is less than 15 cm in diameter, although 22 cm or 25 cm or even 30 cm is better. A telescope over 15 cm – one in the 22 cm to 30 cm range – will probably become a permanent fixture. To buy a 25 cm reflector and have it housed in an observatory costs a lot, but fortunately you can make your own mirror, or you can buy the optics and construct the tube and mounting. You can also build for yourself what you need in the way of an observatory. The three books in the *Amateur Telescope Making* series (page 200) give much useful information, and if you join an active local astronomical society, you should be able to get some practical advice. You would probably do best to start by making a 15 cm reflector.

Refracting telescopes are expensive. They tend to be long and require a large mounting, and for useful work you need one in a permanent observatory. The telescope should have an aperture of not less than 10 cm and preferably 15 cm, but then you are getting into the £2,500 ($5,000) range (plus the cost of an observatory). If you are thinking of hundreds rather than thousands, you would be better off with a telescope of Maksutov design which some firms like the American Questar or Celestron manufacture, and in Europe is obtainable from small specialist suppliers.

A project that is not too advanced for the amateur is to look at stellar spectra. For this you need a 'direct vision' spectroscope or a diffraction grating. Direct vision spectroscopes contain a series of prisms which disperse the colours into a spectrum without making them deviate too far from the line of sight of the telescope. Unfortunately such instruments are hard to come by; you can more easily get a plastic grating and try this out in conjunction with your telescope, using the grating at the eyepiece end.

Probably the most exciting area for the amateur is that of celestial photography. Begin by taking black and white photographs, moving on to colour only when you have gained some experience. For black and white you will need a telescope with a good finder (i.e. a small telescope of small magnification) to track the celestial objects. This is fixed to the tube of the larger instrument (which carries the camera) and is accurately aligned so that when a celestial object is bisected by its cross-wires, the object is in the centre of the field of view of your main telescope. But, above all, you need a good equatorial mounting (pages 70–73). This must be sturdy and rock-steady. Secondly, you will require some kind of drive on the telescope mounting so that the telescope follows the stars

right
This shed runs on tracks to cover up Patrick Moore's reflecting telescope when it is not in use.

below
An amateur's solar radio telescope designed and built by Ron Ham in Sussex, England. It is south-facing and a time-switch allows it to make daily solar observations between 11.30 and 14.30. These are recorded on the chart (*below right*).

above
An amateur's equatorially mounted reflecting telescope with an electric drive and a camera mounted on the telescope.

automatically. Today this is best done using an electric motor and possibly a variable-frequency control so that you get the exact speed required. (Make sure that the electrical equipment is properly 'earthed': *never* use a public electrical supply unless you have had the wiring checked by a competent electrician.) For any advanced photography it is, of course, essential to have a permanently mounted telescope in a small observatory or, at least, a permanently fixed mounting from which you detach your reflector.

The camera itself can be a 35 mm, which should be mounted on the eyepiece or in place of it. A single-lens reflex is desirable because it enables you to see precisely what you are taking. Your single-lens reflex camera must have a detachable lens so that you can use the body alone, and the mirror mechanism in the camera should give a minimum of vibration. For colour photography you must use a camera that keeps the film very cold indeed if you want to get good results on objects like the Orion Nebula. You can make a special camera for such work, but will have to use solid carbon dioxide (dry ice) to keep the film cool.

Designs for this are available in specialist periodicals, for example, the *Journal* of the British Astronomical Association.

Solar activity is a good subject for observation. You can readily see and photograph prominences, and even examine the solar surface in the light of hydrogen alone with a special filter or a spectrohelioscope. The diagram shows the spectroheliograph (a spectrohelioscope for taking photographs). Here one slit moves across the image of the Sun's disc while a second slit isolates one line of the spectrum (the hydrogen line, for instance). It thus builds up a photograph of the Sun in the light of one colour. The sky round the limb of the Sun appears black, making prominences easier to detect. The spectrohelioscope differs from the spectroheliograph in that its two slits vibrate to build up an image. Details of how to build this equipment are given in *Amateur Telescope Making*, but the construction is not at all easy and you do need a permanent site for the instrument, which has to be fed with sunlight by a moving mirror. An easier method is to use a 'narrow band' filter. Such filters are expensive (over £100 or $200), but

they are advertised in the American magazine *Sky and Telescope*.

It is also possible for the amateur astronomer to do some radio astronomy. Magnetic storms, which cause radio fade-outs, can be detected on a shortwave receiver. For more advanced work you can construct a radio telescope; however, do not expect that such an instrument will allow you to probe deep space and record quasars or radio galaxies – it will not. But some useful and interesting work can be done on the Sun. Radio telescopes have large aerials or antennae and you will need a good-sized outdoor area to accommodate one (and, possibly, local government permission). You also need to know at least the rudiments of radio engineering and electronics if you are going to construct such an instrument, or even in order to adapt available equipment.

In all these advanced projects it is better not to work alone, but to be a member of a local or national astronomical society, or both. In this way, you will be able to draw upon the valuable experience of other members to ensure the success of your own projects.

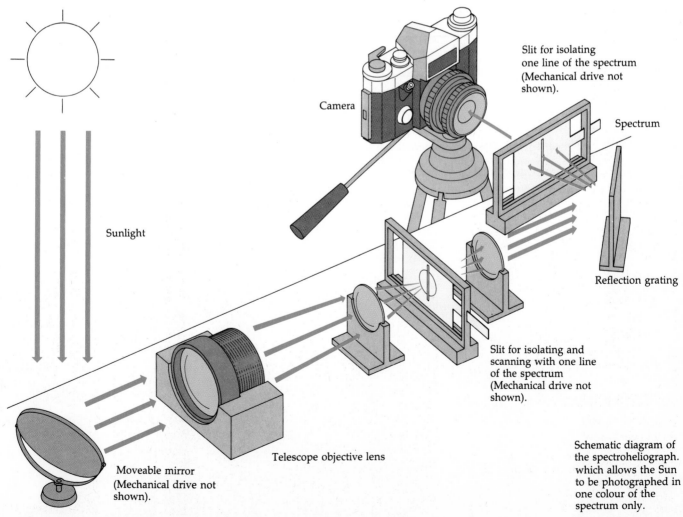

Camera

Sunlight

Slit for isolating one line of the spectrum (Mechanical drive not shown).

Spectrum

Reflection grating

Slit for isolating and scanning with one line of the spectrum (Mechanical drive not shown).

Moveable mirror (Mechanical drive not shown).

Telescope objective lens

Schematic diagram of the spectroheliograph. which allows the Sun to be photographed in one colour of the spectrum only.

BOOKS AND PERIODICALS

Books on Astronomy

Astronomy: An Introduction Jacqueline Mitton (Faber & Faber, London and Boston 1978)

Cambridge Encyclopaedia of Astronomy Simon Mitton (ed) (Cape, London 1977; Crown, New York 1977)

Encyclopaedia of Astronomy Colin A. Ronan (ed) (Hamlyn, London and New York 1979)

The Guinness Book of Astronomy Facts and Figures Patrick Moore (Guinness Superlatives, London 1979)

New Horizons in Astronomy John C. Brandt and Steven P. Maran (W. H. Freeman & Co, San Francisco 1979)

University Astronomy Jay M. Pasachoff and Marc L. Kutner (Saunders, Philadelphia and London 1978)

Books for the Observer

The American Ephemeris and Nautical Almanac (US Government Printing Office, Washington DC 20402, published annually)

Burnham's Celestial Handbook (Dover Publications, New York 1979; Constable, London 1979)

Guide to the Moon Patrick Moore (Lutterworth Press, London 1976)

Handbook of the British Astronomical Association (British Astronomical Association, London, published annually)

Norton's Star Atlas Arthur P. Norton (Gall & Inglis, Edinburgh 1973; Sky Publishing Corporation, Cambridge, Mass. 1973)

The Messier Album John H. Mallas and Evered Kreimer (Sky Publishing Corporation, Cambridge, Mass. 1978; Cambridge University Press, Cambridge 1979)

Yearbook of Astronomy Patrick Moore (Sidgwick & Jackson, London, published annually)

Book for the mathematically minded

Practical Astronomy with Your Pocket Calculator Peter Duffet-Smith (Cambridge University Press, Cambridge, 1979)

* More advanced books

Books about making astronomical instruments

Amateur Telescope Making Albert G. Ingalls (ed) (Scientific American, New York Book 1 1974; Book 2 1972; Book 3 1974)

Make Your Own Telescope Reg Spry (Sidgwick & Jackson, London 1978)
Telescope Making for Beginners Roy Worvill (Kahn & Averill, London 1974)

Philip's planispheres are available from George Philip Ltd., 12 Long Acre, London WC2, and from some bookshops and astronomical suppliers. A plastic astrolabe and booklet is available from Science Studio (Oxford) Ltd., 7 Little Clarendon Street, Oxford OX1 2HP, UK. Cardboard astrolabe kits are available from Paul MacAlister & Associates, Box 157, Lake Bluff, Illinois 60637, USA and the National Maritime Museum, Greenwich, London SE10. A reflection grating for use in a spectroscope can be obtained from Paton Hawksley Electronics Ltd., Rockhill Laboratories, Wellsway, Keynsham, Bristol BS18 1PG, UK. In the USA readers should consult the advertisements in *Sky and Telescope* for the addresses of suppliers.

Periodicals

Hermes (Junior Astronomical Society)

Journal of the British Astronomical Association (British Astronomical Association)

Mercury (Astronomical Society of the Pacific)

Sky and Telescope (Sky Publishing Corporation, 49 Bay State Road, Cambridge, Mass. 02238; available in Britain from Astro Books and Supplies, 47 Riddlesdown Avenue, Purley, Surrey CR2 1JL)

Useful addresses

Australia
Astronomical Society of New South Wales, PO Box 208, Eastwood, New South Wales 2122.
Astronomical Society of South Australia, PO Box 199, Adelaide, South Australia 5001.

Britain
British Astronomical Association, Burlington House, Piccadilly, London W1V 0NL.
Junior Astronomical Society, c/o Mr V. L. Tibbott, 58 Vaughan Gardens, Ilford, Essex IG1 3PD.
For local societies, ask at the local Public Library or consult The Federation of Astronomical Societies, c/o Mr G. S. Pearce, 1 Valletort Cott, Millbridge, Plymouth, Devon PL1 5PU.

Canada
Royal Astronomical Society of Canada, 124 Merton Street, Toronto, Ontario M4S 2Z2.

New Zealand
Royal Astronomical Society of New Zealand, PO Box 3181, Wellington C1.

South Africa
Astronomical Society of Southern Africa, c/o South African Astronomical Observatory, PO Box 9, Observatory 7935, Cape.

United States
American Association of Variable Star Observers, 187 Concord Avenue, Cambridge, Mass. 02138.
Association of Lunar and Planetary Observers, Box 3AZ, University Park, New Mexico 88003.
Astronomical Society of the Pacific, 1290 24th Avenue, San Francisco, CA 94122.
For local societies consult the Astronomical League, c/o Mr R. R. Young, 329 South Front Street, Harrisburg, Penn. 17104.

Table 1 The Solar System

	Mercury	Venus	Earth	Mars	Jupiter
Equatorial diameter (km)	4,878	12,104	12,756	6,794	142,800
Sidereal period of axial rotation	58.65d	243.16d	23h 56m 04s	24h 37m 23s	9h 55m 30s
Inclination of axis to orbit	0°*	178°	23° 27'	24° 46'	3° 04'
Density (Earth=1)	0.997	0.95	1.0	0.71	0.24
Mass (Earth=1)	0.06	0.81	1.0	0.11	317.89
Surface gravity (Earth=1)	0.38	0.90	1.0	0.38	2.64
Escape velocity (km per sec)	4.3	10.36	11.2	5.03	60.22
Albedo	0.06	0.76	0.36	0.16	0.73
Mean distance from Sun (millions of km)	57.9	108.2	149.6	227.9	778.3

	Saturn	Uranus	Neptune	Pluto	Sun
Equatorial diameter (km)	120,000	52,800	48,400	3,300–2,800**	1,392,530
Sidereal period of axial rotation	10h 14m	**	20h*	**	25d 9h 7m 12s
Inclination of axis to orbit	26° 44'	97° 53'	28° 48'	50°*	7° 15'
Density (Earth=1)	0.13	0.23	0.31	0.36*	0.25
Mass (Earth=1)	95.14	14.52	17.25	0.10*	3.33×10^5
Surface gravity (Earth=1)	1.16	1.11	1.21	**	28.0
Escape velocity (km per sec)	32.26	22.5	23.9	**	617.3
Albedo	0.76	0.93	0.62	0.4–0.6*	——
Mean distance from Sun (millions of km)	1,427	2,869.6	4,496.7	5,899	——

* Value uncertain ** Value not known

Table 2 The Constellations

Latin/Greek	Translation	Latin/Greek	Translation	Latin/Greek	Translation
Andromeda	Andromeda	Cygnus	Swan	Pavo	Peacock
Antlia	Pump	Delphinus	Dolphin	Pegasus	Winged Horse
Apus	Bird of Paradise	Dorado	Swordfish	Perseus	Perseus
Aquarius	Water Carrier	Draco	Dragon	Phoenix	Phoenix
Aquila	Eagle	Equuleus	Foal	Pictor	Painter
Ara	Altar	Eridanus	River (Eridanus)	Pisces	Fishes
Aries	Ram	Fornax	Furnace	Piscis Australis	Southern Fish
Auriga	Charioteer	Gemini	Twins	Puppis	Poop
Boötes	Herdsman	Grus	Crane	Pyxis	Compass
Caelum	Chisel	Hercules	Hercules	Reticulum	Net
Camelopardalis	Giraffe	Horologium	Clock	Sagitta	Arrow
Cancer	Crab	Hydra	Water Monster	Sagittarius	Archer
Canes Venatici	Hunting Dogs	Hydrus	Sea Serpent	Scorpius	Scorpion
Canis Major	Great Dog	Indus	Indian	Sculptor	Sculptor
Canis Minor	Little Dog	Lacertà	Lizard	Scutum	Shield
Capricornus	Goat	Leo	Lion	Serpens	Serpent
Carina	Keel	Leo Minor	Little Lion	Sextans	Sextant
Cassiopeia	Cassiopeia	Lepus	Hare	Taurus	Bull
Centaurus	Centaur	Libra	Scales	Telescopium	Telescope
Cepheus	Cepheus	Lupus	Wolf	Triangulum	Triangle
Cetus	Whale	Lynx	Lynx	Triangulum	Southern
Chamaeleon	Chameleon	Lyra	Lyre	Australe	Triangle
Circinus	Compasses	Mensa	Table	Tucana	Toucan
Columba	Dove	Microscopium	Microscope	Ursa Major	Great Bear
Coma Berenices	Berenice's Hair	Monoceros	Unicorn	Ursa Minor	Little Bear
Corona Australis	Southern Crown	Musca	Fly	Vela	Sails
Corona Borealis	Northern Crown	Norma	Rule	Virgo	Virgin
Corvus	Crow	Octans	Octant	Volans	Flying Fish
Crater	Cup	Ophiuchus	Serpent bearer	Vulpecula	Fox
Crux	Southern Cross	Orion	Hunter		

Table 3 Some of the Nearest Stars

Star	Right Ascension h m	Declination deg. min.	Apparent Magnitude	Absolute Magnitude	Distance light-years	Spectral Type
Groombridge 34 A	0 18	+43 54	8.1	10.3	11.6	M1
τ Ceti	1 43	−16 03	3.5	5.7	11.9	G8
ε Eri	3 32	−09 32	3.7	6.1	10.7	K2
Kapteyn's	5 11	−44 59	8.8	10.9	12.7	M0
Sirius A	6 44	−16 42	−1.5	1.4	8.6	A1
B			7.2	11.2		wd
BD+5°1668	7 27	+ 5 27	9.8	12.0	12.2	M4
Procyon A	7 39	+ 5 17	0.3	2.6	11.4	F5
Groombridge 1618	10 10	+49 33	6.6	8.3	15.0	M0
Lalande 21185	11 03	+36 07	7.5 .	10.4	8.1	M2
Centauri C	14 28	−62 36	11.0	15.1	4.3	M5e
Centauri A	14 38	−60 46	0.1	4.4	4.3	G2
B			1.5	5.8		K5
BD−12°4523	16 30	−12 36	10.0	12.0	13.1	M5
CD−46°11540	17 28	−46 53	9.4	11.0	15.1	M4
Barnard's	17 56	+ 4 36	9.5	13.2	5.9	M5
Σ 2398A	18 42	+59 36	8.9	11.2	11.5	M3.5
Ross 154	18 49	−23 50	10.6	13.3	9.4	M5e
61 Cyg A	21 06	+38 38	5.2	7.5	11.2	K5
Lacaille 8760	21 16	−36 58	6.7	8.7	12.5	M1
ε Ind	22 03	−56 52	4.7	7.0	11.2	K5
Kruger 60 A	22 27	+57 36	9.7	11.8	12.8	M4
B			11.2	13.4		M6
Ross 780	22 52	−14 22	10.2	11.7	15.8	M5
Lacaille 9352	23 05	−35 59	7.4	9.6	11.7	M2

Based on a table in *University Astronomy* by J. M. Pasachoff and M. L. Kutner

Table 4 The Brightest Stars for Epoch 1980

Star	Right Ascension h m	Declination deg. min.	Apparent Magnitude	Absolute Magnitude	Distance light-years	Spectral Type
α Andromedae (Alpheratz)	0 07	+28 59	2.1	−0.5	90	A0
β Cassiopeiae	0 08	+59 02	2.3	1.5	45	F5
α Phoenecis (Ankaa)	0 25	−42 24	2.4	0.2	93	K0
α Cassiopeiae (Shedir)	0 39	+56 25	2.2	−1.3	150	K0
β Ceti	0 43	−18 05	2.0	0.8	57	K0
γ Cassiopeiae	0 55	+60 37	2.2	−0.9	96	B0
β Andromedae (Mirach)	1 08	+35 31	2.1	0.2	76	M0
α Ursae Minoris (Polaris)	1 26	+89 11	2.0	−4.5	680	F8
α Eridani (Achernar)	1 37	−57 20	0.5	−2.2	118	B3
γ Andromedae	2 02	+42 14	2.2	−2.3	260	K3
α Arietis (Hamal)	2 06	+23 22	2.0	0.3	76	K2
α Ceti (Menkar)	3 01	+ 4 01	2.5	−1.0	130	M0
β Persei (Algol)	3 07	+40 53	2.1	−0.5	105	B8
α Persei (Mirphak)	3 22	+49 47	1.8	−4.1	570	F5
α Tauri (Aldebaran)	4 34	+16 29	0.8	−0.8	68	K5
β Orionis (Rigel)	5 14	− 8 13	0.1	−7.0	900	B8
α Aurigae (Capella)	5 15	+46 00	0.1	−0.6	45	G8
γ Orionis (Bellatrix)	5 24	+ 6 21	1.6	−4.1	470	B2
β Tauri (Alnath)	5 25	+28 28	1.7	−2.9	300	B7
δ Orionis	5 31	− 0 18	2.2	−6.0	1,500	O9
α Leporis (Arneb)	5 32	−17 50	2.6	−4.8	900	F0
ε Orionis	5 35	− 1 13	1.7	−6.8	1,600	B0
ζ Orionis	5 40	− 1 57	1.8	−6.2	1,600	O9
κ Orionis	5 46	− 9 40	2.1	−7.1	2,100	B0
α Orionis (Betelgeuse)	5 54	+ 7 24	0.4	−5.9	520	M2
β Aurigae	5 57	+44 57	1.9	−0.2	88	A0
β Canis Majoris	6 21	−17 56	2.0	−4.5	750	B1

Table 4 The Brightest Stars for Epoch 1980 (continued)

Star	Right Ascension h m		Declination deg. min.		Apparent Magnitude	Absolute Magnitude	Distance light-years	Spectral Type
α Carinae (Canopus)	6	23	−52	41	−0.7		650	F0
γ Geminorum	6	36	+16	25	1.9	−0.5	105	A0
α Canis Majoris (Sirius)	6	44	−16	37	−1.4	1.41	8.7	A1
ε Canis Majoris	6	58	−28	56	1.5	−5.0	680	B1
δ Canis Majoris	7	07	−26	21	1.8	−7.0	2,100	F8
α Geminorum (Castor)	7	33	+31	57	1.6	0.8	45	A0+A5
α Canis Minoris (Procyon)	7	38	+ 5	18	0.4	2.7	11.3	F5
β Geminorum (Pollux)	7	44	+20	05	1.2	1.0	35	K0
ζ Puppis	8	02	−39	56	2.2	−7.3	2,400	O5
γ Velorum	8	08	−47	14	1.9	−4.2	520	0a
ε Carinae (Avior)	8	21	−59	26	1.9	−3.1	340	K0+B
δ Velorum	8	44	−54	38	1.9	0.1	76	A0
λ Velorum	9	07	− 4	21	2.2	−4.3	750	K5
β Carinae	9	13	−69	38	1.7	−0.4	86	A0
ι Carinae	9	16	−59	11	2.2	−4.2	750	F0
α Hydrae (Alphard)	9	27	− 8	35	2.1	−0.7	94	K2
α Leonis (Regulus)	10	07	+12	04	1.3	−0.8	84	B7
α Ursae Majoris (Dubhe)	11	03	+61	51	1.8	−0.6	105	K0
β Leonis (Denebola)	11	48	+14	41	2.1	1.6	43	A3
α Crucis (Acrux)	12	25	−63	00	0.8	−3.7	370	B0.5
γ Crucis	12	30	−57	00	1.7	−2.5	220	M3
γ Centauri	12	40	−48	51	2.2	−1.7	160	A0
β Crucis	12	46	−59	28	1.3	−4.3	490	B1
ε Ursae Majoris (Alioth)	12	53	+56	04	1.8	−0.2	68	A0
ζ Ursae Majoris (Mizar)	13	23	+55	02	2.1	0.0	88	A2+A6
α Virginis (Spica)	13	24	−11	03	1.0	−3.1	220	B1
ε Centauri	13	39	−53	22	2.3	−3.6	570	B1
η Ursae Majoris	13	47	+49	25	1.9	−2.3	210	B3
β Centauri	14	02	−60	16	0.6	−5.0	490	B1
θ Centauri	14	05	−36	16	2.1	0.9	55	K0
α Boötis (Arcturus)	14	14	+19	20	−0.1	−0.2	36	K2
α Centauri (Rigel Kent)	14	39	−60	46	−0.3	4.2	4.3	G2
α Lupi	14	40	−47	19	2.5	−2.5	430	B2
β Ursae Minoris (Kocab)	14	50	+74	14	2.0	−0.6	105	K5
α Coronae Borealis (Alphekka)	15	33	+26	47	2.2	0.5	76	A0
δ Scorpii	15	58	−22	34	2.3	−4.0	590	B0
α Scorpii (Antares)	16	27	−26	24	0.9	−4.7	520	M1
α Trianguli Australe	16	46	−69	00	1.9	−0.4	82	K2
ε Scorpii	16	49	−34	16	2.3	0.6	65	K0
λ Scorpii	17	32	−37	06	1.6	−3.2	610	B2
α Ophiuchi (Rasalhague)	17	33	+12	35	1.9	0.9	58	A5
θ Scorpii	17	35	−42	59	2.1	−4.0	650	F0
γ Draconis	17	55	+51	29	2.2	0.8	117	K5
ε Sagitarii	18	23	−34	24	1.8	−1.7	124	A0
α Lyrae (Vega)	18	36	+39	02	0.0	0.5	26.5	A0
σ Sagitarii	18	54	−26	19	2.1	−2.4	300	B3
α Aquilae (Altair)	19	49	+ 8	48	0.8	2.3	16.5	A7
γ Cygni	20	21	+40	11	1.9	−4.8	750	F8
α Pavonis	20	23	−56	48	2.2	−2.9	310	B3
α Cygni (Deneb)	20	40	+45	12	1.3	−7.2	1,600	A2
α Cephei (Alderamin)	21	18	+62	30	2.4	1.5	52	A5
α Gruis (Alnair)	22	07	−47	04	1.8	−0.2	64	B5
α Piscis Australis (Fomalhaut)	22	56	−29	43	1.2	1.9	22.6	A3
α Pegasi (Markab)	23	04	+15	06	2.5	0.0	100	A0

(From information given in *Essentials of Astronomy* by Motz and Duveen with right ascensions and declinations updated by Colin Ronan)

α=Alpha	ε=Epsilon	ι=Iota	ν=Nu	ρ=Rho	φ=Phi
β=Beta	ζ=Zeta	κ=Kappa	ξ=Xi	σ=Sigma	χ=Chi
γ=Gamma	η=Eta	λ=Lambda	o=Omicron	τ=Tau	ψ=Psi
δ=Delta	θ=Theta	μ=Mu	π=Pi	υ=Upsilon	ω=Omega

GLOSSARY

Absolute magnitude: the magnitude which a *star* would have if put at a distance of 32.6 *light-years* or 10 *parsecs* from us. It is a measure of the real brightness of a *star*.

Altazimuth: the name given to a telescope mounting which allows a telescope to move up and down in *altitude* and horizontally in *azimuth*.

Altitude: the vertical distance of a celestial body measured vertically upwards from the horizon.

Aphelion: the most distant point from the Sun reached by a *planet* on an elliptical *orbit* in the Solar System.

Apparent magnitude: the apparent brightness of a celestial body.

Azimuth: the angle of a celestial body measured clockwise from the north in a direction parallel to the horizon.

Binary system: a pair of *stars* orbiting around one another.

Black hole: an extremely superdense celestial body emitting no *radiation*.

Celestial equator: the equator of the *celestial sphere*. It is a *great circle* and is the projection on the sphere of the Earth's equator.

Celestial sphere: an imaginary sphere centred on the Earth and with the *stars* on its inside surface. It is useful for measuring co-ordinates (positions) of celestial bodies.

Cepheid variable: a type of *variable star* whose period of variation depends on its real brightness. The star δ Cephei is typical of this class, which is named after it.

Comet: a collection of ice and rocky particles which orbits the Sun in a very elliptical path. Comets may display tails when close to the Sun.

Conjunction: the apparent close approach in the sky of celestial bodies.

Constellation: an artificial grouping of *stars* based on their apparent positions in the sky.

Corona: the faint, outermost atmosphere of the Sun.

Declination: the angular distance of a celestial body north or south of the *celestial equator*.

Ecliptic: the apparent path of the Sun on the *celestial sphere*.

Ellipse: a closed figure which curves around two points (foci). It can be obtained by slicing obliquely through a cone. Planetary *orbits* are all ellipses.

Elongation: the angle between the Sun and a celestial body.

Equatorial mounting: a telescope mounting in which the telescope rotates about one axis parallel to the Earth's polar axis and also rotates at right-angles to it (i.e. in *declination*). It allows the telescope to track the apparent motion of a celestial body in a single movement.

Equinox: when day and night are equal (i.e. 12 hours each). At these points in the year, the Sun is at those places where the *celestial equator* and the *ecliptic* cross one another.

Galaxy: an island of *stars*, together usually with dust and gas.

Gamma (γ) rays: very short wave radiation, more penetrating than X-rays. (Wavelengths 10^{-14} to 10^{-12} metres.)

Gibbous: the phase of a celestial body that lies between the half illuminated disc and the full disc.

Gravity: the force with which bodies attract one another (nb it is quite different from magnetic attraction).

Great circle: a circle on a sphere with a diameter equal to that of the sphere. The *celestial equator* is a great circle on the *celestial sphere* and the terrestrial equator is a great circle on the Earth.

Infrared radiation: *radiation* with a wavelength longer than red light (10^{-6} to 10^{-4} metres).

Libration: an oscillation of the Moon which results in its nearer face not always being directly towards us. It allows us to see a 'little round the corner' on to the hidden side of the Moon. Consequently, over a period of time, an Earth-based observer can see almost 60% of the lunar surface instead of only 50%.

Light-year: the distance light travels in one year: 9.4607×10^{12} km.

Magnetic field: the region of magnetic influence of a magnet or of a celestial body which acts like a magnet.

Magnetosphere: the *magnetic field* around a celestial body.

Meteor: a lump of rock or metal which comes from outer space and falls towards the Earth's surface. Friction, or rubbing against the air, causes it to heat up and emit light. A meteor ordinarily burns away before it drops down as far as the Earth's surface.

Meteorite: interplanetary material which has not been consumed completely in its passage through the atmosphere and which therefore lands on the ground.

Nebula: a cloud of gas in space. Nebulae may be dark or, if set glowing by nearby *stars* or *stars* embedded in them, they may be bright.

Neutron star: a very dense compact *star* which often behaves like a *pulsar*.

Nova: a *star* which throws off a shell of hot gas and thereby appears brighter for a short time, looking just as if a new *star* had been born.

Occultation: an occultation occurs when one celestial body moves in front of another.

Opposition: when a *planet* lies on the side of the Earth opposite to the Sun.

Orbit: a path of one body moving around another.

Parabola: a curve which is closed at one end and open at the other. Such a curve can be obtained by cutting a slice down a cone parallel to one side.

Parallax: the apparent shift in position of a body when it is observed from two different positions.

Parsec: a distance of 3.26 *light-years*, i.e. the distance at which a *star* would display a *parallax* of 1 arc second.

Perihelion: the nearest point to the Sun on an elliptical *orbit* of a *planet* in the Solar System.

Planet: a body attendant on another. In astronomy, the term is usually used to describe a non-radiating body in *orbit* around a *star*.

Precession: the backward (i.e. westward) movement of the point of intersection of the *celestial equator* and the *ecliptic*. This apparent effect is caused by the movement of the Earth's polar axis.

Prominence: a flame-like projection of hot, glowing hydrogen gas, sometimes seen at the Sun's limb during a total solar eclipse and, at other times, by using special equipment, such as a spectrohelioscope.

Pulsar: an extremely dense collapsed *star* which emits rapid pulses of *radio waves* and sometimes other *radiation*.

Quasar: a 'quasi-stellar' source, i.e. a body which looks like a *star* but which emits far too much *radiation* to be one. It may be a bright core of a *galaxy*.

Radiation: short for 'electromagnetic radiation', which ranges from *radio waves* to *gamma-rays* and includes light.

Radio waves: long wavelength *radiation*; in astronomy the range goes from a few millimetres up to 20 metres.

Red giant: a very large *star* which radiates mainly in red light.

Refraction: the bending of a light ray when it passes from one transparent substance to a denser or less dense transparent substance.

Relativity: the theoretical consequences of the realization that all motion is relative and that, however an observer is moving, the observed velocity of light never changes.

Right ascension: angular distance of celestial objects measured eastwards along the *celestial equator*.

Satellite: a natural or artificial body in *orbit* around a *planet*.

Sidereal time: time measured by the Earth's rotation with reference to the *stars* instead of to the Sun. A sidereal day is about 4 minutes shorter than a solar day.

Solar wind: an outflow of atomic particles from the Sun, travelling through the Solar System.

Solstice: a 'standstill point' applied to the apparent motion of the Sun when it changes the direction of its apparent movement in *declination*. The change from a movement northwards to southwards is summer solstice in the northern hemisphere and winter solstice in the southern hemisphere. The change from southwards to northwards is winter solstice in the northern hemisphere and summer solstice in the southern hemisphere.

Spectroscope: an instrument for looking at *spectra*.

Spectrum: the range of wavelengths of a particular section of electromagnetic *radiation*. The spectrum of sunlight runs from red (long wavelength) to violet (short wavelength).

Star: a gaseous body which generates all the energy it emits.

Star cluster: a group of *stars* clustered together by the gravitational forces between them.

Synodic period: the period between two successive alignments of celestial bodies. For a *planet* the synodic period is the time between successive *conjunctions* with a particular *star* or between *oppositions*.

Transit: a passage of a celestial body across the disc of another (e.g. the transit of Venus across the face of the Sun), or its passage across a given point (e.g. the transit of a *star* across the meridian or south point).

Ultraviolet light: light shorter in wavelength than violet light but longer than *X-rays*. (Range about 10^{-6} to 10^{-8} metres.)

Variable stars: *stars* which vary in brightness over specific periods of time.

White dwarf: a very compact *star* close to the end of its life and which emits white light. A white dwarf is not as dense as either a *pulsar* or a *black hole*.

X-rays: short wave *radiation*. (Range about 10^{-8} to 10^{-11} metres.)

Zenith: the point directly overhead.

Zodiac: the band of *constellations* through which the Sun, Moon and *planets* appear to move.

INDEX